Transnational German Studies

Transnational Modern Languages

Transnational Modern Languages promotes a model of Modern Languages not as the inquiry into separate national traditions, but as the study of languages, cultures and their interactions. The series aims to demonstrate the value – practical and commercial, as well as academic and cultural – of modern language study when conceived as transnational cultural enquiry.

The texts in the series are specifically targeted at a student audience. They address how work on the transnational and the transcultural broadens the confines of Modern Languages; opens an extensive range of objects of research to analysis; deploys a complex set of methodologies; and can be accomplished through the exposition of clearly articulated examples.

The series is anchored by *Transnational Modern Languages: A Handbook*, ed. Jenny Burns (Warwick) and Derek Duncan (St. Andrews), which sets out the theoretical and conceptual scope of the series, the type of research on which it is based and the kinds of questions that it asks. Following on from the *Handbook*, the series includes a text for the study of the following Modern Languages:

Transnational French Studies, ed. Charles Forsdick (Liverpool) and Claire Launchbury (Leeds)

Transnational German Studies, ed. Rebecca Braun (Lancaster) and Benedict Schofield (King's College London)

Transnational Spanish Studies, ed. Catherine Davies (IMLR) and Rory O'Bryen (Cambridge)

Transnational Italian Studies, ed. Charles Burdett (Durham) and Loredana Polezzi (Cardiff)

Transnational Portuguese Studies, ed. Hilary Owen (Manchester/Oxford) and Claire Williams (Oxford)

Transnational Russian Studies, ed. Andy Byford (Durham), Connor Doak (Bristol) and Stephen Hutchings (Manchester)

Transnational German Studies

edited by
Rebecca Braun and Benedict Schofield

LIVERPOOL UNIVERSITY PRESS

First published 2020 by
Liverpool University Press
4 Cambridge Street
Liverpool
L69 7ZU

Copyright © 2020 Liverpool University Press

The right of Rebecca Braun and Benedict Schofield to be identified as the editors of this work has been asserted by them in accordance with the Copyright, Designs and Patents Act 1988.

All rights reserved. No part of this book may be reproduced, stored in a retrieval system, or transmitted, in any form or by any means, electronic, mechanical, photocopying, recording, or otherwise, without the prior written permission of the publisher.

British Library Cataloguing-in-Publication data
A British Library CIP record is available

ISBN 978-1-78962-141-9 (HB)
ISBN 978-1-78962-142-6 (PB)

Typeset by Carnegie Book Production, Lancaster
Printed in the UK by CPI Group (UK) Ltd, Croydon CR0 4YY

Contents

Illustrations — ix

Acknowledgements — xi

Contributors — xiii

Introduction: Transnationalizing German Studies — 1
   Rebecca Braun and Benedict Schofield

Part 1: Language: Local and Global Voices

1. Translation, Transposition, Transmission: Low German and Processes of Cultural Transformation — 17
   Elizabeth Andersen

2. Developing a Polyglot Poetics: The Power of Testimony and Lived Literary Experience — 43
   Ulrike Draesner

3. German Writers from Abroad: Translingualism, Hybrid Languages, 'Broken' Germans — 57
   Dirk Weissmann

4. Collaboration and Commitment: German-language Books Across Borders — 77
   Charlotte Ryland

Part 2: Spatiality: Mapping Nations, Mapping Networks

5. Networks and World Literature: The Practice of Putting German Authors in their Place   97
   Rebecca Braun

6. Who is German? Nineteenth-century Transnationalisms and the Construction of the Nation   115
   Benedict Schofield

7. Co-Producing World Cinema: Germany and Transnational Film Production   133
   Sebastian Heiduschke

8. Towards a Collaborative Memory: Networks and Relationality in German Memory Cultures   151
   Sara Jones

Part 3: Temporality: Experiences of Time

9. It's About Time: The Temporality of Transnational Studies   177
   Anne Fuchs

10. Transnationalizing Faith: Re-imagining Islam in German Culture   193
    James Hodkinson

11. Transnational Imaginaries: The Place of Palestine in Gershom Scholem, Franz Kafka and Early Cinema   213
    Nicholas Baer

12. Securing the Archive: On the Transience of (Latin) American German Identities   229
    Paulo Soethe

Part 4: Subjectivity: Ideology and the Individual

13. Radical Germans and Their Anglophone Interpreters: Exploring and Translating 'The Unconscious' and Psychoanalysis   249
    Angus Nicholls

14.	Patterns of Global Exile: Exploring Identity through Art *Birgit Lang*	269
15.	Representative Germans: Navid Kermani and the German Literary Tradition of Critical Cosmopolitanism *Claire Baldwin*	285
16.	Contrite Germans? The Transnationalization of Germany's Memory Culture *Stuart Taberner*	307

Index 323

Illustrations

Fig. 1.	Map of Low, Central and High German Dialects, *c.*1400	18
Fig. 2.	Map of the Hanseatic League, *c.*1400	22
Fig. 3.	The Burgomaster, from *Des Dodes Dantz*	28
Fig. 4.	Death, from *Des Dodes Dantz*	29
Fig. 5.	'Saint Birgitta, Bride of Christ, Pray for us', from *Sunte Birgitten Openbaringe*	33
Fig. 6.	'Saint Katarina of Vadstena', from *Sunte Birgitten Openbaringe*	34
Fig. 7.	End of prologue and title page of the Low German *Ship of Fools*	38
Fig. 8.	BStU Network 2009–2010	159
Fig. 9.	BStU Network 2011–2012	160
Fig. 10.	Degree Centrality in BStU Networks 2009–2012	162
Fig. 11.	Component 1, BStU 2009–2010	164
Fig. 12.	Component 2, BStU 2011–2012	164
Fig. 13.	Component 3, BStU 2011–2012	165
Fig. 14.	Homophily in BStU Networks 2009–2012	166

Fig. 15.	The 'Hafis-Goethe Denkmal' – the Hafez-Goethe Monument, Weimar, Germany	194
Figs. 16, 17 and 18.	Bronze inscription in the plinth of the Hafez-Goethe Monument, Weimar, Germany	195
Fig. 19.	Frontispiece of first edition of the *Divan* (Stuttgart, 1819)	200
Fig. 20.	Cinema as 'a torn-open grave'. Still from Ya'acov Ben-Dov's *Shivat Zion* [*Return to Zion*, 1921].	226
Fig. 21.	The concentration of German-language newspapers in Brazil	235
Fig. 22.	17 March 1888 issue of *Der Pionier*	236
Figs. 23 and 24.	Freud's diagrams for the second topographic model [*zweite Topik*] of the human psyche in its German and English versions	258
Fig. 25.	Louis Kahan, Portrait of Australian writer Patrick White	277
Fig. 26.	Louis Kahan, Portrait of a young man	283

Acknowledgements

Edited volumes such as this one are always the product of collaboration and co-creation, but this book in particular has been shaped since its inception by the generous support, input and knowledge of colleagues from across the Modern Languages, and beyond.

Like its companion volumes in the *Transnational Modern Languages* series, this book has its roots in a large project on the future shape of the Modern Languages that began in 2015, and which came out of the AHRC-funded Translating Cultures project 'Transnationalizing Modern Languages', which ran from 2013–2016. In particular we would like to thank Charles Burdett, Jenny Burns, Derek Duncan and Loredana Polezzi, who were central to arranging that initial project, and who subsequently became the editors of the series of which this volume is part. Together with the editors of the other volumes, they ensured that our collaborative work on the *Transnational Modern Languages* series became a creative space for thinking not just about the shape of this specific book, but about the future shape of the Modern Languages more broadly, and German's place in that future.

We would also like to acknowledge the significant financial support from our institutions, Lancaster University and King's College London, that has enabled both the behind-the-scenes work that has gone into this volume and its final publication. We thank our translator, Sarah Pybus, for her work on making two of our chapters accessible in English, and our indexer, Julia Goddard. The 2019 'Transnational German Studies' workshop team – a postgraduate research network involving students and colleagues from Amherst College, King's College London, Michigan State University, the University of Massachusetts Amherst and the University of Michigan-Ann Arbor, and originally initiated by colleagues at Warwick University in 2012 – provided valuable feedback on this project in its final stages.

Finally, our thanks go to Liverpool University Press for their support of this book and the *Transnational Modern Languages* series as a whole, above all Chloe Johnson, Katherine King and Anthony Cond.

Contributors

Elizabeth Andersen is a Visiting Fellow in the School of Modern Languages at Newcastle University, UK, from where she retired in 2016. She is a medievalist who has published in the fields of Arthurian literature and women's mystical and visionary writing. She has had a particular interest in the intertextuality and articulation of identity in women's writing. The focus of her recent research has been the circulation of Latin and Low German devotional texts throughout the Hanseatic region, with a particular interest in the dissemination, adaptation and impact of the revelations of St Birgitta of Sweden.

Nicholas Baer is Assistant Professor of Film Studies at the University of Groningen in the Netherlands. He co-edited the award-winning *The Promise of Cinema: German Film Theory, 1907–1933* (2016) and *Unwatchable* (2019). Baer has published on film and media, critical theory and intellectual history in journals such as *Cinéma & Cie*, *Film Quarterly*, *Leo Baeck Institute Year Book*, *Los Angeles Review of Books*, *Public Seminar* and *October*, and his writings have been translated into six languages.

Claire Baldwin is Associate Professor of German at Colgate University, USA. Her research focuses on conceptions of cosmopolitan knowledge and authorial practice in late eighteenth-century and contemporary German-language literature and culture, questions of gender and textual authority, and relationships between literary and visual arts. Publications include *The Emergence of the Modern German Novel* (2002) and *The Construction of Textual Authority in German Literature* (co-edited with James F. Poag, 2001).

Rebecca Braun is Professor of Modern Languages and Creative Futures at Lancaster University, UK, where she directs the multidisciplinary Institute for Social Futures. She has published widely on twentieth and twenty-first-century German-language literature and culture, as well as working comparatively on the topics of authorship and creative futures. Publications include *Constructing Authorship in the Work of Günter Grass* (2008), *Literary Celebrity*, special issue 7.4 of *Celebrity Studies* (co-edited with Emily Spiers, 2016) and a handbook on *World Authorship* in Oxford University Press's Twenty-first-century Approaches series (co-edited with Tobias Boes & Emily Spiers, 2020).

Ulrike Draesner is a poet, a writer of long and short fiction and cultural essays. She has published five major poetry collections, six novels, two of which were nominated for the German Book Prize, three collections of stories, two collections of essays and a personal reflection on ageing. Draesner has received numerous literary prizes, most recently the Gertrud-Kolmar-Prize for Poetry (2019) and the Prize of Literatour Nord (fiction), both of which relate to work inspired by crossing the English Channel. She has been awarded poetic readerships at German and international universities. Draesner lived at Oxford as poet in residence in 2015–2017; in 2018 she was appointed Professor for Creative Writing at the Deutsches Literaturinstitut [German Literature Institute], Leipzig, Germany.

Anne Fuchs (FBA, MRIA) is Professor and Director of the Humanities Institute at University College Dublin, Ireland. She has published widely on German cultural memory, W. G. Sebald, modernist and contemporary German literature and, more recently, on aesthetic representations of time and temporality. Recent publications include: *Precarious Times: Temporality and History in Modern German Culture* (2019), *Ästhetische Eigenzeit in Contemporary Literature and Culture*, special issues 46.3 and 46.4 of *Oxford German Studies* (co-edited with Ines Detmer, 2017) and *Time in German Literature and Culture, 1900–2015: between Acceleration and Slowness* (co-edited with J. J. Long, 2016).

Sebastian Heiduschke is Associate Professor of German with appointments in the School of Language, Culture and Society and the School of Writing, Literature and Film at Oregon State University, USA. His publications on film include the books *East German Cinema: DEFA and Film History* (available as English (2013) and Japanese (2019) language editions) and *Re-Imagining DEFA: East German Cinema in its National and Transnational Contexts* (co-edited with Seán Allan, 2016), as well as numerous articles on aspects of gender, film history, reception and production in German cinema.

James Hodkinson is Reader in German at Warwick University, UK. His research areas are the thought and literature of late-eighteenth and nineteenth-century Germany, Islam and Orientalism in German culture, religion in contemporary society, and music and sound studies in modern German culture. His work on Islam has led to large scale public engagement projects in the UK and abroad, and recent publications include *Postsecularisms*, special issue 41.3 of *Poetics Today* (co-edited with Silke Horstkotte, 2020) and *German in the World: The Transnational and Global Contexts of German Studies* (co-edited with Benedict Schofield, 2020).

Sara Jones is Professor of Modern Languages at the University of Birmingham, UK. Her research focuses on the social, cultural and political processes of remembering, particularly in the context of post-socialism in Germany and Central and Eastern Europe. She is author of *Complicity, Censorship and Criticism* (2011) and *The Media of Testimony* (2014) and is currently working on her third monograph with the provisional title *Towards a Collaborative Memory: German Memory Work in Transnational Context* (2021). She was PI on the AHRC-funded network *Culture and its Uses as Testimony* and the follow-on project *Testimony in Practice*, also funded by the AHRC.

Birgit Lang is Associate Professor of German Studies at the University of Melbourne, Australia. She is a cultural historian of Germany and Austria, with expertise in the interdisciplinary exchange of knowledge and émigré intellectual and cultural history. She has published on the cultural history of refugees from National Socialism and their acculturation to and impact on the English-speaking world, on psychiatry and psychoanalysis and on translation studies. Recent publications include *What is Translation History? A Trust-Based Approach* (with Anthony Pym & Andrea Rizzi, 2019) and *A History of the Case Study. Sexology, Psychoanalysis, Literature* (with Joy Damousi & Alison Lewis, 2017).

Angus Nicholls is Professor of Comparative Literature and German at Queen Mary University of London, UK. He was formerly co-editor of two journals: *Publications of the English Goethe Society* and *History of the Human Sciences*. Nicholls has published widely on German thought and its reception in the Anglophone world, in volumes such as *Friedrich Max Müller and the Role of Philology in Victorian Thought* (co-edited with John Davis, 2017) and *Thinking the Unconscious: Nineteenth-Century German Thought* (co-edited with Martin Liebscher, 2010). His monographs include *Goethe's Concept of the Daemonic* (2006) and *Myth and the Human Sciences* (2015).

Charlotte Ryland is Director of the Stephen Spender Trust and founding Director of the Queen's College Translation Exchange, Oxford, UK, both organisations which aim to engage people of all ages and backgrounds in literary translation, to promote language-learning and to bring inspiring translation activities into UK schools. Until 2019 Ryland ran New Books in German, a UK-based project that promotes German-language literature across the world and facilitates English translations of the best contemporary literature from Austria, Germany and Switzerland. From 2007–2018 she was Lecturer in German at the Queen's College, Oxford, where she is still based.

Benedict Schofield is Reader in German and Director of the Centre for Modern Literature and Culture at King's College London, UK. His research spans the nineteenth, twentieth and twenty-first centuries and is situated at the intersection of German Studies and Comparative Cultural Studies, exploring the representation of the German-speaking countries and 'Germanness' in transnational contexts, with a particular focus on US–German and UK–German cultural relations. Publications include *The German Bestseller in the Late Nineteenth Century* (co-edited with Charlotte Woodford, 2012) and *German in the World: The Transnational and Global Contexts of German Studies* (co-edited with James Hodkinson, 2020).

Paulo Soethe is Professor in the Department of Polish, German and Classical Languages and Literatures at the Federal University of Paraná, Brazil. He was chairman of the Latin-American Germanists' Association (2012–2015) and is a board member of the Internationale Vereinigung für Germanistik [International Association for Germanic Studies]. His research interests are in the fields of German-language literature and intercultural relations between Germany and Brazil, with a particular focus on cultural mobility, network theory, archive history and the digital humanities. Recent publications include articles on Thomas Mann (2019), digital humanities approaches to German-language materials in Brazil (2018) and the history of the German language in Brazil (2019).

Stuart Taberner is Professor of German at the University of Leeds, UK. His research focuses on the relationships between politics and writing, the role of the German intellectual in the period after 1945, and literature after 1989. He has written on the Holocaust, its impact on post-unification Germany, 'normalisation' and national identity, and relationships between Germans and Jews in film, literature and intellectual debate. Major publications include *Transnationalism and German-language Literature in the 21st Century* (2017), *Aging and Old-Age Style in Günter Grass, Ruth Klüger, Christa Wolf, and Martin Walser* (2013) and *German Literature of the 1990s and Beyond* (2005).

Dirk Weissmann is Professor of German at Toulouse University, Jean-Jaurès, France, where he is a member of the research group Centre de Recherches et d'Etudes germaniques [Centre for Germanic Studies and Research]. His research spans German speaking literature and culture from 1770 until today, with a particular focus on transnational, transcultural and translingual issues. Recent publications include an authored book on Elias Canetti (*Métamorphoses interculturelles: Les 'Voix de Marrakech' d'Elias Canetti* [*Intercultural Metamorphoses: Elias Canetti's 'The Voices of Marrakesh'*], 2016) an edited book on Emine Sevgi Özdamar (*Istanbul–Berlin: interculturalité, histoire et écriture chez Emine Sevgi Özdamar* [*Istanbul–Berlin: Interculturality, History and Writing in Emine Sevgi Özdamar*], co-edited with Bernard Banoun and Frédéric Teinturier, 2019) and *Mapping Multilingualism in 19th Century European Literatures* (co-edited with Olga Anokhina and Till Dembeck, 2019).

Introduction

Transnationalizing German Studies

Rebecca Braun and Benedict Schofield

Where is German?

This deceptively easy question stands at the heart of this book on Transnational German Studies. Although it begs a simple answer, posing it uncovers a host of practical and existential issues that run right through our approach to studying German language, culture and society in universities today. On the one hand, discovering that studying the German language can extend your geographical and political horizons across much of Central Europe and, through patterns of trade and migration, all around the world, is an early kick for curious students of German, encouraging them to see and explore the 'wider worlds' beyond Germany, Austria and Switzerland that their studies can unlock. The challenge that then follows, though, is how to make sense of what suddenly becomes a potentially vast area of study – an area that cuts across not only nations (from Austria to Australia, if you will) but also time periods, languages and artistic genres (from medieval books of devotion printed in Low German to modernist painting and film, and beyond) – and all of this in the course of just three or four years of a standard degree programme. German Studies, seen in this light, can both excitingly eschew any sense of regionalism or parochialism and expand to such an extent that we might be forgiven for asking 'where in the world' we should begin when studying it.

At the same time, the question of 'where' German is to be found has been accompanied by the question of 'why' one should study it at all, with concerns about the decline of German as a subject in schools becoming an entrenched source of angst in UK higher education. Indeed, UK universities have now almost entirely followed American colleagues, who have been well

1

used to offering German from scratch on their programmes, in order to make up for its near extinction from high school curricula. Even professors of German in Germany are coming under increased pressure to explain the broader worth of *Germanistik* [German Studies] to cohorts of students needing to make their way in a specialized labour market. This is, in fact, not a new phenomenon at all: as Nicola McLelland has shown, German Studies (especially in the UK) has always been a moving target, with the answers to the questions 'why to learn German' and 'who should learn German' evolving over the past 500 years, from scholarly to touristic to commercial reasons.[1] Intriguingly, though, McLelland's historical survey reveals that, ultimately, it is 'cultural rather than purely instrumental reasons [that] have remained crucial' motivating factors for studying German. McLelland concludes:

> If there is a moral to the tale for Germanists and teachers of German, it is perhaps this: we must continue to make the case 'upwards' to policy-makers, that German is indeed a useful language, and, in this era, one of the most useful ones [...]. However, [...] it is not hard-headed commercial reasoning that wins *individual learners* to languages in general and to German in particular, but the promise of enriching cultural encounters, both in travel [...] *and* in travels of the mind.[2]

Nevertheless, there has been a shift in the institutional representation and approach to German (and the Modern Languages more widely) away from German as an inherently valuable subject of study in its own right. At the same time, this has led to new and creative ways of finding the fruits of German writers', politicians' and scientists' work, albeit at times a little to the side of the subject's traditional heartlands. For German culture, broadly defined, translated and adapted, continues to flourish in theatre, music, philosophy, politics, religious studies, science and medicine, whether in university curricula or in the broader worlds of practice to which each of these disciplines attend. Finding new ways of linking language-based expertise in all things German with these cognate areas has led to some startling combinations, whether in bringing computational analysis of data to bear on our understanding of culture, encouraging communities to explore fixed notions of identity through material objects or helping scientists parse their research questions differently,

---

[1] Nicola McLelland, 'German as a Foreign Language in Britain. The history of German as a 'useful' language since 1600', *Angermion* 8.1 (2015), pp. 1–34 (p. 2).

[2] McLelland, 'German as a Foreign Language in Britain', p. 33 (emphasis in the original).

through the lens of language and metaphor, to name just a few examples. These transformative uses of German Studies require that we ask the question again, seriously now, and not on the back foot, but for a new set of students and researchers within and beyond German Studies: *Where is German?*

The Transnational as Transformational

In providing an answer, this volume captures a transformation, not just as the German-speaking countries in Europe reassess their relationship to the wider world in political and economic terms that map on to twenty-first-century realities – an aspect of transnationalism that has been captured in other recent volumes on the topic – but as the whole discipline itself asks why being a repository for the study of a particular, linguistically defined culture matters.[3] Of course, on one level, any structures that we use to stake out parameters for our discipline – such as the categories of 'Language', 'Spatiality', 'Temporality' and 'Subjectivity', which are used to structure this book, and all the other volumes in the *Transnational Modern Languages* series too – are inherently subject to flex. This is partly the paradox of making any living language and its attendant cultures into an object of study, as if these could ever truly be caught and analysed through a microscope to yield broader results that might be scalable and universally true in some reliable sort of way. The very thing that makes the study of languages and cultures worthwhile is the fact that they are constantly changing, often in ways that appear to contradict themselves and frustrate neat categorizations along the lines of familial resemblance or basic laws.

But there is also a certain productive instability to the disciplinary boundaries offered by the categories of 'language', 'spatiality, 'temporality' and 'subjectivity' that we may like to consider as particularly Germanic – not in essential terms (in other words, not promoting the idea that the German language is inherently more slippery or German history more circular than any other languages or histories), but in contextual ones. In *The Shortest History of Germany* (2017), James Hawes, for instance, has entertainingly

---

[3] Recent approaches to a transnational or global German Studies include Elisabeth Hermann, Carrie Smith-Prei and Stuart Taberner, *Transnationalism in Contemporary German-Language Literature* (Rochester, NY: Camden House, 2015); Stuart Taberner, *Transnationalism and German Language Literature in the Twenty-First Century* (Basingstoke: Palgrave Macmillan, 2017); Thomas Oliver Beebee, *German Literature as World Literature* (London: Bloomsbury, 2014); Anke S. Biendarra, *Germans Going Global. Contemporary Literature and Cultural Globalisation* (Berlin: de Gruyter, 2012); and Randall Halle, *German Film after Germany. Towards a Transnational Aesthetic* (Urbana: University of Illinois Press, 2008).

linked the waxing and waning of German space in Europe over the last two millennia to specific religious and political drivers, especially the power of Prussia, arguing that to really understand Germany today we must 'throw away a great deal of what we think we know about German history, and start afresh'.[4] Meanwhile, Heinz Schlaffer provocatively gave German culture a very short time in the sun during the last 200 years of world literary achievement, arguing in *Die kurze Geschichte der deutschen Literatur* [*The Short History of German Literature*, 2002] that, since German literature's heyday, far too much has been made of far too little: 'Critics, literary historians, and even authors themselves will hardly refute the judgement that the past fifty years of German literature is unable to stand comparison with either international literature of the same period, or the earlier national literature [of Germany].'[5] Both accounts of 'Germanness' either implicitly (Hawes) or explicitly (Schlaffer) invoke foundational insecurities about Germany and the value of the German language and its ability to sustain a distinct identity over time and in contradistinction to its neighbours. What unites these popular accounts is the underlying paradoxical notion that, historically, German culture, ideology and politics are *everywhere* and *nowhere* on the world stage, as likely at any point in time to be found leading the way into new areas as they are collapsing back in on themselves. In looking again at where and what German is or might be, the contributors to our volume are consciously exploring what happens when you embrace such ambivalence and instability.

Deterritorializing the Nation

The transnational is certainly a term that invites reflection on a stable concept of nation-based identity (in logical grammatical terms, it presumes a nation to go beyond) and at the same time unpicks it (it goes beyond the nation). This paradoxical movement is very helpful for our troublesome 'German Studies' slide on the microscope. In political terms, national unity appears only very late in the day for what we now think of as Germany, when the loose collection of German states were joined under the Prussian Chancellor Otto von Bismarck in 1871, a result of Prussian victory in the Franco-Prussian war. Austria must point to an even younger official birthday as a nation state: the First Austrian Republic came into existence in 1918, after the collapse of the

---

[4] James Hawes, *The Shortest History of Germany* (London: Old Street Publishing, 2017), p. viii.
[5] See Hans Schlaffer, *Die kurze Geschichte der deutschen Literatur* (Munich: Hanser, 2002), p. 151. All translations are by the authors.

Austro-Hungarian Empire (itself frequently seen as a transnational construct), while contemporary Austria marks its creation with the proclamation of the Second Republic in 1945. Meanwhile, Switzerland – or to use its official title, the Swiss Confederation – was formed in 1848, that year of revolutionary tumult across Europe, with the adoption of the Swiss Federal Constitution creating a federal republic out of its many cantons. Our current nation states of Germany, Austria and Switzerland, then, are merely the latest iteration of alliances, confederations and indeed transnational empires that came and went prior to our contemporary forms of statehood or nationhood. Indeed, taken together, the vast swathe of the European continent – from Lisbon to Lillehammer, from Barcelona to Bucharest – is a model example of how 'culture', as the expression of important values and intellectual ambitions that shape communities of people across the ages, emerges from across ever-shifting combinations of geopolitical boundaries, religious divisions and global economic forces.

Indeed, for much of their history, the various peoples operating across these European regions who might call themselves 'Germanic' have, in this paradoxical sense, always been transnational (all the way back into the first millennium BC). Lacking a nation as a medium-sized container for identity across a surveyable number of people, they have been intensely regional, if not to say parochial, in their everyday lived experience, while their activities have also formed part of something far larger than a nation: not least the Holy Roman Empire (962–1806), which, in fruitful tension with France and a global Iberia, could be considered the very cradle of European letters. The transnational too only makes sense when seen as emerging from the interplay between the macro and the micro, the grand historical tableau of quasi-universals and their local, contingent manifestations. Taking a transnational approach to German Studies thus allows us to indulge in this historical oddity: the transnational not only manifests in German-speaking Europe as going *beyond* the nation in our contemporary moment of globalization, but also comes *before* the nation with its standardized dialects (and well before globalization was ever considered a particular phenomenon).

The transnational thus provides an oblique angle on our traditional subject of study (German language and letters) that forces us to question some of the bases of a discipline that, like all Modern Languages, has emerged from the study of a literature inflected, in line with the nation state itself, by foundational late nineteenth-century values. The periods, genres and, above all, the canon that this nation-bound approach has constructed have, to borrow a phrase from Ulrich Beck, tended to end in a form of 'methodological nationalism' that must look increasingly suspect in an era both of globalization and of rising nationalist populism.[6] The transnational, by contrast, asks us what value still lies in the traditional model of German Studies, and at the same time it asks us to start to unpick some of that canonicity and allow new voices to arise: a form of deterritorialization of German-language culture that shows how we can approach the problematic, ultimately reductive, concept of the nation without denying its existence and continued power.

Local and Global German Studies

With this in mind, far from dismantling the discipline, the transnational has the potential to strengthen what engaging with the discipline might have to offer. It invites us to think big and at the same time to care about the local detail, to argue for real global relevance while not losing sight of relative strengths and weaknesses, and, in so doing, to tread the fine line that divides world-leading from world-domineering, religious devotion from ideological obsession and innovation from emulation when trying to make sense of German political, cultural and literary history. As students of Modern Languages, we do all of this in order to see better what is in front of us, both in the German-speaking countries we care about and also, by innate comparison, in our own. Grasping German language and culture transnationally entails reflecting on structures of inclusion and exclusion, whether these cut along geographic, ethnic, gender or class lines, and better understanding why some things are elevated to areas of apparently universal cultural significance while others are not. But we also want to know why German matters beyond the walls of a Languages Department, and how it can help us transform the nations in which we are currently resident by making us reflect harder and differently on the stories we tell about ourselves and the local and global communities of which we feel ourselves to be part.

The multiple award-winning writer Ulrike Draesner provides us with a first major point of orientation in this respect when, in her contribution to this volume, she emphasizes the inherently transnational and indeed translingual nature of stories that are passed down from generation to generation, crossing thousands of kilometres and different political regimes, and in so doing containing the germ to transform any individual subject's sense of 'the nation' and his or her place within it. Origins are always complex and almost never readily contained, as her own story in becoming a German writer through deep engagement with Anglo-American literature and British culture, grafted on to a familial journey through Silesian and

---

[6] See Ulrich Beck, 'The Cosmopolitan Condition: Why Methodological Nationalism Fails', *Theory, Culture & Society* 24.7–8 (2007), pp. 286–90.

Bavarian dialects and Protestant and Catholic religions, underscores. The later chapters by Birgit Lang and Claire Baldwin provide further examples of individual artistic careers: those of twentieth-century Austrian émigré artist Louis Kahan and the contemporary Muslim German writer and political commentator Navid Kermani, respectively. Both chapters tell fascinating stories of how individuals weave multiple origins and artistic credos into their work that will be seen differently by different people. They also illustrate, on a practical level, how to work with a mixture of biographical and philological (close textual analysis) approaches to analysing how complex processes of cultural cross-fertilization lead not just to new takes on being German but also to finding new subjects of study that open out the discipline towards wider arts practice and politics.

Finding and exploring the limits of different voices within the discipline of German Studies is also the focus of Dirk Weissmann's contribution on the presence, both historic and contemporary, of translingual writers in German literature. While on the one hand dealing in depth with the increased profile in the present moment of 'writers from abroad', as Weissmann terms it (in other words, those writing in German as a second language), such as Zé Do Rock, Tomer Gardi and Feridun Zaimoglu, Weissmann also historicizes this phenomenon, underlining the multilingual origins and/or parallel manifestations of work by writers often thought of in simple canonical terms as wholly German – not least Heinrich Heine and Rainer Maria Rilke. Through these historical and contemporary examples, Weissmann pursues writers' own conscious questioning of when experimental linguistic play shifts from creating a distinctive literary canon in German to breaking down not just the canon but the very legitimacy of literature itself as a bastion of 'pure' language. Benedict Schofield and James Hodkinson similarly explore such issues, but this time by taking contemporary monuments (Walhalla on the Danube and the Hafez-Goethe Monument in Weimar, respectively) as their way into asking who gains access to the German cultural canon and how new readings of the transnational and intertextual imbrications of those who have been placed there might change the way we deal with both the achievements and the shortcomings of this canon today – in these cases, Heinrich Heine, Gustav Freytag, Johann Wolfgang von Goethe and Gotthold Ephraim Lessing.

All of the chapters mentioned so far also share a profound concern with how concepts and legacies travel across time. A second major point of orientation for our unfolding of transnational German Studies is provided by Anne Fuchs's chapter, which argues against the idea, very popular in understandings of the transnational that focus solely on the late twentieth and early twenty-first centuries, that transnational connectivity necessarily brings about universally transformative opportunities. Rooting her contribution firmly in a German intellectual and cultural tradition, but ranging across the world, Fuchs is at pains to bring to the fore the persistence of unequal experiences around areas of the globe that are often glibly claimed to be connected in 'real time' by reinserting a differentiated understanding of time and diverse temporal experiences back into concepts of the transnational. Paulo Soethe and Nicholas Baer provide examples of how keeping such concerns in full view also gives us a new angle on historical corpora. Soethe sets out the challenge of digitally securing an archive – the German-language newspapers and periodicals published in the Americas of the nineteenth and early twentieth centuries that, for both political and economic reasons, have been long neglected. In so doing, he shows how tracing a *histoire croisée* [crossed history] approach – tracing how inter-related discourses and narratives unfold quite differently in different places but at the same time – can change not just what we know about the historical presence of German-speaking communities in the Americas but also how North and South America each told their own stories of one another through the German-language press. Baer, meanwhile, shows how the specific medium of early cinema is used to facilitate imaginary journeys to impossible places that are also explored in the writings of Gershom Scholem and Franz Kafka. In this instance, we are travelling East as part of a foundational doctrine of hope, or, in Scholem's words, the attempt to give real contours to the Jewish 'life lived in deferment' in the Holy Land. Both Kafka's work and the early Zionist cinema he is known to have watched give expression to the incommensurable temporalities of the land that is experienced as a deferred hope and the actual perspective of the Jew in German-speaking Europe.

The way in which concepts, whether of religious devotion or artistic practice, travel through time and take on different expressions in different places, which then in turn transform those very concepts, is also a core concern of Elizabeth Andersen's chapter. Andersen sets out how the Hanseatic League, a maritime trading network that underpinned the global economic significance of medieval and early modern Germany, led to a particular form of cross-cultural and trans-lingual exchange through multiple media and genres (church paintings, devotional literature and political satire) produced in the city of Lübeck on the Baltic coast. In tracing the circuitous journeys travelled through the multiple dialects in play across far-flung trading points, Andersen also helps us understand the significance of fully grasping how economic networks shape cultural practices that unfold in particular social settings, and vice versa.

This third major point of orientation for the transnational is taken up in the chapters by Rebecca Braun and Sara Jones, both of whom work with forms of network analysis developed in Science & Technology Studies, a sub-discipline of Sociology, as well as in Sebastian Heiduschke's practical overview of how shifting transnational alliances have significantly affected the history and contemporary orientation of the German film industry. Braun's focus is on showing how the abstract concept of 'World-literature', the phrase famously coined by Goethe in 1827, was always underpinned by the practice of world authorship: the multiple people, processes and even material objects that are involved in both producing and circulating literary texts. Braun traces the networks of people, media streams and material objects that have coalesced around the contemporary Austro-German writer Daniel Kehlmann and the Northern German Felicitas Hoppe to probe further whether contemporary German-language literature is capable of aesthetic and conceptual renewal in a way that can both promote and look beyond canonical author figures on a world stage. Jones, meanwhile, shows in a very practical way how to apply computational methods to analysing the intent and success of institutional networks, as set out for the international collaborations sustained by the Federal Office for the Files of the State Security Service of the former GDR (BStU) between 2009 and 2012. These networks evolved as part of the BStU's commitment to sharing best practice in the curation of memory documents and to developing broader and more dynamic forms of collaborative memory that acknowledge the fact that memory practices do not necessarily remain confined by geopolitical or linguistic borders.

The inherent translatability of experiences that are also marked as significantly German forms the fourth and final major point of orientation for our volume. Stuart Taberner, Angus Nicholls and Charlotte Ryland each provide their own perspective on how legacies from the German twentieth century are picked up and circulated in transnational politics, science and the cultural sector. Each bring startling findings to well-known topics. Nicholls shows how the transnational legacy of Freudianism together with its somewhat uncomfortable positioning as a pseudo-science has much to do with the way Sigmund Freud's work was first translated into English, obscuring many of his more metaphorical, if not to say literary, allusions when putting forward ideas about the unconscious. Taberner and Ryland, meanwhile, return us to questions of inclusivity within the curation of the German cultural mainstream. Taberner reveals how the gesture of being contrite becomes part of a powerful German political toolkit, but one that is increasingly subject to the radical relativism of much larger looming planetary problems. Ryland, meanwhile, explores, from a position within the publishing industry, how transnational networks support German-language literature in translation. This global flow of German-language culture in translation has, she argues, had the effect of encouraging a greater diversity within German-language literature itself, enabling a broader than ever range of German-language voices to find success both in the German-speaking countries and around the world. Here, Ryland neatly captures the core premise of this volume: that the transnational is both present throughout what we might traditionally define as 'German-language' culture as well as to be found in global contexts that such national frameworks often obscure. Crucially, as all the contributions to this volume make clear, these two positions are not mutually exclusive, but are constantly informing each other.

Structuring the Transnational:
Language, Spatiality, Temporality, Subjectivity

The chapters outlined above are grouped together in this book in four parts: (i) 'Language', (ii) 'Spatiality', (iii) 'Temporality' and (iv) 'Subjectivity'. Deliberately conceived as broad and inclusive in scope, each of these parts nevertheless constitutes an area, and a methodological practice, that students of Modern Languages engage with during their studies, including (but not limited to):

(i) Their experience of language, multilingualism and translation;

(ii) Their interrogation of the construction and deconstruction of borders and boundaries (geographic, social, political, cultural, historical and others);

(iii) Their engagement with competing memory cultures and histories and their exploration of different visions of the future expressed through culture and politics; and

(iv) Their dissection of the relation of self to other, and their critical investigation of identity politics.

Such parts are, of course, open to manifold interpretations, and the chapters in this volume could conceivably be placed into more than one of them. In this sense, these parts are not designed to be prescriptive, and the contributions should be read flexibly across them (indeed, precisely as we have done when outlining their content in the preceding section). At the same time, though, they provide readers with an initial and ultimately necessary pathway through the diverse themes and questions addressed in this volume. In addition, these parts are replicated in the other volumes in the *Transnational Modern Languages* series, thus actively encouraging readers to explore related themes across the books and across different languages and cultures, which in turn helps dissolve any latent 'methodological nationalism' that might still partially be inscribed by the existence of a 'nationally specific' volume on German Studies in a series that explores the 'transnational'. In being able to trace issues of 'Language', 'Spatiality', 'Temporality' and 'Subjectivity' across the series, these parts thus demonstrate to our readers how diverse languages and cultures continually interact across linguistic and geographic differences, and can be fruitfully studied in tandem, rather than in isolation. In turn, all the books in the series can be read alongside the volume *Transnational Modern Languages: A Handbook*, which contains over 30 short essays, each of which takes a key term in cultural criticism (such as 'Diaspora', 'Queer', 'Autobiography', et cetera) and explores how these work methodologically across the many different areas of study, and language zones, that comprise the Modern Languages.

In this German volume, the four parts of 'Language', 'Spatiality', 'Temporality' and 'Subjectivity' are also designed to help readers articulate new ways of thinking about 'where' and 'what' German Studies is. Each part thus contains a spread of chronological examples and showcases a range of different methodologies for approaching the transnational. Part One on 'Language', subtitled 'Local and Global Voices', thus addresses the perhaps surprisingly thorny question of 'who speaks German', tracing debates around language and self-identity, language and national belonging, and language and power (especially questions of exclusion and inclusion) that have raged from the Middle Ages to the very present. These chapters deploy approaches derived from historical linguistics, from the close reading of literary works and visual artefacts, as well as from the practical experiences of multilingual authors, translators and figures in the publishing industry. In doing so, Part One reveals the central role of language in developing transnational communities that cut across the local, national and global, and demonstrates how language can be the source of exclusive cultural identities, yet, through processes of translingualism and translation, can also become the vehicle for more inclusive modes of transnational communication.

The idea that language can be used both as a marker of the boundaries of a specific culture but also as the means to overcome those boundaries is not only linguistic but spatial. This demonstrates the innate permeability of our parts, the second of which approaches explicitly the issue of boundaries and borders, focusing on 'Spatiality'. Subtitled 'Mapping Nations, Mapping Networks', Part Two takes the notion of mapping literally as well as figuratively: tracing authors and filmmakers, as well as institutions and individuals, as they criss-cross borders, but also innovatively showcasing how methodologies from other disciplines, such as Sociology, Comparative Literature and Film Studies, can be applied to key questions in German Studies. This part ultimately reveals how transnational entanglements arise even when mapping what appear to be the most 'national' of spaces, and how that mapping of space always goes hand in hand with the exercise of power: power over the culture we get to consume, and power over the things we are allowed to remember.

In turning to 'Temporality' in our third part, our book considers not only the inherent connection between the transnational and the trans-period – that crucial awareness that the transnational is both the precursor as well as the result of the nation – but also, as our subtitle makes clear, different 'Experiences of Time'. This exploration of time is not solely about the past, and the ways in which we remember the past, but also about the mechanisms with which time is captured, preserved and instrumentalized. This can take the concrete form of archives and monuments – those symbols both of preservation (in what they choose to store or memorialize) and precarity (in what they choose not or are unable to preserve or remember). Yet time is technologically mediated in other ways too, such as cinema's ability to bridge space–time and bring new worlds to us with speed, or through the digital world's insistence on instantaneous communication. The ways in which time, considered transnationally, can become a form of space–time, is a core concern of these chapters: something that suggests the existence of a global community, yet one that can exclude as many people as it includes. Part Three thus explores how our experience of time and the means with which we measure and preserve time impact on the way we imagine ourselves as part of wider national and transnational communities that span space–time.

The final part of this volume is called 'Subjectivity'. As our subtitle 'Ideology and the Individual' makes clear, in Part Four we focus on discourses of power, and how we as individuals are positioned, labelled and prescribed within wider group identities. A core concern for all the chapters in Part Four is the issue of alterity, and how that state of being 'other' or 'different' is culturally and historically constructed – and how, in turn, this can be culturally dismantled. As people, cultures and ideologies move around the globe, different discourses of gender, race, identity, class and religion come into contact: a transnational mobility of peoples, concepts and policies that is at the heart of all the contributions to Part Four. This mobility – which is also across time and space, and which also involves multiple languages – often leads to misunderstanding, exclusion and prejudice. But, as this part shows, it can also result, through acts of linguistic and cultural translation, in increased understanding and the creation of transnationally imagined communities – communities that stretch in surprising and dynamic ways far beyond the geo-political borders of the German-speaking countries.

Decentring and Recentring German Studies

We began this introduction by posing the question 'where is German'? The concept of the 'nation' is, of course, never something we can entirely escape or eliminate, and this is not our intention in this book: fundamentally, the transnational does not negate the national, it coexists with it. But the chapters in this book do demand that we question, as students and researchers of German, the cultural and linguistic construction of the nation, nation states and national identities. The chapters enable this questioning by at once displacing the centrality of 'Germanness' through transnational perspectives – what we earlier called its deterritorialization – but, crucially, in ways that also allow us to return to an expanded German Studies with new critical questions.

Our concern is thus not only 'where is Germany', but 'who' makes Germany, and 'how' – concerns that demand a creative transnational approach that traces the mobility of different peoples, languages, ideas, institutions and ideologies as truly 'trans' – in other words, *across, through, between, before* and *beyond* what we define today as the geo-political entities of Germany, Austria and Switzerland. With this, transnational German Studies also encourages us to think *trans-period*, to operate *trans-lingually* and consider the *trans-lational* potential of our work for other fields of enquiry that might stand to gain from a relational knowledge of German history and culture: a *trans-disciplinary* approach that also allows German Studies to benefit methodologically from these other fields. In recognizing that German-language culture never corresponds neatly to clearly defined national identities or linguistic and geographic entities, but can be both decontextualized and recontextualized through transnational approaches, the contributions to this volume together demonstrate the transformative potential of the transnational for our understanding of 'where' German might be, and 'why' we choose to continue to study it.

Suggestions for Further Reading

Beebee, Thomas Oliver, *German Literature as World Literature* (London: Bloomsbury, 2014), 256 pp.

Biendarra, Anke S., *Germans Going Global. Contemporary Literature and Cultural Globalisation* (Berlin: de Gruyter, 2012), 256 pp.

Halle, Randall, *German Film after Germany. Towards a Transnational Aesthetic* (Urbana: University of Illinois Press, 2008), 258 pp.

Hermann, Elisabeth, Carrie Smith-Prei and Stuart Taberner, *Transnationalism in Contemporary German-Language Literature* (Rochester, NY: Camden House, 2015), 293 pp.

Taberner, Stuart, *Transnationalism and German Language Literature in the Twenty-First Century* (Basingstoke: Palgrave Macmillan, 2017), 365 pp.

Part 1

Language: Local and Global Voices

1

Translation, Transposition, Transmission

Low German and Processes of Cultural Transformation

Elizabeth Andersen

Introduction

Germany, in the modern sense of a nation state, did not truly exist until the founding of Kaiser Wilhelm's German Empire in 1871. In the preceding centuries, the German-speaking lands were incorporated in the Holy Roman Empire, a territory that varied in size and composition during its existence (962–1806). The evolution of this empire into a German political unit was first acknowledged in 1474 in the official use of the expanded imperial name 'Holy Roman Empire of the German Nation', a title ratified in a decree following the Diet of Cologne in 1512. This political unit comprised many smaller sub-units, such as principalities, duchies, counties and free imperial cities. The nature of this loose union of territories has led to debate about how far the term 'transnational' can be used with reference to border crossings in the pre-modern period. Simon Macdonald makes the case for using the concept as an investigative tool, arguing that 'transnational approaches to the history of ideas are concerned with taking seriously the questions of the reception, negotiation and appropriation of given texts as they cross cultural and linguistic boundaries.'[1] There is certainly no difficulty in applying the related concepts of the 'transcultural' and the 'translingual' (the latter discussed in detail by Dirk Weissmann in Chapter 3 of this volume) to the literature and culture of late medieval Germany. Thus, a recent volume authored by medieval historians entitled *Transkulturelle Verflechtungen. Mediävistische*

---

[1] Simon Macdonald, 'Transnational history: a review of past and present scholarship' (2013), p. 12, https://www.ucl.ac.uk/centre-transnational-history/sites/centre-transnational-history/files/simon_macdonald_tns_review.pdf [accessed 4 March 2020].

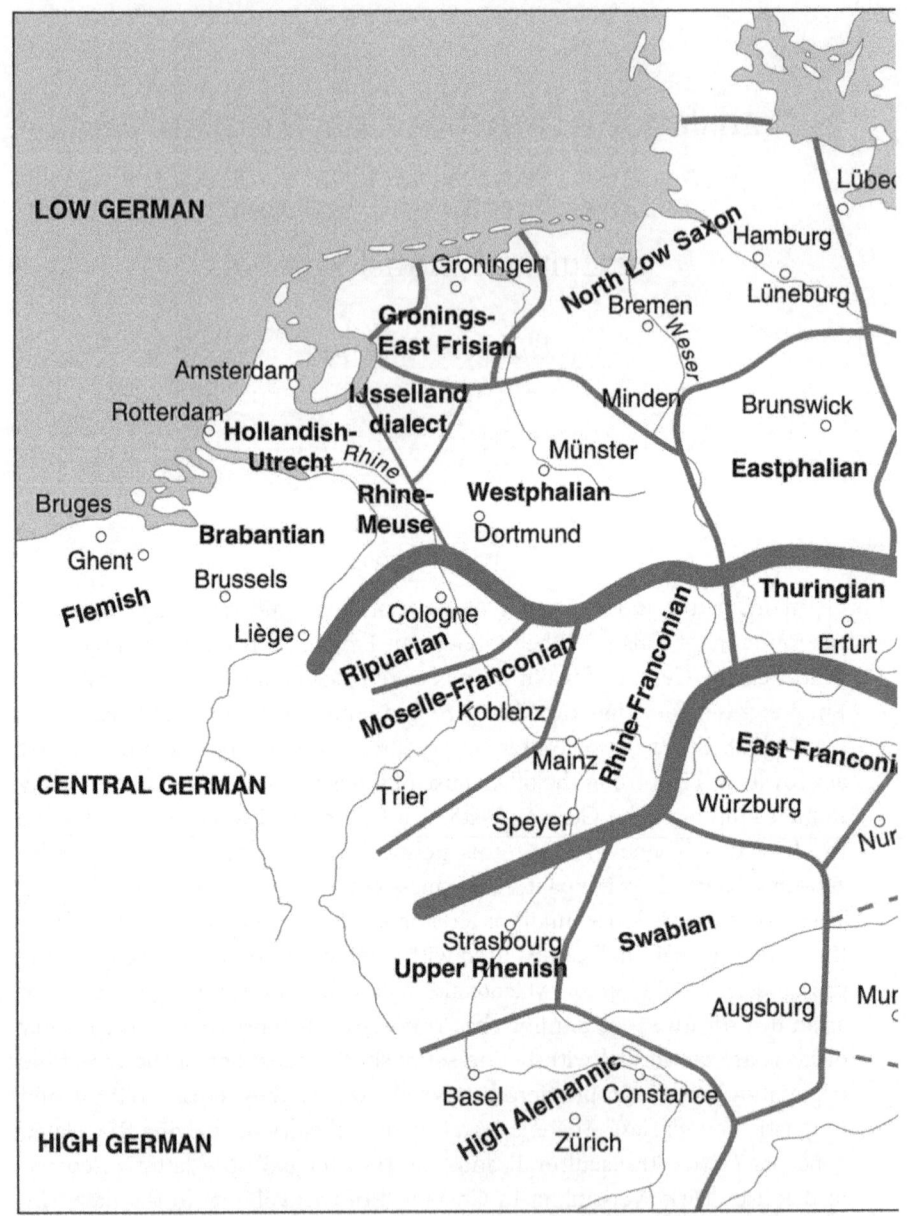

Fig. 1. Map of Low, Central and High German Dialects, *c.*1400, taken from *A Companion to Mysticism and Devotion in Northern Germany in the Late Middle Ages*, ed. by Elizabeth Andersen, Henrike Lähnemann and Anne Simon (Leiden: Brill, 2014), by kind permission of Brill.

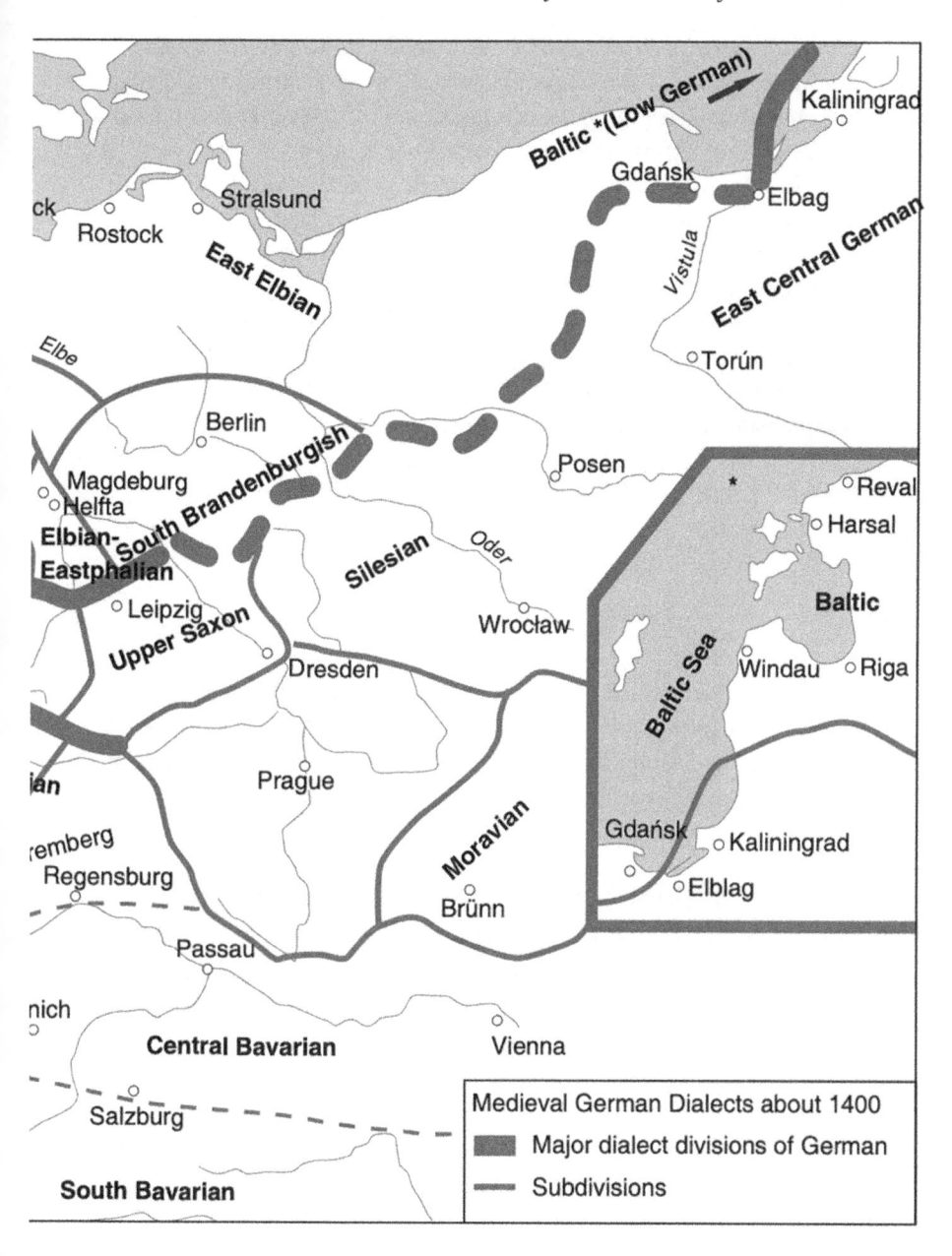

Low German and Processes of Cultural Transformation   19

Baltic *(Low German)
Kaliningrad
Gdańsk
Stralsund
Elbag
Rostock
East Elbian
East Central German
Elbe
Vistula
Torún
Berlin
Posen
Magdeburg
Reval
Helfta
Harsal
Elbian-
South Brandenburgish
Eastphalian
Silesian
Oder
Baltic
Leipzig
Wrocław
Upper Saxon
Baltic Sea
Dresden
Windau
Riga
Prague
Moravian
Gdańsk
Kaliningrad
remberg
Regensburg
Brünn
Elblag
Passau
nich
Central Bavarian
Vienna

Medieval German Dialects about 1400
Salzburg
■ Major dialect divisions of German
South Bavarian
— Subdivisions

Perspektiven (*Transcultural Entanglements: Mediaevalist Perspectives*, 2016),[2] avoids the term 'transnational' and talks instead about 'cultural interaction' and the 'transcultural paradigm' in discussions about networks that cross borders, such as those of merchants or monastic orders.

Although it is customary within the context of medieval scholarship to talk about the 'German-speaking lands' as a way of circumventing the anachronistic concept of nationhood, it must nonetheless be borne in mind that in the late Middle Ages there was no standard language as we would understand it today. Instead, there was a set of 'regionally marked dialects' (Fig. 1).[3]

The strongest marker of difference in these German dialects is that between Low and High German. Where the First Sound Shift, which affected the plosive consonants (voiceless: p, t, k; voiced: b, d, g),

Proto Indo-European	Latin cognate	Germanic cognate
*peter[4]	pater	father
*treyes	tres	three
*korn	cornu	horn

distinguished the Germanic family of languages[5] from Indo-European, it was only in High German that these plosives were shifted again. As Low German did not undergo the Second Sound Shift (also known as the High German Consonant Shift), it is closer in phonology to Dutch and English than it is to High German:

HG	Pfeife	Apfel	Schaf	Zeit	setzen	groß	Kalb	machen	Dach
LG	Piep	Auppel	Schoop	Tiet	setten	groot	Kaulf	moken	Dack
Eng	pipe	apple	sheep	tide	set	great	calf	make	thatch
Dutch	pijp	appel	schaap	tijd	zetten	groot	kalf	maken	dak

---

[2] Georg Christ et al. (ed.) *Transkulturelle Verflechtungen. Mediävistische Perspektiven*, (Göttingen: Universitätsverlag, 2016). https://doi.org/10.1785/gup2016-981 [accessed 6 January 2018].

[3] C. J. Wells, *German: A Linguistic History to 1945* (Oxford: Clarendon Press, 1987), p. 31.

[4] The symbol * indicates a reconstructed rather than an attested form of the word.

[5] The Germanic languages are normally divided into three groups: West Germanic (including Dutch, English and German), North Germanic (including Danish, Swedish, Icelandic, Norwegian and Faroese) and East Germanic (now extinct but comprising Gothic and the languages of the Vandals, Burgundians and a few other tribes).

Standard Modern German evolved from the separate, though related, dialects of Central and High German, while modern Low German has remained a dialect. However, in the heyday of the Hanse Low German enjoyed the status of a *lingua franca*. The Hanseatic League dominated trade in Northern Europe, stretching from the Baltic to the North Sea and inland during the late Middle Ages and early modern period (around the thirteenth to the seventeenth century) (Fig. 2). At its height, this economic alliance comprised 70 major cities and 100 to 130 smaller cities, some of which enjoyed the privileges afforded by the Hanseatic League without formally becoming members of it. Among merchants and seamen in Northern Europe Low German competed with Latin as a 'supra-regional koine'.[6] The widespread use of Low German as the language of administrative, commercial and legal matters also meant that there was a readership for religious and secular texts in Low German in the countries bordering the Baltic.

With a population of *c.*25,000–30,000, late medieval Lübeck was the second largest city after Cologne in the German-speaking lands and by far the largest and most powerful member of the Hanse. The Imperial Free City of Lübeck derived its wealth and its political power from its strategic location. It stood at a crossroads of trading routes that ran west to east from Bruges in Flanders to cities on or near the Baltic, such as Gdánsk, Tallinn and Novgorod, and from north to south connecting Scandinavia with Nuremberg, Augsburg and Venice.

Following the invention of printing with moveable type in 1450 by Johannes Gutenberg, printing offices were quickly established in Bamberg and Strasbourg in 1460, in Cologne in 1465, in Basel in 1468 and in Nuremberg in 1470. In the north of the Holy Roman Empire Lübeck led the way. In the decades on either side of 1500 Lübeck, 'Queen of the Hanse', was still at the height of its power. The social composition, economic strength, political autonomy and well-developed trading and personal networks of the Free City provided very favourable conditions in which the new business of the book trade could take root.[7] Between about 1473 and 1525 nine print workshops set up business in Lübeck. Throughout the German-speaking lands it was the norm for Latin, as the European *lingua franca* of the Church, education, administration and commerce, to dominate in the production of the printing

---

[6] Wells, *Linguistic History*, pp. 198–99.

[7] Dieter Lohmeier, 'Die Frühzeit des Buchdrucks in Lübeck', in *Die Lübecker Buchdrucker im 15. und 16. Jahrhundert. Buchdrucker für den Ostseeraum*, ed. by Dieter Lohmeier and Alken Bruns (Heide in Holstein: Boyens & Co, 1994, pp. 11–53; Wolfgang Undorf, *From Gutenberg to Luther – Transnational Print Cultures in Scandinavia 1450–1525* (Leiden: Brill, 2014).

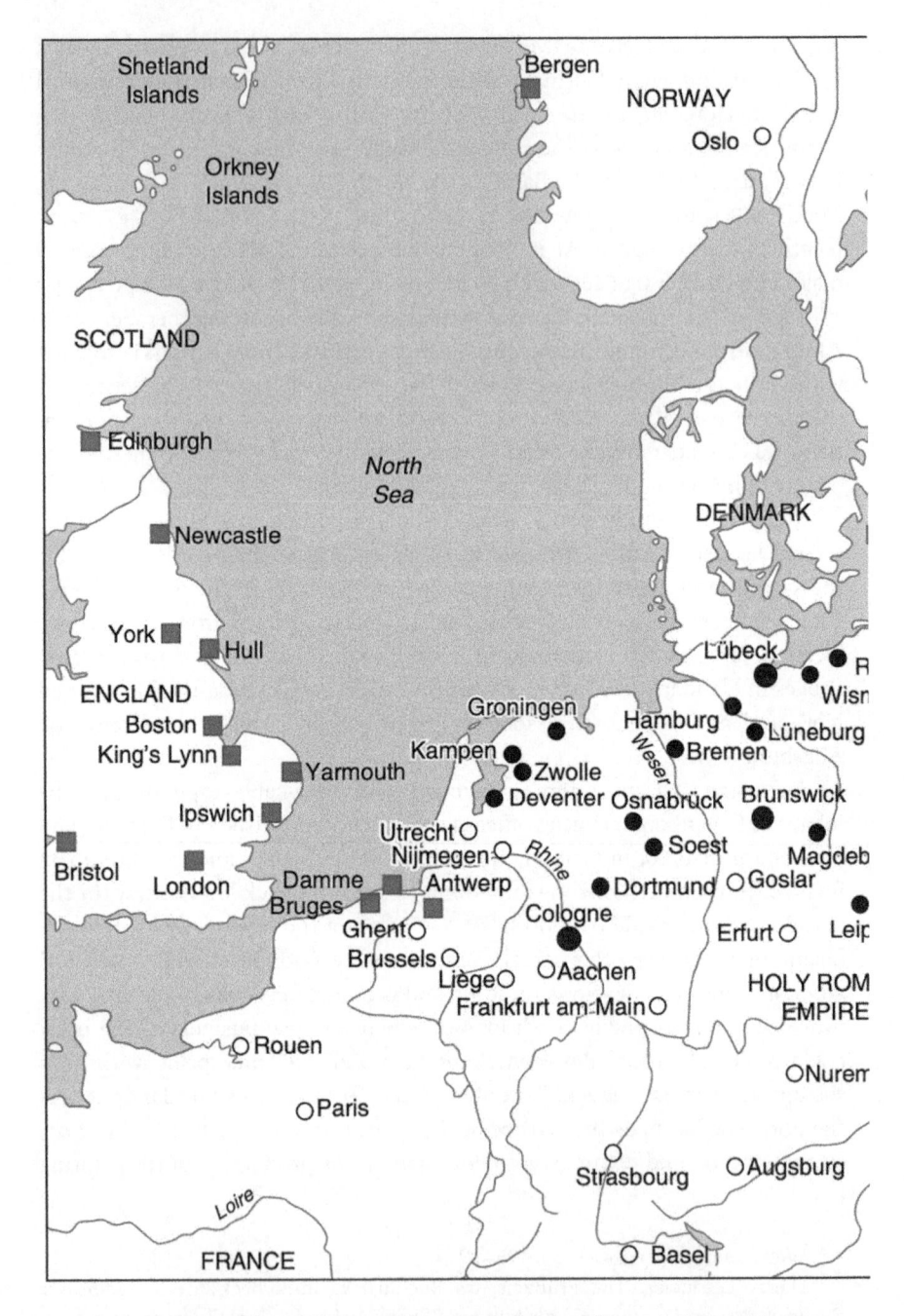

Fig. 2. Map of the Hanseatic League, c.1400, taken from *A Companion to Mysticism and Devotion in Northern Germany in the Late Middle Ages*, ed. by Elizabeth Andersen, Henrike Lähnemann and Anne Simon (Leiden: Brill, 2014), by kind permission of Brill.

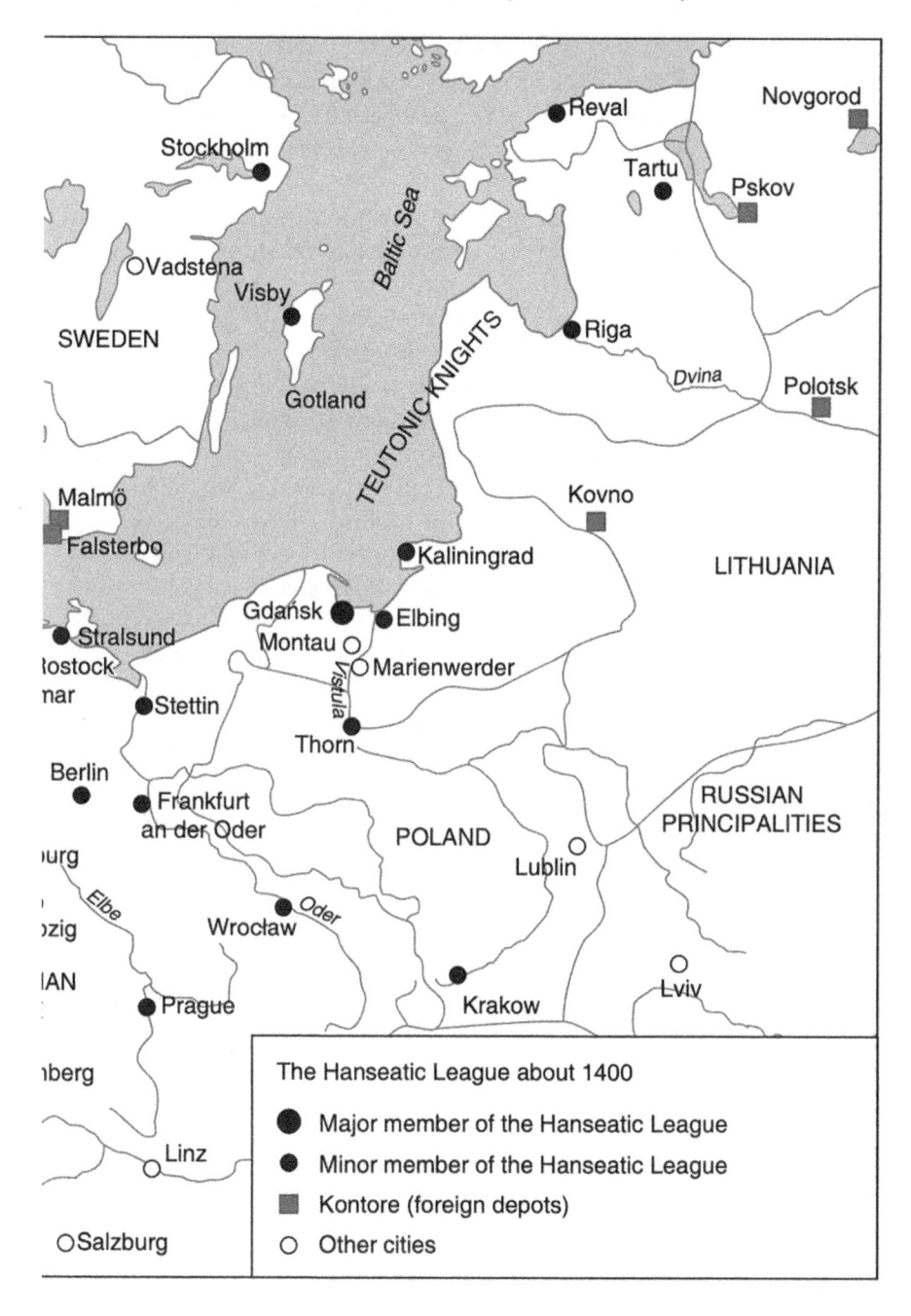

Map: The Hanseatic League about 1400
- ● Major member of the Hanseatic League
- ● Minor member of the Hanseatic League
- ■ Kontore (foreign depots)
- ○ Other cities

houses. This was no different in Lübeck, with the notable exception of the Mohnkopf Press. Where in the other Lübeck presses output in Latin constituted between 65 and 80 per cent of the total production, the majority of the 31 texts printed by the Mohnkopf Press between 1487 and 1527 are in the Low German vernacular.

The literature published by the first generation of Lübeck printers is pre-eminently characterized by its devotional nature, with its overriding concern to cater 'for those not schooled in scholastic learning who do not understand Latin thoroughly'.[8] The development of this urban literary culture was influenced strongly by the mendicant orders, the contemporary reform movements and the *Devotio moderna*, with their common interest in making the teaching of the Church accessible to lay people. The Mohnkopf Press exemplifies this trend to a greater degree than the other printing houses in Lübeck, not least in the texts that are the focus of this chapter. The distinctive output of the Mohnkopf Press may serve as a microcosm for pointing up how the intersections of geography, culture and language shaped the production of western European literary culture in the late Middle Ages. To demonstrate this three incunable texts have been selected as complementary case studies:[9] *Des Dodes Dantz* [*The Dance of Death*], *Sunte Birgitten Openbaringe* [*The Revelations of St Birgitta*] and *Dat Narrenschyp* [*The Ship of Fools*].[10] Although markedly different in origin and genre, these texts are all shaped by the devotional purpose that defines the literary production of the Mohnkopf Press. Significantly in the context of this volume, they reveal shared patterns of linguistic, cultural and visual translation that both 'transnationalize' and localize.

---

[8] *De salter to dude* (GW M36239), 274v: 'vor de ungelerden de dat latyn nicht gruntlicken vorstaen'. All German prints of the fifteenth century are catalogued in the Gesamtkatalog der Wiegendrucke (GW) [Union Catalogue of Incunabula Database] which is available online: http://www.gesamtkatalogderwiegendrucke.de/ [accessed 17 November 2019].

[9] An 'incunable' is a term used to classify books printed before 1501, i.e. in the infancy of printing.

[10] In this chapter I refer to: *Dat Narren Schyp* (Lübeck: Mohnkopf, 1497) [GW 05053]; *De salter to dude* (Lübeck: Mohnkopf, 1493) [GW M36239]; *Diarium Vadstenense: Latinsk text med översattning och kommentar*, ed. by Claes Gejrot. Kungl. Samfundet för utgivande av handskrifter rörande Skandinaviens historia, Handlingar del 19 (Stockholm, 1996); *Des Dodes Dantz* (Lübeck: Mohnkopf, 1489) [GW M47262]; *Revelationes Sanctæ Birgittæ* (Lübeck: Bartholomäus Ghotan, 1492) [GW 04391]; *The Revelations of St. Birgitta of Sweden*, translated by Denis Searby with Introductions and Notes by Bridget Morris, 4 vols (Oxford: Oxford University Press, 2006–2015); and *Sunte Birgitten Openbaringe* (Lübeck: Mohnkopf, 1496) [GW 04395].

Case Study 1: *The Dance of Death* (1489)

The allegorical concept of the Dance of Death functions as an arresting reminder of both the mortality of humankind and death as the great leveller. It confronts this life with the next, temporality with eternity and power with powerlessness. The concept had its origins in late thirteenth-century or early fourteenth-century poems on the subject of death.[11] It became widespread in the late Middle Ages, fuelled by events such as the Black Death in the mid-fourteenth century and the devastation wreaked by the Hundred Years War between France and England (1337–1453). The earliest known example of the fully developed concept is a series of paintings in the open arcade of the charnel house of the Cemetery of the Holy Innocents in Paris (1424/25). The wall painting depicts the inevitability of death in a series of human figures (all male) accompanied by skeletons cutting capers in a long procession. The figures are ordered according to the hierarchy of church and state, from pope and emperor to shepherd and farmer, with a verse below each explaining the person's station in life.

The Parisian *danse macabre* spread throughout France and then to Italy, Spain, Switzerland, Austria, Germany, Flanders, England, Denmark, Finland and Estonia.[12] The concept reached Lübeck in the second half of the fifteenth century, via the Dutch-speaking territory of the Netherlands. Throughout the Middle Ages the Low Countries functioned as a mediating link between the Romance and Germanic trading and cultural regions. Thus, they facilitated the impact and influence of the *Devotio moderna*, the most successful religious movement in late medieval Europe and of central importance to the business of the Lübeck printers. The aim of the *Devotio moderna* was the reform of the spiritual life according to the ideals of early Christianity, with a focus on personal spiritual regeneration through reflective immersion in and imitation of the life of Christ. This was coupled with a concern for lay education and social ministry to the poor.[13]

In 1463 Bernt Notke, an artist and sculptor who worked across the Baltic region, painted a Dance of Death on the Parisian model for the Church of

---

[11] Wolfgang Stammler, *Der Totentanz. Entstehung und Deutung* (Munich: Carl Hanser Verlag, 1948).

[12] Elina Gertsman, *The Dance of Death in the Middle Ages. Image, Text, Performance* (Turnhout: Brepols, 2010).

[13] Anne Bollmann, 'The Influence of the *Devotio moderna* in Northern Germany', in *A Companion to Mysticism and Devotion in Northern Germany in the Late Middle Ages*, ed. by Elizabeth Andersen, Henrike Lähnemann and Anne Simon (Leiden: Brill, 2014), pp. 231–60.

St Mary in Lübeck.[14] This depicted 24 figures, half of them drawn from the clergy and half from secular life. The painting is no longer extant because of Second World War bombing. However, a sizeable fragment (1.60m × 7.50m with 13 life-size figures) of a very similar Dance of Death, also thought to have been painted by Notke for the Church of St Nicholas in Reval (present-day Tallinn), does exist. This, together with a series of documentary photographs, both allows us to reconstruct what the Lübeck painting would have been like and to gain some insight into the migration of the trope of the Dance of Death across the Hanseatic region.[15] We know that in the original painting the figures were projected against a background that was recognizably Lübeck and that the text below the images was in Middle Low German with traces of Middle Dutch, revealing the channel of transmission from France through the Netherlands. The familiarity of the Lübeck landscape and the vernacular language would no doubt have impressed even further upon the church-goers the relevance of the subject matter to them and their condition. Some further changes were made with regard to the identity of the figures (which in this version included women); those not relevant to the Lübeck context (e.g. the sergeant) were omitted, while others, most notably the burgomaster, the chief magistrate of the town,[16] were added, reflecting more closely the particular social composition of the Imperial Free City with its ruling urban patriciate. Free and Imperial cities were enclaves that ranked alongside the Imperial States with a seat and a vote in the Imperial Diet. This was in sharp contrast to the majority of cities in the Empire, which belonged to a territory and so were governed by either a secular lord (e.g. a duke, margrave, count) or an ecclesiastical lord (e.g. a prince-bishop or prince-abbot). In the Free and Imperial cities the source of political power and legitimacy shifted from religious or dynastic authorities to the urban élite.[17]

---

[14] Hartmut Freytag (ed.), *Der Totentanz der Marienkirche in Lübeck und der Nikolaikirche in Reval (Tallinn)* (Cologne/Weimar/Vienna: Böhlau Verlag, 1993).

[15] The original Lübeck wall painting had begun to deteriorate by the seventeenth century and was copied on canvas in 1701 by Anton Wortmann. At the same time the fifteenth-century text, all but illegible, was transcribed by the pastor Jacob Melle and subsequently replaced by new verses composed by Nathanael Schott. Documentary photos taken by Wilhelm Castelli between the two World Wars are all that remains of the original painting. Hildegard Vogeler, 'Zum Gemälde des Lübecker und des Revaler Totentanzes', in *Der Totentanz*, ed. by Freytag, pp. 73–108.

[16] The role of the burgomaster in the city is comparable to that of a mayor; the burgomaster is typically to be found in the Netherlands, Flanders, Austria and Germany.

[17] Kerstin Petermann, *Bernt Notke. Arbeitsweise und Werkstattorganisation im späten Mittelalter* (Berlin: Reimer, 2000).

The seminal influence of Notke's Dance of Death painting on the anonymous author of *The Dance of Death* is evident. However, this work is not simply a copy in book form but rather an independent and extended adaptation that is aligned with the concerns of the devotional literature so prevalent in Lübeck. It is recast into a didactic book that is both catechetical and entertaining; it has 36 leaves (72 pages), includes four additional figures and runs to 1,686 lines, which is four times the length of the text in Notke's painting. In the switch in medium from wall painting to book the ratio of image to text has been inverted. The human figures appear on the left-hand page and the figure of Death as a skeleton on the right. With the exception of the Rider who is mounting his horse, the human figures appear rooted to the spot, as if frozen in the face of imminent death. Their bodies face to the left (with the exception of the Nun and the Knight Templar) and they look back at Death, whose gaze is fixed on them. Death is portrayed conventionally as a skeleton. Where in the Lübeck and Reval paintings Death leads the procession, playing the flute and bagpipes respectively, in *The Dance of Death* he has variously four attributes – a scythe, an arrow, a spade and a sword, which he brandishes while riding a lion. The order in which the figures appear is, as established in the Parisian *Danse macabre*, hierarchical, with the pope at the head of the procession, followed by the dignitaries of the religious and secular estates. They are followed by representatives of the urban population, such as the burgomaster, the doctor, the student and the merchant. The dance concludes with the nurse and infant.

The title page, with its quote from the epilogue, confronts the reader with the chilling words: 'Oh human, consider where you have come from and what you are now and what you will become in a short space of time.'[18] The encounter of the individual figures with Death is presented as a series of discrete text units, all of which follow the same pattern of narrative development. The dialogue between the Burgomaster and Death may serve to exemplify this (Figs. 3 and 4).

The Burgomaster opens the dialogue with Death, although this term is not quite accurate, as, rather than talking to one another, they each deliver a monologue. The Burgomaster muses on the heavy responsibility he carries for the welfare of the community, lamenting that the community can ill afford to lose him, but recognizing at the same time the inevitability of death. He reassures himself that he has done his best and prays to God to have mercy on him. This self-righteous projection is called into question by Death, who, while acknowledging the responsibility the Burgomaster carries for his community, probes into the integrity with which he has discharged

---

[18] 'O mynsche dencke wor du bist her ghekomen unde wattu nu byst. unde wat du schalt werden in korter vryst.'

Borgermester

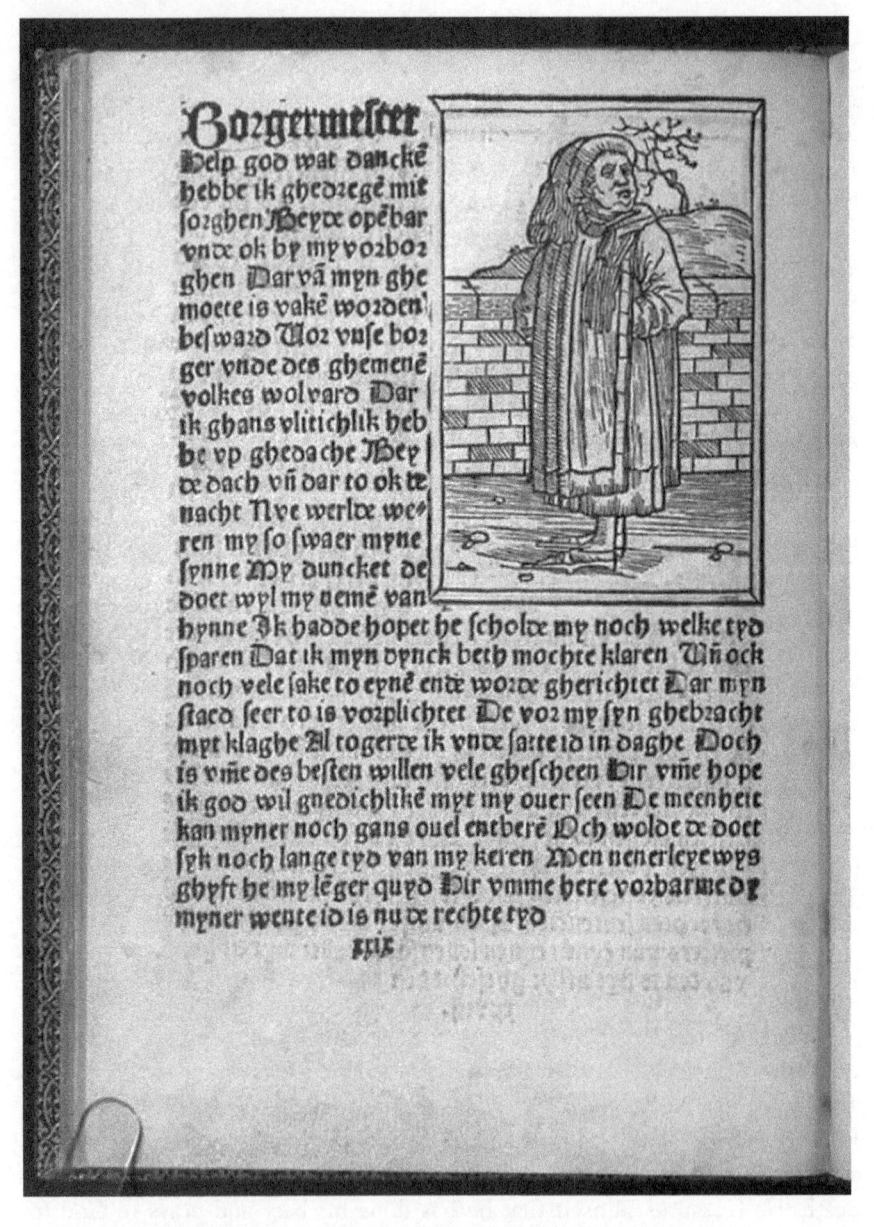

Help god wat dancke
hebbe ik ghedzege mit
sorghen Heyre opēbar
vnde ok by my vorbor
ghen Dar vā myn ghe
moete is vake worden
beswaro Vor vnse bor
ger vnde des ghemenē
volkes wolvaro Dar
ik ghans vlitichlik heb
be vp ghedache Hey
de dach vn dar to ok te
nacht Nye werlde we-
ren my so swaer myne
synne My duncket de
doet wyl my nemē van
hynne Ik hadde hopet he scholde my noch welke tyd
sparen Dat ik myn dynck beth mochte klaren Vñ ock
noch vele sake to eyne ende worde gherichtet Dar myn
staed seer to is vorplichtet De vor my syn ghebracht
myt klaghe Al togerde ik vnde satte id in daghe Doch
is vme des besten willen vele ghescheen Dir vme hope
ik god wil gnedichlike myt my ouer seen De meenheit
kan myner noch gans ouel entberē Och wolde de doet
syk noch lange tyd van my keren Men nenerleye wys
ghyft he my leger quyd Dir vmme here vorbarme dy
myner wente id is nu de rechte tyd

Fig. 3. The Burgomaster, taken from *Des Dodes Dantz*
(Lübeck: Mohnkopfdruckerei, 1489), available with creative commons
licence from the Germanisches Nationalmuseum
(http://dlib.gnm.de/item/4Inc28260/11/html).

De doet

Der borghermester de sorge vn ok dat arbeyt dattu hefst gehat vor de borger vn meenheyt Vnde hefstu de sake vlitich ouerghedacht Vñ nicht de personen efte gelt gheacht Vñ hefst den riken gherichtet so den armen So wyl syk god diner wol erbarmē Vñ wil dyn arbeit hochlykē belonē Wen dy ne missedaet en wert he ok nicht schonen Also efte du dyn eghē ghenuth meist hefst gesocht Dar mede vyllichte de meenheyt were in last ghebrocht Efte du hefst ghekoft rēte efte tolle Dat sy in acker, in wysche in dorper efte in mollen Dar a me du vor den vorstē de warheyt icht hefst ghespard Vñ in dagēde dyne worde so nicht gheklart Up dattu dyne rēte alle mochtest krygē to dyne vromen Dar vā de meenheyt icht were in welke last ghekomē To allē weldigē rētenerē is dit alsus gheseche Vñ dy nicht dy allene to ghelecht: wē te dyn staed is myt groter sorge beladē Hefstu den wol gheholdē so en schal dy nicht schadē Vñ de bode godes vor dy ghesath in al dyne dingē So vrochte dy nicht dy schal wol ghelingen God wert an seen dyn arbeyt vñ dyne rechtuerdicheit Vñ wert dy dar vor gheuē de ewygben salicheyt xxx.

Fig. 4. Death, taken from *Des Dodes Dantz*
(Lübeck: Mohnkopfdruckerei, 1489), available with creative commons
licence from the Germanisches Nationalmuseum
(http://dlib.gnm.de/item/4Inc28260/11/html).

his duties. If, Death says, the Burgomaster has acted in the best interests of the community, treating the rich and the poor alike, and has not sought his own advantage through the unfair imposition of taxes, then God will have mercy on him and reward him richly. Death then moves from the individual to the collective, addressing in the same vein all those who hold the office of burgomaster. Whether the conduct of the particular Burgomaster addressed is exemplary or not is left open. All burgomasters and, by extension, the reader are challenged to consider the probity of their actions. The accent falls on the responsibility of the individual for his own salvation through leading a life according to Christian principles, in harmony with God's plan for the salvation of mankind.

In the paintings of the Dance of Death the tone of the verses spoken by Death is generally parodic, mocking the human figure's futile ambition on earth. *The Dance of Death*, by contrast, sits in the broader context of catechetical instruction so typical of late medieval Lübeck and of the Mohnkopf Press in particular. Where the life-size figures of the Lübeck and Reval paintings intimidate the viewer, the illustrations of the human figure and Death in *The Dance of Death* function more as devotional images, focusing the reader's private meditation on the congruence of action and motivation in the context of a God-fearing life.

The *danse macabre* resonated in the late medieval psyche, becoming a construct of European relevance, as is evidenced through the wide dissemination of the trope. At the same time, *The Dance of Death* demonstrates how a motif that has become transnational may also be inflected in a manner specific to a particular context, in this case late fifteenth-century Lübeck.

Case Study 2: The *Revelations of St Birgitta* (1496)

While the impact of the *danse macabre* is achieved through its stark images, the appeal of the *Revelationes Sanctae Birgittae* lay in the detailed visuality of the visions that draw the reader into the presence of the divine. Through her visionary revelations, St Birgitta of Sweden (1303–1373) exercised a profound influence on the spirituality of the late Middle Ages in Europe, not least in Northern Germany and in particular in Lübeck. The transformation of a personal religious vocation into a model of European relevance was initiated and supported in Sweden by three of her confessors: Master Matthias Ovidi, canon of Linköping; Prior Petrus Olavi of the Cistercian Abbey of Alvastra; and his namesake Prior Petrus Olavi of Skänninge, who translated Birgitta's revelations from Swedish into Latin, thus making them widely accessible across Europe. Birgitta's fourth confessor, Alfonso Pecha, whom Birgitta met during her period of residence in Rome, edited and shaped the revelations with a view to her canonization. After the establishment of the Birgittine Order in the 1380s, the canonization of Birgitta in 1391 and the spread of the Birgittine cult across Europe,[19] interest in the *Revelationes* grew rapidly. The Latin text circulated widely throughout Germany, with the translation of extracts into German appearing as early as the late fourteenth century.[20]

The trading and cultural exchange around the Hanseatic Baltic area meant that Birgitta was almost a local saint to Northern Germany and thus it is not surprising that the *Revelationes* was taken up by the first generation of printers in Lübeck. Most significantly, the motherhouse of the Birgittine Order at Vadstena in Sweden commissioned the printing of the *editio princeps* from the press of the Lübeck printer Bartholomäus Ghotan in 1491. The importance of this commission is evident both in the imposing dimensions of the resulting volume (large folio in format, 422 leaves, with 46 lines to the page in double columns and 15 woodcuts as a series of full page and smaller illustrations) and in the print run, as recorded in the relevant entry in the memorial book of Vadstena (800 paper copies and a further 16 on vellum).[21]

The *Revelations of St Birgitta*, printed by the Mohnkopf Press in 1496, is a reworking in Low German of the *Revelationes* a century after the canonization of Birgitta (1391), by which time she was a well-established saint and her daughter Katherina also recently canonized (1484). Although the interval of time between the printing of the *editio princeps* and the *Openbaringe* was only four years, they represent different stages in the cult of Birgitta. The *Revelationes*, including the *Ordo Sanctissimi Salvatoris* [*The Rule of the Saviour*] as communicated to Birgitta by Christ, is the legitimizing founding document of the Birgittine Order. Through the medium of Latin the *Revelationes* were already accessible to the educated élite of Europe. However, the advent of moveable type printing presented the motherhouse at Vadstena with an opportunity to enhance the impact of Birgitta across Europe through the wider dissemination of the work. In a more restricted way, the Mohnkopf *Revelations of St Birgitta* also extended the linguistic reach of Birgitta's revelations in the Hanseatic Baltic area through the recasting of the Latin text into Low German. Furthermore, the use of the

---

[19] Bridget Morris and Veronica O'Mara (eds.), *The Translation of the Works of St Birgitta of Sweden into the Medieval European Vernacular* (Turnhout: Brepols, 2000).
[20] Ulrich Montag, 'The Reception of St Birgitta in Germany', in *The Translation of the Works of St Birgitta*, ed. by Morris and O'Mara, pp. 106–16.
[21] Claes Gejrot (ed.), *Diarium Vadstenense: Latinsk text med översättning och kommentar* (Stockholm: Samfundet för utgivande av handskrifter rörande Skandinaviens historia, 1996), XXXX, 889 (p. 378).

vernacular in *The Revelations of St Birgitta* extended the social reach of the *Revelationes* by unlocking them for a lay urban readership.

The Revelations of St Birgitta was both an abridgement and an adaptation of the *Revelationes*. Quarto in format with 204 leaves and 29 lines to the page, it was a book that could be owned by urban patrician families. Rather than an anthology of extracts, as earlier adaptations into Low German had been,[22] the Mohnkopf *Revelations of St Birgitta* is a carefully crafted book. Where the *Revelationes* has eight books plus extensive supplementary material, *The Revelations of St Birgitta* has just five. The anonymous adaptor has not only made a selection from the material, he has restructured it, modifying the visionary profile. He supplemented the material by drawing on the genre of the saint's life, once for Birgitta (Books I–IV) and again for her daughter Katarina (Book V). Throughout *The Revelations of St Birgitta* the adaptor makes clear what his didactic intentions are, supporting these by drawing on the Bible, ecclesiastical writers and contemporary authors. In this way *The Revelations of St Birgitta* becomes less of a visionary text and more of a saint's life as well as a didactic book of devotion.

The guiding philosophy behind the Mohnkopf Press was that the new art of printing was a divine gift for the instruction of the lay reader in devotional matters.[23] Thus, in Book III of *The Revelations of St Birgitta* (88ᵛ–89ʳ) the adaptor inserts a lengthy excursus on the new art of printing. He manifests a sense of cultural nationalism in the expression of gratitude for what he perceives to be a divine gift to the German people:

> Oh what grace God has shown to these German lands, these German cities into which God has sent so many preachers, so many teachers and in particular this new art which was invented on German soil and which has flourished vigorously.[24]

He is convinced of the efficacy of the printed word for ensuring a God-fearing life and he warns of the greater responsibility placed on the individual for his own salvation given his increased exposure to instruction.

---

[22] Elizabeth Andersen, 'Birgitta of Sweden in Northern Germany: Translation, Transmission and Reception', in *A Companion to Mysticism*, ed. by Andersen et al., pp. 205–30 (p. 209).

[23] Elizabeth Andersen, 'Religious Devotion and Business. The Pre-Reformation Enterprise of the Lübeck Presses', *Ons Geestlijk Erf* 87 (2016), pp. 200–23 (pp. 211–13).

[24] 'Eya wat gnade heft god de here gegeven dessen dudeschen lande. desse dudeschen steden in welken god sendet so vele predikers. so vele lerer. unde sunderliken dessen nyen kunst. de in dudeschen landen erst is ghevunden. unde overvloedighen bloyet.'

Fig. 5. 'Saint Birgitta, Bride of Christ, Pray for us',
taken from *Sunte Birgitten Openbaringe*
(Lübeck: Mohnkopfdruckerei, 1496), by kind permission
of SUB Göttingen, 8 H E SANCT 176/33 INC, fol. 9^v.

34   *Elizabeth Andersen*

Fig. 6. 'Saint Katarina of Vadstena', taken from *Sunte Birgitten Openbaringe* (Lübeck: Mohnkopfdruckerei, 1496), by kind permission of SUB Göttingen, 8 H E SANCT 176/33 INC, fol. 178ᵛ.

Although images are not so prevalent and are not integrated into the text as they are in both *The Dance of Death* and *The Ship of Fools*, *The Revelations of St Birgitta* nonetheless has 11 woodcuts, including the printer's signature marks at the end of the volume. Each of the five Books is opened by a woodcut: the same image of Birgitta (Fig. 5), with varying captions, is used for the frontispiece and the first four books; an image of Katherina opens 'her' book, Book V (Fig. 6).

In keeping with the manner in which *The Revelations of St Birgitta* has been adapted, the focus in the image of Birgitta is on her as an individual, as an author, rather than on her prophetic role as a channel for God to address mankind. Dressed as a widowed matron, she sits writing in the conventional pose of the Gospel writers and the Church Fathers. The focus is firmly on the book, with Birgitta's eyes trained on it as she writes. The visionary aspect of the work is represented in the depiction of the heads of Christ and Mary, as her main interlocutors, in the top left- and right-hand corners. However, the scale of these two heads reinforces the shift in emphasis that the adaptor made in his reworking of the *Revelationes* from a pre-eminently visionary work to one which is in equal measure a work of devotion, a saint's life and a book of revelations. The woodcut image of Katherina suggests a different type of saint. She appears as a nun and it would seem a Birgittine nun, wearing the distinctive headdress of the Birgittines.[25] The image is in fact a woodcut recycled from *The Dance of Death*, where the Birgittine represents the social category of the nun. Taken out of the pairing with Death, the image becomes in *The Revelations of St Birgitta* a model of saintliness, although different in kind from Birgitta. The girdle book hung from Katherina's belt would typically have contained devotional reading and so casts her as a reader, not as an author.

In the context of fifteenth-century Lübeck the text of the *Revelationes* is reframed in *The Revelations of St Birgitta* to meet the spiritual needs of a lay, and possibly particularly female, audience.[26] Thus, the imposing and authoritative Latin text of the Birgittine Order is recast as a book of devotion for private reading and reflection, with the charismatic, visionary figure of the

---

[25] The Birgittine headdress has two bands that form a cross over the head, the arms of which are connected by a circular band. Set in this cross-band crown, one at each joint, are five red stones recalling the five wounds Christ suffered on the Cross.

[26] A handwritten inscription to one of the 13 extant copies of the *Openbaringe*, held in Göttingen University library, gives a clue as to the typical owner of this work. According to the inscription, written by Tybekke Grönhagen, one Sister Katharina Grönhagen gave the book to her dear aunt. Cf. Andersen, 'Birgitta of Sweden in Northern Germany', pp. 221–22.

fourteenth-century aristocratic Birgitta presented as an accessible role model for a fifteenth-century urban lay readership.[27]

Case Study 3: *The Ship of Fools* (1497)

Although the source text for the Low German *The Ship of Fools* is in German, it is in High German, from deep in the south of the Holy Roman Empire – to all intents and purposes a different language. Sebastian Brant's *Narrenschiff* (also *The Ship of Fools*, referred to henceforth as *Narrenschiff* to distinguish it from the later 1497 *Dat Narren Schyp*) was first published in 1494 in Basel. It is a satirical allegory of a ship laden with fools setting sail for the imaginary land of *Narragonia*, a 'fools' paradise'. The satire is biting and the commentary on such topics as the folly of pedantry, boastfulness, gluttony, gambling, false learning, adultery, greed, envy, hatred and pride is delivered in lively rhyming verses that are both aphoristic and humorous, and are rich with insights into the foibles of human nature. The work holds up to its readers a mirror of multi-faceted folly, cutting across social class, with the intention of showing them the dangers of such behaviour and encouraging them to live in the world more wisely. The *Narrenschiff* has a prologue and an epilogue, but there is no narrative framework as such. Instead, it is a compendium of 112 separate examples of folly, ranging from the vicious to the silly, to be read and digested individually. Each of the examples is constructed according to the same tripartite pattern: a three-line rhyming verse stanza is followed by a woodcut image that offers either a literal or an allegorical interpretation and then a passage of rhyming verse (ranging from 30 to 200 lines) enlarges upon the particular folly or vice.

Sebastian Brant (1457–1521) was born in Strasbourg. He studied philosophy and law at the newly established university of Basel (1460) and went on to teach law there until 1501, when he returned to his native Strasbourg to practise as a lawyer and hold the office of town clerk. During Brant's time, Basel was at the forefront of German Humanism, with its aim to revive the cultural and literary legacy as well as the moral philosophy of classical antiquity, this not least in the service of the renewal of Christianity after the more utilitarian and narrower focus of medieval scholasticism. Brant himself was well versed in the Latin classics, in particular the satires of Horace, Persius and Juvenal, the formal influence of which is evident in the *Narrenschiff*.[28] The text of the *Narrenschiff* is complemented by woodcuts, thought to be

---

[27] Elizabeth A. Andersen, 'Heiligkeit auf Niederdeutsch: Birgitta und Katharina von Schweden in Lübecker Frühdrucken', *Niederdeutsches Jahrbuch* 136 (2013), pp. 37–58.
[28] Edwin H. Zeydel, *Sebastian Brant* (New York: Twayne, 1967), pp. 24–33.

principally the work of Albrecht Dürer, who, like Brant, was at the forefront of German Humanism. The skilful integration of the lively and entertaining woodcuts with the pithy verses in the vernacular ensured the wide appeal of the *Narrenschiff*, but it is also clearly a work of some scholarly erudition. It anthologizes traditional wisdom and morality, drawing on classical Latin literature, the Church Fathers and teachers of patristic theology while at the same time incorporating the traditions of the court fool and the carnival fool.

The *Narrenschiff* quickly became a bestseller, going into six authorized and seven unauthorized editions within Brant's lifetime. Furthermore, it became a European bestseller through the adaptation into Latin by Jakob Locher, entitled *Stultifera navis* (1497). This free translation was executed in collaboration with Brant himself, whose student Locher had been. The arrangement of the chapters in the *Stultifera navis* does not conform faithfully to that of the original and new material is introduced, more classical allusions are inserted and shifts in emphasis are made.[29] Paradoxically, while the *Stultifera navis* extends the readership internationally through the *lingua franca* of Latin, at the same time it restricts it to the educated élite of those who understood Latin. Nonetheless, the *Stultifera navis* was also key to the wider accessibility of the *Narrenschiff* in that it was the main source text from which all the translations into European vernacular languages (Dutch, English, Flemish, French) were made – that is, with the exception of the Low German translation, which drew on the original High German text.

The anonymous adaptor who translated the *Narrenschiff* into Low German substituted High German place-names and the names of people for those that were familiar and local in the Lübeck context.[30] The main source text was the Basel edition in the unauthorized but reliable edition printed in Nuremberg by Peter Wagener in 1494, supplemented by the edition printed by Johannes Grüninger in 1494/95 in Strasbourg. The Mohnkopf *The Ship of Fools* is an impressive volume: quarto in format, it runs to 238 leaves, with 140 woodcuts from 83 printing blocks. Of these 72 were newly made, while seven are probably from a text, no longer extant, about the Antichrist.[31] Significantly in the context of this chapter, a further four are drawn from *The Dance of Death*: Death, the Junker, the monk and the nun (the same image of

---

[29] Michael Rupp, *'Narrenschiff' und 'Stultifera navis'. Deutsche und lateinische Moralsatire von Sebastian Brant und Jakob Locher in Basel 1494–1498* (Münster et al.: Waxmann, 2002).

[30] Timothy Sodmann (ed.), *Dat Narren Schyp Lübeck 1497. Fotomechanischer Neudruck der mittelniederdeutschen Bearbeitung von Sebastian Brants Narrenschiff* (Bremen: Schünemann, 1980), p. 10.

[31] Sodmann, *Dat Narren Schyp*, pp. 11–15.

ü

Gaudeamus oēs ad narragoniam

Dat narren schyp

¶ Hi sūt qui descēdūt mare in nauibus faciē
tes operationē i aquis multis Ascēdūt vsq3
ad celos et descēdūt vsq3 ad abyssos. aia eo
rū i malis tabescebat Turbati sūt et moti sūt
sicut ebrius et ois sapiētia eorū deuorata est
Psalmo C v i

Fig. 7. End of prologue and title page of the Low German *Ship of Fools*, taken from *Dat Narren Schyp* (Lübeck: Mohnkopfdruckerei, 1497), reproduced from *Dat narren schyp, Lübeck 1497: Fotomechanischer Neudruck der mittelniederdeutschen Bearbeitung von Sebastian Brants Narrenschiff*, ed. and supplemented with an afterword by Timothy Sodmann (Bremen: Schünemann, 1980).

the nun, as noted above, that was used in *The Revelations of St Birgitta* (see Fig. 6)). The multiple use of these images by the anonymous artist reinforces the association of these three Low German texts within the devotional programme of the Mohnkopf Press and demonstrates how, in very practical terms, cultural images and thus ideas circulated from one context to another. The sense of common purpose is reinforced by comments in *The Ship of Fools* that echo those in *The Revelations of St Birgitta* on the nature and purpose of the printing business: 'If the printer uses his art so that he has God's favour by honouring God, then he does right by teaching it in this way.'[32] Furthermore, close examination of those passages where the text of *The Ship of Fools* has been amplified has revealed that the sources of this expansion were largely drawn from other devotional works printed in Lübeck by Ghotan and, most frequently, the Mohnkopf Press.[33]

Careful comparison of the *Narrenschiff* with *The Ship of Fools* [*Dat Narren Schyp*] has revealed a guiding principle in the adaptor's approach to his task.[34] Where Brant, fully engaged in the Humanism that had found fertile ground in Basel, had drawn liberally on classical literature to illustrate his narrative and to reinforce the message of his work, the Low German adaptor reduces significantly the range of erudite references from classical antiquity, replacing them instead with increased numbers of examples from the Bible and religious literature. This is accompanied by an increase in moralizing comments that emphasize the individual's responsibility for his own actions in the eyes of God. Lübeck in the north and Basel in the south are both frontier cities within the context of the Holy Roman Empire, geographically as far away from one another as possible. This distance is reflected in the different prevailing cultures of these two Imperial Free Cities. The cultural production of Basel, with its proximity to Italy, is clearly marked by Humanism with its roots in the Italian Renaissance, whereas the urban literary culture of the Hanseatic City of Lübeck, remote from Italy and without a university to champion Humanism, is marked strongly by a pronounced devotional character, with texts of widely differing genres being adapted as vehicles for the communication of pastoral instruction.

---

[32] 'Brucket de drucker alzo syne kunst / Dat he wyl hebben godes gunst / Dat god dar uth wert gheeret / He deyt recht wan he so leret' (11^v).

[33] From the Ghotan printing house *Dat levent sunte jeronimi* (1484) and *Dat lycht der selen* (1484); and from the Mohnkopf Press itself *Boek der prophecien, lectien, epistolen unde ewangelien* (1488 and 1492), *Des Dodes Dantz* (1489), *De salter to dude* (1493) and *Speygel der leyen* (1496).

[34] Friederike Voss, *Das mittelniederdeutsche Narrenschiff (Lübeck 1497) und seine hochdeutschen Vorlagen* (Cologne/Weimar/Vienna: Böhlau, 1994).

Conclusion

The use of Latin as a *lingua franca* meant that there was always a 'transnational' culture in medieval Europe that transcended linguistic and political borders among the educated élite, whether in the worlds of the Church, monastic orders, universities, law or commerce. In the late fifteenth century in Northern Europe, Low German was an additional *lingua franca*, both in the Low Countries, where it was closer to Middle Dutch than it was to High German, and in the Hanseatic trading area around the Baltic. The many Low German words borrowed into Danish and Swedish attest to the importance of the Hanse as a channel of mercantile and cultural influence. Those texts printed by the Lübeck presses in the *lingua franca* of Low German were assured of a readership beyond Northern Germany.[35] The Imperial Free City of Lübeck, with its ruling urban patriciate, fostered a thriving network of printers and the city became a hub for the development of a literary production that was in its essence transcultural and translingual. The case study of three works printed by the Mohnkopf Press has demonstrated the linguistic complexity of channels of dissemination across Europe as texts written in Latin were translated and adapted into the vernacular and, conversely, texts written in the vernacular were translated and adapted into Latin. In the hands of the Mohnkopf Press, who saw the new business of printing as a divine gift for the religious and moral education of the lay population, the three case-study texts, so very different in origin and genre, were assimilated to a programme of didactic devotional literature. The reception of these texts throws into sharp relief the complex dynamics that shaped the interaction between the local and the 'transnational' in a specific context, that of late medieval Lübeck.

Suggestions for Further Reading

Andersen, Elizabeth, Henrike Lähnemann and Anne Simon (eds.), *A Companion to Mysticism and Devotion in Northern Germany in the Late Middle Ages* (Leiden: Brill, 2014), 451 pp.

Bruns, Alken, and Diester Lohmeier (eds.), *Die Lübecker Buchdrucker im 15. und 16 Jahrhundert. Buchdrucker für den Ostseeraum* (Heide in Holstein: Westholsteinische Verlagsanstalt Boyens & Co., 1994), 104 pp.

Freytag, Hartmut (ed.), *Der Totentanz der Marienkirche in Lübeck und der Nikolaikirche in Reval (Tallinn)* (Cologne: Böhlau, 1993), 484 pp.

---

[35] Cf. Wells, *Linguistic History*, p. 128 and Undorf, *From Gutenberg to Luther*.

Jones, Howard, and Martin H. Jones, *The Oxford Guide to Middle High German* (Oxford: Oxford University Press, 2019), 736 pp.

Morris, Bridget, and Veronica O'Mara (eds.), *The Translation of the Works of St. Birgitta of Sweden into the Medieval European Vernaculars* (Turnhout: Brepols, 2000), 264 pp.

Schulte, Brigitte, *Die deutschsprachigen spätmittelalterlichen Totentänze. Unter besonderer Berücksichtigung der Inkunabel ‚Des dodes dantz'. Lübeck 1489* (Cologne/Vienna: Böhlau, 1990), 330 pp.

Selzer, Stephan, *Die mittelaterliche Hanse* (Darmstadt: Wissenschaftliche Buchgesellschaft, 2010), 144 pp.

Voss, Friederike, *Das mittelniederdeutsche Narrenschiff (Lübeck 1497) und seine hochdeutschen Vorlagen* (Cologne: Böhlau, 1994), 290 pp.

Wells, C. J., *German: A Linguistic History to 1945* (Oxford: Clarendon Press, 1987), 608 pp.

2

Developing a Polyglot Poetics

The Power of Testimony and Lived Literary Experience

Ulrike Draesner

My essay aims to show how a German writer evolved into being a polyglot writer. Raised in post-war West Germany in the 1970s, it took me years to realize that my personal background wasn't as monolithically 'German' as it had seemed to be. My father's family were (German) migrants from Poland in 1945, with the consequence that I was brought up in a split family (Protestants versus Catholics, farmers versus middle-class citizens, Bavarian versus Silesian rites, recipes, songs, traditions, clothes and so on). The dialects varied as widely as the respective feelings of belonging, roots and loss. English became my second, self-chosen tongue; Anglo-American literature has ever since formed the (hidden) basis of my literary writing. This essay will focus on the development of a literary identity that transgresses national and linguistic borders.[1] It will investigate how findings on long-term consequences of exile inspire changes in fiction writing and will discuss the invisible processes of intergenerational translation.

Language?

My first encounter with English happened through song: the Beatles' *Norwegian Wood* (1965) made perfect sense to my German ears, since I had been taught the meaning of wood at school (where I had started to learn English at the age of ten, and now I was ten and a half), whereas 'Norwegian' suggestively aligned itself with the German 'quietschen' (squeaking) – my

---

[1] For further accounts of cultural figures whose careers cross linguistic and geographic borders, see also the chapters in this volume by Birgit Lang on Louis Kahan (Chapter 14) and Claire Baldwin on Navid Kermani (Chapter 15).

German mind made sense of the world in close complicity with my ears. I was taught by teachers who had seen the war, but had never been to England, and I particularly remember the teacher in my second year at the *Gymnasium* (high school), where even we, 11 and 12 years old at the time, realized that what he spoke wasn't English but Appalling. English would have remained a school language, artificial and as dead as Latin, had it not been for even more songs, films, graphic novels and some books in later years.

When I was 15 I was taken to Welwyn Garden City to spend a fortnight with an English family and at an English school. It was amazing, I liked the water, the tea in the mornings, the afternoons of more tea, even the weather; I discovered punning in English and the art of understatement. As I felt that it was time to give other languages a chance as well, my English was fairly poor the next time I set foot on the island. I had just turned 21 and was about to study at Oxford for a year on an exchange scheme that introduced me to northern accents and to practical words like 'socket' and 'nurse'. Had it not been for a Classics student, I would have been lost. The first term was hard; I really encountered the language, my first 'foreign' one, my first non-mother-tongue, my first non-automatic-one, my chosen first. I hadn't known that this meant to be changed as a person, too. That 'it' – using English sounds, using English grammar, using its time structures and idioms – would transform my perception of 'the world' (all and everything). Thanks to my fellow students and my English boyfriend, I started to live in another tongue (not just an attire, something in the very body). My identity changed with the metaphors I used. Even my voice did.

Surprises continued when I returned to Germany. In the 1980s immersion was full and inescapably real: no internet, no flat rates on phones, no mobiles. On coming back, my 'native' (natural?) tongue had grown foreign to me. Only now had I lost my linguistic first-language naivety – the (wonderful) illusion of the child that the world (things) just *is* (*are*) these words, where it feels utterly bizarre that anybody would not call a Baum (tree) 'Baum'. New dimensions of what it means to 'use' a language had been opened up to me: words and sentences had become as much bodily as 'rational': deeply inscribed, powerful and encompassing. Psychological and physical, emotional and argumentative tools that, constantly changing, proved highly intelligent (collectively fed) hot houses of people's lives and time. I had lived from 'hand to mouth' in German (not implying poverty in this case but rather a natural flow of what was fed into my system). Now I realized how any language is built from sets of metaphors and didn't know how else to think or express what I perceived. It – no, I rather – had been turned into a receiver on two different wave lengths.

I started to write literary texts. In German.

Studying English literature, I was taught narrative and poetic forms and means through English-language writing. I started to translate this into German or, rather, forwarded it into a German of my own making, an invention of my voice.

This took ten years.

In the midst of this process (at the time, of course, there was no midst), I lost my home country.

This came quite as a surprise. The Berlin wall was opened in 1989, a year later we lived in a reunified Germany. The surprise came in two steps. Who would have thought that the post-war order in which we had been brought up would dissolve that quickly? I had been brought up in Munich and studied there. We greeted a plethora of Saxonians in Munich in their *Trabi*-cars, everybody talked about how the GDR disappeared and the *Bundesrepublik* [federal republic] grew and had acquired five new *Bundesländer* [states], and, as we did so, the *Bundesrepublik* of my childhood and youth disappeared as much as the GDR.

The transformation of the western parts wasn't as spectacular as the one in the east, but was nonetheless real. The most extraordinary experience of being a foreigner befell me when I moved to Prenzlauer Berg in 1996. I lived in Germany, same supermarkets as in the south, same currency, same language (almost, but dialects were everywhere), but was treated as a most unwelcome stranger.

Again, my identity had changed. The move to Berlin didn't happen by chance. There had been yet a third surprise for me, a 'present from the past', well hidden in the political changes that transformed Europe around 1990. It shocked and exhilarated me. In autumn 1989 I lived in a kind of college in Munich. There was a common room with a TV set; jointly we watched the coverage of Monday demonstrations in Leipzig and the night of 9 November 1989. I remember that I started to cry – for joy, empathy and relief, feeling how something that had been depressingly out of joint was set right. But most of the others, some very good friends, remained calm and aloof. We had been brought up as Europeans, learnt English and French or Spanish at school and travelled in West Europe. Everybody knew people in France or England or the US; this was, they said, part of their identity. But 'the east'?

The east. Oh, what a bell this rang. So familiar, so part of my clandestine history. Another language was hidden there, another reservoir of family memories, family nightmares and dreams, of cuts and losses, desire and sorrow. I wouldn't have been able to name all this at the time. It was to take another decade to unearth it, and after that a second decade working on intra-generational memory and the reverberations of forced migration for a story that turned itself into nine stories of four generations and two families, one

German, the other Polish. The novel was finally published in 2014 with the title *Sieben Sprünge vom Rand der Welt* [*Seven Leaps from the Edge of the World*].[2]

But let's start from the beginning (let's invent one, for the sake of communication). My writing space consists of a language on (not 'with' – rather on, in, by) which I grew up (a variant of High German with Bavarian tinges), a language I learnt to understand but never actively used (the strong Bavarian dialect spoken in my maternal family), a third variant of German, Silesian, that I loved for its sounds and smells (words, melody of sentences, songs and food, used by my paternal family), a brawl of memories not mine, and a language chosen and adopted at the very end of my childhood, stepping into my adult life (English).

The Dachshund in the Oven

A cousin and I are travelling through Poland and are struck by a completely mad idea: where does our name come from? It's never interested us before, but we have nothing to do here. They've never seen the likes of us in the State Archives in Wroclaw (formerly Breslau), we're too young for what we want, they tell us. 'The German register? Oh …water damage, it's disappeared, been deleted, yet since 1989 it's been waxing like the moon.' When it finally turns up, it's all back-to-front: at first it's all nicely typed up, at the start of the twentieth century the typewritten script vanishes, then the lines of the tables dry up, the scrawl grows ever denser. Only one thing remains the same: names constantly pop up that are erased. They're in Polish or in German, half there, half between the lines – ticks here, sibilants there, oblique wings, feminine eyes. What a mess of entries and exits. And the family name? It obviously gobbled up quite a number of female birthnames names over the centuries, offering but the male side of the story, intertwining the German with the Polish and vice versa. It doesn't faze us, we're educated and immediately decide that inexplicable is a good thing. We don't have to shout it from the rooftops, this hiding ourselves under a cloak of a name that rose up from Slavic swamps and does nothing other than represent corruptibility, tenacity and green-eyed impenetrability, meaning – of course – our green eyes, though not everyone in the family tree inherits them.

Origin – 'Herkunft' in German – is a technical word.[3] It applies to timetables and product lines, to places, to tales. Applied to people it casts a

---

[2] Ulrike Draesner, *Sieben Sprünge vom Rand der Welt* (München: Luchterhand, 2014).

[3] See Ulrike Draesner, *Zauber im Zoo. Vier Reden zu Herkunft* (Göttingen: Wallstein, 2007).

shadow. A shadow warm and soft, bloody, often enough forgotten yet present; 'origin' is dubious, useful and once more turning into an ambivalent concept in an increasingly globalized world. The shadow of the word 'origin' is 'home'. It has a shape. In Bavaria, home's shadow is prone to taking the form of a sausage or a cake or even a *Schmarrn* (a type of dessert), and it smells like cheese from the neighbouring village; it has a colour (sky, fields, a tram braking, a brook gurgling); it has a particular light, in winter, in autumn; it has a sound (the wind in the wooden roofs, in the grass); a twist of the tongue.

Home as *Heimat* is a word of the emotions: half forbidden when I was growing up, rarely used, suspect from the outset – like those half-criminals who populated the newspapers' 'miscellaneous' columns.

Home, for my paternal grandparents, was something lost. Something wonderful, in hindsight. But even that home they'd rather not see again. Too suspect. They could have travelled to Poland. It was brought up nearly every time they met with friends and acquaintances; some left and crossed the border once again, while others, among them my grandparents, stayed put.

Home, glorious, was a thing of the past.

Home, now: a place that no longer resembled itself.

They knew that home was a construct. Home, a luxury. A surplus.

I didn't know this, although I sensed that something in that talk of home, a talk that never ceased in this branch of the family, wasn't right. Was suspect. But that was exactly what appealed to me – the feeling of excess, the authentic inauthenticity. The way x was used to talk about y. Home was interesting, ambivalent: x shone through y, through z.

All of this meant 'home'.

The shining. The secretiveness. Gaps and gasps.

Hannes Grolmann, the grandfather figure in the novel *Seven Leaps from the Edge of the World*, isn't my grandfather, but without my grandfather he wouldn't be Hannes Grolmann. Does that make sense? It's not a metaphor. It describes, very precisely, a condition of non-biographical biography. A way of being rooted in rootlessness, within a field charged with the personal and the political, the historical and the social, within a shadow that is warm, soft, cold. Questions sitting on the shelf mean nothing if nobody asks them. It takes questions and a questioner, questions and a mouth, to take them off the shelf and voice them.

Forty years ago my grandparents were anxious to share something of their early lives with me. They picked and chose, of course, recounting only the good things. When they told me their story they had been living in Bavaria for a quarter of a century. In their tales they were 'at home', yet in the present, during the telling, they were sitting in Munich. With me. An origin story, tailored, cut down to a bearable size. But my grandparents' faces, their sheer physical presence, the apartment that surrounded us – they always told a different tale. And so it was that the 'Dachshund in the Oven' became my favourite story.

It was about a trick, and it still made my grandparents laugh. My grandfather had bought a Dachshund puppy against my grandmother's express wish that there would be no dogs in her house. Early in the morning of 24 December 1937 he stole out of bed at dawn, walked to the breeder, tucked the puppy under his coat and brought it home. Silently he entered the still dark and cold kitchen, put on the oven – lowest level, of course – nested the puppy onto a tray, closed it, went into hiding behind the kitchen door. He knew that my grandmother would be coming down any minute to start her day's work. And it worked out well: her surprise, his charm, the puppy's trust. The dog had stayed with them, my grandmother growing especially fond of him. Till they had to leave their Silesian home in January 1945. Till my father, aged 14, was charged with bringing the Dachshund to the local butcher. Forced migration. You weren't allowed to take pets along.

This my grandparents didn't tell. They ignited a warm *Heimat*-fire in an oven, they laughed and made me laugh, but the story nevertheless held a second truth: I saw or sensed a dachshund in a dark oven that suddenly grew hot, the dachshund, vulnerable, threatened, placed in a trap, saved or lost in the nick of time – it was my grandparents themselves. It was us. All of us. In the middle of the Cold War.

My grandparents' and my father's history as refugees made sure one thing was clear: origin is no fact, no fixed place. It is always a story, a process, no end.

Origins

My Catholic grandmother spoke Bavarian. In her language 'home' was the parental farmstead. It wasn't much spoken of, it was there. And it was useful.

My sister and I were the opposite: Protestant.

Little devils?

Certainly our Catholic grandmother's gifts to us were always significantly smaller than those she gave our Catholic cousins (which was all of them).

When I went to school in 1968, they set up a top-stream class for Catholics only. Protestants, by official definition, were stupid? Nobody would have said so, but it seemed implied.

How do you fight something you can't put your finger on? Unknowingly, I inherited part of my refugee father's lineage.

My mother's homelessness only struck me later.

Then there was home number three, the great land of my father's family: broad as the mind, the imagination. Behind an iron curtain, which for years

I pictured as a literal iron edifice straddling Eastern Europe. I imagined you could burrow underneath it, at least as a child.

There were stories to be found there: grandfather as a Silesian hunter. As the heir to a brewery. As a horseman. Grandfather, who, being a hunter, took his dachshund out. The story was told over and over again. As were some other – anecdotes. Over and over again, in the same meagre words. My sister and I soon got fed up, tried to flee from it. The babble and stammer of trauma. We didn't know, we felt. It was ghostly. Bodies, half alive, something 'between' seemed to enter the room. Unreal space, half-contained in a shape, half-materialized. We tried to fend it off by not listening.

But it stayed on. My sister can't bear to be alone overnight. She owns a huge, well-trained dog that sleeps in her room, if her three sons and her husband should all happen to be out. Dreams and fears. My father told us the end of one of the stories, in passing: The dachshund at the butcher's. It was part of a bigger story that could never come to a rest. It was obliquely referred to in many sentences, single words, gasps, stammers, broken refrains, chokes: the flight.

I felt it my task, my heirloom – my gift – to try to give language to this, to voice the unspeakable.

Being in a Place, of a Place – being a Place?

When I knew my grandparents, they were living in a dark ground-floor apartment in Munich. Three rooms, one of them always rented to a student. Living room, bedroom. I was impressed by the large bed that fit grandfather's belly and grandmother's goitre. Stomachs drew men like him taut and held them upright; otherwise they would have folded up like switchblades. Grandmother couldn't lower her head, because her goitre bulged out like a Halloween pumpkin. During the holidays they travelled to Bad Tölz, grandmother wearing the salvaged coral necklace that made her look like she had bloody finger-marks around her throat, and when I met her in the street my heart flew. But where?

Grandmother had fled with my 14-year-old father and his 24-year-old handicapped brother. They arrived in Bavaria in the late summer of 1945, and now there were only two of them. Before that they had been staying in a small town in what later became the GDR, sheltering with relatives, but had been bombed out. The older brother, injured, weakened, caught pneumonia and died. Grandmother and father reached a refugee camp at Oberwiesenfeld in Munich, today the Olympic Park, then were sent on to a holiday cottage in the country. Their table was one of the suitcases brought from Silesia, which they'd held on to. The makeshift bed was burned for fuel next winter.

Had they arrived?

The beginning of their flight is easily identified: the night between 19 and 20 January 1945. Two hours to pack, it was emphasized again and again. It's always seemed strange to me: 17 years later, midday on 20 January, I came into the world.

Arrived?

But when does any 'flight' stop?

It was Ernst Bloch who said: home is where no one has yet been.[4] The dispossessed, as they're called, like so many others dispossessed before them and so many afterwards, had two things broken off them: first the concrete place, then its language. And, with the language, the place was broken once more, in their memories. And with it – also once more – were their own selves. Although many people found it difficult to believe, this infringement of their integrity was as real and threatening as the bullets shot at their bodies.

Grandfather never 'fled'. He had been recruited as a *Volkssturm* soldier (Hitler's home guard of men above 50 and boys aged 16–18) in January 1945 to defend his home town Breslau, where he was taken prisoner by the Red Army in May 1945 and transported to the Soviet Union. He survived the journey and ended up in a camp for prisoners of war near Leningrad. I write this without really knowing what this means: life in a Soviet camp in 1945, 1946. Half is missing, the rest distorted. He was old, by comparison. They worked in the quarries. All he ever told was that he traded his ration of cigarettes against bread. That they ate grass. He came back, not home. His origins now had a kink that veered east. The photo taken to celebrate his reappearance was paid for with apples my father stole from the cloister garden at night. They didn't tell me that, not explicitly – but I understood. The picture tasted of apples and truth, of mildness and something peeled. It's the photograph where, for me, my grandfather can be seen most acutely as the man he was when nothing sustained him any longer.

Fourteen days after his return he went into the forest.

It too was wrong.

Stony, shot through by a mountain stream. Grandfather plucking belladonna berries from their twigs, shoving them into his mouth. Belladonna, which costs nothing. One after another. They taste sweet. Then handfuls. His green-grey eyes, the leaves' lush green. He was found, and pumping his stomach cost his father's silver pocket watch, preserved from home only with

---

[4] Ernst Bloch, *Das Prinzip Hoffnung*, vol. 3 (Frankfurt/Main: Suhrkamp, 1969), p. 1628: '… etwas, das allen in die Kindheit scheint und worin noch niemand war: Heimat'.

great difficulty. Grandfather with wide, black pupils. Grandfather on drugs. Speechless, his tongue swollen.

In German, 'Heimat' – 'home' – is connected to 'heimlich' and 'unheimlich' – 'secret' and 'uncanny'. To apparitions, spectres, ghosts. The home, the hidden, the box where nobody is allowed to look. But also the uncanny, the gingerbread house with an evil witch inside. 'Heimat' involves magic and secret-keeping, lure and threat. Thus home is always double, x and y, the ugliest and the most beautiful of things, one always visible through the other. For 'home' is another word for intimacy – with things, with people – that doesn't gloss over abysses. Twenty-five years after resettling, my grandparents had a clear picture of home. For them, by then, it was simply something beautiful, surgically excised, and everything else was gone. For those born later, it doesn't work like that. Even my father had to deal with his history very differently, and the bits he couldn't manage still trouble him today. For me, third in the chain, home was always nowhere. It had to be, I'd like to think, but that's only half true. Home both surrounded me and was absent. My sister and I were the only ones in our eastern family who didn't come from the east (we were born in Munich). In our mother's Bavarian family we were the only ones who didn't speak Bavarian and didn't pray properly, so we never belonged there either.

All told it created a kind of 'de-rootedness', by which I don't mean 'rootlessness', but rather movability. Surrounded by roots, but standing beside them. Rootable, yet easily detached. Half rooted down, half elsewhere – and always longing for both. Which in turn means constant motion, tending towards paradox: you're nomadically rooted.

And as for writing? A poetics that considers itself polyglot. Multilingual, even if the first layer of the text seems to be written in a single language. There's always another underneath.

My Silesian grandparents had, as they said, lost everything. But that wasn't true. Their legacy, all of it, was transmuted into stories.

Nomadically overgrown. Polyglotally poetic. Coming and going, roots and air.

Falling Aloud

People communicate by words and deeds, gestures, murmurs, songs, by grunting, hissing, tickling, in dreams – and silently. They express what they think or feel or think to feel and feel they should be feeling in many ways, trying to direct, manipulate, forget, support, efface. They want to shine, want to hide. Conscious or half-conscious acts of communication are accompanied by legions of semi- and sub-conscious signs – ungovernable bodily giveaways such as blushing, tears or this movement of the muscle in the left corner of grandma's mouth.

This has been known for a long time. It is the stuff literature is made of. A lot of our daily comedies (in reality, plays, TV series, cartoons and novels) rely on the inexhaustible plethora of how body-signs and words tell intransigent stories, how intentions, half-intentions and actual acts diverge – and wonderful blunders bloom from it. Freudian slips of the tongue are notorious, blushing and sweating give away secret thoughts.

There is more to it, less well known: an area of uncanny and weird communication, *not* defined by spatial presence or contemporaneity. Our thinking about how the members of a family are connected with each other through time underwent substantial revisions when, 20 to 30 years ago, psychologists started to observe the grown-up children of Holocaust survivors. It was found that traumatization jumped generations. It also affected the memories and abilities to vocalize of daughters and sons and their offspring. Even decades after the end of WWII some wordless, involuntary transmission of knowledge, emotion and pain resulted in inexplicable bodily symptoms, uncanny fears, barren or deprived emotional and spiritual frames of psyches and minds. Traumata or severe injuries of psyche or soul in one generation seem to be passed onto children and grandchildren through forms of secondary communication, using our capacities of projection and mind-reading, of compassion and guilt, of empathy and identification with 'the other'.[5]

Literature has been trying to tell us about these phenomena of intergenerational traumatization (postmemory) for ages.[6] Biologists and neuroscientists marvel about epigenetics, the changes induced in an individual's DNA by that individual's life experience. Epigenetic mutation is a form of knowledge transfer, creating legions of new questions about cellular encoding and reading processes. The inscription of life experience into our physical letters, however, has always been paralleled by another track of a more or less letterized transfer, comprising anything transmitted between the generations in real life communication. These acts are equally difficult to read: encoded and, often enough in these contexts, consisting of a 'no': a hug *not* granted, a

---

[5] See Sabine Bode, *Die vergessene Generation. Die Kriegskinder brechen ihr Schweigen*, (Stuttgart: Klett-Cotta, 2004).

[6] The term 'postmemory' was coined by Marianne Hirsch, *The Generation of Postmemory: Writing and Visual Culture After the Holocaust* (New York: Columbia University Press, 2012), in order to open an intersubjective, transgenerational space of remembering. It differs from memory by generational distance and from history by deeply personal and emotional engagement. The connections between the generations are brought about not through actual memory, but through imaginative investment and creation.

kiss *not* given, an emotion *not* even felt (in the grown-up). They are difficult to spot since we are dealing with negative rather than positive shapes – with voids and loopholes, breaches and gaps, with gasps at best, ghosts of encapsulated events-feelings-spaces, spectres of absence. Nevertheless: even these 'nons', that never become nouns and names, grasp our minds as much in single acts as in our mind-sets, and equally transform single emotions and entire emotional landscapes. Intangible and notoriously hard to assess as these influences must by nature be, they tend to escape our attention, which doesn't make any of it less real, powerful or fast.

I would not have been able to find language(s) for these voices if my German had not been ruptured several times. It was never monolithic (I had to turn 22 in order to learn to pronounce the German standard 'r'). The cuts and splits had been coated so very well that I was hardly aware of them; my English settled on top of this coat, adding different marks, cracks and mistakes. Two layers of ice on a lake, cracked and reflecting, a view, distorted, though alluring, onto what lay 'beneath'. Skating the ice, you wouldn't really want to see it more directly. It needed to stay beyond. I learnt to write using different point of views; Virginia Woolf's *Mrs. Dalloway* (1925) and *The Waves* (1931) startled me into writing, James Joyce cost me a lot of time and Vladimir Nabokov's English works told such a different story about authorship and control, but were equally amazing. Reading split my heart in two (well, that had happened before, but now it became reflected in my set-up as a writer): I loved narrative and plot and needed to think not about, but in, language. I found myself involved in a twofold process of translating: some of the traumatized, suppressed voices I tried to capture travelled to English more easily than to German. National and, above all, family taboos didn't grasp me with their entire strength when I changed into my English identity. Quite a splitting procedure: using my knowledge about writing, deduced from literature written in English, profiting from the elaborate discourse on forced migration's consequences in the Anglo-American world and, above all, hiding and emerging in my own English identity, I found access to topics (voices, characters) buried in the collective body of Berlin-Germany-family-change. By estranging myself into my second identity – being Ulrike in English, at least as a reader – I could feed my German-written voices with the emotions of the German child I had been when my grandparents were still alive.

The stories actually *told* within the family were barren of detail, reiterated over and over again. No plot, no narrator, no audience, no end. In literature and research in English I found (more) context for my intergenerational fears (afraid of snow; shaky at the howl of sirens; an avid packer of suitcases as a child, fantasizing awake about which doll I would take along if we had to leave on an hour's notice; periodically dreaming about trains and luggage lost – I am sure this is telling and multi-faceted and a long story with many wellsprings, since it actually is a long story, a melody of my life, stemming from people loved and parentified by me as a child). So here, starting with Virginia Woolf's character Septimus Warren Smith in *Mrs. Dalloway*, they were: others, telling tales that could not be told, personal witnesses, notorious memory forgers, introducing me to the travels of murmur, of oblivion, of aggression, of hope.

Gauging Languages

So 'polyglot' combined with 'poetics' doesn't refer to countable nations and languages in the first place. It is founded on a combination of biographical traces and the thoughts they provoked, on turns of truth and the experience of difference, the richness and loneliness equally implied by an identity experienced as a story of continual change.

Any single one of us might be more of a familial and collective being than the dominant narratives of individualism so characteristic of Western culture have been telling us for more than two centuries.

Findings on intergenerational memories and traumatization necessitate changes in fiction writing. They are enhanced by post-postmodern uses of meta-fictional awareness and multi-faceted shifts in the category 'real', splayed into layers and fragments, possibilities and hybrids, such as new forms of collective existence. It is time to experiment with new forms of historical narrative in order to envision and question our own time through intelligent translation and retranslation. Refrains, inaudible but to the damaged ear, songs sung by no-voice, stories never told but conveyed. In *Seven Leaps from the Edge of the World* six characters tell the story of their forced migration: they had to leave the world hitherto known to them and dive into something entirely unfamiliar. The seventh leap or 'spring' of the title, though, has to be performed by the novel itself – it is, on its last page, pushed out of its traditional printed form, this cosy (readers') bed, and forced to go digital – whereby it becomes reversed as you might reverse a jumper in order to see how it was made. The website www.der-siebte-sprung.de opens into seven chapters, offering various sources, historical photos, recordings of Polish and Polish–German eye witnesses, parts of a chapter spoken by an ape that never made it into the printed book, an essay on the making of the narrative and, in the last chapter, a blog element. And they contain a dictionary of travelling words, offering explanations of unusual words, old or new, fun definitions and more material on some of the concepts mentioned above, opening up an undocumentary documentation.

In an ultimate, unforeseen eighth leap, however, I found myself pushed to writing the next novel in English. It tells the story of Kurt Schwitters, the artist and writer, who came to England in 1940, having had to flee Germany in 1937 because of his 'degenerate art'. He stayed in London and then the Lake District, where he died in 1948. His English naturalization documents lay on his bedside table, but he was too weak to sign them. Two languages, two identities, or none, an existence in-between. A struggle, a war, continued. The novel needed to be many-voiced and doubly-lingual: I wrote it in English and am now translating it into German, whereby the German version reverberates back into the English tale, changing it in parts, diverging from it, too. Schwitters's identities move, Kurt or Körrt differ in each of their voices. Depending on the language present, different memories become accessible or (can be) blocked; different ideas and emotions arise.

I love to watch films, series, to be online. But there is one thing I find only in literature: the intensity of inner talk. The facility to switch worlds. Literature, through voicing what goes unheard or is considered as unreal, is part of my mixed rootedness: it expresses it, it consoles me in it, it makes it clear and sharp – and makes me feel what it might mean to belong.

Un-fearing me.

Showing how to cope with multi-faceted simultaneous universes.

So yes: let the ghosts talk. In their many-tongues![7]

Suggestions for Further Reading

Draesner, Ulrike, *Zauber im Zoo. Vier Reden zu Herkunft* (Göttingen: Wallstein, 2007), 111 pp.

Draesner, Ulrike, *Sieben Sprünge vom Rand der Welt* (Munich: Luchterhand, 2014), 561 pp.

Draesner, Ulrike, *Grammatik der Gespenster. Frankfurter Poetikvorlesungen* (Ditzingen: Reclam, 2018), 200 pp.

Draesner, Ulrike, *Schwitters* (Munich: Penguin, 2020), 471 pp.

Hirsch, Marianne, *The Generation of Postmemory: Writing and Visual Culture After the Holocaust* (Columbia: Columbia University Press, 2012), 319 pp.

Woolf, Virginia, *Mrs. Dalloway* (London: Penguin, 1992; orig. 1925), 176 pp.

Woolf, Virginia, *The Waves* (London: Penguin, 1992; orig. 1931), 240 pp.

---

[7] Taken up in Ulrike Draesner, *Grammatik der Gespenster. Frankfurter Poetikvorlesungen* (Stuttgart: Reclam 2018).

3

German Writers from Abroad

Translinguralism, Hybrid Languages, 'Broken' Germans

Dirk Weissmann
Translated by Sarah Pybus

A New 'German' Literature

One of the most interesting aspects of the current transnationalization of German culture and the associated transnational reorientation of German Studies is the fact that an increasing proportion of German-language literature is now being written either by authors whose mother tongue or native language is not German or by authors who grew up in multilingual environments. For example, in recent years, more and more of the most important German literary prizes have been awarded to authors who were not born into a German-speaking environment or who use both German and other languages in their everyday lives and literary works.

These intercultural and multilingual language biographies usually result from the migration of the author themselves or from forms of post-migration socialization following the settlement of their parents. 'Moved' in to the German language,[1] these writers confirm the idea that, for the most part, today's world literatures cannot be classified using the traditional model of national literature. Approaches based on the national framework generally assume congruence between culture, language and national affiliation; in the globalized, post-colonial age, such points of view have become increasingly questionable.[2] In place of the organic and holistic concept of literature

---

[1] Uwe Pörksen and Bernd Busch (eds.), *Eingezogen in die Sprache, angekommen in der Literatur, Positionen des Schreibens in unserem Einwanderungsland* (Göttingen: Wallstein Verlag, 2008).

[2] Marie-Andrée Beaudet, '[Littérature] Nationale', in *Le dictionnaire du littéraire*,

originally popularized in the eighteenth century by Johann Gottfried Herder and others, multi-faceted relationships between identity and language are now emerging in literary writing.

Developing further the work of Steven Kellman, this new variety of German or German-speaking writers could be described as 'translingual' authors. Translingual writing takes place against a backdrop of linguistic diversity in a zone of permanent language contact, whereas the national literature model of the nineteenth century (which has remained potent to this day) is based on a monolingual vision of individuals and societies. In contrast to rival concepts such as interculturality and transculturality, this approach emphasizes (migrant) language biographies, processes of linguistic borrowing, interference and idiosyncrasies.

Translingual authors are highly influenced by forms of multilingualism that can be both individual (their own command of multiple languages in an otherwise largely monolingual environment) and collective (for example in the case of minority languages that exist as a significant set of spoken languages within a community). Their writing is marked by a change of language usually induced by migration, resulting in various forms of latent or manifest linguistic interference. These authors may write their texts in their new, 'adopted' language exclusively or in several languages simultaneously. Writers' language biographies and the criteria by which they choose their writing language are manifold and highly personal, as shown by Kremnitz and others.

Following a deep shift in language conceptions around 1800, the language of literature can no longer be reduced – as in the premodern era – to a simple tool or transparent communication medium. Since the works of Herder and Humboldt at the latest, language choice also implies questions of personal and collective identity. Today, translingual forms of literary writing in German demand a reassessment of the relationship between language and cultural or national affiliation. As Kellman puts it: 'Perhaps even more than ethnicity, language is a useful way to approach questions of identity, individual and collective.'[3]

If the Romantics of Herder and Humboldt's day considered German literature to be a privileged expression of genuine German identity based on ethnocentric and nationalistic conceptions of subject and society, the literary language of translingual writers is subjected to hybridization, creolization and even pidginization. Now that the criteria of nation and culture no longer have the power to define literature, translingual writing – with its implicit

ed. by Paul Aron, Alain Viala and Denis Saint-Jacques (Paris: PUF, 2002), pp. 393–94 (p. 393).

[3] Steven Kellman, *The Translingual Imagination* (Lincoln/London: University of Nebraska Press, 2000).

questioning of the 'monolingual paradigm'[4] – is shaking what is perhaps the last foundation of literary identity: the classification of world literature on the basis of self-contained (national) languages.

This development, which will be outlined here using selected examples, is undoubtedly valuable and refreshing in expanding and opening up current German literature – even if, as we shall see, it is not an entirely novel occurrence within the longer history of German literature. In some cases, this new German literature seems to challenge literary criticism by questioning traditional literary criteria such as the need for sophisticated and refined poetic language and linguistic purity. Ultimately, the question arises as to how much German literary language can or should open itself up to the hybrid languages used by migrant authors. To what extent can forms of literary pidginization be read as a symptom of the levelling globalization of the literary market? Or, on the contrary, are these new literary idioms the vital antithesis to such a levelling effect?

Writing Beyond the National Language

Translingual and multilingual authors in contemporary Germany write against the backdrop of a new relationship between language and cultural or national affiliation. Recently, Jacques Derrida, in *Monolingualism of the Other*, has attempted to rethink the inscription of the subject into the collective language in the postcolonial and postnational condition.[5] For Derrida, language is no longer controlled and owned by a national subject, but determined by an infinite process of change he called 'différance'. From an individual's perspective, too, a language always remains for Derrida the 'language of the other', to be reappropriated each time anew. Yet the literature of German writers from abroad provides a particular opportunity to explore this complex inscription of identity into texts.

In refusing to defer to the stylistic and aesthetic norms of standard literary language, many authors currently involved in the German literary scene highlight the way in which writing by translingual (post)migrants combines linguistic strategies with questions of origin, identity and belonging in exemplary fashion. Owing to their multilingual identity, these authors create singular idioms that contain traces of both individual and collective minority identities via inferences, loan translations and language mixing. As

---

[4] Yasemin Yildiz, *Beyond the Mother Tongue: The postmonolingual condition* (New York: Fordham University Press, 2012), introduction.

[5] Jacques Derrida, *Le monolinguisme de l'autre, ou la prothèse d'origine* (Paris: Galilée, 1999).

Alfons D. Knauth states, such writing is 'the most visible mark of an efficient cross-cultural process and of a plural identity, both in the individual and in the collective domain'.[6] In this way, those authors break – by means of aesthetic creativity – with the dominant norm of monolingualism, one of the cornerstones of German and European literary history since the end of the eighteenth century.

In her seminal study, Yasemin Yildiz defines this 'monolingual paradigm' as follows: 'According to this paradigm, individuals and social formations are imagined to possess one "true" language only, their "mother tongue", and through this possession to be organically linked to an exclusive, clearly demarcated ethnicity, culture, and nation.'[7] Even before German studies was established in the nineteenth century monolingualism was an essential condition for German literature. Since the Baroque period German literature has been regarded as the 'defence and illustration' of a specific national character embodied in the German native language.[8] Over the centuries, the nexus of language and ethnicity has led to a nationalistic idealization of literature driven not least by German Studies as a 'Science of Germanness'.[9]

The homogenizing policies of the national state have declared cultural and linguistic otherness to be the exception that proves the rule. German mother tongue and German ethnicity became a necessary condition for a literary work to be counted as a part of 'German national literature'. This was supported by exclusionary mechanisms that have become increasingly institutionalized since the mid-nineteenth century. After the 1813 Wars of Liberation, the derogatory term *Blendling*, or bastard, was used to refer to the 'impure' use of language, including all traces of foreign languages in German.[10] Although the ethnocentric, xenophobic and anti-Semitic excesses of this native language ideology have fortunately disappeared from German Studies, it is important to acknowledge the current success of translingual writers (who have moved

---

[6] Alfons K. Knauth, 'Literary Multilingualism I: General Outlines and Western World', in *Comparative Literature: Sharing Knowledges for Preserving Cultural Diversity, Encyclopedia of Life Support Systems (EOLSS), Developed under the Auspices of the UNESCO*, ed. by Márcio Seligmann-Silva et al. (Oxford: Eolss Publishers, 2007).

[7] Yildiz, *Beyond the Mother Tongue*, p. 2.

[8] Here I reference Joachim Du Bellay's seminal 1549 essay, 'Défense et Illustration de la Langue Française' ['Defence and Illustration of the French Language'].

[9] Eberhard Lämmert et al., *Germanistik – eine deutsche Wissenschaft* (Frankfurt/Main: Suhrkamp, 1967).

[10] See Anja Stukenbrock, *Sprachnationalismus, Sprachreflexion als Medium kollektiver Identitätsstiftung in Deutschland (1617–1945)* (Berlin et al., 2005); Claus Ahlzweig, *Muttersprache – Vaterland, Die deutsche Nation und ihre Sprache* (Opladen: Westdeutscher Verlag, 1994).

into the German language) given the historic position of glottophobia, or linguicism, that underpins the discipline.[11]

The decolonization processes, globalization movements and waves of migration in the post-war period, particularly the phenomenon of 'guest workers' (*Gastarbeiter*), have massively called into question the monocultural and monolingual paradigm. As in other world literatures, German-speaking authors 'from a migrant background' (according to the German expression 'mit Migrationshintergrund') have emancipated themselves from the fixations of monolingual and monocultural norms. For these German writers from abroad, German is not a language of national community, but an open, hospitable language that enriches itself with foreign identities, experiences and idioms.

In this context, Yasemin Yildiz talks of the transition from the concept of German as a national language to the idea of German as a type of lingua franca.[12] Other scholars use the term 'Germanophonie', inspired by 'Francophonie', to mark the end of the narrow bond between nation and language.[13] As in Anglophone literature, with its 'new Englishes', the transformative writing of translingual authors seems to present an opportunity for German literature to attain the status of a new world literature.[14]

The Success Story of Translingual German Writers

Having set out this political and theoretical framework, we will now look at some prominent examples that illustrate the actual importance of those German writers from abroad.

The prestigious Kleist Prize, officially Germany's oldest literary prize, could be used as an initial example of the growing success of translingual writers in Germany. In 2016 the prize was awarded to Yoko Tawada (born 1960, Tokyo), a Japanese author who first came to Germany at the age of 22. For the first time, the prize was awarded to a bilingual writer who has published roughly the same number of works and received approximately

---

[11] See Robert Phillipson, 'Linguicism. Structures and ideologies in linguistic imperialism', in *Minority Education: From Shame to Struggle (Multilingual Matters)*, ed. by Tove Skutnabb-Kangas and Jim Cummins (Clevedon et al., 1988) and Philippe Blanchet, *Discriminations: combattre la glottophobie* (Paris: Textuel, 2016).

[12] Yildiz, *Beyond the Mother Tongue*, p. 210.

[13] Christine Meyer (ed.), *Kosmopolitische 'Germanophonie'. Postnationale Perspektiven in der deutschsprachigen Gegenwartsliteratur* (Würzburg: Königshausen & Neumann, 2013).

[14] See Elke Sturm-Trigonakis, *Global Playing in der Literatur, Ein Versuch über die Neue Weltliteratur* (Würzburg: Königshausen & Neumann, 2007).

the same number of awards in each of her literary languages, German and Japanese. Another fitting example from recent times would be the Ingeborg Bachmann Prize, one of the German-language literary awards with the greatest media impact. In 2016 the prize was awarded to Sharon Dodua Otoo, who was born in London in 1972 to Ghanaian parents and only recently began to write in German. She too writes in both German and her native language, English.

However, literary prizes cannot serve as the sole indicator of the current significance of translingual writers in German literature. The mechanisms and processes involved in recognizing and establishing literary excellence and cultural value are far more complex than that. We must also take into consideration not only the many awards and grants for up-and-coming writers but also nominations on longlists and shortlists, academy memberships, lectureships and residencies, and many other essential factors.

Book sales are, of course, central in assessing the status of this new German literature. Many bestselling authors from recent years – such as Saša Stanišić (born 1978, Višegrad, Bosnia and Herzegovina), Ilja Trojanov (born 1965, Sofia, Bulgaria) and Terézia Mora (born 1971, Sopron, Hungary) – are among the growing number of writers who have 'migrated' into the German language.[15] A high-profile name from within popular fiction would be Wladimir Kaminer (born 1967, Moscow), an author of Russian–Jewish heritage who may not have won any notable literary prizes but has reached an audience of millions with his book *Russendisko* [*Russian Disco*, 2000] and further titles.[16] We also cannot fail to mention Emine Sevgi Özdamar (born 1946, Malatya, Turkey), the grande dame of Turkish–German literature, who came to Germany in 1965 with no knowledge of German and in 1991 became the first non-native speaker to receive the Ingeborg Bachmann Prize. Özdamar, who has also published in Turkish, is undoubtedly one of the most-read translingual authors on the German literary market.

As this first overview shows, the phenomenon can by no means be reduced to a 'Turkish turn',[17] the now well-known Turkish–German constellation in today's literature and other arts. Alongside the home languages of the 'guest workers', who have been active within the literary field since the mid-1960s,

---

[15] See bestselling titles such as Saša Stanišić, *Wie der Soldat das Grammofon repariert* (Munich: Luchterhand, 2006); Saša Stanišić, *Vor dem Fest* (Munich: Luchterhand, 2014); Ilja Trojanov, *Der Weltensammler* (Munich: Hanser, 2006); Terézia Mora, *Das Ungeheuer* (Munich: Luchterhand, 2013).

[16] Wladimir Kaminer, *Russendisko* (Munich: Goldmann, 2000).

[17] Leslie A. Adelson, *The Turkish Turn in Contemporary German Literature, Toward a New Critical Grammar of Migration* (New York: Palgrave-MacMillan, 2005).

today the phenomenon extends around the whole globe, encompassing a large variety of languages from America to Eastern Europe, from Africa and the Middle East to Asia. One of the last German-speaking recipients of the Nobel Prize for Literature (2009) – Herta Müller (born 1953, Nițchidorf), who comes from the Romanian Banat region – is another example of a prominent writer who is 'not only German'. Although she writes (almost) exclusively in German, the Romanian language is always underlying and actively influencing her German writing, as Müller herself has emphasized many times.[18]

In short: the list of German 'immigrant' or multilingual literature prize winners and successful writers 'with a migration background' is getting longer every year, and the so-called refugee crisis – that is, the massive wave of immigration to Germany in 2015–2016 – suggests that this phenomenon will by no means be a temporary fad.

In a globalized world characterized by mass migration, the increasing prominence of these and other translingual writers – which has grown more and more noticeable since the 1990s – appears first and foremost to be a contemporary reflection of current geopolitical trends. However, we should not forget that German literature has a long tradition of multilingualism. This historical perspective has often been overshadowed by literary research into multilingualism, which was initially very much focused on the present. Long before Herta Müller, internationally acclaimed German authors were enriching German literature from the margins of the German-speaking region. Esther Kilchmann thus talks of a 'hidden history of multilingual writing in German literature'.[19] It would be easy to trace this timeline all the way back to the fifteenth century, to, for example, the multilingual songs of Oscar von Wolkenstein (1377–1445), who hailed from South Tyrol.

Were we to restrict ourselves to the post-war period and focus solely on the recipients of the Georg Büchner Prize (a kind of virtual hall of fame for German literature), we would see writers such as Paul Celan (1920–1970), a French citizen of Romanian origin, Elias Canetti (1905–1994), a British citizen born in Bulgaria, and Manès Sperber (1905–1984), a French Citizen from Galicia. Were we to expand the field to include native-German-speaking multilingual writers, we could add many writers in exile to the body of translingual authors, provided they have adopted and been published in new literary languages while in exile. This would apply, for example, to the

---

[18] Herta Müller, 'In jeder Sprachen sitzen andere Augen', in *Der König verneigt sich und tötet* (Munich: Hanser, 2003), pp. 7–39 (p. 27).

[19] Esther Kilchmann, 'Mehrsprachigkeit und deutsche Literatur', *Zeitschrift für interkulturelle Germanistik* 3.2 (2012), pp. 11–17 (p. 11).

work of Heinrich Heine (1797–1856), who pursued a dual career in Paris as a German–French author (something discussed in detail by Benedict Schofield in Chapter 6 of this volume). Twentieth-century examples include Klaus Mann (1906–1949), who wrote works in English during his American exile, including his second autobiography. We could also add Peter Weiss (1916–1982), who wrote in Swedish while in exile.

George Tabori (1914–2007), winner of the Georg Büchner Prize, is an extreme case in this context. Born in Hungary and persecuted as a Jew, Tabori came to Germany later in life via the Middle East, Great Britain and the USA, and wrote his works exclusively in English; they were then translated into German by his wife. Tabori is clearly a translingual Anglophone writer although he grew up with German as a second language and was received as a German-speaking author in Germany and Austria.

Naturally, the current territory of German-language writing – perhaps with the exception of countries such as Luxembourg and Switzerland – cannot be compared with decidedly multilingual literary systems such as Canada, India and the Maghreb. In contrast to Commonwealth or Francophone literatures, German literature does not benefit from the translingual 'writing back' of authors from former colonies. Nevertheless, from a historical perspective literary multilingualism plays a significant role as an individual and collective phenomenon on the margins of the former Holy Roman Empire (of the German nation), from Lorraine to Bohemia and Silesia, and from Schleswig to Transylvania.[20] Thus, when this chapter talks of 'German' literature, we must always remember this incongruity, deeply rooted in history, between linguistic, cultural and political territories.

Similar constellations can be seen in the Habsburg Empire and the Austro-Hungarian Dual Monarchy, whose multilingual and multicultural legacy continued to bear fruit until well after 1919 for, for example, members of Jewish ethnic groups, as shown by Celan, Canetti and many others. The great renown enjoyed by German culture enticed many writers into the German language (from Central Europe, for example); however, the National Socialist dictatorship and its crimes put an abrupt end to this literary radiance. Prague, the birthplace of Franz Kafka (1883–1924) and Rainer Maria Rilke (1875–1926), deserves a special mention in this context. In addition to Czech and Yiddish, French should also be mentioned here, which Rilke chose as the language of his poetry at the end of his life. Bilingual Alsatian

---

[20] To illustrate this phenomenon, see this 'map of the peoples of Central Europe'. While highly problematic from a modern perspective, it is still extremely illuminating: https://upload.wikimedia.org/wikipedia/commons/6/65/Central_Europe_%28ethnic%29.JPG [accessed 17 November 2019].

authors such as René Schickelé (1883–1940) and Hans Arp (1886–1966) are also worth considering as part of these geopolitically determined multilingual constellations.

Without looking to further expand this historical overview, we should also refer here to the case of Louis Charles Adélaïde de Chamissot de Boncourt, born in 1781 near Châlons-en-Champagne in eastern France. After his parents fled the French Revolution he adopted the name Adelbert von Chamisso and became one of the most important German Romantic poets. In addition to the historical depth provided by Chamisso's case, he also deserves to be mentioned here because his name has close links with the intercultural (and translingual) German literature of the last four decades; at least for a time, it was customary to refer to this as 'Chamisso literature'. This stems from the annual award, from 1985 to 2017, of the Chamisso Prize, sponsored by Germany's Robert Bosch Foundation, to authors writing in German whose works are shaped by changes in culture and/or language.[21] With a few exceptions, the contemporary authors mentioned here have all received the Chamisso Prize. The decision in 2017 to discontinue the award, which played a leading role on an international level in promoting intercultural German literature, has been condemned by many people.[22] And yet the concept behind the prize was frequently criticized during its lifetime, being seen by some as a literary equal opportunities programme and by others as an essentializing ostracism of foreign authors.

Throughout the history of this prize, the criteria for recipients slowly shifted from biographical factors (migrant background, non-native speaker of German) to a sole focus on their literary works; from 2012, works by native speakers of German were also formally considered, provided they tackled the issue of cultural otherness. Ultimately, as many 'Chamisso authors' became increasingly successful on the book market and, in particular, began to win other literary prizes, there was no reason for the prize to continue; apparently, this literature was now perfectly integrated into the German literary landscape.[23]

---

[21] For the history and concept of the prize, see Über den Chamisso-Preis, http://www.bosch-stiftung.de/content/language1/html/14169.asp [accessed 17 November 2019].

[22] Ilija Trojanow and José F. A. Oliver, 'Ade, Chamisso-Preis?', http://www.faz.net/aktuell/feuilleton/debatten/kritik-an-bosch-stiftung-ade-chamisso-preis-14443175.html [accessed 17 November 2019].

[23] Stefan Kister, 'Klassenziel erreicht – ohne Auszeichnung, Chamisso-Preis wird eingestellt', http://www.stuttgarter-nachrichten.de/inhalt.chamisso-preis-wird-eingestellt-klassenziel-erreicht-ohne-auszeichnung.964383b1-3b2c-44e0-98d3-85b7ac2e0388.html [accessed 17 November 2019].

The Limits of Ethnobiographical Determinisms

Considering that this prize for intercultural German literature was named after Chamisso, who first wrote in French, the terms 'intercultural' and 'translingual' appear to be closely intertwined. In order to better distinguish between these terms, a 'translingual' approach (beyond biographical issues) should concentrate first and foremost on specific linguistic processes that can be attributed to language contacts or the multilingual author's specific attitude to the German language. However, we cannot precisely separate these terms because interculturality almost automatically involves the crossing of linguistic boundaries. Rather, this is about shifting the perspective from literature (and language) as an intrinsic attribute of culture to the specific linguistic strategies of multilingual authors.

Naturally, these linguistic strategies also include language assimilation processes, which can be observed in those writers who apparently strive to avoid all forms of interference in their German texts. This results in a sort of 'grey area' of authors who, if we consider their biography, would be described as translingual by critics such as Kellman but whose literary idiom does not, in my opinion, truly earn this label.

The work of Elias Canetti could be taken as an example here. The Bulgaria-born Sephardic Nobel laureate (1981) learned German as his fifth language. Nevertheless, he chose German as his sole literary language and maintained this loyalty throughout his life, despite being expelled and living through the Holocaust. He adopted a rather classical form of German influenced by Goethe, which fulfilled the strictest purist standards. Contemporary literature also offers numerous examples of such German authors from abroad whose writing bears no manifest traces of their language of origin or of other languages. One example would be *Tauben fliegen auf* [*Fly away, pigeon*, 2010] by the Hungarian–Swiss writer Melinda Nadj Abonji (born 1968), which was awarded the German Book Prize and the Swiss Book Prize in 2010.[24] The aforementioned Wladimir Kaminer could also be included in this category, as the 'foreign' in his case is addressed more on a thematic than a linguistic level.

If nothing else, these (counter)examples clearly show the limits of biographical approaches, insofar as specific experience of migration does not necessarily lead to a change of language or to the development of multilingual, hybrid-linguistic or heterolingual writing processes. Conversely, translingual strategies can also be observed in authors who would certainly not be identified as multilingual migrants based on the common perception

---

[24] Melinda Nadj Abonji, *Tauben fliegen auf* (Salzburg: Jung und Jung, 2010).

or within the framework of research on exile literature. A good example of this would be the poetic work of Stefan George (1868–1933), particularly his early work, which displays a high degree of multilingualism.

Writing in diatopic variations by using dialects and regiolects in standard-language texts is another complex intermediate area, since the designation of an idiom as a dialect or language cannot always be scientifically determined. Similar questions are raised by the numerous traces of other languages, such as Yiddish, Hebrew, Polish, Bohemian, Dutch, Swiss and French, as can be observed throughout history in the German-speaking area. With this in mind, the Anglicisms in German so frequently criticized today are simply the latest form of a long-standing phenomenon. Linguists have described this phenomenon, which is also relevant to translingual literature, as 'inner multilingualism'.

As we can see, translingual writing is simply a new, post-colonial phenomenon, nor can it be attributed solely to biographical migrant experiences. The booming globalization of the last few decades and the associated mass circulation of information, goods and people worldwide act as catalysts for long-existing processes of contact, exchange and hybridization (processes also discussed by Paulo Soethe in Chapter 12 of this volume). While these conditions are more than conducive to the rise of translingual authors in contemporary literature, translingual writing largely eludes any schematic approach to individual linguistics and literary aesthetics. Instead, shared migration experiences, similar lives and common countries of origin can lead to totally different, singular literary works on a spectrum ranging from pure monolingualism to multilingual oeuvres and 'babelizing' idioms. Sociological studies also conclude that the languages chosen and the writing practices employed by translingual authors result from a complex interplay of external conditions, social circumstances, sociological assessments, biographical fortuities and individual decisions influenced not least by personal taste and aesthetics.[25]

A Variety of Linguistic Strategies and Processes

Interdisciplinary research into multilingualism and literature has been growing significantly for years, producing a range of standard works, including some from the field of Germanic studies and even a first handbook. This chapter does not have sufficient scope to explore the phenomenon of

---

[25] Georg Kremnitz, *Mehrsprachigkeit in der Literatur. Wie Autoren ihre Sprachen wählen. Aus der Sicht der Soziologie der Kommunikation* (Vienna: Edition Praesens, 2004), p. 253.

translingual authors in German literature in detail. Some authors, such as Yoko Tawada, combine a wealth of highly complex linguistic processes at the lexical, morphological, graphical and syntactic level that are difficult to express in a concise manner. In what follows, I simply provide a brief overview of the variety of translingual writing processes, including – for example – literal translations, the use of foreign words, multilingual language games and mixing sociolects and idioms.[26]

First, we must make a basic distinction between the text-internal perspective (the language of an individual text) and a cross-text, work-based perspective. This latter perspective refers to authors who create their works in different languages or do so according to period or genre. Several recipients of the Ingeborg Bachmann Prize over the last few years – such as Olga Martynova (born 1962 in Leningrad) and the Carinthian–Slovenian author Maja Haderlap (born 1961, Bad Eisenkappel/Železna Kapla) – practise such cross-text multilingualism, writing literature in Russian and Slovenian respectively alongside their German texts. These cross-text practices also include the phenomenon of literary self-translation, now a major focal point for researchers.[27] Cross-text multilingualism does not automatically involve translingual phenomena in the texts themselves; theoretically, authors can employ a standard style in each of their languages without manifest translingual interferences.

Translingual writing is immediately noticeable above all at the text-internal level when other languages appear on the surface of the text. Undoubtedly the simplest form of this is the peppering of texts with other languages, from individual words to entire passages of dialogue (code switching). Such linguistic material – also described as heterolingual[28] by researchers – is often accompanied by metalinguistic commentaries through to glossaries. In this case, the translingual dimension of the writing is explicitly marked and conveyed to the reader.

However, text-internal multilingualism is not always so clearly visible on the surface of a text. Intratextual loan translation is a widespread practice, explored at an early stage in Emine Sevgi Özdamar's work, in which certain

---

[26] Interdisciplinary research into multilingualism and literature has been growing significantly for years, producing a range of standard works, including some from the field of Germanic studies, and even a first handbook, Till Dembeck and Rolf Parr (eds.), *Literatur und Mehrsprachigkeit: Ein Handbuch* (Tübingen: Narr, 2017).

[27] See Jan Walsh Hokenson and Marcella Munson, *The Bilingual Text. History and Theory of Literary Self-Translation* (Manchester: St. Jerome, 2007).

[28] Rainier Grutman, *Des langues qui résonnent, L'hétérolinguisme au XIXe siècle québécois* (Montréal: Fides-CÉTUQ, 1997).

words, expressions and figures of speech are transferred literally into the German. In many of her texts Özdamar develops a personal idiom that recreates Turkish phraseology and expressions as foreignisms in the German, creating a deliberately foreignizing effect. Yet such processes must not always be seen as interference phenomena – that is, as being motivated by a foreign language – but can also be attributed to the general literary licence in creating new words and images. A reader or literary scholar competent in the other language can often help to identify the hallmarks of translingual authors.

In this context, it is particularly difficult to grasp the 'latency' of a foreign language in German-language writing. Some literary scholars, such as Carmine Chiellino, describe linguistic latency as the key characteristic of intercultural literature.[29] That means that a writer who actively masters another language will automatically see the German literary language in a different light and, in doing so, tap into new creative potential. However, such writing 'with an accent', as one might call it, or the interference of the other language, as stated by Nobel laureate Herta Müller, is often quite difficult to define precisely, as it tends to remain a matter of interpretation.

Idiosyncratic literary idioms created against a multilingual background are a particular form of linguistic interference in the literature of translingual authors. These idioms decisively break both with the norm of monolingualism and with the 'classic' German literary language. These literary idioms may invoke everyday examples, such as certain group languages, sociolects or ethnolects, or may be experimental on an aesthetic level. *Finnegans Wake* by James Joyce would be a prime example from literary history of 'artificial' language mixtures whose primary intention was not mimesis but invention. A historic example of mixed languages anchored in real-life experience would be *Die Schönste Lengevitch* [*The most beautiful lengevitch*, 1927] by Kurt M. Stein, which imitates in amusing fashion the English–German hybrid language ('Denglisch') used by German immigrants in the USA.[30]

The most famous example from contemporary German literature of an idiosyncratic literary idiom rooted in group language and the everyday world is without doubt *Kanak Sprak* [*Kanak-Talk*, 1995] by Feridun Zaimoğlu (born 1964 in Bolu, Turkey).[31] Based on semi-fictional interviews, the book – which quickly developed a cult following and has been extensively praised by literary scholars – employs features such as simplified grammar, sound shifts and

---

[29] Carmine Chiellino, *Interkulturelle Literatur in deutscher Sprache: Das große ABC für interkulturelle Leser* (Bern: Peter Lang Verlag, 2016), pp. 191–92.

[30] Kurt M. Stein, *Die Schönste Lengevitch* (Chicago: Pascal Covici, 1927).

[31] Feridun Zaimoğlu, *Kanak Sprak, 24 Mißtöne vom Rande der Gesellschaft* (Hamburg: Rotbuch, 1995).

generous sprinklings of Turkish and English. Due to the almost documentary feel of the language he captured, Zaimoğlu was seen as the mouthpiece of a new generation of German Turks, who adopt the German language in their own special way. With a title that uses the derogatory, racist term *Kanake* and his uncensored and brazen documentation of 'discords from the margins of society', the author provocatively exposes the connection between race, class, gender and language. While Zaimoğlu's text may be considered to employ 'weak' forms of literary multilingualism, his aesthetically reflected, translingual hybridization of German literary language points not least to the agency such writing strategies have within cultural and linguistic politics.

Another example of the deliberate creolization of German literature is the various artificial idioms of Claudio Matschulat, alias Zé do Rock. Born in Porto Alegre in 1956, he writes predominantly in German but also in Portuguese and English. His German idiolects, which bear such bizarre names as *ultradoitsch* [ultra-German], *kauderdeutsch*, a play on *Kauderwelsch* meaning 'gibberish', and *siegfriedisch* [Siegfriedish], strongly deviate not least from German orthography. In contrast to Zaimoğlu, his anarchic-seeming literature, bursting with witty language, can be ascribed to the tradition of macaronic verse, which also includes Kurt M. Stein. However, his satirical texts are also decidedly critical of language and ideology, as seen in the name *siegfriedisch*, which plays with the cliché of linguistic and racial purity, or the book title *Deutsch gutt sonst geld zuruck* [*German good or money back*, 2002].[32] In his texts, Zé do Rock takes a subversive approach to stereotypical images of the Other and monocultural definitions of languages and cultures.

When classifying such linguistic experiments, it is important to note that Zaimoğlu in particular, who grew up bilingual in Germany, and Do Rock, whose forebears include Lithuanian, Russian and German immigrants, are perfectly capable of respecting the linguistic standards of literary German, as demonstrated by some of their other texts. Their virtuoso, aesthetically and politically motivated pidginization of German inspired by many different language regions has to be placed against the background of their perfect mastery of the German language.

Their writing strategy must therefore be distanced from other migrant literary experiments based on an actual lack of mastery of the linguistic rules. The most prominent current example of this new form of writing in German is *Broken German* by Tomer Gardi, who was born in 1974 in the Dan kibbutz in Galilee.[33] When Gardi was invited to the 2016 Ingeborg Bachmann Prize

---

[32] Zé Do Rock, *Deutsch gutt sonst geld zuruck, a siegfriedische und kauderdeutshe ler- und textbuk* (Munich: Kunstmann, 2002).

[33] Tomer Gardi, *Broken German, Roman* (Graz: Dröschl, 2016).

reading competition with an extract from this German-language novel, the Israeli author's limited knowledge of German – which became evident when he was interviewed – caused the jury to debate whether he should actually be allowed to enter the competition with his error-strewn text. In contrast to Zaimoğlu and Do Rock, Gardi not only employs the aesthetic strategy of concocting an artificial language but truly lacks the ability to communicate correctly or fluently in the language – something he deploys in an aesthetically conscious manner and uses as a sign of migrant authenticity: 'I am a migrant worker in the German language.'[34]

Although Gardi left Klagenfurt empty-handed, his book was published by the prestigious Droschl publishing house and enjoyed a very positive critical reception. The linguistically idiosyncratic text was praised for reflecting on the fate of migrants in modern-day Berlin and for pleading against ostracism, language monopolies and the fear of foreign invasion. The publisher advertised the book as 'an allusive, challenging and enjoyable plea for linguistic diversity within one language, for the transgression of the rules, for the non-standard'.[35] In fact, despite its simple mode of expression and its many violations of linguistic standards, the text has a highly developed literary style and is aesthetically pleasing, as shown in this passage, in which the author artfully and humorously plays with a grammatically incorrect composite word:

[...] Your shop is the placeofbrokenspokenGerman.
They all find it funny and then play a game. The first to say it ten times fast. PlaceofbrokenspokenGerman.
Placeofbr.
Placeofbrokenspok.
PlaceofbrokenspokenG.
PlaceofbrokenspokenGerman.

[[...] Dein Shop ist das Gebrochenesdeutschsprachigesraum.
Die finden es alle lustig und dann spielen zusammen ein Spiel. Wer kann zehnmal schnell sagen. Gebrochenesdeutschsprachigesraum.
Gebrochenesde.
Gebrochenesdeuschp.
Gebrochenesdeutschpapige.
Gebrochenesdeutschsprachigesraum.][36]

---

[34] Gardi, *Broken German*, p. 101.
[35] Gardi, *Broken German*, blurb.
[36] Gardi, *Broken German*, pp. 23–24.

Gardi's ultrarealistic aesthetics of migrant 'broken German' and his claim that 'everyone should be allowed to write in German'[37] – regardless of their linguistic and stylistic abilities – is an extreme case, and perhaps a kind of endpoint in translingual writing. Gardi's statement that 'we are Babylonian'[38] embodies an important shift where a speech previously denigrated as 'foreigner German' (*Ausländerdeutsch*) or 'guest worker German' (*Gastarbeiterdeutsch*) is now deliberately requisitioned as a literary idiom in line with the contemporary, globalized urban culture: 'My prose is bio sonar. I seek out sounds and follow them. Where they lead me. I write in sounds and set them free in the space. German-speaking. Language is a public space.'[39]

Gardi's book is controversial and highly political, not least because, as a Jewish author, he deconstructs a language long regarded by Germans as a veritable national treasure – in their racial fanaticism, the National Socialists went as far as to deprive the Jews of the right to speak the language at all. This historical background becomes apparent in the text when the narrator relates the words of a group of skinheads: 'That is not German. That is not German. What WE speak is German. That is not German!'[40]

Toward German as a Lingua Franca?

More than 70 years after the end of the Second World War, the economic success and cultural prestige of Germany (and the German-speaking countries) are attracting people from all over the world. Thanks to migrant and translingual writing, the last few decades have seen the German literary language develop into a culturally open and multicentric system. But how far can the German literary language open itself up to the hybrid linguistic idioms of migrant authors? What value can we attach, for example, to the development of a pidgin-like literary German? Will German literature automatically be enriched and revitalized, or is there also a danger of dumbing down, of dissolving it into a global literary non-space?[41]

As yet, there appears to be no consensus on transformative extreme positions such as Tomer Gardi's *Broken German*. His literary idiom is

---

[37] Hannah Lühmann, 'Jeder sollte auf Deutsch schreiben dürfen' [interview with Tomer Gardi], in *Welt Online*, 18 August 2016. https://www.welt.de/kultur/literarischewelt/article157738156/Jeder-sollte-auf-Deutsch-schreiben-duerfen.html [accessed 17 November 2019].
[38] Gardi, *Broken German*, p. 91.
[39] Gardi, *Broken German*, p. 109.
[40] Gardi, *Broken German*, p. 11.
[41] See Marc Augé, *Non-lieux: introduction à une anthropologie de la surmodernité* (Paris: Le Seuil, 1992).

rejected not only by 'glottophobes' and language purists; there has also been criticism from some within the intercultural literature community, such as Zafer Şenocak, a renowned writer born in Ankara in 1961 who strictly rejects creolizing and pidginizing speech. While Şenocak rebels against German society's enduring tendency toward cultural and ethnic segregation by calling for ambiguous and hybrid identities and multilingualism, he is also extremely critical of the 'decline of the language', even in the range of experimental literature: 'I cannot fathom that there are people who can find anything approaching creativity or even avant garde creativity in this halving, quartering, this disappearance of languages. For me, these fragmented languages are an expression of homelessness.'[42] A rift emerges here between those who wish to assimilate to the 'un-broken' or 'accent-free' dominant language and those who wish to deconstruct the national literature paradigm and 'break up' linguistic and literary norms as part of a multicultural self-criticism of 'Germanness'.

Şenocak does not stand alone with his linguistic criticisms. Ultimately, even an experimental, deconstructive author such as Zé Do Rock criticizes certain signs of linguistic deterioration in his performances and through his mixed language *kauderdeutsch*. In some of his texts we can discern a dystopian vision in which all of the world's languages are merged to form a simplified Globish that goes hand in hand with the commercialization of all spheres of life and a loss of authentic forms of expression. From this point of view, 'Broken German' would be an open and hospitable language that anyone could adopt – even as a literary language – but also a depleted, dumbed-down language whose potential for genuine expression has waned and whose innovative character appears doubtful.

While literary texts may be singular objects, language is never purely individual; it is always a collective language that binds a speaker or author to the group. In German history in particular, language has generally served as a strong identity marker; this is clear from the way that the term 'German' is based on the correspondence between 'lingua' and 'natio'. Given the historically rather uncertain sense of identity felt by the German people, the language appears to be a strong support in the aim to define identity. In this context, the literary canon embodies a national style, and literary language serves as an integrative medium to establish and impart social and national cohesion. Even though Johann Gottlieb Fichte's statement in *Reden an die deutsche Nation* [*Addresses to the German Nation*, 1808] that 'a writer's most precious privilege and most sacred office is to bring his nation

---

[42] Zafer Şenocak, *Deutschsein, Eine Aufklärungsschrift* (Hamburg: Edition Körber-Stiftung, 2011), p. 19.

together'[43] may no longer apply, language – including literature – remains a strong bearer of identity.

As Jürgen Roche has shown, both monolingualism and multilingualism can act as cultural and social integrators. The question of how a given idiom might operate in a given space and time as a medium of either integration or disintegration is highly complex and has a decisive influence on how we understand and evaluate translingual literature. From an optimistic point of view, the largely positive reception of Tomer Gardi's *Broken German* could be interpreted as a sign that German identity today is so firmly established that it can openly and calmly receive such a literary 'attack' on common linguistic rules.

Conversely, though, one has to ask which collective or personal identities such a 'Broken German' might still feasibly carry? Of course it would be absurd to enact normative and discriminatory language standards, with the linguistic permissibility of non-native-language texts systematically examined as if part of a naturalization procedure. But, by the same token, can we really conceive of a new German (world) literature in which everyone is free to create – in a 'glotto-anarchical' way – his or her private language beyond linguistic standards, as it were, a form of deregulated language utopia that Gardi seems not only to envisage but to demand? Doesn't the idea of cultural openness and inclusivity meet a limit when it comes to assimilating linguistic substance itself? That is to say, isn't a degree of standardization and a claim to aesthetic discrimination indispensable in the realm of literature? Not only writer colleagues and conservative voices from culture and politics but Gardi himself seems to ask the question when he lets his narrator say: 'What is an author without linguistic dominion?'

Yet experimental writing including subversive or even destructive treatments of language have never been the sole preserve of German authors from abroad; throughout literary history, such strategies have often occurred from within the 'native language', as evidenced by texts from the Dadaism movement. However, this comparison also shows that such attacks on literature as a 'fine art' have never been mere literary play, but have always affected language and society, as suggested by Deleuze and Guattari in their reflection on a minor literature.[44] With this in mind, German writers from abroad play an important role in redefining German (linguistic) identity, the boundary between creative 'Babylonian' (Gardi) enrichment of the language

---

[43] Johann Gottlieb Fichte, *Reden an die deutsche Nation* (Hamburg: Meiner, 1955), p. 201.

[44] Gilles Deleuze and Felix Guattari, *Kafka: Toward a Minor Literature*, trans. D. Polan (Minneapolis/London: University of Minnesota Press, 1986).

and vandalizing 'fragmentation' (Şenocak) of German raising many questions of aesthetics and language politics.

The limits of the term 'lingua franca', proposed by Yildiz and others, become clear here; theoretically, this would require such a literary language to be neither the native language nor the national language of any speaker or writer. Only in this way – for the sole purpose of communication and with no issues of legitimacy and ownership – could symmetrical balances of power be guaranteed, as in the case of Latin for the Humanists or the Mediterranean trading language known as *sabir*. Such a concept hardly seems realistic for German, neither from the perspective of native speakers nor for the translingual authors who often place questions of (linguistic) power at the forefront of their writing.

Translingual writing could, therefore, be understood as a complex negotiation between the (national) linguistic collective and the singular (linguistic) identity of the (migrant) writer. Literature can – and should – challenge and break up linguistic norms and the dichotomy of the 'native' and 'foreign'; however, it can only take agency against the backdrop of linguistic communities and their traditions and values. While Derrida may state that a (national) language is always the language of the Other, insofar as it is nobody's commodity or possession (not even the 'native' speaker's), the inclusion of literary language within the complex interplay of origin, race and nation is an indispensable part of modern writing.

This would suggest that the German literary language is far from becoming a lingua franca in the sense of a mere language of communication for migrant authors; ultimately, language always refers back to complex and multi-layered questions of national and cultural identity and affiliation. However, the rise of translingual authors requires the traditional binary categories (native/foreign, national/foreign, native language/foreign language) to be replaced by more nuanced and open concepts. This will be one of the main challenges facing current and future scholars.

Suggestions for Further Reading

Arndt, Susan, Dirk Naguschewski and Robert Stockhammer (eds.), *Exophonie. Anders-Sprachigkeit (in) der Literatur* (Berlin: Kulturverlag Kadmos, 2007), 302 pp.

Bürger-Koftis, Michaela, Hannes Schwaiger and Sandra Vlasta (eds.), *Polyphonie – Mehrsprachigkeit und literarische Kreativität* (Vienna: Edition Praesens, 2010), 481 pp.

Forster, Leonard, *The Poets Tongues: Multilingualism in Literature: The de Carle Lectures at the University of Otago 1968* (Cambridge: Cambridge University Press, 2009), 118 pp.

Kellman, Steven, *The Translingual Imagination* (Lincoln/London: University of Nebraska Press, 2000), 164 pp.

Knauth, K. Alfons, 'Literary Multilingualism I: General Outlines and Western World', in *Comparative Literature: Sharing Knowledges for Preserving Cultural Diversity, Encyclopaedia of Life Support Systems (EOLSS), Developed under the Auspices of the UNESCO*, ed. by Márcio Seligmann-Silva et al. (Oxford: Eolss Publishers, 2007), pp. 41–64.

Yildiz, Yasemin, *Beyond the Mother Tongue. The Postmonolingual Condition* (New York: Fordham University Press, 2012), 375 pp.

4

Collaboration and Commitment

German-language Books Across Borders

Charlotte Ryland

'You're sitting in his swimming pool'.

As we took this in, a ripple of laughter went round the horseshoe of tables. The room we were sitting in, with a wall of windows looking out onto a small garden, had once been Carl Hanser's swimming pool. One of the most important European publishers of the twentieth century, Hanser founded Carl Hanser Verlag in 1928, and the offices of the publisher are still in his beautiful villa. His swimming pool is now a bright and airy seminar room, the perfect setting for this unique meeting of editors from the UK, USA and Germany. As I looked around the room, at the posters on the wall celebrating Hanser's long history, at the piles of books stacked on the tables at the back, ready for our visiting editors to pore over during coffee, and at the editors themselves, it became clear that I was witnessing the core ingredients of a literature that travels: committed individuals, motivated by a sense of mission, working together in transnational networks.

I was in Munich in my role as editor of *New Books in German* (NBG), a twice-yearly magazine that recommends the latest German-language books for translation. Since its inception in 1996 NBG has become more than just a magazine; it is now a major programme promoting intercultural relations in the UK, US and beyond. NBG is one of a growing number of international organisations engaging in literary advocacy of this kind, working together against the insularity of English-language reading culture. Any conversation about this insularity will inevitably at some point reference 3 per cent: the estimated percentage of books in the UK and US market translated out of another language into English.[1] NBG is supported in its endeavours by a fantastic network – itself transnational – of partners in Germany, Austria, Switzerland, the UK and the US.

One of NBG's partners is the *Frankfurter Buchmesse* [Frankfurt Book Fair], the company that runs the world's largest publishing trade fair. The *Buchmesse* regularly organizes themed 'Editors' Trips', taking publishers from across the world on a tour through Germany's publishing scene, facilitating new relationships and networks. In 2018 they ran a trip composed mainly of editors from the UK for the first time: 11 UK editors, three US editors, and me.

That moment in Carl Hanser's swimming pool brought home to me why the last nine years at the helm of NBG and immersed in the world of literary translation have been such a thrilling and stimulating experience: because I have never before worked in a field that is so essentially collaborative, that thrives on partnerships. In recent years we have begun to theme each issue of NBG, and a personal favourite was our 'Cooperation and Collaboration' issue in spring 2017. Conceived initially as an opportunity to focus on the rising numbers of co-translations being published, the articles and interviews in that issue ultimately reflected the huge range of ways in which collaboration feeds international literature, from masterclasses to publisher–translator partnerships, translator collectives to 'triangular talks'.[2]

What became evident as that issue of NBG developed is that – where it is successful – this collaboration is always fuelled by passion and ideological commitment, where the 'ideology' is the belief that English-language culture will be enriched by translations from other languages, and that publishing them and finding readers for them is therefore an ethical *good* that transcends any considerations of market value. Gisèle Sapiro has identified ideological motivations of this kind in a study of commissioning editors of translated literature in American publishing houses. The quotations from editors when giving their reasons for publishing translated literary fiction disavow economic concerns in favour of 'mission', 'identity'

---

[1] The first study to investigate the 3 per cent claim was conducted by Literature Across Frontiers, the European Platform for Literary Exchange, Translation and Policy Debate, based at Aberystwyth University in Wales. Their report, published in 2015 and updated in 2017, shows that translations indeed represent approximately 3 per cent of the total market, while among literary publications the proportion is 4–5 per cent. https://www.lit-across-frontiers.org/wp-content/uploads/2013/03/Translation-Statistics-UK_2017-1.pdf [accessed 7 December 2018].

[2] *New Books in German* 42 (Autumn 2017). This issue opened with a feature on 'Triangular Talks', a day of panel discussions between editors from English-, French- and German-language publishing houses (pp. 2–3).

and 'worthy' acts.³ My experience of working with UK editors of translated literature over the past nine years reflects Sapiro's findings exactly. This is what motivates literary translation into English: in the insular book markets of the UK and US, both commitment and collaboration have to be in place for literature to travel.

Networks of Passionate Individuals

Such thoughts about collaboration and commitment were going through my mind as I sat in that swimming pool and looked around the table. As I did so, a network of individuals working together to move literature across borders swam into view. On behalf of NBG, I'd worked together with the *Frankfurter Buchmesse* team to put together a list of UK invitees for the Editors' Trip; this particular meeting was facilitated by Hanser's Rights Director Friederike Barakat, with whom I'd been working closely since my early days at NBG; next to her sat Jo Lendle, Hanser's Publisher since 2014 but also an author whose novel *Alles Land* [*All the Land*, 2011] – a personal favourite of mine – we'd reviewed in NBG in 2011. Lendle's book had subsequently been published in English by Seagull Books of India, in a translation by one of the most important and influential translators from German, Katy Derbyshire.⁴ This nexus of personalities and stories is striking and yet not surprising: these are the ingredients that combine to enable literature to cross borders; these are the players whose interaction spurs that transnational movement.

Katy Derbyshire first came to my attention online. Her *lovegermanbooks* site was a very early example of a translator's blog and – as Derbyshire put it in a recent interview with NBG – an effective way of gaining visibility: 'My blog has made me visible. I'm far from London publishers and editors, but they can still be aware of me. Some of my book reviews have functioned as part of pitches to publishers, sometimes that's even worked out'.⁵ At the time of the Editors' Trip I was preparing a new edition of NBG, themed around literary blogging and social media. We called that issue 'Digital Encounters', because our research turned up two key elements in the digital world of literary translation: firstly, the role of the impassioned individual; and, secondly, the importance of the encounter – in particular where digital means generate physical encounters. Again and again we found moments where, for it to have

---

³ Gisèle Sapiro, 'Globalization and cultural diversity in the book market: The case of literary translations in the US and in France', *Poetics* 38 (2010), pp. 419–39 (p. 425).
⁴ Jo Lendle, *All the Land*, trans. Katy Derbyshire (London: Seagull Books, 2018).
⁵ Interview with Katy Derbyshire, *New Books in German* 44 (2018), p. 22.

its full effect, the digital gave rise to some kind of encounter, be it an author's lively response to comments on her own blog, or the reading groups and 'German literature months' promoted by blogger Lizzy Siddal.[6]

Our research on those 'digital encounters' thus reconfirmed the impression I had had since starting out at NBG: that the individuals interacting in a network are the essential components of a literature that travels. Literary translation is not a one-way street. Literature does not find its way into English translation by being pushed onto the market from its source culture. That push has to be accompanied by a pull: the target market must seek to receive and absorb texts from other cultures. Which texts these are, and which cultures and languages they hail from, depends very much on the advocacy and support present in both the source and target cultures.

'The fundamentally collaborative nature of literary labour'

Advocacy for international literature in the UK is growing, and is accordingly receiving increasing attention within academic research, most prominently in a recent AHRC-funded project on 'Translating the Literatures of Smaller European Nations' (2014–2016). Although the project focused on 'smaller' countries, its findings are strikingly relevant to the field of translated German-language literature.[7] The final report highlighted 'the variety of actors who collaborate to bring a text to an international audience', a phrase that recalls Rebecca Braun's work on literary celebrity and world authorship (the latter discussed by Braun in Chapter 5 of this volume). Drawing on sociologist Bruno Latour's 'actor network theory' and work on entrepreneurship by Fred Turner and Christine Larson, Braun highlights the role of the 'network intellectual', whereby 'agency is dispersed between multiple actors', underlining the 'fundamentally collaborative nature of literary labour'.[8] This is precisely what was at play in Hanser's swimming pool, as the chains of individuals that had contributed to various transnational publications came into focus. By 'following the actors themselves' and thereby building up a 'map of relations', Latour argues that 'a large number of actors will emerge on this map as

---

[6] *New Books in German* 44 (2018). See in particular pp. 3, 21, 26.

[7] The project's findings are summarized in Rajendra Chitnis, Jakob Stougaard-Nielsen, Rhian Atkin and Zoran Milutinović, 'Translating the Literatures of Smaller European Nations: A Picture from the UK, 2014–16' https://www.bristol.ac.uk/media-library/sites/arts/research/translating-lits-of-small-nations/Translating%20Smaller%20European%20Literatures%20Report(3).pdf [accessed 7 December 2018].

[8] Rebecca Braun, 'The world author in us all: conceptualising fame and agency in the global market', *Celebrity Studies* 7.4 (2016), pp. 457–75 (pp. 458–60).

discernible nodes'.[9] These concepts of the map, the actor and the node are useful in conceptualising what happens when a book travels into another language and is received in another culture, and they inform my reflections here on that transnational movement from a German-language perspective.

New Books in German: Collaboration and Committees

Literature travels most effectively when a push from the source culture coincides with a pull from the target culture, and when the network of actors functions successfully. These mechanisms are perfectly exemplified in the collaborative structure of the New Books in German project, which involves individuals from UK, US, Austrian, German and Swiss publishing at every stage of its processes, largely working together in committees.

This collaborative approach goes back to NBG's founding in 1996. That summer, the UK Translators Association (TA) and British Centre for Literary Translation (BCLT) organized a seminar to discuss 'the general problem of why so few German books are translated into English', and 'to attempt to create a framework in which these problems can be addressed, and eventually overcome'.[10] The seminar was a triumph of transnational cooperation, with representatives from the TA, BCLT, the Austrian, German and Swiss embassies in London, the cultural institutes and foreign ministries of those countries, Arts Council England, publishers, translators, literary critics, booksellers, scouts and agents. The breath-taking guest list is testament to the strength of feeling at the time, that 'there is a wealth of German writing which is known through translation in many countries, but which never finds its way into English translation'.[11] A further collaborative meeting six weeks later, also hosted by the TA, put in place the first building blocks for what would become NBG – funding from the cultural institutes of Germany, Austria and Switzerland, a steering committee, editor, copywriter and editorial advisors – and by autumn of that year a leaflet was circulating the halls of Frankfurt Book Fair, proudly announcing 'Ein neues Journal aus London' ['A new journal from London']. The first edition of that journal was published in spring 1997, and so NBG was born.

That founding story is key to understanding NBG and the world it inhabits: we witness a group of concerned individuals coming together to seek a solution to a problem communally identified. This communal approach has remained central to NBG's systems and is key to the project's success. For its first issue

---

[9] Braun, 'World author', p. 459.
[10] 'New Books in German Turns Twenty', New Books in German 40 (Autumn 2016), pp. 2–3.
[11] 'New Books in German Turns Twenty', p. 2.

the translator Rosemary Smith and literary editor Rivers Scott collaborated with 'editorial advisors on book selection' Katharina Bielenberg, Karin Scherer and Martin Chalmers to assemble a selection of books that were both well written and likely to appeal to UK publishers. These advisors – a UK publisher, bookseller and translator respectively – reflect the importance that NBG has always placed on the 'pull' factor, taking seriously the advice it receives from the UK publishing industry. From its second issue onwards, the small group of advisors developed into an 'editorial committee' composed of NBG's partners (mainly cultural institutes and embassies from Austria, Germany and Switzerland) and of representatives from the publishing industry – editors, agents, scouts, booksellers and translators. Each committee member brings their own expertise, experience and professional judgement to the table. This structure has a two-fold impact: it brings gatekeepers and influencers (in this case editors, agents, booksellers, translators) into the NBG organisation, giving them early and privileged access to the latest books; and it ensures that the books reviewed by NBG have stood the test of a selection process that includes industry experts from the target culture.

To enable that editorial committee to make informed decisions, NBG commissions book reports by a large team of freelance 'reader–reviewers'. Primarily translators, these readers are also often drawn from academia, publishing and education. Each reader is sent a book that NBG is considering for its forthcoming selection, in the most part books that have not yet been published in German. Collaboration with German-language publishers means that NBG is given privileged access to these new books, mostly working with manuscripts, proofs and review copies. Although this system was designed to ensure that NBG can swiftly gain a broad and deep impression of a large number of unpublished books, this reader–review process has a secondary impact that is perhaps more important. It means that every year over 100 UK- and US-based individuals are engaging actively and collaboratively with the cutting edge in German-language literature: they tweet about these books, recommend them to their friends, add them to university reading lists, translate sample passages into English and pitch them to English-language publishers. This community of reader–reviewers thus immeasurably broadens NBG's impact, ensuring that even the books that don't make NBG's final cut receive greater exposure within the English-language sphere.

It is in the context of reader–reviewers that NBG's partnership with the Frankfurt Book Fair New York comes most strongly into play. NBG's New York partner commissions some of the book reports and holds its own editorial committee meeting with a similar constitution of cultural diplomats and publishing professionals. This partnership has been in place since 2011, when the two organisations agreed that the practice hitherto of producing two lists of recommended German-language books, one for the US market and one for the UK, was an unhelpful duplication. NBG and the Frankfurt Book Fair New York now consequently have combined fiction lists but separate lists for non-fiction and children's books.

From its inception, books reviewed in NBG have been *de facto* guaranteed funding for translation into English from one of its partners (the Goethe-Institut, the Austrian Federal Chancellery or Pro Helvetia, the Swiss arts council, depending on the nationality of the author). In 2007 this mechanism was made explicit, with the guarantee printed in each issue of NBG and on the website. In this way a further impediment to German-language books reaching English-language audiences was circumvented: UK editors were given not only the confidence that these books had been selected by a trusted group with expertise in the field, but the assurance that the inevitable risk involved in publishing a title in translation would be mitigated by some funding for the translation costs. It is this upfront cost – in addition to the cost of buying the rights from the original publisher or agent – that is understood to act as a deterrent to the publication of foreign fiction. Of course, there are always upfront costs in publishing: an English-language author's advance will often dwarf the translation costs for a non-English book; but sales figures remain low and unreliable enough to make the publishing of translations a risky business for all.

Ondrej Vimr has recently embarked on much-needed research into the funding of literary translations, working with the concepts of supply- and demand-driven translation models. He defines a 'supply-driven' model as one where the source culture pushes a book onto the target market, often through state-funded mechanisms, while 'demand-driven' translation requires the target culture to have a 'genuine interest' in the source text or culture.[12] The books reviewed in NBG are the result of transnational debate and consensus, and as such provide an example of what Vimr calls the 'intertwined approaches' of supply- and demand-driven models.[13] This balance of both models – in particular the fact that the books selected for recommendation are chosen by both source and target culture representatives – is relatively unusual in the field of international literature in the UK.[14]

---

[12] Ondřej Vimr, 'Supply-driven Translation: Compensating for Lack of Demand', in *Translating the Literatures of Small European Nations*, ed. by Rajendra Chitnis (Liverpool: Liverpool University Press, 2019), p. 49.

[13] Vimr, 'Supply-driven Translation', p. 64.

[14] The project New Spanish Books uses a similar model to New Books in German, whereby the recommended books are selected by a jury of six representatives from the publishing and literary translation sector in the UK. http://www.newspanishbooks.com/uk-panel-choice [accessed 7 December 2018].

NBG was founded through and continues to consist in collaboration between individuals committed to a common cause and to changing the status quo. In mapping network relations like these, Latour places the 'local' and the 'global' on a level playing field, giving primacy to neither but insisting on their necessary interconnectedness. Our experience at NBG reinforces this idea: it is as important for us to support the avid reader of a debut Swiss novelist and assist that reader in pitching the novel to UK publishers as it is to continue our high-profile media partnership with the German Book Prize. Both of these acts support our aim of promoting German-language literature internationally. Holding together the large group of supporters and partners, attending to both the local and the global in equal measure, and thus making sure that this broad-based and energetic collaboration creates a project that is greater than the sum of its parts is where the real labour of NBG lies.

Ideology and Independence

Retaining the balance between the 'push' and 'pull' of source and target cultures is essential for NBG to be effective. The magazine is co-funded by German-language publishers, who pay a subsidy if their book is selected for review. In this way there are two types of 'push' from the source culture, with differing priorities: the cultural institutes and the publishers. Similarly, the 'pull' needs further nuance. If our prime aim is to increase the *number* of German-language books in English translation, then are we only selecting books that are *a priori* likely to appeal to UK editors and readers, thereby flattening a diverse literary world, filtering out the more challenging texts? In our world of German-language literature, this can be crudely parsed as: are we simply facilitating the translation of more books about Nazis, to confirm and sustain what might be considered a UK reader's existing view of German history and culture?

To answer this we need to go back to the question of ideology and commitment, and to consider the role of independent publishers. An unexpected delight when I began to edit NBG was that I could witness the founding of exciting new publishers who have since changed the UK literary landscape. I recall meeting German-born journalist Meike Ziervogel at an event at the Goethe-Institut in London while preparing my first issue of NBG. Ziervogel had just founded Peirene Press, which has since become a renowned independent publisher dedicated to literature in translation, with a fine list of translations from German. I soon found myself at one of her first 'salons': gatherings of international literature lovers at her North London home for readings by the author and translator of her latest book. Similarly, in my first months at NBG I met Stefan Tobler just as he was in the process of setting up the innovative publisher And Other Stories (AOS). Tobler, who himself translates from German as well as Spanish and Portuguese, had been a reader–reviewer for NBG for several years, and duly published a book recommended by NBG.[15] AOS has also harnessed collaborative energies, establishing its support base through reading groups for particular languages. These groups brought like-minded individuals together to discuss potential books, before pitching the most popular ones to the AOS team for publication. The members of these groups were some of the first subscribers to AOS, which – like Peirene and numerous other new independent publishers since then – uses a subscription model to ensure a consistent foundation of support on which to grow.

What we are witnessing here is ideology in action. These publishers were founded in hugely risk-taking endeavours by individuals pursuing an ideological cause: to diversify the UK book market, to find readers for books that they believed in but that the mainstream publishing houses refused to take on. They are explicitly not interested in commercial gain, with many of them functioning as not-for-profit entities: any profit is reinvested into the enterprise and so contributes directly to producing more cutting-edge literature in English translation. And they have built up intercultural organs through collaboration, with a great emphasis on physical networks – the salon, the book club, the reading group, the 'family' of subscribers. The entry for 2009 in AOS's online timeline charmingly sets out how the publisher developed through a combination of collaboration, commitment and 'magic'.[16]

Since those early days Peirene and AOS have been joined by Fitzcarraldo Editions, Tilted Axis Press and several others, with AOS and a group of independent presses based in the north of England establishing a further collaboration through the Northern Fiction Alliance (founded in 2016). Similar developments have taken place in North America. Both Sapiro and the AHRC researchers have identified similar phenomena, with the former's research on American independent presses highlighting their use of words like '"vision", "labor of love", "pleasure", "magical", all terms opposed to the rationalization of profit governing the commercial logic of the large conglomerates'.[17] Similarly, the AHRC project has highlighted the marked increase in the number of independent presses publishing translated literature over the past decade, and the 'boundary-pushing ethos' of most advocates for

---

[15] Christoph Simon, *Zbinden's Progress*, trans. Donal McLaughlin (High Wycombe: And Other Stories, 2012).
[16] 'About Us: Timeline', https://www.andotherstories.org/about-us/ [accessed 7 December 2018].
[17] Sapiro, 'Globalization', p. 434.

translated literature.[18] Independent publisher Pushkin Press, for example, was bought by Stephanie Seegmüller and Adam Freudenheim (both formerly of Penguin) 'precisely because they believed that there was not enough foreign literature being published in the UK'.[19]

NBG and similar organisations work closely with these new independent presses, along with more established publishers with a similar mission to publish literature in translation: MacLehose Press, Granta Books, Harvill Secker and Oneworld Publications, among others. By privileging literary quality over immediate commercial viability, and by vigorously promoting literature in translation, these publishers broaden the UK and US readership's appetite for literature in translation, opening up new possibilities and leaving behind established but limited views of foreign cultures.

Creating Space for Translation

Ideologically driven independent publishers can also often provide the space that is needed to establish an author in translation. It is by no means a given that a bestseller in German will translate into one in English, and potential bestselling authors are often dropped if the first book in English does not realize that sales potential. The chequered publishing histories of German-language bestsellers Arno Geiger and Martin Suter in English translation are a case in point here: each of their books has been published by a different English-language publisher, a situation which severely limits their capacity to become established in English. In NBG's 'Cooperation and Collaboration' issue we featured a piece on US publisher Barbara Epler, which perfectly exemplifies the role of sustained commitment in publishing literature in translation: an editor prepared to take the initial risk and to stay the course. Epler is president and publisher of the independent American firm New Directions, which has published a range of exceptional literature in translation since its founding in 1936. Award-winning translator Susan Bernofsky, who has worked with Epler on numerous books, wrote in NBG about the publisher's direct commitment to individual authors. Bernofsky acknowledges that translated literature remains a hard sell in the English-language market, and that success rarely comes from one-off publications and far more frequently from sustained commitment to publishing an author's oeuvre and gradually building their readership. Her two prime examples come from her own experience, as translator of German author Jenny Erpenbeck and Japanese–German Yoko Tawada. Both of these authors now count among the few whose books NBG no longer reviews – because we no

---

[18] Chitnis et al., 'Translating the Literatures of Smaller European Nations', p. 6.
[19] Chitnis et al., 'Translating the Literatures of Smaller European Nations', pp. 2–6.

longer need to. Erpenbeck and Tawada have a substantial international audience that has grown book by book, because of careful and committed curation by New Directions and latterly their UK publisher, Granta and Portobello Books: 'Now Tawada joins Erpenbeck as one of the most beloved mid-career German-language authors in English, and without Barbara's willingness to take risks – including significant financial risks – for the literature she believes in, it's likely that neither author would be in that position.'[20]

Translators as Co-creators

Susan Bernofsky exemplifies many of the processes already identified here: she is a digital influencer through her blog *Translationista*, and she forges physical networks through her academic role in the Faculty of Arts at Columbia University and regular participation in literary events in the US.[21] Bernofsky is consequently a highly visible translator, both on and offline, and in this way represents a key development in the literary translation scene over recent years. Just as the new independent publishers discussed above have tended to involve their readers and potential translators in the various stages of the publishing process, they have also platformed their translators more than has traditionally been the case in mainstream publishing. Whether cause or symptom, this reflects a more general development across publishing in the UK, with translators now routinely functioning as unofficial (not to mention unpaid) scouts and agents.

A very familiar term in translation studies is that of the translator's 'invisibility' – associated most closely with the great translator Anthea Bell. The irony of Bell's insistence on this status must be noted as I write, less than one week after her death at the age of 82 (in October 2018). So far her son's tweet announcing her death has been retweeted 1663 times and 'liked' by a further 4735 individuals and organisations. During her lifetime, too, Anthea Bell was anything but invisible, being included in the *Observer*'s list of the 100 most influential people in publishing in 2011. Her 'invisibility' notion referred to how she saw the role of the translator as writer. For Bell, a successfully translated text was one that read as though it had been written in the target language, where the translator was therefore – necessarily – completely elided within the text itself.[22]

---

[20] *New Books in German* 42 (Autumn 2017), p. 18.
[21] Bernofsky was, for example, one of the first curators of New York's 'Festival Neue Literatur', an annual festival of German- and English-language literature.
[22] Anthea Bell, 'Translation: walking the tightrope of illusion', in *The Translator as Writer*, ed. by Susan Bassnett and Peter Bush (London: Bloomsbury, 2008), pp. 58–67.

There is a debate on the subject in Translation Studies which we shall set aside for now, since our interest is in how the translator's role has become – and became even for Bell – one of visible co-creator in an extra-textual, structural sense.

To say that this is a complete change in the role of the translator would do a disservice to the generations of translators who have pitched beloved books to publishers, successfully launching international careers; but nobody disputes today that this translatorly role has expanded hugely in the past 20 years. Translators are now regularly pitching books, pro-actively networking with publishers and other translators, setting up cooperatives, attending and running summer schools, reviewing translated literature in the mainstream press, blogging, running translation workshops in schools, going on tour with their authors and engaging in multiple forms of public engagement as part of translation residencies.[23]

In this way translators have become the co-creators of particular books, of author's international careers (for a practical example of this, see Angus Nicholl's discussion of Freud in Chapter 13 of this volume), and of the heightened status of translated literature in the UK. As such, the translator has become an increasingly significant 'node' in Latour's network. This is why, after two years at NBG, I set up our 'Emerging Translators Programme' (ETP), the result of two observations that I had made in those early years. Firstly, NBG needed more and better sample translations to accompany our reviews. These translated extracts are essential to the process of rights sales, because they give editors unable to read German a taste of the book in English, but at the time they were often commissioned by German-language publishers and sometimes translated by inexperienced literary translators and not adequately edited.[24] In addition, the growing influence of translators as nodes within international literature meant that giving them additional training and broadening their professional network would fortify and build that network. The ETP brings both elements together by commissioning six as-yet-unpublished translators to complete sample translations of books published in NBG, and we co-edit those samples in a workshop

---

[23] Katy Derbyshire discusses the pro-active translator in 'Translators Acting Up', *New Books in German* 40 (Autumn 2016). Cedilla & Co. and the Starling Bureau are translators' collectives in the US and UK respectively. The British Library and Free Word Centre in London have both run translator residencies.

[24] In the last ten years this phenomenon has almost vanished from German-language publishing, yet the AHRC project identified it as an existing problem in the 'literatures of small nations', a symptom of the dominance of supply-led translation (Chitnis et al., 'Translating the Literatures of Smaller European Nations', p. 11).

facilitated by NBG and leading translator Shaun Whiteside. As I write, we are developing this workshop into a two-day event that will include visits to publishing houses for meetings with editors, mindful of the ever-increasing importance of the network, and of translators' place within it, as a way of making books travel.

A Whole Life

The year 2012, the ETP's second, was an auspicious one. Of the 11 graduates of that year's programmes, eight have gone on to develop careers in literary translation: from Niall Sellar, who went on to translate Volker Kutscher's crime series set in interwar Berlin (adapted for television as *Babylon Berlin*, 2017–ongoing), to Charlotte Collins, translator of Robert Seethaler's *Ein ganzes Leben* (*A Whole Life*, 2014) and *Der Trafikant* (*The Tobacconist*, 2012), hugely successful books in English translation. I highlight Sellar and Collins in particular because their published translations followed on most directly from involvement in the ETP. Impressed by Sellar's ETP translation, I recommended him to Sandstone Press shortly after they had acquired the rights to the first in Kutscher's series. Shaun Whiteside, who had facilitated the workshops and so got to know each translator's work well, similarly recommended Charlotte Collins to editors at Picador, who had asked him to suggest new readers for reports and new translators for samples. Kate Harvey, then editorial director at Picador, takes up the story, which becomes a fascinating potted history of how a German-language book makes it into English and – crucially – how it becomes a success.

At a London Book Fair party in 2014 Harvey met Karsten Kredel, publisher of Hanser Berlin (the Berlin imprint of Carl Hanser Verlag), who talked to her at length about a new book he was particularly excited about: *A Whole Life*, the fifth novel by Austrian author Robert Seethaler. Hanser Berlin had commissioned a sample translation by Katy Derbyshire, so Harvey – who does not read German – was immediately able to get a sense of the book's quality and style. Excited by the prospect, she decided to commission a reader's report and so turned to Whiteside's recent recommendation: Charlotte Collins. By this point, time was of the essence, as Hanser had already received an offer for the book from another publisher. Collins did not have time to read the book and write the report as quickly as Harvey needed, as she was working on another project in Germany at the time, but she agreed to read it as quickly as possible and then to give an oral report to Harvey over the phone. Harvey attributes the book's ultimate success to a 'chain of passionate individuals', and at this stage in the process Collins joined that chain, sending the publisher an unprompted email after a couple of days telling her how much she 'loved' the book.[25] That 'human touch', followed by the phone call a day or two later in which Collins spoke passionately about the book, contributed to Harvey's resolve to make an offer on the novel.[26] As the AHRC researchers note, at large publishers it is 'not just one person but a team, ultimately including sales people, who need to be persuaded to go ahead with a translated book'.[27] Harvey cites the double confidence that came from Derbyshire's excellent sample translation and Collins' highly positive report, coupled with the fact that the broader team at Picador could read the opening pages in English, as central to the book's acquisition. Along with 'passion', the word 'trust' loomed large in my discussion with Harvey – Kredel, Derbyshire, Whiteside, Collins were all trusted individuals whose immense confidence in the book imbued Harvey with her own.

During their discussions about *A Whole Life* Collins had asked to be considered for its translation, and after completing a sample for Picador she was contracted to do so. Harvey considers their close working relationship part of the book's success: Collins lived in London at the time and so the pair were able to meet for a 'real-time' editorial session, rather than the email-only edits that are often the case with translated literature.

The chain of passionate individuals did not end here: next came Richard Baker from Picador's sales department, cover designer Matthew Garrett, and Camilla Elworthy, director of publicity. Baker had great success selling the book to London's independent bookshops, with Daunt's requesting a special edition for window displays in the run-up to Christmas. This success in an independent built a following for the book, which led to mainstream attention as Waterstone's Book of the Month in its paperback edition. Here Harvey notes the benefit of some structural features – the modest length of the book versus its epic narrative scope, and the striking cover image – which made it a book that editorial colleagues 'could take out to lunches'. This extended to Pan Macmillan managing director Anthony Forbes Watson, who loved the book. Elworthy's publicity campaign took *A Whole Life* to the next stage, where it featured as Radio 4's *Book at Bedtime*. The pinnacle was reached when the novel was shortlisted for the Man Booker International Prize in 2016. This new prize, launched that year with significant publicity for the shortlisted titles, is itself further evidence of the heightened status of translated literature in the UK.

These impassioned individuals, and the networks that they form, have produced a highly successful book in translation which has its own legacy: Collins has gone from emerging translator to highly visible 'node' within

---

[25] Author's interview with Charlotte Collins, October 2018.
[26] Author's interview with Kate Harvey, October 2018.
[27] Chitnis et al., 'Translating the Literatures of Smaller European Nations', p. 9.

literary translation networks; those of us advocating translated literature have another example for publishers and booksellers that these books can and do sell; and the star rises a little further for books by German-language authors.

The Translator's Celebrity

One of NBG's core roles is recommending translators to UK, US and German-language publishers – for samples, reader's reports and whole books. When recommending Charlotte Collins now I usually cite both the great success of Seethaler and her award of the prestigious Helen and Kurt Wolff prize in 2017, with publishers more taken by the former and cultural diplomats by the latter. This opens up the question of 'translatorial celebrity' and takes us back to Anthea Bell and all those retweets. Is the translator's celebrity beginning to stand in for authorial celebrity? Can and should the translator provide a physical presence on book tours, at signings, at literary festivals where the author cannot be present? This authorial absence is yet another factor that works against literature in translation, deterring UK editors from buying translation rights. In German-language literature this is much less of a problem than for other languages, since the authors are geographically close in the case of the UK, and usually able to speak English well, but there is still work to be done in mitigating this problem.

The new translator's celebrity presents a potential solution to this, by foregrounding the art of translation. A further solution to this problem lies in yet more collaboration, in particular with literary festivals and between cultural institutes. European Literature Night, the European Writers' Tour and the European Literature Network are three examples (resolutely Eurocentric, admittedly) that seek to move beyond national categories by advocating multiple foreign literatures as well as the *idea* of translation regardless of the language. The recommendations of the AHRC project are striking here, encouraging further collaboration and less 'implicit competition' between languages.[28]

This is the direction that we are moving in at NBG too. A trilateral French–German–English event, 'Triangular Talks', in London in March 2017, resulted from collaboration between New Books in German, the French Book Office in London and the London embassies and cultural institutes of France and Germany. Now that organisations such as NBG, that promote single-language literatures, are well established, transnational networks of this kind are the obvious next step in the process. In this context, collaboration trumps competition: organisations work together to grow the readership for translated literature, rather than seeking to shift existing readers from one country's literature to another's.

[28] Chitnis et al., 'Translating the Literatures of Smaller European Nations', p. 9.

A Transnational Literature

Contemporary German literature lends itself to this transnational, triangulating approach because it itself is so often already transnational. The central position of the German-speaking countries within Europe – both geographically and politically – has resulted in cultures greatly influenced by migration, and in a strong position to transmit that hybrid culture beyond their own borders. Bosnian–German author Saša Stanišić, Azerbaijani–German Olga Grjasnowa and Georgian–German Nino Haratischwili are just three prominent examples of German-language authors writing from transnational perspectives who have been translated into English. In each case, a UK publisher has gained access to an 'exotic', hard-to-access culture through the relatively accessible German language. For all our concerns about the limited numbers of German-language books making it into English translation, there is no doubt that the resources available – both financial and in terms of trained translators and networks – for the German language are hugely greater than that for Bosnia, Azerbaijan or Georgia.

Philip Gwyn Jones, who acquired Haratischwili's *Das achte Leben* (*The Eighth Life*, 2014) for Scribe UK, confirms the role of German as 'bridge language' for literatures from further East. 'Without question,' he remarks of *The Eighth Life*, 'the book would not exist in English had it been written in Georgian.'[29] Gwyn Jones puts this down largely to 'structures and systems', citing 'very well established, funded, marketed and discriminating systems for promoting German-language literature'.[30] 'Networks and connections' come next, with the numerous well-trained and networked translators – and a competitive market among them – giving publishers the confidence that, if they buy the rights to a book, they will find a translator who can do it justice.[31]

When Collaboration meets Commitment

Haratischwili's translators are Charlotte Collins and Ruth Martin, who first met the author at the BCLT Summer School in 2012 and proceeded to advocate her work to British publishers in the years that followed. This gives us a final example of the power of the real-time encounter, of physical

---

[29] Author's interview with Philip Gwyn Jones, November 2018.
[30] Author's interview with Philip Gwyn Jones, November 2018.
[31] The AHRC project confirms the importance of good translators by citing a 'severe shortage of gifted native English-speaking translators' as a challenge for 'smaller European literatures' (Chitnis et al., 'Translating the Literatures of Smaller European Nations', p. 11).

networks and of what happens when collaboration meets commitment. Just as the AHRC report concludes with the remark that 'the strength, status and diversity of literary translation [...] will continue to grow best where advocates find paths to cooperation', so my experience at NBG has been that real, committed transnational collaboration is the key to a literature that travels.[32] It is a sign of the relative health of the field that the focus in debates on international literature is shifting away from concerns about the *numbers* of books translated into English to the *types*, with diversity now a major focus of advocates. Two recent initiatives, the Warwick Prize for Women in Translation and the Tilted Axis Mentorship for an emerging BAME translator, are prominent early results of this new advocacy. Arising from collaboration between impassioned individuals, they showcase these new ideological motivations and light the way for an increasingly diverse UK literary culture.

The transnational networks and processes supporting German-language literature in translation have contributed to a diversity even within that literature, too. The collaborative commitment to expanding the global readership for German-language literature is bearing fruit, with a broader than ever range of German-language voices now finding expression across the world, in multiple genres and in numerous languages. This transit is most successful when the advocacy and support systems in both source and target cultures function effectively, from national funding bodies through to committed publishers and pro-active translators. English is central in this constellation not only as a language with a large and prominent readership but as a bridge that makes translations into other languages more likely. A second bridge is formed by the increasingly transnational nature of German-language literature in terms of authorship and setting, a new hybridity that has enhanced the literature's appeal for cultural mediators and publishers across the world. These linguistic bridges, formed of individuals and networks, enable a diverse German-language literature to cross borders, reinventing as it does the global image of that literary culture.

Suggestions for Further Reading

Bernofsky, Susan and Esther Allen (eds.), *In Translation: Translators on Their Work and What It Means* (Columbia: Columbia University Press, 2013), 290 pp.

Braun, Rebecca, 'The World Author in Us All: Conceptualising Fame and Agency in the Global Market', *Celebrity Studies* 7.4 (2016), pp. 457–75.

---

[32] Chitnis et al., 'Translating the Literatures of Smaller European Nations', p. 14.

Chitnis, Rajendra, Jakob Stougaard-Nielsen, Rhian Atkin and Zoran Milutinović (eds.), *Translating the Literatures of Small European Nations* (Liverpool: Liverpool University Press, 2019), 272 pp.

Hungerford, Amy, *Making Literature Now* (Stanford: Stanford University Press, 2016), 225 pp.

Sapiro, Gisèle, 'Globalization and Cultural Diversity in the Book Market: The Case of Literary Translations in the US and in France', *Poetics* 38 (2010), pp. 419–39.

Spencer, Sally Ann, 'Prizing Translation: Book Awards and Literary Translation', in *Perspectives on Literature and Translation: Creation, Circulation, Reception*, ed. by B. Nelson and B. Maher (New York: Routledge, 2013), pp. 195–209.

Vassalo, Helen, Translating Women Research Project blog, http://blogs.exeter.ac.uk/translatingwomen/ [accessed 16 November 2019].

Walkowitz, Rebecca, *Born Translated* (Columbia: Columbia University Press, 2017), 383 pp.

Part 2

Spatiality: Mapping Nations, Mapping Networks

5

Networks and World Literature

The Practice of Putting German Authors in their Place

Rebecca Braun

On 31 January 1827 Johann Wolfgang von Goethe famously called the modern period of literature into being, pronouncing, 'National literature is now rather an unmeaning term; the epoch of World-literature is at hand, and everyone must strive to hasten its approach.'[1] Although the term 'World-literature' – *Welt-Literatur* – was not his coinage and was already in isolated use some 20 years earlier by Martin Christoph Wieland and other contemporaries at Anna Amalia's court in Weimar, it has gone down in literary history as the concept that he brought to life.[2] Today the term has come back to prominence as a research area. World Literature programmes have been increasingly introduced across Western institutions of higher education to mitigate the tendency, common across the twentieth century, of studying literature as an aesthetic medium solely in accordance with the boundaries of language and/or nation states. More broadly, research across the humanities is exploring how to account for the 'real world' considerations of global cultural production in a way that might allow us to capture the value of art and literature for society in new ways, and sectors as diverse as design, defence and health are all investing in both the idea and practice of creativity. In this respect, the similarities between the turn of the nineteenth and the twenty-first centuries

---

[1] Johann Wolfgang von Goethe, *Conversations of Goethe with Johann Peter Eckermann*, trans. John Oxenford, ed. by J.K. Moorhead, introduced by Havelock Ellis (n.p: Da Capo, 1998), pp. 165–66.

[2] See Dieter Lamping, *Die Idee der Weltlitertur: Ein Konzept Goethes und seine Karriere* (Stuttgart: Kröner, 2010) for a very accessible discussion of this and related terms; see also Manfred Koch, *Weimaraner Weltbewohner: Zur Genese von Goethes Begriff 'Weltliteratur'* (Tübingen: Niemeyer, 2002), esp. ch. 1 and ch. 2.

98 Rebecca Braun

are striking. At the beginning of both, the catchy concept of world literature, used broadly to signify transnational processes of creative exchange that carry high cultural value, has been used by influential people and/or institutions to convey a step change in the way creative–intellectual activity is linked to interpersonal and intercultural relations. But what did the term really mean 200 years ago, what might it mean now, and how does thinking about world literature help us better understand how authors relate to their various locations, both in books and in the world?

The Author in the World: Nineteenth-century Networks

For all the drama of his pronouncement, Goethe did remarkably little, either at the time or afterwards, to specify exactly what he meant by his new 'epoch of World-literature' (this non-standard orthography of 'World-literature' will be retained throughout to distinguish between general contemporary usage of the term 'world literature' and Goethe's specific coinage of *Welt-Literatur*). Was he delighting in enhanced access to an agreed global canon of great writing or praising instead the spectacular boom in translations of contemporary, as yet largely undiscovered, texts?[3] Might there be an echo of 'worldly' in his 'world', as he celebrates literature's new relevance to an emergent set of international relations?[4] Or is it precisely the opposite, as he pits the world of the literary text, with its own morals and aesthetics, against that of international trade and the global citizen, the so-called 'Weltbürger', who was emerging at the same time?[5] Scholars have been left to intuit answers from the range of literary activities noted by Goethe's faithful aide and diary-writer, Johann Peter Eckermann, along with various further isolated references to the term sprinkled into forewords and other short pieces written by the ageing Goethe before his death in 1832.

From even a very cursory glance at these sources, it is clear that in Goethe's day connectivity across the literary world certainly did mean the circulation of well-regarded texts through translation – he delighted in reading a Chinese

---

[3] On the massive boom in translation activity in Germany, France, Great Britain and North America in the first half of the nineteenth century see Andrew Piper, *Dreaming in Books: The Making of the Bibliographic Imagination in the Romantic Age* (Chicago, IL: University of Chicago Press, 2009), pp. 160–62.

[4] For this take on literature's growing social relevance, see William St. Clair, *The Reading Nation in the Romantic Period* (Cambridge: Cambridge University Press, 2004).

[5] See Lamping, *Die Idee der Weltliteratur*, and also Tobias Boes, *Formative Fictions: Nationalism, Cosmopolitanism, and the Bildungsroman* (Ithaca, NY: Cornell University Press, 2012).

novel, and felt instructed by reading some of his own work in French, for example.[6] He also actively promoted his own Scottish translator Thomas Carlyle's *Life of Schiller* (1825), using a generous foreword to the German-language edition in 1830 to familiarize German readers with Scottish folk traditions that might provide them with a new angle on their own linguistic heritage, and thus a new angle on Schiller. This mediatory activity was deliberately flagged by Goethe as supporting 'World-literature' in his foreword, which he glosses as part of 'the more or less free trade in intellectual goods'.[7] Heralding the dawn of world literature thus also meant promoting the circulation of the underpinning intellectual ideas and foregrounding the actual people shaping and expressing them. The books themselves were just one aspect of a whole world literature system that encompassed the physical and epistemological world of literary practice (literally: where people sit and write, how they develop their ideas, the extent to which personal and economic circumstances allow them to travel or otherwise access new sources, who is able to read the resulting writings and so on). Indeed, as Goethe would remark, invoking his concept of 'World-literature' to the Assembly of German Scientists and Doctors in Leipzig in 1827, authors must embrace the concept to find a common sense of purpose in their intellectual work, '[b]ut this is effected more by travellers than by correspondence, since personal presence alone succeeds in determining and cementing the true relationship between people'.[8]

To illustrate how the ideal and the practice of world literature coalesce, we can consider the extent to which Carlyle and Goethe's transnational networking is the product of both intellectual ideas and material circumstances. The two never met, but they corresponded at length, mutually promoting one another's work and taking the temperature of the contemporary British and German literary scenes. When preparing the

---

[6] The former is captured in Eckermann's diary entry for 31 January 1827, the latter in a piece published in the introduction to the sixth volume of Goethe's periodical, *Über Kunst und Altertum*, reproduced in vol. 22 of *Sämtliche Werke: Briefe, Tagebücher und Gespräche*, ed. by Dieter Borchmeyer et al., 40 vols. in 2 sections (Frankfurt: Deutscher Klassiker Verlag, 1985).

[7] Thomas Carlyle, *Leben Schillers: aus dem Englischen, eingeleitet durch Goethe* (Frankfurt a.M.: Wilmans, 1830), p. vii.

[8] Johann Wolfgang von Goethe, *Sämtliche Werke: Briefe, Tagebücher und Gespräche*, ed. by Dieter Borchmeyer et al., 40 vols. in 2 sections (Frankfurt: Deutscher Klassiker Verlag, 1985), section 1, vol. 25, p. 79. This speech is discussed and referenced in John K. Noyes, 'Writing the Dialectical Structure of the Modern Subject: Goethe on World Literature and World Citizenship', in *World Authorship*, special issue of *Seminar* 51.2 (2015), ed. by R. Braun and A. Piper, pp. 100–14, p. 101.

German-language edition of Carlyle's *Life of Schiller* for recommendation to the Berlin Academy for Foreign Literature, Goethe personally requested an image of Carlyle's rural Scottish homestead in Craigenputtock. He included this in the frontispiece and wrote at some length about Carlyle's home in the foreword, lending the whole endeavour the distinct flavour of a travelogue that captures a meeting of minds in a mutually admired landscape. The fact that Carlyle chose this isolated, hilly location as the place in which to deepen his understanding of German literature only underscores the geophysical connection prized by both that arose from shared aesthetic sensibilities (he lived there for six years, to the dismay of his wife).[9] Goethe's intellectual network, to which Carlyle was thrilled to accede as the self-styled foremost promoter of German culture in Great Britain and which effectively gave him a free pass into the Berlin academy, was, alongside the shared intellectual ideals, also grounded in an eagerness to apprehend others through their physical and material circumstances. The conceptual aspirations of 'World-literature', in other words, are brought to life through a solid network of mutually supportive authors actively taking an interest in one another's lives.

On the matter of access to this network, Goethe would appear to have been surprisingly egalitarian, introducing a sense of 'the whole world' to his term. In the same diary entry of 31 January 1827, Eckermann records him relativizing the act of writing and universalizing the Romantic idea of poetic vision:

> 'I am more and more convinced,' he continued, 'that poetry is the universal possession of mankind, revealing itself everywhere and at all times in hundreds and hundreds of men. One makes it a little better than another, and swims on the surface a little longer than another – that is all.'[10]

While the grandiloquent and culturally egalitarian Goethe who emerges from Eckermann's diaries should be seen as itself a literary construction (see below), the spirit in which he is recorded launching the concept of world literature and using it to inspire others can nevertheless be captured here. For perhaps the purest ideological core of Goethe's thinking about world literature is that the activity of producing literary texts captures something transcendent from

---

[9] See Rosemary Ashton, 'Carlyle's Apprenticeship: His Early German Criticism and His Relationship with Goethe (1822–1832)', *The Modern Language Review* 71.1 (1976), pp. 1–18, esp. p. 12.

[10] Goethe, *Conversations*, p. 165.

across the human condition. Formulated from within the heart of the Weimar circle but with a deep appreciation of the real interpersonal exchanges across the European continent and beyond that this circle had come to facilitate, Goethe's concept of world literature conveys a sense of the socio-cultural interconnectedness that can be achieved through the practice of literature – sharing existing texts and ideas, collaborating on new intellectual ventures and, in so doing, recognizing points of commonality across otherwise diverse environments. From his perspective, tucked away in provincial Germany just as Carlyle toiled in Craigenputtock, writers who consciously positioned themselves within the 'epoch of World-literature' through their really existing transnational connections with one another were thereby lifting themselves out of their particular circumstances to be part of a grander intellectual whole that knows neither national nor linguistic boundaries and celebrates a coming together of intellectual and personal interactions.

In this respect, Goethe's 'World-literature' is in the first instance a concept that necessitated a certain practice on the part of its principle producers, authors, if it were to become more than an empty ideological slogan. This practice, as John Noyes explores in detail, can be called 'world authorship', and it requires a writing style that is able to keep sight of multiplicity and diversity even as it points to overarching shared experiences, as well as a personal ability to seek out meaningful interaction across different fora. Drawing on speeches and letters Goethe addressed to learned recipients, Noyes stresses how Goethe consciously actively embodied processes of cultural exchange and, in so doing, worked on 'developing representational and communicative practices that do justice to whatever it is that humanity has in common, while still respecting the diversity of phenomena'.[11] Indeed, Eckermann's diaries, along with the vast bibliographic activity Goethe undertook re-presenting both his own work and that of his friends and contemporaries in his later years, testify to a kind of author who lived in a world made by literary practice. With this I do not mean to indicate an author fooled by his own fictions and living at a far remove from everyday life. Rather, I follow Andrew Piper's line in taking seriously the vastly expansive gesture that defines Goethe's later years, and in particular the way he navigated multiple media and literary systems throughout the extended gestation and publication period of his novel *Wilhelm Meisters Lehjahre* (*Wilhelm Meister's Travels*, which appeared in multiple variants from 1808 to 1829). Goethe is so convinced of the inter-relatedness of all things under the umbrella of human experience – science and art, life and death, east and west, plants and poetry – that his intellectual

---

[11] Noyes, 'Writing the Dialectical Structure', p. 107.

raison d'être becomes one of capturing the whole world in his collected works or, as Piper calls it, his 'larger textual cosmos'.[12]

What Goethe's launch of the whole area of world literature as both a concept and a practice sets in motion is therefore a preliminary staking out of parameters around literary agency, viewed from the broader perspective of how people live and act together in the world: what can literature do, what kind of intellectual worlds can it sustain, how do fictional worlds relate to historical and contemporary ones? For Goethe, these questions directly concern the actions of human beings, rather than, as late twentieth-century theory will make popular, the seemingly independent circulation of texts and/or language itself. This leads us to a broader methodological question: if world literature as both an intellectual concept and a product of an expanding international book market is first and foremost carried by authorial practice, how can the nature and significance of the network sustained by those actions be traced? How, in other words, can literary historians study Goethe's 'World-literature' as a meaningful process that gives a broader purchase on society and extends well beyond individual biographical connections, rather than just as a canon of select texts written by famous people?

> 'Even if, for my part, nothing has been invented and *everything is completely true*, it has nevertheless been *chosen*':[13]
> Recording the Legacy of Goethe's World

Not only did one of the most significant attempts Goethe actually made at enacting his concept of 'World-literature' happen in his support of Carlyle's literary biography of Schiller, but the medium in which his 1827 pronouncement was recorded, Johann Peter Eckermann's *Gespräche mit Goethe in den letzten Jahren seines Lebens* [*Conversations with Goethe in the Last Years of his Life*, 1836–1848], also belongs to this genre. Broadly speaking, literary biography is the written reconstruction of authorial lives, and it offers a form of particularly self-aware social networking when undertaken by near contemporaries on one another. Eckermann's diary-style record of his life with Goethe from 1823 to 1832, which runs to three hefty volumes in total, paints a picture of Goethe repeatedly personally enacting the broader interconnectedness of all things that can be known by man. In this sense, his whole life as captured by

---

[12] Piper, *Dreaming in Books*, p. 33.

[13] Eckermann in a letter to Heinrich Laube, 5 March 1844; quoted in Johann Peter Eckermann, *Gespräche mit Goethe in den letzten Jahren seines Lebens*, ed. by Christoph Michel with Hans Grüter (Berlin: Deutscher Klassiker Verlag, 2011), p. 918 (my translation, original emphasis).

Eckermann is already linked to the term 'World-literature' in quite a practical sense, as he is shown acting out the core underlying principles of multiplicity and universality well before he actually wields the term. Around the time Goethe pronounces on world literature, for example, Eckermann reports how the author is also eagerly gathering scientific evidence of mankind's ability to renew itself, formulating arguments to prove the value of pushing oneself beyond one's own horizon of experience and actively testing out and reshaping his emergent literary novella, *Novelle* [*Novella*, 1828], in discussion with others. In Eckermann's portrait of Goethe's life, the author's multiple actions lie at the heart of a series of diverse but interlinked worlds of academic enquiry and social interaction – Goethe himself calls them 'Weltgegenden' [world areas] as early as 1817.[14] This vast intellectual effort can be seen as the natural flipside of Goethe's desire to capture the whole world in his collected works, and it underscores again the implicit existence of a 'world author' as a central practical figure alongside the explicit turn to world literature as an idealized intellectual concept in his late work.

It is presumably this very dynamic and relational aspect of the kind of intellectual activity he promotes that also leads Goethe to caution against fetishizing any one particular model when evoking the different cultural traditions that can be apprehended through the practice of world literature. Following immediately on from his call to hasten the dawn of the new 'World-literature' epoch he adds, 'But while we thus value what is foreign, we must not bind ourselves to some particular thing, and regard it as a model.'[15] Significantly, this important qualification to the notion of finding a common cause or overarching aesthetic in literature warns against the kind of essentialist, emulative reading that frequently drives the very genre of literary biography in which his pronouncement has been captured. In fact, and quite paradoxically, Goethe's own enactment of world literature as a willed and interactive authorial practice leads precisely to ossification, as others seek to profit from his exemplary embodiment of the broader intellectual ideal that underpins it by paying homage to his greatness in material form – they turn him into a model.

When read with a careful eye for composition, Eckermnn's diary-style conversations provide a direct example of how multiple material and circumstantial factors have given rise to a highly circumscribed narrative construction both of Goethe and the concept of 'World-literature'. Eckermann himself lived much of his life in near penury, yearned to be published as an author in his

---

[14] Goethe's early use of 'Welt' compounds is discussed in Noyes, 'Writing the Dialectical Structure', p. 109.

[15] Goethe, *Conversations*, p. 166.

own right and repeatedly looked to the commercial success of his books to sustain him in his old age. In his younger years he initially hoped to launch his own literary career – he was particularly keen to grow a readership for his poetry – on the back of publishing his conversations with Goethe during Goethe's lifetime. Yet, although Goethe was sympathetic to the project and periodically reviewed and intervened in the early drafts, he repeatedly refused to consent to their publication. He also significantly slowed down Eckermann's work by giving him other editorial tasks.[16]

Goethe's direct influence would inevitably wane after his death, but not before he had introduced a significant time lag into the texts that made narrative shaping and, to some degree at least, fabrication into a necessity. This was for the simple reason that Eckermann could not possibly have accurately remembered Goethe's exact words years after they were uttered, and the only logic for continuing with such a venture at such a temporal remove can have been to convey some underlying essence about the author that is best presented through significant deliberate arrangement: not what Goethe actually said in the manner of a blow-by-blow transcript, but a broader image of how Goethe the world author tended to act and speak, tied back to the facts of what he was working on and thinking about when. Eckermann presents his project very much in this spirit, as evidenced in his 1844 letter to a friend quoted at the beginning of this section. Arguably, however, Goethe had masterminded it by leaving his acolyte with no other choice.

Yet, if Goethe indirectly continued to shape the literary nature of Eckermann's records after his death, other factors also played an increasingly significant part. The success of each volume was highly dependent on broader political events at the time. The first two volumes, published by Brockhaus in 1836, struggled to find a readership in the heady build-up to the failed revolution of 1848, where Goethe's conservative perspective was rapidly falling out of fashion. This, combined with an argument between Eckermann and Brockhaus that stemmed from Eckermann's wounded pride and financial worries about the poor sales figures of the first two print runs, in turn affected the publishing apparatus available to Eckermann, as the prominent publisher refused to take on the third book, his 1848 sequel, which subsequently threatened to sink without trace with a lesser Magdeburg publisher. The three German volumes finally found a domestic readership only when they were ultimately united by Brockhaus and republished in 1868 as a result of their

---

[16] Captured in the section 'Entstehung und Charakter der Gespräche mit Goethe' of the critical commentary provided in the German-language edition, Eckermann, *Gespräche mit Goethe*, pp. 915–66.

proven commercial success abroad.[17] In this sense, the global book market here quite literally sustained the passage of Goethe's 'World-literature' into lasting literary history.

In all of this, it was clearly in Eckermann's interests to produce an image of Goethe that would chime with the expectations of his readership. Following the 'authentic' format of recording their conversations in chronological order and creating for Eckermann himself what David Damrosch describes as a timid 'maidenly' reserve, Eckermann's texts create a relentlessly linear Goethe, striving ever forwards in all he does and developing his ideas in perfectly pitched monologues and pronouncements that cannot but awe his most immediate interlocutors.[18] Alongside the strictures of his chosen literary form, material circumstances sway the picture further. The fact that Eckermann was remunerated for his work with Goethe primarily in dinners and lodgings explains why they always appear to be having dinner, for example. The very prosaic fact of needing to eat drives the creation and dissemination of Goethe's world author persona in multiple ways. Bearing all in this in mind, the Goethe who emerges from the volumes must be first and foremost understood as Eckermann's literary creation, designed to serve Eckermann's own career and accordingly held up as a model that can be grasped and sold on the global book market.

More broadly, however artificially shaped by Eckermann's financial circumstances and the contrasting demands of the publishing industry and political movements this record of Goethe's life may be, the whole horizon of his life was in any case already pre-determined by Weimar as a geopolitical place under Anna Amalia and Carl August, complete with the representational buildings and sense of provincial importance this entailed. Although Goethe was a great draw to their court, he was nevertheless also a subject of that court and, in this sense, reliant on the social networks the court sustained. These pre-existing structures to no small extent determined what conceptual connections Goethe could make and into which worlds he could have insight. The extent to which there is a whole way of life that pre-exists Goethe and is linked to Weimar as a physical place is neatly captured by Eckermann in the way the passage of time in this provincial setting determines their thoughts and conversations. The second half of the diary entry from 31 January 1827, in which Goethe expounds on Alexander Manzoni's work and the question of

---

[17] Recounted with some inaccuracies in David Damrosch, *What is World Literature?* (Princeton: Princeton Univeristy Press, 2003), pp. 32–34. A more precise and detailed German-language account is available in Eckermann, *Gespräche mit Goethe*, pp. 917–65.

[18] Damrosch, *What is World Literature?*, p. 29.

historical accuracy in literature, for example, is neatly framed by the tinkling of sleigh bells. Goethe and Eckermann rush to the window each time the bells are heard, at the beginning and end of Goethe's pronouncements, as they are on the lookout for the return of a carriage that headed to Belvedere Palace that morning. The detail underscores the slow passage of time and comparative scarcity of people in their surroundings, as well as providing a framing device for Goethe's excursus that is well suited to marking out the slippage between literary and historical worlds it entails – it is as if the bell works as a cue for refocusing attention at the beginning and end of his pronouncements. Thus we see Eckermann arranging narrative time, on the one hand, but with reference to a generally slower pace of life that has also pre-conditioned the very existence of his narrative, on the other, and made the details and relationships he focuses on pertinent in the first place.

This brief sojourn into the material, social and intellectual circumstances that underpin the genesis of Eckermann's *Conversations* gives us a different angle on the extent to which the biographical person of Goethe is able to enact agency within the most famous biographical account of him. This is important because the text has gone on to become the mainstay for those seeking to understand Goethe's literary ideals. Goethe may well have initiated Eckermann's project of scrupulous note-taking in order to have an image of himself produced that stressed his material comforts and the polite after-dinner society he kept alongside his capacious learning and practical aesthetic ideals. But when all of the above factors are taken together, it is also clear that his control over Eckermann's literary record of the way he navigates between multiple worlds is minimal. He is as much the product of Eckermann's need for social advancement, which unfolds in line with the largely predetermined socio-historical and geopolitical opportunities available to Eckermann, as he is the powerful self-styled prophet of world literature.

'Follow the Actors Themselves': Reading and Writing Networks in the Twenty-first Century

If the preceding analysis made use of one of the staple methodologies in literary studies – a mixture of philological close reading of textual sources (the style and structure of Eckermann's *Conversations*) and socio-historical contextualization of these sources – it was also guided by an adapted form of actor–network theory (ANT), a method of social analysis stemming from Science and Technology Studies within Sociology. The French sociologist Bruno Latour has particularly developed his ANT approach with a view to the question of agency and mapping out local and global networks, and for this reason some of his thinking is directly applicable to how we might set about trying to grasp the nature and significance of the different worlds and kinds of activity that can be discerned in the practice of literature. (For a further model of mapping networks see Sara Jones's account of Social Network Analysis in Chapter 8 of this volume.) Under the rallying call to 'follow the actors themselves', Latour sets out the basics in his 2005 *Reassembling the Social*:

> Even though the question seems really odd at first – not to say in bad taste – whenever anyone speaks of a 'system', a 'global feature', a 'structure', a 'society', an 'empire', a 'world economy', an 'organization', the first ANT reflex should be to ask: 'In which building? In which bureau? Through which corridor is it accessible? Which colleagues has it been read to? How has it been compiled?'[19]

These questions are directly applicable to the phenomenon of world literature. I began asking them in what I wrote above about Eckermann's account of his conversations with Goethe, linking what could be readily deduced from and known about the text with some of the forms of agency that Latour points to in his work: the food that was eaten, the buildings where encounters took place, the various vested financial and political interests in different parts of the world, even the geophysical surroundings and an epochal sensitivity to the passage of time all exerted an influence on the text's genesis and, with this, the genesis of the concept of world literature and its accompanying practice of world authorship. Reflecting on these non-human forms of agency allows us to extend our understanding of literary networks from purely interpersonal affairs – 'networking', in common parlance – to an interplay of human and non-human agents (or actors, in ANT terminology) that determine what literature is and how authors, readers, publishers and any number of social and cultural institutions relate to it.

By focusing on the construction of the devices in which Goethe's concept of 'World-literature' and the accompanying practice of world authorship have been captured – Eckermann's diary, Carlyle's biography – I was able to begin a line of enquiry that encourages us to consider the network significance of 'mediators' that are themselves affected by multiple actors. Latour defines mediators as things that carry a message, but in so doing 'leave a trace' on the networks they help create. Thus the devices themselves (the diary and the biography) are clear and substantial mediators, while the pictures of Craigenputtock, the food shared at Goethe's table and the tinkling of the

---

[19] Bruno Latour, *Reassembling the Social: An Introduction to Actor-Network-Theory* (Oxford: Oxford University Press, 2005), p. 183.

sleigh bells all too play a role in shaping what we might now call the 'world literature process' carried within Eckermann and Carlyle's work. By this latter term, I mean the fusing together of a concept of intellectual interaction and exchange ('World-literature') and the practice of agency as these play out in the world of literature (both in literary texts and in the – broadly defined – literature network).

Latour's invocation of non-human agency thus opens up the purview of literary study, encouraging us to think harder and deeper about why society comes to value a certain set of writings, who or what might get left out and where the agency of individuals begins and ends within this discernible world literature process (a process that can also apply to world cinema, as discussed by Sebastian Heiduschke in Chapter 7 of this volume). In the remainder of this chapter I am going to turn my attention to the early twenty-first century and two distinct examples of transnational networking that can help us extend our understanding of the ways authors and the texts they write are positioned in society by recasting or otherwise querying what and where the literary world is.

My first example is the Austro-German writer Daniel Kehlmann and the ongoing interaction he has had with the US writer Jonathan Franzen. Both Kehlmann and Franzen are literary celebrities in their national contexts, having sold millions of copies of their novels on both domestic and foreign markets, received multiple literary prizes and routinely appearing in the global media and at major literary events. Franzen is the older and more globally established of the two, and he first entered into prolonged contact with Kehlmann when he met him at a literary event in Vienna, just as he (Franzen) began working on *The Kraus Project* (2013).[20] This publication is the result of an unlikely transnational project that consisted of Franzen translating two of the early twentieth-century Viennese author Karl Kraus's satirical essays, and in so doing using the translations to formulate his own intellectual journey in attaining a degree of fluency in German culture. One might add that it is almost certainly a vanity project that Franzen could afford on the back of his previous success, for the text is never going to sell in large quantities. For help with both the nuts and bolts of translation and in navigating the German-language canon of world literature, the American author consulted a US academic and Karl Kraus specialist, Paul Reitter, and Kehlmann. The Austro-German author, renowned for being particularly well read, brought both his own cultural cachet to the project and functioned as something of a gatekeeper in providing informed access to the German-language literary canon.

---

[20] At least, this is how Franzen presents their initial acquaintance in *The Kraus Project* (London: Fourth Estate, 2013), p. 189.

I have written elsewhere about the detail of this text and the uneven power dynamics between the four authors, as well as how these dynamics alter when the text is translated back into German and Franzen becomes the guest on Kehlmann's turf.[21] What is useful for our purposes here is to reflect on Goethe's fear of fixity, of what happens within the world literature process if one example is taken as a model and this, rather than authorial exchange and the circulation of ideas, comes to dominate. This is in fact exactly what happens in Franzen's text. Even though he documents his email exchanges with Reitter and Kehlmann and makes space in his narrative for their voices, they remain nothing more than adjuncts to his personal project of appropriating Karl Kraus, together with the German philosophical and Austrian satirical traditions of which Kraus is a part. He does this, by his own confession, to build his own intellectual author persona, which thunders throughout the accompanying autobiographical text on the degeneracy of early twenty-first-century media (Kraus's essays take aim at the same issue a century earlier). The extent to which Franzen uses both Kraus and his aides Reitter and Kehlmann to lay claim to a whole tradition of literature is evident in the book's cover. This vampirically reproduces the front page of Kraus's satirical journal, *Die Fackel* [*The Torch*, 1899–1936], but with Franzen's name printed where Kraus's would have appeared and Reitter and Kehlmann relegated to a copyright acknowledgement in the small print of the front matter inside.

While all of this can be read from the text, it is even more obvious when we turn to other biographical traces of the authors' lives. Eckermann's reconstructed diary functioned as a mediator that left a significant trace on Goethe's world author persona. A twenty-first-century version of this mediator is an official YouTube clip, produced by the German House at New York University, showing the three authors speaking together as the self-named 'Kraus-Troika'.[22] It provides us with a similar kind of broader biographical record that is itself part of a series of actors exerting agency within the (unequally) shared practice of world authorship as it unfolds between several authors. Just as Eckermann crafted his diary for publication to achieve various aims, both pecuniary and poetic, the German House's clip has been shot with a number of needs in mind, from selling the English-language book to promoting German culture in New York. It is unlikely that Franzen was involved in

---

[21] Rebecca Braun, 'The World Author in Us All: Conceptualizing Fame and Agency in the Global Literary Market Place', in *Literary Celebrity*, ed. by R. Braun and A. Piper, special issue of *Celebrity Studies* 7.4 (2016), pp. 457–75.

[22] This clip can be viewed at <https://www.youtube.com/watch?v=AcZbHiUkATQ> [accessed 1 April 2020].

setting up the room or ordering the splicing of the clip, yet the physical setting and the social assumptions conveyed by the recording directly echo those underpinning Franzen's fixation on appropriating Kraus for his own purposes. The setting itself is grand, a smartly lit room with windows giving out over a night-sky of high-rise buildings in central New York; the audience is predominantly white, older and middle class; the official from the German House is male, the three speakers are male and all wear the casual jackets and open-necked shirts of twenty-first-century academia. A couple of 2D pictures of Kraus in his early twentieth-century garb are shown on screens to either side of the podium, but the main focus is clearly on the contemporary Anglophone Franzen in the middle, with Kehlmann and Reitter flanking him; at the end, Franzen signs a copy of his book with a flourish, his name scrawled ostentatiously over the title of *The Kraus Project*.

Everything about this is set on recreating a model: German-language culture is presented in clearly demarcated lines, represented by one living and one dead famous author, both of whom are positioned in such a way in the room as to lead to Franzen. English is spoken throughout. The clip's own production advertises its importance – a 'breaking news' style pulsating musical beat accompanies it, and the power of the cultural establishment is evident in both the buildings and the technology they have been able to use to capture and disseminate the event. All of this underscores the canonical positioning of Franzen's work within a fixed understanding of world literature's broader cultural value, even before Franzen opens his mouth. In this sense, his world author persona has already been created by the place, people and recording machinery set up to capture him.

My second example, by contrast, focuses on an author who has been directly involved in shaping and communicating a more dispersed notion of world authorship. Büchner-Prize-winning Felicitas Hoppe first came to wider public attention in Germany with her fictional autobiography *Hoppe* [Hoppe, 2012]. This text represents the culmination of a literary career that had been built up to that point on self-reflexive writing that deliberately blurs fiction with reality and has a particular affinity with the imaginary worlds and literary motifs of early nineteenth-century German Romanticism. Multiple worlds run through the structuring author's consciousness, with the effect that the biographical author, for all her protestation to the contrary, appears to have divine control over the text's meaning very much in the mould of the Romantic genius. Although it would be aesthetically interesting to compare the way she manipulates different literary worlds with some of the techniques developed by Goethe and his contemporaries in their writing, and then compare that with Franzen's self-serving emulation of Kraus's polemics on literature and the media, that is not the angle I am taking here. Rather, I am interested in how she has subsequently set about opening up her writing to different networks and media precisely by turning away from the fixed world author model in which Goethe's World-literature too most frequently ends (as witnessed by the cases of both Eckermann and Franzen), despite its original intentions in the opposite direction.

In 2015 Hoppe set off, with funding from the North American Goethe Institutes, to recreate a journey across America that was first undertaken by two satirical Russian authors, Ilja Ilf and Jewgeni Petrow, in the pay of *Prawda*, the Communist party newspaper, some 80 years earlier. Like Ilf and Petrow, she travelled in a team of four, this time including a Ukrainian-born installation artist, an East German photographer and a Viennese–American émigré working in the United States as a professor of German (Ilf and Petrow travelled with a naturalized Russian–American engineer and his wife). As part of the funding agreement, Hoppe appeared at Goethe Institutes on all the staging posts of her journey, where she read from her work and presented the current project. Although no YouTube clips were made, the readings were captured photographically as part of a blog and (now defunct) dedicated web space that was set up by the German Goethe Institute: http://blog.goethe.de/little-golden-america-revisited/.[23] This site made available a wealth of material about the trip that Hoppe shared as she travelled – alongside transcripts from interviews she gave at the Goethe Institutes and brief blog reports on each stage of the journey, accompanied by photographs of both Hoppe's team travelling today and of the historic journey undertaken by Ilf and Petrow.

While this site is primarily a historic record, put together at the time and not updated since, another site exists, http://www.3668ilfpetrow.com, which uses some of this material but as part of a self-confessedly 'ongoing' project (the English word is used in the top banner, demarcating the contemporary project materials from those of the 1935 archive).[24] The web domain is officially copyrighted to Hoppe herself, although she elsewhere refers to the website managers.[25] The main difference between it and the Goethe blog is the significantly greater space made available not just to show the work of the other people involved in both journeys (including Russian- and German-language excerpts from Ilf and Petrow's work, as well as pictures of the accompanying installation artist's resultant exhibition in 2017), but also to re-present the travel blog as guided far less by people and more by objects and concepts that are inspired by both everyday and literary culture. This is

---

[23] Accessed 20 July 2018.
[24] Accessed 1 April 2020.
[25] In the acknowledgements of *Prawda: Eine Amerikanische Reise*, she thanks 'the managers of 3668.Ilfpetrow.com'.

achieved by including many more photographs of things encountered along the way (drawing on the work of the accompanying photographer), as well as interspersing spontaneous poems and hyperlinks to local newspapers or points of information thrown up by the journey throughout the extended, at times bilingual, prose travelogue.

This second website scopes out a far larger network than the first by focusing much less on the sponsored author and her set of practices and experiences and much more on what the whole venture itself has to tell. Significantly, 'Empires Facing Each Other' is the title introducing its home page, as if the West and East themselves are being made to talk through the material signs of their cultural and political history that the troupe of travelling authors, artists and academics have been able to record from 1935 to the present. The most obviously literary work, the lightly fictionalized *Prawda: Eine Amerikanische Reise* [*Prawda: An American Journey*, 2018], which Hoppe subsequently published, sits within this network. In this text, in keeping with the relativizing gesture towards her own authorship that was set in motion by the collaborative nature of the whole project across time, space, genre and media, she repeatedly casts herself as little more than a travelling scribe, notably having an anonymous voice from the text address her directly on occasion as 'Frau Eckermann'.

This unexpected reference back to Eckermann seems a good place to conclude. If the real Eckermann made his name by creating the mediator that would carry both Goethe's early nineteenth-century notion of 'Worldliterature' and his practice of world authorship for posterity, Hoppe's fictional Frau Eckermann receives her name in recognition of her attempts to catalogue the early twenty-first-century world by traversing a large portion of it in real life and online. However, her mediation also records the world that has been seen previously by two Russian authors, and the intellectual gesture driving her literary text, the earlier websites, and the actual journey itself is to link up the multiple mediators she and her companions find to both disseminate and generate their transnational literary project along the way. This 'Frau Eckermann' has come a long way from Johann Peter Eckermann. J.P. Eckermann transmits an approach to world literature that, for all of Goethe's awareness of the danger of fixity, is underpinned by a canonical and normative gesture – one that is still very much alive and well and which drives the global book market, as the example of Kehlmann and Franzen illustrates. Hoppe's Frau Eckermann, by contrast, puts literature back in its place as just one way of engaging with the world and one mediator through which to shape it. Departing from the self-referentiality of her earlier work, the author is also relativized here as just one form of creative artist working alongside others, and one who is not necessarily better adapted to foregrounding the value of literary exchange in the contemporary moment than her predecessors. Rather, she is prepared to travel and forge new interactions with people, places and things in ways that cannot be foreseen or directly controlled. This is a refreshingly open-ended and humble position from which to think again about what it might mean to be a world author writing in German today.

Suggestions for Further Reading

Biendarra, Anke, *Germans Going Global: Contemporary Literature and Cultural Globalization* (Berlin: de Gruyter, 2012), 256 pp.

Braun, Rebecca and Andrew Piper (eds.), *World Authorship*, special theme issue of *Seminar: A Journal of Germanic Studies* 51.2 (2015), 133 pp.

Lamping, Dieter, *Die Idee der Weltlitertur: Ein Konzept Goethes und seine Karriere* (Stuttgart: Kröner, 2010), 151 pp.

Latour, Bruno, *Reassembling the Social: An Introduction to Actor-Network-Theory* (Oxford: Oxford University Press, 2005), 312 pp.

Mani, B. Venkat, *Recoding World Literature: Libraries, Print Culture, and Germany's Pact with Books* (New York: Fordham, 2017), 510 pp.

Piper, Andrew, *Dreaming in Books: The Making of the Bibliographic Imagination in the Romantic Age* (Chicago, IL: University of Chicago Press, 2009), 321 pp.

Tautz, Birgit, *Translating the World: Toward a New History of German Literature around 1800* (University Park: Pennsylvania State University Press, 2018), 189 pp.

6

Who is German?

Nineteenth-century Transnationalisms and the Construction of the Nation

Benedict Schofield

I'm standing in front of a temple, surrounded by a forest of oak trees, high above a river. The temple is made of marble, imposing in its classical monumentality. Inside, hundreds of busts are lined along the walls, also in marble, gazing impassively below. The scenography gives the impression of immutability and timelessness; the neoclassical building triggering associations of Ancient Greece or Rome. The reality, inevitably, is rather more prosaic: I'm in modern-day Germany, the river below is the Danube, and I'm surrounded by fellow tourists and school groups. This temple is called Walhalla, and the busts inside are celebrated Germans, gathered together, according to its website, to act 'as an inspiration and reference point for the nation'.[1]

First conceived by Ludwig I of Bavaria in 1807, and ultimately opening in 1842, Walhalla was designed to be a synecdoche for the German 'imperial nation'[2] – a nation that had recently been lost with the collapse of the 'Holy Roman Empire of the German Nation' in 1806 after the defeat of Austria at Austerlitz by Napoleon. This was a time of tumult in the German-speaking lands, with Napoleon also defeating Prussia at Jena-Auerstedt and creating the 'Confederation of the Rhine', essentially a German satellite state of France, that same year. For Ludwig, Walhalla was to be a point of continuity in this constantly shifting geopolitical landscape; a project to foster a sense of national community through its presentation of a pantheon of 'notable,

---

[1] See https://www.schloesser.bayern.de/englisch/palace/objects/walhalla.htm [accessed 11 September 2018].

[2] Stefan Berger, 'Building the Nation Among Visions of German Empire', in *Nationalizing Empires*, ed. by Stefan Berger and Alexei Miller (Budapest: Central European Press, 2015), p. 272.

distinguished Germans' who would be preserved in Walhalla for 'eternity'.[3] These aims, literally inscribed on a stone tablet next to the building, from today's perspective speak as much to the national anxieties that led to the creation of Walhalla as to its function as a home for German pride and identity: 'May Walhalla be beneficial for the strengthening and propagation of the German spirit! May all Germans, whatever lineage they have, always feel that they have a common fatherland; a fatherland which they can be proud of.'[4] Of course, Germany was not unique in its attempt to enshrine in a building certain individuals as 'representatives' of the nation. The Panthéon in Paris, for instance, was opened in 1791 as a 'secular temple' in order to 'celebrate national heroes with statues'.[5] It shares with Walhalla a neoclassical façade – indeed, both buildings are modelled on the Pantheon in Rome – which establishes a similar sense of temporal continuity between the national present and a more ancient past as Walhalla. In Britain, Westminster Abbey and Poet's Corner fulfil an equivalent function, also helping to 'consolidate a feeling of belonging that lends itself to a national consciousness'.[6] Though not a product of the nineteenth century, even the Abbey could not escape the fervent nation-building of that century, with Arthur Stanley, the dean of the Abbey from 1864 to 1881, specifically 'invoking the Bavarian "Walhalla"' as its model, resulting in 'the term "Valhalla"' becoming inextricably linked with the history of the Abbey[7] and leading to multiple plans by ambitious Victorians to expand Poet's Corner into a 'new English "national Valhalla"'[8] worthy of comparison – and, above all, competitive in scale – with Ludwig's monumental temple in Germany.

In their role as crucial points of reference for nation building and as sites of cultural memory, each of these monuments makes visible the nation: in the case of Germany, a nation that was still firmly in the process of being 'imagined' (to borrow Benedict Anderson's influential term),[9] given that German unification would not occur until 1871. This 'imagining' is to be

[3] König Ludwig den ersten von Bayern, *Walhalla's Genossen* (Munich: Literarische-artistische Anstalt, 1847), pp. vii, v. (Translations from German in this chapter are by the author.)

[4] Inscription at Walhalla, ascribed to Ludwig.

[5] Jessica Goodman, 'Between celebrity and glory: Textual after-image in late eighteenth century France', *Celebrity Studies* 7.4 (2017), pp. 545–60 (pp. 548–49).

[6] Thomas Prendergast, *Poetical Dust: Poet's Corner and the Making of Britain* (Philadelphia: University of Pennsylvania Press, 2015), p. xi.

[7] Prendergast, *Poetical Dust*, p. 116.

[8] Prendergast, *Poetical Dust*, p. 118.

[9] See Benedict Anderson, *Imagined Communities. Reflections on the Origins and Spread of Nationalism* (London: Verso, 1983).

found not only in the canonization of national heroes in Walhalla, though, but also in the creation of the German literary canon. For Jeffrey Sammons, this 'German canon was formed under the pressure of compelling nationalistic imperatives'[10] – something it shares with Walhalla – while Matt Erlin and Lynne Tatlock identify the canon as a crucial 'feature of imperial culture in [...] nineteenth-century Germany'.[11] Hinrich Seeba has argued in turn that the canon was fundamental for the creation of a German 'National Literature [...] into which a nation's collective sense of imagined history [could be] inscribed in images that invoke historical continuity and social unity'.[12] For Anderson, however, it is not simply the creation of a formal literary canon that powers the creation of an imagined national community, but also the wider spread of print culture (what he terms the dual impact of 'the novel *and* the newspaper')[13] and the rise of literacy.[14] Nineteenth-century Germany was a world leader in both respects: book production in Germany increased dramatically over the century, to the extent that by 1910 Germany published more books than anywhere else in the world (more than treble the production in England, for instance);[15] and a 'reading revolution' was accompanied by a 'democratisation of reading', with literacy increasing by '10% per decade [from 1830] until virtually everyone could read' by 1900.[16] Nineteenth-century Germany was thus what Tatlock has termed a 'reading nation',[17] its path to nationhood shaped by the creation of an extensive literary market formed of both the canon and many best-selling non-canonical works, which were all bound in the service of Germany's 'national enterprise'.[18]

[10] Jeffrey Sammons, 'The Nineteenth Century Novel', in *German Literature of the Nineteenth Century, 1832–1899*, ed. by Clayton Koelb and Eric Downing (Rochester, NY: Camden House, 2005), p. 183.

[11] Matt Erlin and Lynne Tatlock, '"Distant Reading" and the Historiography of Nineteenth-Century German Literature', in *Distant Readings. Topologies of German Culture in the Long Nineteenth Century*, ed. by Matt Erlin and Lynne Tatlock (Rochester, NY: Camden House, 2014), p. 6.

[12] Hinrich Seeba, 'Germany: A Literary Concept. The Myth of National Literature', *German Studies Review* 17.2 (1994), pp. 353–69 (p. 354).

[13] Anderson, *Imagined Communities*, p. 25 (my italics).

[14] Anderson, *Imagined Communities*, pp. 79–82.

[15] Lynne Tatlock, 'The Book Trade and "Reading Nation" in the Long Nineteenth Century", in *Publishing Culture and the "Reading Nation". German Book History in the Long Nineteenth Century*, ed. by Lynne Tatlock (Rochester, NY: Camden House, 2010), p. 4.

[16] Tatlock, 'The Book Trade', p. 6.

[17] Tatlock, 'The Book Trade', p. 6.

[18] Charlotte Woodford, 'German Fiction and the Marketplace in the Nineteenth

In many respects, this picture of a German national culture, enshrined in Walhalla, the literary canon and national bestsellers, appears to allow little space for the theme of this volume: the *trans*national. In the following, however, I will argue that even this most 'national' of centuries was profoundly shaped by the transnational and that, throughout Germany's era of nation building, German authors resourcefully turned to other cultures and nations to help construct Germany's self-image. Two case studies will be presented. The first is of the German lyric poet Heinrich Heine, canonized as one of 'the [German] classics'[19] and who today can be found in the halls of Walhalla. The second is Gustav Freytag, a name now largely forgotten and outside the canon, but an author who was the most widely read novelist of his day and who on his death was a popular candidate for inclusion in Walhalla. In this chapter I will outline how each of these figures sought to become the dominant cultural voice of Germany, and explore the different ends to which they put their status as the national voice – in Heine's case, critiquing the nation and nationalism; in Freytag's case, in acts of nation building. Ultimately, I will argue that a series of crucial transnational structures underpin the national literary projects of both authors – structures that include (i) the mobility of authors and texts; (ii) processes of translation and translingualism; (iii) models of hybridity and appropriation; and (iv) acts of intercultural rapprochement. In their work *Minor Transnationalism*, Françoise Lionnet and Shu-mei Shih argue that 'cultures as we know them are products of transmigrations and multiple encounters; [and] are already mixed, hybrid and relational'.[20] In this chapter, I will demonstrate that this is equally true for so-called 'national poets' such as Heine and Freytag: figures that consistently engaged with worlds beyond Germany to critique, but also to sustain, nineteenth-century narratives of nationhood.

'The emancipation of the entire world': The Case of Heinrich Heine

Heinrich Heine was not impressed with Walhalla, dismissing it, mockingly, as a 'marble skull-site' that had somehow managed to fill its halls with the 'fish' rather than the 'whales' of German culture and history.[21] In *Atta Troll.*

Century', in *The German Bestseller in the Late Nineteenth Century*, ed. by Charlotte Woodford and Benedict Schofield (Rochester, NY: Camden House, 2012), p. 7.

[19] Renate Stauf, *Heinrich Heine. Gedichte und Prosa* (Berlin, Erich Schmid, 2010), p. 9.

[20] Françoise Lionnet and Shu-mei Shih, 'Introduction: Thinking through the Minor, Transnationally', in *Minor Transnationalism*, ed. by Françoise Lionnet and Shu-mei Shih (Durham, NC: Duke University Press, 2005), p. 10.

[21] Heinrich Heine, 'Lobgesänge auf König Ludwig', in *Historisch-kritische Gesamtausgabe der Werke (Düsseldorfer Ausgabe)*, ed. by Manfred Windfuhr

Ein Sommernachtstraum [*Atta Troll. A Midsummer Night's Dream*, 1841] – a satire of Germany's tendency to appropriate culture and poetry to uphold reactionary nationalism – he goes even further, fully undermining Walhalla's claim to be the home of the German 'greats' by interring into its halls his protagonist, a bear named Atta Troll, with the following inscription under his bust:

> Atta Troll, biased bear, [...]
> Led astray by the *Zeitgeist* [...]
> Often also very stinky
> No talent – yet a character![22]

As B. Venkat Mani has argued, Heine had an 'uneasy relationship with the dominance of [...] nationalist discourse and the cooption of literature as a national artefact':[23] tendencies that come together powerfully in Heine's depiction and distrust of Walhalla. Given this, there is considerable irony to be found in the fact that Heine himself would ultimately be inducted into the halls of Walhalla in 2010, on the advice of the Bavarian Academy of Sciences.

Already in his lifetime, though, Heine was seen as the 'greatest lyrical and political voice of his generation'[24] and thus 'one of the leading figures in the canon'[25] – this fame spreading abroad, where Heine became 'internationally the best-known German-language author in the nineteenth century [...] after Goethe'.[26] Indeed, despite his distrust of the nationalization of literature and culture, Heine vigorously pursued the goal of becoming the leading cultural voice in Germany. 'A new song, a better song/ Friends! This I will compose for you',[27] he boldly stated at the start of *Deutschland. Ein Wintermärchen* [*Germany. A Winter's Tale*, 1844], dismissing the past and emphasizing his own role in the future of German culture. Nothing was sacred in Heine's

---

(Hamburg: Hoffmann und Campe, 1975), vol. 2, p. 143. Referred to henceforth as *DHA*, followed by volume and page number.

[22] Heinrich Heine, *Atta Troll. Ein Sommernachtstraum*, *DHA*, 4, p. 79.

[23] B. Venkat Mani, *Recoding World Literature. Libraries, Print Culture, and Germany's Pact with Books* (New York: Fordham University Press, 2017), p. 102.

[24] Willi Goetschel, 'Heine's Displaced Philology', *The Germanic Review* 93.1 (2018), pp. 30–38 (p. 30).

[25] Roger Cook, 'Introduction', in *A Companion to the Works of Heinrich Heine*, ed. by Roger Cook (Rochester, NY: Camden House, 2002), p. 2.

[26] Sandra Richter, *Eine Weltgeschichte der deutschsprachigen Literatur* (Munich: Bertelsmann, 2017), p. 228.

[27] Heinrich Heine, *Deutschland. Ein Wintermärchen*, *DHA*, 4, p. 92.

process of authorial self-fashioning, with even Goethe, that central figure of the German literary canon, facing Heine's iconoclastic critique. For Heine, Goethe's canonical dominance had become deadly for German culture. In an image reminiscent of Walhalla, he depicts Goethe's literary 'masterpieces' as marble statues, which 'grace our country, like attractive statues grace a garden – but they are statues. One can fall in love with them, but they are infertile.'[28] Far from propagating new art, Heine argues that Goethe's works are incapable of producing a fresh generation of poetic voices for Germany. Instead, they are literally petrified, 'unhappy mixtures of divinity and stone',[29] which, just like the busts in Walhalla, can be fetishized for nationalistic purposes. As Mani deftly summarizes, Heine's works consistently show a 'disregard for iconicity and cult worship, especially the kind that is constantly in the service of the nation.'[30]

It was not easy, however, for Heine to assume the mantle of the national voice, and he faced both religious and political persecution. As Cook has outlined, 'while Heine's poetry established him as a Romantic poet par excellence, he found it necessary to continually affirm that he was a *German* poet of the highest order',[31] the result of anti-Semitism that saw Heine's Jewishness as 'at odds with the ethnocentric nationalist view of the Romantic soul'.[32] Heine also faced political repression for his liberalism, and extensive censorship of his writings: factors that motivated his relocation from Germany to France in 1831, where he would remain until his death.

Once in Paris, Heine began a long-term project of intercultural communication between France and Germany, including extensive journalism and translation work, and produced two transnationally orientated cultural–historical studies: *Zur Geschichte der Religion und Philosophie in Deutschland* [*On the History of Religion and Philosophy in Germany*, 1834] and *Die romantische Schule* [*The Romantic School*, 1836]. Together, these books aimed not only to narrate German history but to shape the future of Europe by 'mediat[ing]' between French and German cultures and therefore [contributing] to peace among the peoples by opposing the war-mongering ruling class'.[33] Significantly, though, these works were not only transnational in theme but also translingual: Heine wrote *The History of Religion* in French,

---

[28] Heinrich Heine, *Die romantische Schule*, DHA, 8.1, p. 155.
[29] Heine, *Die romantische Schule*, p. 155.
[30] Mani, *Recoding World Literature*, p. 98.
[31] Cook, 'Introduction', p. 17 (my italics).
[32] Cook, 'Introduction', p. 17.
[33] Jeffrey Sammons, *Heinrich Heine. A Modern Biography* (Princeton: Princeton University Press, 1979), p. 188.

and much of *The Romantic School* first appeared in French too. Heine's life and works are thus an important iteration of the 'intercultural and multilingual language-biographies [which] result from the migration of the author'[34] and which Dirk Weissmann identifies as central to contemporary transnational writing in Chapter 3 of this volume. Significantly though, the case of Heine reminds us that such transnational and translingual biographies are not solely a feature of contemporary culture and that, even before the creation of the German nation state, forms of transnational interaction and exchange were firmly embedded within its cultural practice.

Heine's status as a 'German' national poet must thus be seen as shaped by processes of dislocation (his transnational mobility; his translingualism) and forms of interculturalism. Indeed, the culture and history of France fundamentally shaped his poetics and politics, even prior to his emigration to Paris. Above all, the French Revolution of 1789 was central to his worldview. 'Freedom is a new religion', he wrote in the *Englische Fragmente* [*English Fragments*, 1830], 'the religion of our time':

> The *French* are, however, the chosen people of this new religion; the first gospels and dogmas were noted in their language; Paris is the new Jerusalem, and the Rhine is the Jordan, which divides the promised Land of Freedom [France] from the Land of the Philistines [Germany].[35]

It is tempting to speculate that Heine's decision to write in French was motivated not only by practical concerns (for instance, his need to earn a living and gain a new audience through the newspapers and publishing opportunities of Paris) but also by an *ideological* sense that French was the language of freedom, and thus the language of the future. What is certain, however, is that Heine was invigorated by the French revolutionary spirit, with the 'dogma' of freedom he refers to above being the *Déclaration des droits de l'homme et du citoyen* [*Declaration of the Rights of Man and of the Citizen*, 1789]. Heine saw this French declaration as the starting point for a new intellectual tradition of freedom – this in direct opposition to the constructors of Walhalla, who were attempting to politically and culturally free themselves of the yoke of France. In this belief Heine was not alone, and he is often placed within a loose grouping known as *Junges Deutschland* [Young Germany],[36]

---

[34] See Weissmann's chapter in this volume, p. 57.
[35] Heinrich Heine, *Englische Fragmente*, DHA, 7.1, p. 269 (my italics).
[36] See Eda Sagarra, *Germany in the Nineteenth Century. History and Literature* (New York: Peter Lang, 2001), p. 7.

who all strove for 'political liberalism, free speech, and the emancipation of individuals'[37] in Germany, drawing on the political inspiration of France.

In *The History of Religion* Heine charts the progress of this spirit of freedom throughout history, predicting its ultimate victory in the form of a final revolution that will lead – crucially – not just to *national* but to *global* emancipation. This vision is clearly outlined in *Reise von München nach Genua* [*Journey from Munich to Genoa*, 1830]. Based on an actual trip, yet containing multiple moments of imaginative digression, Heine outlines a conversation he had with a 'Latvian Russian'[38] on the Italian battlefield of Marengo (symbolically, the site of a Napoleonic victory over Austria) in which they discuss the state of the Balkans, the potential dominance of Russia over the West and the fate of Turkey within Europe. Against this highly transnational backdrop, Heine asks: 'But what is this great task of our age? It is emancipation. Not only of the Irish, Greeks, Frankfurt Jews, West-Indian Blacks and similarly oppressed peoples, rather it is the emancipation of the entire world.'[39] Heine begins to envisage an alternative geo-political future in which national tensions, and political and social oppression, are superseded by the 'new song, the better song'[40] that he promised to compose for the nation in *Germany. A Winter's Tale*. Indeed, in that poem, this song precisely is revealed as one of a transnational community that has defeated war and inequality and has enabled the creation of a heaven on earth (for more on the contemporary legacy of this, see the discussion by Claire Baldwin in Chapter 15 of this volume):

> The lamentations are over/
> The funeral bells are silent [...]
> The old-maid Europe is engaged/
> To the beautiful genius of freedom [...]
>
> We wish to establish here, on earth/
> already the realm of heaven.[41]

For Heine, then – especially in the pre-1848 period – the emancipatory spirit of the French Revolution becomes a model: a model not just for Germany but also, in an imaginative act, for the exploration of a global emancipation of

---

[37] Mani, *Recoding World Literature*, p. 91.
[38] Heinrich Heine, *Reise von München nach Genua*, DHA, 7.1, p. 71.
[39] Heine, *Reise von München*, p. 69.
[40] Heine, *Deutschland. Ein Wintermärchen*, p. 92.
[41] Heine, *Deutschland. Ein Wintermärchen*, p. 92.

peoples and races in a moment of transnational solidarity – an image he then provocatively places at the heart of his national epic, *Germany. A Winter's Tale*.

Of course, Heine was aware that this was an act of imagination, and he was equally capable of foreseeing some of the potentially dangerous consequences of this radical emancipation of France, Germany, Europe and, ultimately, the world – not least the potential destruction of his own art. After the failure of the 1848 Revolutions to bring about his 'heaven on earth', Heine seemed – at least at first – far less convinced about the need for world-historical change.[42] Once again writing in French, in the 'Préface' to *Lutetzia* [*Lutetia*, 1855], he expresses his fear of the iconoclasm that might come from a future communist uprising, with the 'calloused hands' of the oppressed 'mercilessly shattering all the marble statues of beauty so dear to my heart'.[43] Yet he cannot deny the claims to freedom of the oppressed, and ultimately accepts that his poetic role might just be to act as both prophet and victim of the world revolution. Continuing in French, he writes:

> Blessed be the grocer who one day will make my poems into cones into which he will pour coffee and tobacco for those good old women who, in our current unjust world, have had to deprive themselves of such a pleasure: *fiat justitia, pereat mundus!*' [Let justice be done, though the world perish!][44]

Once again, French becomes the 'revolutionary' language through which Heine can express an imagined community: not, however, an imagined community of a nation in the sense of Anderson, but a transnational community beyond the nation state, powered by the emancipation of the people.

Heine's writing is thus rooted in multiple transnational mechanisms: (i) the physical movement of individuals (his exile in France); (ii) acts of intercultural understanding (through works such as *The History of Religion* and *The Romantic School*); and (iii) his translingualism (across French and German). These transnational features support Heine's sustained critique of nationalism, especially German nationalism, but also enable him to envisage

---

[42] For a comprehensive account of the changes in Heine's political thought, especially either side of 1848, see Nigel Reeves, *Heinrich Heine. Poetry and Politics* (Oxford: Oxford University Press, 1974).

[43] Heinrich Heine, 'Préface' à *Lutèce. Lettres sur la vie politique, artistique et sociale de la France, DHA*, 13.1, pp. 166–67. (Translations from French in this chapter are by the author.)

[44] Heine, 'Préface', p. 167.

a world beyond the nation – as Sandra Richter has argued, 'embodying the idea of "world literature"'[45] – from his position as a German national voice in exile.

'Every land of the world; every race of humanity': The Case of Gustav Freytag

On 30 April 1895 a report appeared in both the *London Times* and the *Manchester Guardian*: 'A telegram from Wiesbaden says that Herr Gustav Freytag, the celebrated author, is suffering from inflammation of the lungs. His condition yesterday showed a slight improvement.'[46] It might come as a surprise that the British press were anxiously following the health of a 79-year-old German author who today can be found neither in the canon nor in the halls of Walhalla. Yet, at the time, Freytag was both the most widely read novelist in Germany and one of the few German authors to 'enjoy enough popularity [...] to merit such attention' in the international press.[47] Freytag's novel *Soll und Haben* [*Debit and Credit*, 1855] was the most widely read German novel of its age, selling almost 1.25 million copies between 1855 and 1965 (excluding translations); and, by the time the copyright expired on Freytag's writings in 1925, over 2.5 million German-language copies of his works had been sold, including a further bestselling novel-cycle, *Die Ahnen* [*The Ancestors*, 1872–1880], and a multi-volume cultural history of Germany, *Bilder aus der deutschen Vergangenheit* [*Pictures of the German Past*, 1859–1867].[48] For the nineteenth-century German 'reading nation', then (to borrow Tatlock's phrase once more), Freytag was without doubt *the* voice of the nation, already 'canonised as a National Poet and Poet of the People' decades before his death.[49] Indeed, his passing in 1895 was mourned specifically as a national tragedy: 'German literature [...] has lost one of its most important representatives', said the *Tagespost* [*Daily Post*]; a loss, for the *Deutsche Rundschau* [*German Review*], that cut across 'the high and low, old and young, men and women, professional and unprofessional, also those

---

[45] Richter, *Eine Weltgeschichte*, p. 228.
[46] *Manchester Guardian*, 30 April 1895, p. 7.
[47] Larry Ping, *Gustav Freytag and the Prussian Gospel. Novels, Liberalism, and History* (Bern: Peter Lang, 2006), p. 16.
[48] See Florian Krobb, '*Soll und Haben* nach 150 Jahren', in *150 Jahre Soll und Haben. Studien zu Gustav Freytags kontroversem Roman*, ed. by Florian Krobb (Würzburg: Königshausen & Neumann, 2005), p. 9.
[49] Philipp Böttcher, *Gustav Freytag. Konstellationen des Realismus* (Berlin: de Gruyter, 2018), p. 10.

Germans beyond the world's oceans' who now came together in a global 'cry of pain' at his death.[50]

Freytag would no doubt have been pleased with these epitaphs. Like Heine, he had actively sought to fashion his reputation as the new poetic voice of his generation – though, unlike Heine, he embraced fully the national (and, at times, the nationalistic), engaging with anti-Semitic and anti-Slavic tropes, above all in *Debit and Credit*. Like Heine, he also rooted this self-fashioning by comparing and contrasting himself with the preceding 'greats' of German culture, including, once again, Goethe. However, unlike Heine, Freytag did not critique Goethe, but saw him as a source of inspiration, 'continually us[ing] the expressions of earlier writers, especially Goethe, as if they were his own', as Eda Sagarra has argued.[51]

France, too, played an important role in Freytag's artistic and national development, but here again his approach is the opposite of Heine's. Far from embracing France, Freytag actively rejected any French influence on German culture, leading an anti-French campaign in the pages of *Die Grenzboten* [*The Border Messenger*], a political and literary periodical he edited between 1848 and 1870 alongside Julian Schmidt, in which he rejected 'all the unhealthy influences that have entered the souls of the Germans through the Young German dependence on French education' (here indeed clearly targeting Heine, though without naming him directly).[52] In their articles, Freytag and Schmidt particularly criticized the inclination of French fiction to focus on social problems; we are told of Victor Hugo, for instance, that he had falsely made 'dissonance (capriciousness, the ugly, the nakedly peculiar), the aims of art'.[53] Against this, *The Border Messenger* argues for a specifically *German* vision of art, focused on 'the dissemination and embedding of moral and ethical ideas into the detail of real life'.[54] Instead of France, Freytag turns to English-language literature as his source of inspiration, especially to Henry Fielding, Oliver Goldsmith, Walter Scott and Charles Dickens. Of these, Dickens is particularly singled out as an appropriate model for German cultural renewal. Here, Freytag mirrors many of his contemporaries. Peter

[50] See Böttcher, *Konstellationen des Realismus*, p. 11.

[51] Eda Sagarra, *Tradition and Revolution. German Literature and Society 1830–1890* (New York: Basic Books, 1971), p. 213.

[52] Gustav Freytag, *Erinnerungen aus meinem Leben*, in *Gesammelte Werke* (Lepzig: Hirzel, 1896), vol. 1, p. 155. Referred to henceforth as *FGW*, followed by volume and page number.

[53] Gustav Freytag and Julian Schmidt, 'Studien zur Geschichte der französischen Romantik', *Die Grenzboten* 8 (1849), 4.50, pp. 401–25 (pp. 409–10).

[54] Gustav Freytag and Julian Schmidt, 'Charakterbilder aus der deutschen Restaurationsliteratur', *Die Grenzboten* 11 (1852), 3.31, pp. 161–71 (p. 167).

Uwe Hohendahl has noted the frequency of this turn to English-language fiction among cultural commentators of the era, who viewed 'writers such as Dickens and Fenimore Cooper as possible models for German literature in its efforts to regain the vitality it had lost'.[55]

Thinking of German culture through transnational relations was thus well established within nineteenth-century literary discourse, and Freytag's obituary for Dickens on his death in 1870 reveals the extent of the latter's impact on both Freytag and Germany. Reflecting on Dickens's literary canonization through his burial in Poet's Corner, Freytag writes: 'In Westminster Abbey, the remains of a poet have been interred, who had a rich and deep impact on his contemporaries [...]. We Germans were hardly any less familiar with him than his compatriots; he was also our good friend, often a treasured educator.'[56] Importantly, Freytag goes on to claim that Dickens had actually 'given more to Germany than to England', since Germany had been mired, before the arrival of Dickens, in a slavish 'dependence on French ways'.[57] Here, Dickens is presented as more than just an *external* 'blessing' for German culture:[58] he is also *transformed* through his transnational circulation into a form of 'honorary German'.

The first hint of this transformation comes when Freytag characterizes Dickens's *The Pickwick Papers* (1836–1837) as a 'melody' that welcomed the German 'wanderer' back to their 'parental home' (in German, *Vaterhaus* – literally 'father-house', with its echo of *Vaterland*/fatherland) after an arduous journey (in other words, the false journey through French literature).[59] In this image Dickens is essentially singing the German song of *Heimat*, or 'homeland' – indeed, Freytag goes on to state this explicitly: 'the language of the poet [Dickens] is transferred into ours; his thoughts become our property.'[60] Dickens is thus not only an 'honorary German' but is actively 'Germanized' through a form of linguistic *and* cultural translation. Transnational exchange does not gesture beyond the nation here (as it did in Heine), but is precisely put in the service of strengthening the nation. Indeed, Freytag's contemporaries saw him as both drawing on Dickens but also transcending his source material. Theodor Fontane, for instance, noted in his review of *Debit and Credit* that

---

[55] Peter Uwe Hohendahl, *Building a National Literature. The Case of Germany, 1830–1870* (Ithaca, NY: Cornell University Press, 1989), p. 276.

[56] Gustav Freytag, 'Ein Dank für Charles Dickens', *Die Grenzboten* 29 (1870), 2.26, pp. 481–84 (p. 481).

[57] Freytag, 'Ein Dank', p. 481.

[58] Freytag, 'Ein Dank', p. 483.

[59] Freytag, 'Ein Dank', p. 482.

[60] Freytag, 'Ein Dank', p. 483.

while Freytag's characterization was Dickensian (citing both *The Pickwick Papers* and *Oliver Twist* (1837–1839) as intertexts), Freytag had successfully transformed 'the formlessness of the English novel' into something more structured: 'a Germanisation – in the most complete and noble sense – of the more recent English novel'.[61] The result of this transnational exchange is thus not a direct *transfer* of Dickens into Germany (what Susanne Stark has called 'Dickens in a German Guise'),[62] but, as noted, a transformation: a *hybrid* work that ultimately both appropriates and nationalizes its non-German sources into a German national bestseller.

The plot of this hybrid bestseller is structured along the lines of a *Bildungsroman* [novel of education] and charts the story of its hero Anton Wohlfart (whose surname, in a highly Dickensian manner, foreshadows his fate, literally meaning 'good journey') as he learns the secrets of German business. At the start of his apprenticeship Anton is shown into the storeroom of the firm he has joined, where he is astounded to see the world represented in miniature: 'Almost every land of the world, every race of humanity, had worked and collected, in order to pile up the useful and the valuable in front of the eyes of our hero.'[63] Inspired by the goods, Anton imaginatively charts the global network of trade and labour that have brought them to Germany:

> The floating palace of the East India Company, the flying American brig, the quaint ark of the Dutchman, had circumnavigated the world; stout-ribbed whalers had rubbed their noses on the icebergs of the South and North Poles; black steamers, colourful Chinese junks, light Malayan canoes with bamboo as their masts – these had all spread their wings and battled with winds and waves to furnish this room. This matting had been woven by a Hindu woman, that chest had been industriously painted with red and black hieroglyphics by a Chinaman; there, that cane had been fixed around those bales by a negro from the Congo in service of a Virginia planter; this trunk of dyewood had been washed up on the beach by the waves of the gulf of Mexico; that square block of zebra or jacaranda wood had stood in the

---

[61] Theodor Fontane, 'Gustav Freytag. *Soll und Haben*', in *Sämtliche Werke*, ed. by Kurt Schreinert, vol. 21.1 (Munich: Nymphenburger Verlagshandlung, 1963), p. 215.

[62] Susanne Stark, 'Dickens in German Guise? Anglo-German Cross-Currents in the Nineteenth-Century Reception of Gustav Freytag's *Soll und Haben*', in *The Novel in Anglo-German Context*, ed. by Susanne Stark (Amsterdam: Rodopi, 2000), p. 165.

[63] Gustav Freytag, *Soll und Haben*, FGW, 4, p. 68.

swampy primeval forests of Brazil, and monkeys and coloured parrots had skipped through its leaves.[64]

Germany here is at the very heart of a globe transnationalized by trade, an experience that leaves Anton with 'a joy in the foreign world [which] never left him from that day forward'.[65] But, of course, for all Anton's joy, the transnational network presented here is powered by the oppression of colonialism and processes of exoticization and othering. Anton diligently seeks 'through reading [...] to get a clearer picture of the landscapes from which [the goods] came, and of the people that had collected them',[66] but this is ultimately part of his wider penchant for exotic and colonial adventure stories, such as James Fenimore Cooper's *The Last of the Mohicans* (1826), which we also find him reading. Furthermore, within the ideological logic of *Debit and Credit*, Germany remains the dominant player in this hierarchized global network, and Anton soon learns that his role is not to feel joy but to raise a profit and thus exploit the network, as the money he earns is the very lifeblood of Germany's body politic: 'The nation was like [...] a body; money, this blood of business life, rolling from one part of the body to the other.'[67]

Indeed, in the second half of the novel, Freytag turns to an even more explicitly colonial mode of storytelling, clearly inspired by Cooper. As noted above, Cooper was seen in nineteenth-century criticism as a figure that might help reinvigorate German culture. This view was not only prevalent among more 'popular' authors such as Freytag or Karl May but was also shared by Goethe, who himself engaged extensively with Cooper as a 'writer whom he considered to be participating in the ongoing project of world literature'.[68] Ben Morgan has argued that Goethe saw Cooper as a means of 'refining and extending [...] his own prose',[69] and thus as part of the intercultural or mediatory project of world literature (a concept explored further by Rebecca Braun in Chapter 5 of this volume). In *Debit and Credit*, however, we encounter something quite different: another moment of hybridity, in which Freytag takes the 'wild west' of Cooper's America and projects it on to 'the

[64] Freytag, *Soll und Haben*, 4, pp. 68–69.
[65] Freytag, *Soll und Haben*, 4, p. 70.
[66] Freytag, *Soll und Haben*, 4, p. 70.
[67] Freytag, *Soll und Haben*, 4, p. 371.
[68] Ben Morgan, 'Embodying and Distributing World Literature. Goethe's *Novelle* in the Context of the 1820s', in *German in the World. The Transnational and Global Contexts of German Studies*, ed. by James Hodkinson and Benedict Schofield (Rochester, NY: Camden House, 2020), p. 37.
[69] Morgan, 'World Literature', p. 42.

wild east'[70] of Poland, as Kristin Kopp has convincingly argued. In doing so, Freytag constructs a narrative in which the German hero 'civilizes' the 'unruly' Polish in an act of colonial expansion. In strongly xenophobic language, we are told: 'There is no race that more lacks the ability to move forwards than the Slavic [...]. It's curious how incapable they are at creating out of themselves the status of civilization.'[71] As he strikes out into Poland, Anton is described as a 'colonist[-] on new ground',[72] and the only civilization to be found in Poland is that sustained by Germans. Coming across a well-maintained farm, Anton is able instantly to identify it as a form of colonial outpost: 'Hooray! Here is a housewife, here is our fatherland, here are Germans!'[73] In these scenes, we see an aggressively nationalistic iteration of the 'othering' of different cultures also outlined by James Hodkinson in Chapter 13 of this volume, with Germany 'presented as active, rational, progressive and civilized'[74] against the negative foil of an 'uncivilized' Poland.

Throughout *Debit and Credit*, then, Freytag engages in mechanisms of transnational exchange: (i) a network of cultural relations (rejecting France and embracing Britain); (ii) acts of cultural hybridity (his Germanization of Dickens and Cooper); and (iii) his literary representation of worlds beyond Germany (especially through his depiction of global trade). Unlike Heine, though, these transnational mechanisms are not used to envisage a world beyond the nation state, or to critique nationalism. Instead, we see 'the fortification of national literature through world literature',[75] as Mani has elegantly termed it: the emergence of a German nation empowered and emboldened through its engagement with the transnational.[76]

---

[70] Kristin Kopp, '"Ich stehe jetzt hier als einer von den Eroberen": *Soll und Haben* als Kolonialroman', in *150 Jahre Soll und Haben. Studien zu Gustav Freytags kontroversem Roman*, ed. by Florian Krobb (Würzburg: Könighausen & Neumann, 2005), p. 228.
[71] Freytag, *Soll und Haben*, 4, pp. 482–83.
[72] Freytag, *Soll und Haben*, 5, p. 298.
[73] Freytag, *Soll und Haben*, 5, p. 25.
[74] See Hodkinson's chapter in this volume, p. 197.
[75] Mani, *Recoding World Literature*, p. 103.
[76] For more on Freytag's engagement with national issues in and beyond *Debit and Credit*, and the more differentiated picture of nationhood across his works, see Benedict Schofield, *Private Lives and Collective Destinies. Class, Nation and the Folk in the Works of Gustav Freytag, 1816–1895* (London: MHRA, 2012).

Conclusion: Transnationalism and the National Within

The 1873 Baedeker guide to *Southern Germany and Austria* tells its readers that a trip to Walhalla makes for 'a most attractive excursion'.[77] Written just two years after Germany's unification, the Baedeker is impressed by Walhalla's monumentality, but rather less certain of its lasting national significance: 'The general effect of the interior is grand and impressive, although the association of classical Greek architecture with an ancient Barbarian paradise and modern German celebrities may appear somewhat incongruous.'[78] The Baedeker points to a number of tensions at the heart of Walhalla: that it is not the timeless monument it pretends to be; that it conflates historical figures with a more modern cult of celebrity; and that it is geographically hybrid, peculiarly drawing on *Norse* mythology and *Greek* architecture in its attempt to enshrine a *German* national identity – what might appear an ironically transnational foundation on which to build a national myth. However, as this chapter has argued, in nineteenth-century Germany transnational relationality and hybridity could just as easily be co-opted in service of the nation as they could be used to criticize and displace the nation. Walhalla could be both the source of Ludwig's pride and the source of Heine's scorn – in this sense, the perfect synecdoche for Germany's troubled path to nationhood.

In its case studies of Heine and Freytag, this chapter has also outlined two different models of transnationalism in the period before German unification in 1871. Both authors have been shown to engage with transnational structures: placing themselves and their works in *networks of cultural relations*; seeking to distinguish themselves from national predecessors; and looking abroad, above all to France and England, for different *models of cultural inspiration*. Both also consistently and deliberately depicted wider worlds beyond the German-speaking countries in their texts. At this point, however, their paths diverge. Heine's transnational trajectory revolved around *acts of migration and translingualism*. Freytag, by comparison, is relatively static and monolingual, with movement restricted to that of trade as it flows into Germany. Indeed, in *Debit and Credit*, Germany's place in the world is not displaced, but rather legitimized by its dominant position in a transnational business network. While Heine's early (pre-1848) works, such as *The History of Religion* and *The Romantic School*, looked beyond German borders in an attempt at *intercultural rapprochement*, Freytag, on the

---

[77] Karl Baedeker, *Southern Germany and Austria, including the Eastern Alps: Handbook for Travellers* (Coblenz, Leipsic: K. Baedeker, 1873), p. 71.

[78] Baedeker, *Southern Germany*, p. 72.

contrary, developed a model of *cultural hybridity as cultural appropriation*, especially in *Debit and Credit*, through his Germanization of Dickens and his symbolic projection of patterns of oppression from Cooper's America onto Poland. It was precisely such patterns of oppression that Heine had sought to overthrow in his imaginative conceptualization of a world revolution to bring freedom to all, whatever the cost. Relationality to other nations can thus build as many walls as it brings down, and the hybridity of cultures can exclude as much as it can include.

In Heine, then, the transnational can help displace the nation, critique nationalism and point to forms of wider global community, while in Freytag it can be put in service of the nation, underpin nationalism and support structures of German expansionism and dominion. Freytag's 'national service' did not, however, secure him longevity in German cultural history: now forgotten, it is instead Heine who is remembered and, indeed, canonized. Perhaps this process, too, is linked to the transnational. Freytag's pragmatic programme of transnational transactions and appropriations ultimately granted his works only a time-limited fame that was rapidly lost as the nineteenth century passed and as historical circumstances changed, above all with the totalitarianism and terror of twentieth-century nationalism. Heine's intercultural imaginary of an intellectual space beyond the nation state, on the other hand – his sense of a world beyond Germany – perhaps helped elevate his works above the specific political concerns of his own era, thus granting them a longer life and legacy. Applying the notion of the transnational to the 'national' nineteenth century thus allows us to better understand the ways in which the 'national voice' is always formed within transnational contexts – contexts that can even dictate the longevity of those voices – and reveals the complex patterns of transnational exchange that German culture deployed in order to imagine what the German nation might become in the years before its unification in 1871.

Suggestions for Further Reading

Erlin, Matt, and Lynne Tatlock (eds.), *Distant Readings. Topologies of German Culture in the Long Nineteenth Century* (Rochester, NY: Camden House, 2014), 396 pp.

Hohendahl, Peter Uwe, *Building a National Literature. The Case of Germany, 1830–1870* (Ithaca, NY: Cornell University Press, 1989), 376 pp.

Mani, B. Venkat, *Recoding World Literature. Libraries, Print Culture, and Germany's Pact with Books* (New York: Fordham University Press, 2017), 510 pp.

Tatlock, Lynne (ed.), *Publishing Culture and the "Reading Nation". German Book History in the Long Nineteenth Century* (Rochester, NY: Camden House, 2010), 360 pp.

Woodford, Charlotte, and Benedict Schofield (eds.), *The German Bestseller in the Late Nineteenth Century* (Rochester, NY: Camden House, 2012), 298 pp.

7

Co-Producing World Cinema

Germany and Transnational Film Production

Sebastian Heiduschke

Just like other national cinemas, German cinema in its early years was transnational by default: films were shot without a soundtrack. Owing to the lack of spoken dialogue, studios sold their silent films easily internationally without the need to subtitle or dub. A German film venturing beyond the German language borders required only new title cards to be written for other markets. Transnationalism remained a necessity for studios when the 'talkies' arrived. Studios adapted to the new challenge and initially shot various language versions of films in order to remain competitive globally.[1] Over the decades, political and cultural changes would tax the transnational character of German cinema, but even during the darkest moments in German history film did not cease to exist in transnational settings. German film production has thus always been both a 'product of global economies'[2] and a 'part of aesthetic and political utopias about universal communication and international co-operation'.[3]

The four case studies presented in this chapter of 'co-productions' as examples of the transnational character of the German film industry will shed light on how various degrees and constellations of political, economic, technological and content convergence shaped the type, frequency and

---

[1] *Der blaue Engel* (*The Blue Angel*) by Josef von Sternberg (1930) is probably the best-known example of the same film shot in two language versions and the earliest example of transnational German sound film. Marlene Dietrich sounds great in both of them.

[2] Randall Halle, *German Film after Germany* (Urbana: University of Illinois Press, 2008), p. 4.

[3] Sabine Hake, *German National Cinema*, 2nd edn (London: Routledge, 2008), p. 1.

manner of collaboration (themes also considered, in the different context of the translation industry, by Charlotte Ryland in Chapter 4 of this volume). The first case study assesses the influence of Paramount and Metro-Goldwyn on UFA's release strategy and the editing of Fritz Lang's *Metropolis* (1927) for the US market via their distribution company, Parufamet, and reveals a global production and distribution process, demonstrating the transnational character of a media conglomerate spanning entire continents. The second case study reveals how, even during National Socialist rule, when German film production gave rise to, for example, the infamous propaganda pieces of Leni Riefenstahl and Veit Harlan, transnational co-productions can be easily located. Arnold Fanck's project *Die Tochter des Samurai* [*The Samurai's Daughter*, 1937] may have ended up a less collaborative German–Japanese co-production than originally envisioned, but the undertaking was considered crucial for the self-representation of two political allies at a time of beginning international isolation. In the third case study we also find evidence of a transnational German cinema in the cinematic output of the Federal Republic of Germany (West Germany) and the German Democratic Republic (East Germany). More often than not we discover curious and unexpected ties in the film production within and across the Iron Curtain. If German westerns were not already transnational by way of genre, additional layers of transnationalism are located in film sets, locations and extras that were shared by East and West German directors; even actors such as the Serbian Gojko Mitić appeared in both East and West German productions.[4] In a fourth and final case study we look briefly at the current co-production arrangements of Europe's second-largest film production facility, Studio Babelsberg, in order to understand the significance of transnational film production in the current global market. Aligning and cooperating with Hollywood studios after a thorough but painful restructuring became instrumental to the resurgence of a studio on the brink of falling into oblivion. It is somewhat fitting that the historic studio once more becomes a signifier of transnational German cinema, even though the films produced there are no longer Fritz Lang's works but those of Roman Polański, Quentin Tarantino and Bryan Singer.

---

[4] DEFA-Foundation, 'DEFA-Indianerfilm', *Google Arts & Culture* (2015) https://www.google.com/culturalinstitute/beta/exhibit/ZQLyVBhH2vfFIA [accessed 15 June 2018] for sets and co-production. Mitić had worked as a stuntman in some of the West German productions and was discovered and selected for the East German DEFA film.

Transnational Marketing

Little by little, Universum-Film (UFA) emerged as the largest German film studio by acquiring and merging with smaller companies.[5] Their biggest competitors were no longer located in Germany but in Hollywood, where rich and powerful studios began to import their films into the increasingly valuable German market.[6] This influx forced UFA and its studio head Erich Pommer to react with a new type of film that offered an alternative to Hollywood's entertainment cinema. These productions had in common 'neoromantic, mythical, or historical plots in exotic, artificial settings, illuminated by stark, evocative contrasts of light and shadow combined with sprawling, slow-moving, probing narratives focusing on the darker sides of the human psyche, often interspersed with elements of the supernatural'.[7] Films such as *Das Cabinet des Dr. Caligari* [*The Cabinet of Dr. Caligari*, 1920] and *Der letzte Mann* [*The Last Laugh*, 1924] allowed UFA to maintain their dominant position in the German market and to compete internationally as well.[8]

Being competitive in international markets called for large financial investments to allow for the production and distribution of these art films. They also yielded lower ticket sales than anticipated – audiences wanted lighter entertainment fare instead and did not turn up at the box office. Combined with the generous budgets UFA handed out to its directors, the lack of revenue created a large deficit and put the studio in a precarious financial position. It became obvious that UFA's most recent futuristic spectacle, the Fritz Lang film *Metropolis*, would not nearly break even in the German market when it grossed a mere 400,000 marks. Lang's original budget allotment for the film had been 1.5 million marks, and the film actually turned out to cost the hefty sum of nearly 6 million marks. UFA was left with no other choice than to look for foreign investors to avoid bankruptcy. In 1925 two Hollywood studios, Paramount and Metro-Goldwyn, stepped up and lent 4 million dollars to UFA in exchange for what became known as

---

[5] For more on UFA, see Klaus Kreimeier, *The UFA Story: A History of Germany's Greatest Film Company, 1918–1945* (Berkeley: University of California Press, 1999).

[6] See Kristin Thompson, *Exporting Entertainment: America in the World Film Market, 1907–1934* (London: BFI, 1985).

[7] Holger Bachmann, 'The Production and Contemporary Reception of *Metropolis*', in *Fritz Lang's Metropolis: Cinematic Visions of Technology and Fear*, ed. by Michael Minden and Holger Bachmann (Rochester, NY: Camden House, 2002), p. 7.

[8] Technically, *Caligari* (directed by Robert Wiene [Berlin: Decla-Bioscop AG (as Decla Film Gesellschaft)], 1920) was a film by the production company Decla, but Pommer was in charge of production there before Decla-Bioskop merged with UFA.

the 'Parufamet agreement'. Along with access to UFA movie theatres and the obligation to show a certain number of US films per year, a newly founded joint distribution company called Parufamet (made up of the three studio names: Paramount, UFA and Metro-Goldwyn) was placed in charge of the distribution of UFA films in Germany and the USA. It was 'nothing less than UFA's unconditional surrender to its American competitors'.[9]

The Parufamet agreement gave the two Hollywood studios unrestricted access to *Metropolis*. Paramount had already decided to alter the film for the US market, a customary practice at that time for films imported from Europe, but the lavish premiere screening in Berlin's renowned moviehouse UFA-Palast am Zoo on 10 January 1927 provided an excellent point of reference for the coming US release.[10] An audience of more than 2,100 people attended a spectacle that UFA had been planning carefully and marketing methodically since the production's start in 1925. *Metropolis* premiered in Berlin as a 'director's cut' with a running time of about 150 minutes, using a score by UFA's famous silent film composer Gottfried Huppertz. Yet the film flopped with audiences and press alike, despite the technical expertise in camerawork, creative set design and innovative special effects. At the final curtain booing and hissing covered up the faint applause.[11] Willy Haas, Herbert Jhering, Paul Ickes and Rudolf Arnheim, Germany's leading film critics of the time, wrote devastating reviews about screenwriter Thea von Harbou's banal script and trivial plot. The film ran in German cinemas for four months but fell dramatically short of expectations. Crucial changes were needed for the US market to salvage whatever could still be salvaged.

Marketing the film proved difficult from the beginning. In Germany, directors and their distinctive status in society were at the centre of film advertising strategies; Hollywood, on the other hand, was used to deploying its stars as vehicles. Concerned about a film without stars recognizable to American audiences and unable to follow the storyline of the premiere screening cut, Hollywood studio executives ordered two major changes. First, the film needed to be shortened to 105 minutes to fit the standard exhibition length.[12] Secondly, a new storyline following continuity editing

[9] Bachmann, 'Production', p. 33.

[10] Holger Bachmann, *Über die Heide ins Herz der Nation: Theodor Storms Novelle Zur Chronik von Grieshuus und ihre Verfilmung durch die Ufa 1925* (Essen: Die blaue Eule, 1996), p. 184.

[11] Hans Pander, 'Filmschau: Metropolis', *Der Bildwart* 4.5 (April/May 1927), pp. 326–29 (p. 326).

[12] See Thomas Elsaesser, *Metropolis* (London: BFI, 2000), p. 30.

customary to a Hollywood release had to be developed from the material. Paramount hired the American playwright Channing Pollock and two supporting writers, Julian Johnson and Edward Adams, to abridge the plot, rearrange scenes and write new intertitles. Pollock eliminated all alcohol and drug orgies in the nightclub Yoshiwara because of the Prohibition era; Americanized Joh and Freder's names to John and Eric; cut out every mention of Hel because the name was too close to the word 'Hell' (which triggered the removal and thus most of the rivalry between Joh and Rotwang); and realigned the storyline around Feder and Maria into a romantic love story. An article in the *New York Times*, written by Pollock's friend Randolph Bartlett, praised the new, Americanized version as superior to the Berlin cut in that the latter was a proof of either UFA's 'lack of interest in dramatic verity or an astonishing ineptitude'.[13] This new, Americanized *Metropolis* was a different film that now expressed the dominance of capital and new technology. It stood in stark contrast to the way the original cut's 'images of the profoundly unstable and problematic relation between the masses and technology clearly mark mass technological culture as dangerous', yet it was exactly what US audiences wanted.[14] *Variety* praised the new version for its continuity after lambasting the German cut only a few weeks before. More than 10,000 people enthusiastically celebrated the US premiere at New York's Rialto cinema on 5 March 1927.[15] In the weeks to follow, American and British movie houses running the new cut sold out and instilled new hope for the German market. Parufamet pulled the original version from German cinemas and released a hybrid version based on the American edit that added 12 minutes of sequences but also dispensed with key sequences, such as those referencing Hel and most of the Yoshiwara.[16] In the decades to follow, the American product and the extended German re-edit became the new standard while the original cut was forgotten and believed lost, until archival footage discovered in Argentina in 2008 allowed the reconstruction and the precise tracking of changes caused by the transnational operation of Parufamet.[17]

---

[13] Randolph Bartlett, 'German Film Revision Upheld as Needed Here', *New York Times*, 13 March 1927, section 7.3, quoted in Bachmann, 'Production', p. 34.

[14] Michael Minden, 'Fritz Lang's *Metropolis* and the United States', *German Life & Letters* 53.3 (2000), pp. 340–50 (p. 346).

[15] Stephen Jenkins, *Fritz Lang. The Image and the Look* (London: BFI, 1981), p. 22.

[16] Bachmann, 'Production', p. 43.

[17] Peter Bradshaw, 'Missing scenes from Fritz Lang's Metropolis turn up after 80 years', *The Guardian* (2008) https://www.theguardian.com/film/2008/jul/03/news.culture3 [accessed 15 June 2015].

Transnational Auteurship

German film production changed dramatically only a few years after the Parufamet agreement. In the 1933 German election, the National Socialist German Workers Party under their leader Adolf Hitler became the strongest party in parliament and gradually realigned all aspects of society into a conforming and centralized totalitarian community. Party doctrines confined film co-productions increasingly to projects that emphasized the dominance of the Aryan race and promoted political alliances. A little-known example of transnational German cinema coming into fruition under these parameters is Arnold Fanck's *Die Tochter des Samurai*.[18] Fanck, who is known for his mountain films starring a young Leni Riefenstahl, travelled to Japan in the 1930s to collaborate with director Itami Mansaku on a feature film.[19] Germany and Japan planned this as a transnational prestige film with the title *The Samurai's Daughter*. The project ended in disaster, however, when Fanck and Mansaku continuously fought about details in the screenplay and on the set. Fanck finished shooting and editing *Die Tochter des Samurai* on his own after Mansaku abandoned the project, while Mansaku took Fanck's material, hired the same actors to shoot additional scenes and combined the material into a new film, the Japanese feature *Atarashiki Tsuchi* [*The New Earth*, 1937]. Looking back to trace the fundamental challenges resulting in the failure of the co-production allows us to gain insight into the way German cinema under National Socialist governance redefined the idea of the transnational by using its German parameters as yardsticks for these productions.

---

[18] This is somewhat curious, as a good number of studies exist that look at this film. See Valerie Weinstein, 'Reflecting Chiral Modernities: The Function of Genre in Arnold Fanck's *Transnational Bergfilm, The Samurai's Daughter (1936–37)*', in *Beyond Alterity: German Counters with Modern East Asia*, ed. by Qinna Shen and Martin Rosenstock (New York: Berghahn, 2014); Christine Böhnkes, 'The Perfect German Woman: Gender and Imperialism in Arnold Fanck's *Die Tochter des Samurai* and Itami Mansaku's *The New Earth*', *Women in German Yearbook* 33 (2017), pp. 77–100; Janine Hansen, *Arnold Fanck's 'Die Tochter des Samurai': Nationalsozialistische Filmpropaganda und japanische Filmpolitik* (Wiesbaden: Harrassowitz 1997); Peter B. High, *The Imperial Screen: Japanese Film Culture in the Fifteen Years' War, 1931–1945* (Madison: University of Wisconsin Press, 2003); Michael Baskett, *The Attractive Empire: Transnational Film Culture in Imperial Japan* (Honolulu: University of Hawaii Press, 2008); and Janine Hansen, '*The New Earth (1936/37)*: A German-Japanese Misalliance in Film', in *Eigagaku No Susume*, ed. by Mark Howard Nornes and Aaron Gerow (Victoria, Canada: Trafford, 2001), pp. 184–98.

[19] See Eric Rentschler, 'Mountains and Modernity: Relocating the Bergfilm', *New German Critique* 51 (Autumn, 1990), pp. 137–61.

It is not surprising that Germany and Japan embarked on cinematic cooperation at a time when German cinema experienced increasing isolation in the global market. The exodus of world-famous Jewish–German directors, actresses and actors, and screenwriters left German cinema with large gaps difficult to fill. European countries restricted the import of German films partly because they hoped to isolate Germany and partly because the quality of German cinema suffered as a result of the Aryanizing of the German film industry.[20] Although the Japanese market was not the German film industry's centre of attention, a selection of Fanck's mountain films had made it to the screens and reached enthusiastic audiences.[21] Japan hoped at the same time to establish a European trade hub for its films, using Germany as the nexus for continental distribution.[22] Fanck's film thus came at the right time for both nations, even though it remains unclear whether the Japanese producer Nagasama Kawakita invited Fanck to join the film project or if the German director offered his services as transnational cinematic ambassador for the German Empire. We know that Japan provided financing, infrastructure and political support during Fanck's 18-month stay, while Fanck used his expertise in Western cinematic practice to ensure that *Die Tochter des Samurai* appealed to European audiences.[23]

Fanck quickly took the lead on the project and foregrounded the film's German elements predominantly in a way that suggested a superior urban Germany over an almost primitive and largely rural Japan. Transnational in this film means an international cast, European and Japanese costumes, a set design that juxtaposes German and Japanese cultures, and even the choice of the mountain film as genre of choice.[24] Yet the film conveys how little Fanck was interested in putting forth a transnational project, and rather how he utilized an exotic locale to proclaim German supremacy. He encourages German viewers to perceive of *Die Tochter des Samurai* as a Japanese film that acknowledges a partnership between the two nations – under German leadership. The blond female lead, German journalist Gerda Storm, functions as the structuring element throughout the film. Played by beauty queen Ruth Eweler, Gerda Storm easily navigates tricky Japanese cultural moments,

---

[20] Eric Rentschler, *The Ministry of Illusion* (Cambridge, MA: Harvard University Press, 1996).

[21] Janine Hansen, 'Celluloid Competition: German-Japanese Film Relations 1929–1945', in *Cinema and the Swastika: The International Expansion of Third Reich Cinema*, ed. by Roel Vande Winkel and David Welch (New York: Palgrave Macmillan, 2007), pp. 62–78.

[22] Hansen, 'Celluloid', pp. 62–78.

[23] Weinstein, 'Reflecting', p. 35.

[24] See Weinstein, 'Reflecting', who delves into most of these issues in much detail.

facing them with a smile and the always-appropriate costume. On the steamer to Japan she often dons the traditional kimono to signal tolerance towards the other culture. Or so it seems: we need to read the choice of wardrobe as cultural appropriation that consistently foregrounds Gerda's superiority over her Japanese antagonist, Mitsuko; Mitsuko is meant to be married to Gerda's male travel companion, Teruo, who is returning to Japan after a long time in Germany. Gerda's natural ability to transition between worlds, signified by her easy transition between kimono, pantsuit and dress, contrasts starkly with Mitsuko's clumsy attempt to wear a European dress, which makes her appear like a schoolgirl instead of a partner for Teruo. On top of the visual disparity, *Die Tochter des Samurai* reinforces the imbalance between the women – and consequently the two cultures – in Gerda's disparaging remarks about Mitsuko's dress when their paths cross accidentally on the way to dinner in their hotel in Tokyo. At this point, Gerda is unaware of Mitsuko's identity and poses the question, 'Why don't Japanese women realize they look nicer in a kimono?' – a comment Mitsuko is able to understand because of the German lessons she took to impress her future husband. Fanck's choice to place the unflattering dress on the Japanese woman side by side with Gerda's authority over the fashion of two countries, and this verbal amplification, implies a cultural hierarchy well beyond a slight bias towards German superiority.

Costuming was but one of the ways Arnold Fanck skews the narrative towards a dominant Germany. Japanese director Itami Mansaku was probably more upset by the way his German counterpart presented Japan as a backward nation with a consistently polarizing mise-en-scene. Fanck situated the majority of the plot in a Japan full of stereotypes to create a visceral and visual pleasure for the German viewer.[25] Before Gerda and Teruo's arrival in Japan Fanck introduces Mitsuko in an extended sequence presumably showing her everyday life: feeding fish, talking with birds and petting deer, followed by leisurely strolls through the Tori gate on the island Miyajima, a visit to the Itsukushima Shrine and, finally, her father's manicured Japanese garden with stone pagodas, after which he shows her domestic skills as she folds a freshly laundered kimono on the traditional tatami floor coverings. When the plot shifts to Tokyo Fanck presents a pulsating city that appears wild and untamed. A constantly moving canted camera first pans across neon signs, then fades to brightly illuminated high-rises, and eventually cross-cuts to buildings with blinking Japanese letters reflecting in the windows of a taxi that takes Gerda and Teruo to their hotel. Not coincidentally, the nervousness of a restless and disorderly Tokyo slows down to a pace manageable to a German audience as

[25] Rentschler, 'Mountains', p. 142.

the cab pulls up in front of the Hotel Europe. Once inside, we are no longer in Japan: the interior furniture, the uniforms of the personnel and even the tea service are all European, placed there to ensure a familiar setting for the first encounter between Gerda, Mitsuko and Teruo. This move allowed Fanck to shift the power dynamics and place agency in the hands of Gerda. The hotel is ostensibly her terrain and not Mitsuko's, even though it is located in Japan's capital city, Tokyo.

Examples such as these, of belittling costuming and mise-en-scene, abound in the film. Arnold Fanck's stereotyping of Japanese culture, his reductive staging of Japan as a mostly rural and backwards society and a filmic Nazi cinema aesthetic that idealized purity sowed discord. The lack of a truly transnational collaboration became painstakingly obvious to Japanese co-director Mansaku when the two Japanese protagonists Teruo and Mitsuko finally end up together as a couple because of their shared love for the German language. Yet, while *Die Tochter des Samurai* may not have been a transnational production success story, Japanese critics and audiences admired Fanck's cinematography and praised his ability to capture nature's beauty.[26] Joseph Goebbels' propaganda ministry capitalized on the positive news, advertised the German premiere heavily and set up a successful theatrical run in the Reich's movie houses.[27] In the end, German cinema dominated and had single-handedly produced a film with 'transnational thematic, aesthetic and ideological appeal'.[28]

Transnational Acting

At the end of the Second World War German cinema divided along political fault lines into West German and East German cinemas that gradually became more distinct. Until the early 1960s we can still detect similarities in the style of filmmaking and find co-productions between East and West German partners – co-operations that largely ended after the erection of the Berlin Wall and other border fortifications.[29] It is thus useful to understand the term co-production less literally during these years, and rather to locate intersections between the two cinemas instead. Perhaps the most interesting

---

[26] High, *The Imperial Screen*, p. 162.

[27] See Arnold Fanck, *Er führte Regie mit Gletschern, Stürmen und Lawinen. Ein Filmpionier erinnert sich* (Munich: Nymphenburger Verlag, 1982), pp. 361–63 and Hansen, *Arnold Fanck*, pp. 57–59.

[28] Weinstein, 'Reflecting', p. 35.

[29] John E. Davidson and Sabine Hake, *Framing the Fifties: Cinema in a Divided Germany* (New York: Berghan, 2007).

case of a transnational, albeit divided, German cinema during the Cold War emerges in the person of Gojko Mitić, a Serbian national who acted in roughly two dozen German westerns in both divided and united Germany.[30] His appearance in German westerns on both sides of the Iron Curtain forms a symbolic cultural co-production of German filmmakers who worked on the same unlikely genre in German cinema and created blockbusters that defined German film production during the 1960s.

West German cinema after 1949 developed a pluralistic system of film production. The three Western allies, France, the UK and the USA, approved the development of small, privately owned, regional studios in their respective occupation zones as a counter model to the former UFA monopoly. East Germany went in the opposite direction and established film monopolies for the production of feature films, documentaries and, later, television programmes. The East German studios were all state-owned companies and named after the first post-war German film studio DEFA.[31] The historic UFA studio premises in Babelsberg became the DEFA feature film studio. Its convenient location just outside Berlin allowed for a number of East–West German co-productions before the erection of the Berlin Wall. Until 1961, many West German actors and directors commuted to Babelsberg to staff East German movies. While there was little cooperation between actual studios, people continued to collaborate and co-produce. Even when the physical border no longer permitted these commuters to cross, a more self-contained flow replaced the fluidity of personnel, allowing us to locate a form of transnational acting during the dual period of German film history, personified in the person of Gojko Mitić.

From 1963 to 1965 Mitić worked on the sets of five West German Karl May film productions as a stuntman and an extra.[32] DEFA directors seeking

---

[30] I counted at least 28 films, the first being *Winnetou* in 1963, the most recent *Winnetou & Old Shatterhand* in 2016. For an account of German co-productions in the 1960s see Tim Bergfelder, *International Adventures: German Popular Cinema and European Co-Productions in the 1960s* (New York: Berghahn, 2006).

[31] For the history of DEFA see, for example, Seán Allan and John Sandford (eds.), *DEFA: East German Cinema 1946–1992* (New York: Berghahn, 1999); Sebastian Heiduschke, *East German Cinema: DEFA and Film History* (New York: Palgrave, 2013).

[32] At that time, DEFA hired a number of actors, directors and cinematographers from the Eastern Bloc to increase the export potential of their films and to signal solidarity with other socialist nations. Compare Pavel Skopal, 'Reisende in Sachen Genre – von Barrandov nach Babelsberg und zurück. Zur Bedeutung von tschechischen Regisseuren für die Genrefilmproduktion der DEFA in den 1960er und 1970er Jahren' in *DEFA international: Grenzüberschreitende Filmbeziehungen vor*

to take on the western genre and turn it into what came to be known as the 'red western' recycled those sets and conceptualized their ideological genre responses as an antithesis to the Wild West films of West Germany. This was also an attempt to win back East German audiences, who were able to watch the westerns made by the political enemy on West German television broadcasts that reached most East German households. For these productions, DEFA turned to its Eastern European socialist neighbours in the hope of creating a transnational socialist cinema. The complex agenda was, in the words of Mariana Ivanova, intended 'to entertain, to educate, to claim scientific or historical accuracy, and to promote the fantasy of identifying with a socialist community that transcends the limits of time and space'.[33] For their westerns, DEFA used not only the film sets at the Plitviče Lakes in Yugoslavia but also Eastern European studios as co-producers, directors in charge of some *Indianerfilme*, cinematographers from Bulgaria and Yugoslavia (and even non-European countries, such as Cuba) working on the sets of the red westerns, and, in addition, actors such as Gojko Mitić.

It may appear bizarre that DEFA chose the western, a 'typically American genre', to bring its citizens back to East German movie screens.[34] One of the reasons was perhaps audience desire for genre films, but the bigger impetus is surely grounded in 'Indianthusiasm', a long-lasting fascination of the German people with Native American culture.[35] Karl May's pulp novels about his imaginary adventures in the 'Wild West' of the nineteenth century cast a spell

und nach dem Mauerbau, ed. by Michael Wedel, Barton Byg, Skyler Arndt-Briggs and Evan Torner (Berlin: Springer, 2013), pp. 249–66.

[33] Mariana Ivanova, 'DEFA and Eastern European Cinemas: Co-Productions, Transnational Exchange, and Artistic Collaborations' (unpublished doctoral dissertation, The University of Texas at Austin, 2011), p. 78. Ivanova's dissertation lays out nicely the intricate connections between filmmaking and international relations between East Germany and other socialist Central and Eastern European nations. Other works to be considered for a better understanding of the relationship between DEFA and Eastern Europe include, for example, Larson Powell, '"Wind from the East": DEFA and Eastern European Cinema', in *DEFA at the Crossroads of East German and International Film Culture*, ed. by Marc Silberman and Henning Wrage (Berlin: de Gruyter, 2014), pp. 223–42; and Katie Trumpener, 'DEFA: Moving Germany into Eastern Europe', in *Moving Images of East Germany: Past and Future of DEFA Film*, ed. by Barton Byg and Betheny Moore (Washington DC: AICGS, 2002), pp. 85–104.

[34] Andre Bazin, *What is Cinema?* 2 vols, trans by Hugh Gray (Berkeley: University of California Press, 1967), II, pp. 140–57.

[35] Hartmut Lutz coined this term. See Hartmut Lutz, 'German Indianthusiasm: A Socially Constructed German National(ist) Myth', in *Germans and Indians: Fantasies, Encounters, Projections*, ed. by Colin Gordon Calloway, Gerd Gemünden and Susanne Zantop (Omaha: University of Nebraska, 2002), pp. 167–84.

over their readers.[36] In the early 1960s West German studios such as Rialto film turned the best-known novels into a sizable number of successful westerns, starting with Harald Reinl's *Der Schatz im Silbersee* [*The Treasure of Silver Lake*, 1962] and following with *Winnetou* (1963), *Old Shatterhand* (1964), *Winnetou II* (1964), *Unter Geiern* [*Amongst Vultures*, 1964] and *Winnetou III* (1965). Both East and West Germans re-enacted the lifestyle of Native American tribes on the weekends, living in teepees and donning 'ethnic drag'.[37] The ethnic appropriation and claiming of a cultural heritage sometimes went as far as Germans seeking to be 'adopted' by a Native American tribe, or to turn into safe keepers of 'lost' Indian traditions.[38] Although Karl May's novels were not sold officially, East Germans still found ways to obtain them. The GDR also had their own, Socialist version of storytelling about Native Americans in the form of 16 novels written between 1951 and 1982 by historian Liselotte Welskopf-Henrich, whose trilogy *Sons of Great Mother Bear* served as a foundation for the screenplay of the very first DEFA western with the same title, which opened in 1966 in East Germany's movie theatres.

DEFA's Indianerfilme are ostensibly distinct from the US genre models by way of their plot structure (the Native Americans are the good guys), landscape (Yugoslavia), language spoken (German) and actors (East Germans playing US soldiers and a Serbian filling in as Native American hero), making them 'almost an affront, not only to conventional "American" connotations, but also to the Western itself'.[39] Yet it is precisely the choice of Gojko Mitić as Indian chief that creates a compelling example of transnational German cinema. Read in conjunction with the West German counterpart Pierre Brice, a French actor with facial features reminiscent of Alain Delon, who played the role of the Apache chief Winnetou in the West German productions based on the Karl May novels, Mitić turns into the same object of desire as Brice did in the West. 'Indianthusiastic' Germans longed for the on-screen presence of an actor who personified their visual imagery of 'Indians' the way Yugoslavia turned into the prairies of North America. Mitić's and Brice's darker complexions, enhanced by 'red-face' make-up and coupled with a physiognomy different

---

[36] See, for example, Richard Cracroft, 'The American West of Karl May', *American Quarterly* 19.2 (1967), pp. 249–58.

[37] Birgit Turski, *Die Indianistikgruppen der DDR: Entwicklung – Probleme – Aussichten* (Pfullingen: Baum, 1994). For the concept of 'ethnic drag' see Katrin Sieg, *Ethnic Drag: Performing Race, Nation, Sexuality in West Germany* (Ann Arbor: University of Michigan Press, 2002), pp. 131–36.

[38] Sieg, *Ethnic Drag*, pp. 131–36.

[39] Vera Ditka, 'An East German *Indianerfilm*: The Bear in Sheep's Clothing', *Jump Cut* 50 (2008) https://www.ejumpcut.org/archive/jc50.2008/Dika-indianer/index.html [accessed 3 January 2018].

to that of other German actors, sufficed as markers of the ethnic 'other'.[40] Audiences did not care that the skin tones were enhanced by make-up and the saturation caused by modern film stock (Eastman Color for the films with Brice, ORWO color for the DEFA films with Mitić); to them, both actors personified the German longing for the Wild West. Mitić and Brice were also known for their heavily accented German, resulting in them being dubbed into accent-free High German during postproduction, lending them an additional layer of authenticity. The actors allowed Germans to encounter a 'real' Indian, regardless of the fact that both actors were European.[41]

After their film careers ended their legacies as German Indians continued on the summer outdoor theatre stages of Germany, where Karl May's novels were adapted into plays. Pierre Brice and later Gojko Mitić played Winnetou in Bad Segeberg's Karl May Festspiele, the best-known of those festivals, during its most successful period from 1988 to 2006.[42] Mitić's role as a transnational cinematic commuter continued on German television, and to this day he still appears as a Native American in film productions such as the Hungarian *Nyomkeresör* [*Pathfinder*, 1993] and the German western *Winnetou & Old Shatterhand* (2016).

Transnational Production

The opening of the Iron Curtain, the fall of the Berlin Wall and German unification in 1990 caused a major shift in the way we need to define transnational German cinema. A federal holding agency, Treuhand, sold East Germany's state-owned companies to private investors who promised to turn them into vital enterprises of Germany's unified market economy. Treuhand's transfer of the DEFA film studio in Babelsberg to the French consortium CGE in 1992 signalled that the historic studios occupied a crucial position and offered the opportunity to orientate the German film industry towards a transnational European cinema. CGE modernized the premises and created a *Medienstadt Babelsberg* (Media City Babelsberg) in the hope of attracting lucrative film projects from all over Europe.

---

[40] See Evan Torner, 'The Red and the Black: Race in the DEFA Indianerfilm *Osceola*', *New German Review* 25.1 (2011), pp. 61–81; and Hake, *German National Cinema*, n8, p. 138.

[41] On his skin tone, see also Evan Torner, 'The DEFA *Indianerfilm*: Narrating the Postcolonial through Gojko Mitić', in *Re-Imagining DEFA: East German Cinema in its National and Transnational Contexts*, ed. by Seán Allan and Sebastian Heiduschke (New York: Berghahn, 2016), pp. 227–47.

[42] Attendance figures jumped in Brice's inaugural year 1988, from 146,791 the year before to 251,554 visitors.

The idea to locate a European film studio on German soil coincided with a widespread and omnipresent optimism across the continent during the early 1990s. Many believed that they were witnessing the dawn of a new era without borders in which cinema would contribute to the unification of Europe. Oscar-winning German director Volker Schlöndorff was among the hopefuls and accepted the position as first CEO of the renamed Studio Babelsberg. He intended to start the project with a clean slate, but created negative headlines when he expressed the opinion that the name DEFA was 'terrible'. East German filmmakers took his remarks as scathing and belittling, and yet, seen in a transnational context of Studio Babelsberg at a historic, political and economic juncture, Schlöndorff was really suggesting that German cinema could no longer successfully function without appealing to Western European markets and positioning itself in this market as a partner for co-productions.[43]

Until 2004 Studio Babelsberg embodied this new type of film production, with co-productions such as Schlöndorff's *Der Unhold* [*The Ogre*, 1996], Chantal Akerman's *Un divan à New York* [*A Couch in New York*, 1996] and Roman Polański's *The Pianist* (2002). Studio Babelsberg's attempt to create a German cinema for a European audience largely failed, however, probably as a result of a misguided hope of capitalizing on the renewed spirit of the European idea that imagined the studio as a continental antagonist to Hollywood.[44] Schlöndorff vacated his post in 1997 and in July 2004 Vivendi Universal eventually sold Studio Babelsberg to a new company, Carl Woebcken and Christoph Fisser's Filmbetriebe Berlin Brandenburg, a move that concluded the short-lived experiment of a German-based European-style transnational cinema. Instead, Woebcken stated his vision for a renewed Studio Babelsberg using Paramount Studios as a standard.[45] They chose to return to the early days of Babelsberg and Parufament with their concept of transnational cooperation instead of competition with Hollywood, and they revived the 'Babelsberg myth' to create an appealing environment for Hollywood producers.[46] Woebcken and Fisser put the new rebranding efforts of the

---

[43] The debate that took place in the German press over the course of many weeks was translated as 'The Schlöndorff Controversy (2008)' in *DEFA after East Germany*, ed. by Brigitta Wagner (Rochester, NY: Camden House, 2014), pp. 320–32.

[44] See especially chapter 3, Halle, *German Film*, pp. 61–88.

[45] Ingrid Poss, 'Gespräch mit Carl Woebcken', in *Spur der Filme: Zeitzeugen über die DEFA*, ed. by Ingrid Poss and Peter Warnecke (Berlin: Links, 2006), pp. 527–38 (p. 538).

[46] The 'Babelsberg Myth' refers to the rich history of the studios and its influence on the history of cinema. Names such as Erich Pommer, Fritz Lang and Marlene Dietrich are tied to Babelsberg. See, for instance, 'Happy Birthday, Studio Babelsberg',

Studio Babelsberg logo into the hands of the well-known corporate branding designer Albert Morell, who visualized the myth as Fritz Lang's iconic film scene of the cyborg becoming Maria in *Metropolis*. The logo he developed features a silhouette of Maria encircled by four undulating electrical beams, 'abstract but immediately recognizable', and a visual metonymy that allowed the instant association of Studio Babelsberg with its famous past.[47]

Their strategy worked. Studio Babelsberg in the year 2018 epitomizes transnational cinema in the global film marketplace. The complete overhaul and restructuring ended the production of films under the old Studio Babelsberg trademark and preceded the current commercial success and the rise of the company into a competitive transnational player. In contrast to its predecessors UFA and DEFA and to its main domestic competitor, Bavaria Film in Munich, Studio Babelsberg redefined the idea of German film co-production. While Bavaria takes on more projects that either target German-speaking audiences or rely on the profound cultural knowledge necessary to decipher the films' nuances – as shown by their production of films such as *Fack Ju Göhte 3* [*Suck Me, Shakespeer 3*, 2017] or *Bullyparade: Der Film* [*Bullyparade: The Movie*, 2017] – Studio Babelsberg embarked on a clearly transnational path.[48] Instead of competing in saturated German and other European markets, the company is now a service provider and co-producer for other production companies and for television.[49] Its backlots and studios host Hollywood productions such as *The Bourne Supremacy* (2004), *Valkyrie* (2008), *Inglorious Basterds* (2009), *The Hunger Games* (2014; 2015) and *Bridge of Spies* (2015), and Epix renewed their contract for a third season of the spy series *Berlin Station* (2016–2018). Studio Babelsberg recently finished a large, multi-million-euro upgrade to create the outdoor metropolitan backlot 'Neue Berliner Straße' [New Berlin Street], which resembles numerous European cities (London, Paris, Berlin), making it ostensibly geared

---

The Berlinale (2012) https://www.berlinale.de/en/archiv/jahresarchive/2012/06b_berlinale_themen_2012/ babelsberg_2.html [accessed 13 June 2018]; 'Myth', *Based in Berlin* (n.d.) http://www.based-in-babelsberg.de/englisch/location/myth/myth.html [accessed 13 June 2018]; and Jana Hasse, '"Babelsberg ist filmisches Weltkulturerbe" Filmhistoriker Friedemann Beyer über den Mythos Babelsberg – und wie er die Zeiten überdauert hat', *Der Tagesspiegel Potsdamer* (2 Dec. 11) http://www.pnn.de/potsdam/622086/ [accessed 13 June 2018].

[47] Morell, Albert, 'About this project', *AM* (2018) https://albertmorell.com/portfolio_page/studio-babelsberg/ [accessed 13 May 2018].

[48] The Bavaria film *Das Boot* is an exception in that respect. It is a German film, but was produced with the intention of appealing to audiences worldwide.

[49] 'Production Services', *Studio Babelsberg* (2018) http://www.studiobabelsberg.com/en/services/production-services/ [accessed 15 June 2018].

towards international productions.[50] A large co-production agreement with the up-and-coming Chinese Wuxi studios suggests the vitality and transnational character of Babelsberg as the current focal point of the contemporary German film industry.[51]

Yet is it legitimate to include these foreign films shot on the premises of Studio Babelsberg, or do we need to take a step back and re-evaluate our parameters? Do these co-productions still qualify as being a part of a transnational German cinema, or is the studio merely a service provider with little to no stake in the production process? Put bluntly, what is 'German' about this aspect of German cinema? Questions like this arise time and again when scholars in German studies define German cinema. Notions of films as products or mirrors of German national sentiments and a conviction that, until recently, German cinema was a monolingual affair have dominated the academic discourse.[52] More than two decades ago, in 1996, Marc Silberman stated that '[f]rom production to distribution, from import to censorship politics, from marketing to reception, from film subsidies to film criticism, the cinema apparatus in Germany has articulated national interests and constructed national traditions'.[53]

Since then, the world – and with it German film production – has become even more globalized and transnational. Transnational in this context means at least co-productions with other European nations, employing a European

---

[50] The 'Metropolitan Backlot' opened in 2017: Klaus Peters, 'At a film studio in Germany, Berlin can be anything you'd like', *dpa International* (2017) http://www.dpa-international.com/topic/film-studio-germany-berlin-can-anything-d-like-170810-99-595831 [accessed 15 June 2018].

[51] Studio Babelsberg and Wuxi announced their deal in February 2017: Scott Roxborough, 'Germany's Studio Babelsberg, China's Wuxi Studios Sign Co-Production Deal', *The Hollywood Reporter* (2017) https://www.hollywoodreporter.com/news/germanys-studio-babelsberg-chinas-wuxi-studios-sign-production-deal-979395 [accessed 15 June 2018].

[52] Most German film histories introduce Fatih Akın's *Gegen die Wand* [Head On, 2004] as a turning point of sorts, and now acknowledge Turkish as an element of German cinema. Some examples include Hake's *German National Cinema*; Stephen Brockmann, *A Critical History of German Film* (Rochester, NY: Camden House, 2010); Tim Bergfelder, Erica Carter and Deniz Göktürk (eds.) *The German Cinema Book* (London: BFI, 2002); and Jennifer Kapczinsky and Michael Richardson (eds.) *A New History of German Cinema* (Rochester, NY: Camden House, 2012). The inclusion of languages other than German remains an afterthought in German cinema histories, in a manner similar to the way German film histories before unification featured films from the German Democratic Republic as an appendix.

[53] Marc Silberman, 'What is German in the German Cinema?' *Film History* 8.3 (1996), pp. 297–315 (p. 297).

cast and personnel, or sparking debates beyond German borders. Film financing and shooting, and the production and post-production processes, are no longer in the hands of just one studio. What causes confusion among German Studies scholars is what might be considered a perceived balancing act between the national and the transnational, when these transnational German films still 're-imagine the German nation and German national identity'.[54] The question of what constitutes the German in German cinema in 2018 might thus be answered best with a reference to a recent exhortation about the state of German film studies. In 2013, Sabine Hake lamented how scholarship was exhibiting a:

> noticeable absence from the most interesting debates in film studies today, including the incorporation of film into screen cultures and its impact on artistic practices and forms of cultural consumption. Even more disconcerting is the continued lack of sustained engagement with the hegemonic aesthetic, institutional, and economic practices associated with both classic and global Hollywood and the corresponding research on film industry, technology, and the star system that could provide some much needed corrective to the continued preference for text-centred analyses.[55]

Applying the transnational as a default frame of reference and overlay might not only provide this much-needed and overdue shift for German film studies but would also reveal how – as argued in the four case studies of this chapter – German cinema never existed in a hermeneutic vacuum and was never solely conceptualized as a mirror of a national sentiment.

Suggestions for Further Reading

Brockmann, Stephen, *A Critical History of German Film* (Rochester, NY: Camden House, 2010), 534 pp.
Elsaesser, Thomas, *Metropolis* (London: BFI, 2000), 87 pp.
Hake, Sabine and John Davidson, *Framing the Fifties: Cinema in a Divided Germany* (New York: Berghahn, 2007), 260 pp.
Heiduschke, Sebastian, *East German Cinema: DEFA and Film History* (New York: Palgrave, 2013), 191 pp.

---

[54] Paul Cooke, *Contemporary German Cinema* (Manchester: Manchester University Press, 2012) p. 129.
[55] Sabine Hake, 'Contemporary German Film Studies in Ten Points', *German Studies Review* 36.3 (2013), pp. 643–60 (p. 645).

Kapczinsky, Jennifer and Michael Richardson (eds.), *A New History of German Cinema* (Rochester, NY: Camden House, 2012), 694 pp.

Rentschler, Eric, *The Ministry of Illusion* (Cambridge, MA: Harvard University Press, 1996), 480 pp.

8

Towards a Collaborative Memory

Networks and Relationality in German Memory Cultures

Sara Jones

The study of memory, particularly in its social, cultural and political forms, has long been a central aspect of German Studies programmes in the United Kingdom and beyond. Memory studies has developed from a niche interest in multiple fields (history, literature and cultural studies, psychology and neuroscience, to name a few) to an international and interdisciplinary field of study in its own right.[1] In the process of this international and interdisciplinary networking, memory studies scholars have begun to call into question the 'methodological nationalism'[2] that has tended to underpin much research in the field: that is, methodological approaches that incorporate the (often unspoken) assumption that the borders of the nation state represent the borders of a memory culture, even while recognizing that that memory culture is itself contested. Indeed, empirical work on memory – whether it focuses on memorialization, culture, society or politics – highlights the difficulty of hermetically sealing one memory culture from another. People, ideas, ideologies, books, films and art travel from one place to another and they take their representations of the past with them (a theme also discussed by the author Ulrike Draesner in Chapter 2 of

---

[1] See Anamaria Dutceac Segesten and Jenny Wüstenberg, 'Memory Studies: The State of an Emergent Field', *Memory Studies* 10.4 (2017), pp. 474–89. For an overview of the state-of-the-art in the field see Lucy Bond, Stef Craps and Pieter Vermeulen (eds.), *Memory Unbound: Tracing the Dynamics of Memory Studies* (New York/Oxford: Berghahn, 2017).

[2] Chiara De Cesari and Ann Rigney, 'Introduction', in *Transnational Memory: Circulation, Articulation, Scales*, ed. by Chiara De Cesari and Ann Rigney (Berlin: de Gruyter, 2014), pp. 1–26 (p. 2).

this volume). National pasts are also interwoven through war, diplomacy, co-operation and migration.

Memory studies scholars have begun to conceptualize these transnational entanglements in diverse ways: as 'transnational memory',[3] 'transcultural memory',[4] 'travelling memory',[5] 'multidirectional memory',[6] 'cosmopolitan memory'[7] and even as memory in a 'global age'.[8] A wide range of empirical work has also been conducted under the banner of transnational or transcultural memory studies.[9] This research tends to fall into two broad categories in terms of method. In the first the national or regional remains the primary unit of analysis, even as authors consider cross-fertilization between different memory cultures or the reception of memory narratives outside of their country of origin.[10] In the second approach researchers focus on supranational structures, notably European Union institutions.[11] These studies have provided important insights into a variety of contexts. However, in the first approach the nation state remains the presumed container of memory; on the other hand, the second approach does not deal sufficiently with this powerful framework. As De Cesari and Rigney note, 'even in a so-called post-national age, "the national" as a framework for identity and memory-making is still a powerful one.'[12]

Sierp and Wüstenberg make a similar point in their discussion of European memory, noting that, rather than 'single local, national, or even global case studies [, ...] what we need to investigate are the mechanisms

[3] De Cesari and Rigney, *Transnational Memory*.

[4] Lucy Bond and Jessica Rapson (eds.), *The Transcultural Turn: Interrogating Memory between and beyond Borders* (Berlin: de Gruyter, 2014).

[5] Astrid Erll, 'Travelling Memory', *Parallax* 17.4 (2011), pp. 4–18.

[6] Michael Rothberg, *Multidirectional Memory: Remembering the Holocaust in the Age of Decolonization* (Stanford, CA: Stanford University Press, 2009).

[7] Daniel Levy and Nathan Sznaider, *The Holocaust and Memory in the Global Age* (Philadelphia, PA: Temple University Press, 2006), pp. 3–4.

[8] Aleida Assmann and Sebastian Conrad (eds.), *Memory in a Global Age: Discourses, Practices and Trajectories* (Basingstoke: Palgrave, 2010).

[9] For a discussion of these two terms and the distinctions made between them in memory studies, see Bond and Rapson, *The Transcultural Turn* and De Cesari and Rigney, *Transnational Memory*.

[10] For example: Erich Langenbacher, Bill Niven and Ruth Wittlinger (eds.), *Dynamics of Memory and Identity in Contemporary Europe* (New York: Berghahn, 2012); Małgorzata Pakier and Joanna Wawrzyniak (eds.), *Memory and Change in Europe: Eastern Perspectives* (New York and Oxford: Berghahn, 2016).

[11] For example, Elisabeth Kübler, *Europäische Erinnerungspolitik: Der Europarat und die Erinnerung an den Holocaust* (Bielefeld: transcript, 2012).

[12] De Cesari and Rigney, 'Introduction', p. 6.

by which memories are (trans)formed, displayed, shared, and negotiated through transnational channels, while maintaining their local rootedness'.[13] By asking us to think about the interconnectedness of national and supranational memories, Sierp and Wüstenberg are asking us to take the 'trans' in 'transnational' seriously. The prefix 'trans' can mean 'across', 'beyond', 'through' and 'changing thoroughly'. 'Transnational memory' can therefore have the meanings 'across national memory', 'beyond national memory', 'through national memory' and, importantly, 'changing thoroughly national memory'. Transnational memory must therefore also always be about a relationship between the national and the 'something' that goes across, beyond, through or changes it thoroughly (on this, see too the discussion of memory by Anne Fuchs in Chapter 9 of this volume). This focus on relationships can point us in new directions in our search for methodologies and frameworks. The ones that I want to explore in this chapter are those developed in the field of Social Network Analysis (SNA).

Social Network Analysis and Relationality

Wassermann and Faust state succinctly that the 'the fundamental difference between a social network explanation and a non-network explanation of a process is the inclusion of concepts and information on *relationships* among units of study.'[14] What this means is that network analysts focus not on the attributes of the actors but on what Emirbayer describes as the 'transactions' between them. For Emirbayer, in the 'relational' perspective, 'the very terms or units involved in a transaction derive their meaning, significance, and identity from the (changing) functional roles they play within that transaction. The latter, seen as a dynamic, unfolding process, becomes the primary unit of analysis rather than the constituent elements themselves.'[15] Such transactions are transformative. The relationships between units of analysis (which might be individuals, groups, artefacts, ideas, narratives and so on) shape those units.

The 'relational' approach to memory studies is gaining momentum,[16] but

---

[13] Aline Sierp and Jenny Wüstenberg, 'Linking the Local and the Transnational: Rethinking Memory Politics in Europe', *Journal of Contemporary European Studies* 23.3 (2015), pp. 321–29 (p. 324).

[14] Stanley Wasserman and Katherine Faust, *Social Network Analysis: Methods and Applications* (Cambridge: Cambridge University Press, 1994), p. 6.

[15] Mustafa Emirbayer, 'Manifesto for a Relational Sociology', *The American Journal of Sociology* 103.2 (1997), pp. 281–317 (p. 287).

[16] See especially Astrid Erll's work on 'mnemonic relationality' and 'relational mnemohistory. Astrid Erll, 'Travelling Memory in European Film: Towards a

is still missing a methodological framework that allows us to focus on the discourses and narratives about the past circulating in a given context at a given point in time and through the relationships between actors within and across national borders. SNA researchers have developed an array of sophisticated tools to track, visualize and analyse just such relationships, including quantitative and qualitative methodologies. There has been some initial application of these methods to memory studies, notably Wüstenberg's analysis of individuals involved in pan-European networks.[17] In my own work, I have combined some of the quantitative methods of SNA with narrative approaches developed in part from literary studies.[18] In the present chapter I focus on the quantitative dimension of this research as the aspect that is most likely to be unfamiliar to the readers of this volume. Nonetheless, I will also point towards how this method can be usefully complemented by traditional humanities methods of hermeneutics: that is, textual analysis and interpretation of meaning.

The emphasis will be on the concept of 'memory regions': that is, the discursive construction of common histories across borders that relate to contemporary politics as much as to shared pasts. My discussion draws on Troebst's work on memory conflicts in contemporary Europe, his division of post-communist cultures of remembrance into four categories and his more recent analysis of different commemorative discourses relating to the sixtieth anniversary of the Second World War.[19] As Aleida Assmann has noted, in the West, the Holocaust remains the 'memory centre of Europe'.[20] However, the understanding of the genocide of the European Jews as a unique human catastrophe is not universally shared, particularly within Eastern European

Morphology of Mnemonic Relationality, *Image [&] Narrative* 18.1 (2017), pp. 5–18 and Astrid Erll, 'Homer: A Relational Mnemohistory', *Memory Studies* 11.3 (2018), pp. 274–86.

[17] Jenny Wüstenberg, 'Vernetztes Gedenken? "Influence Mapping" in der transnationalen Erinnerungsforschung', *Jahrbuch für Politik und Geschichte* 6 (2015), pp. 97–113.

[18] Sara Jones, 'Cross-border Collaboration and the Construction of Memory Narratives in Europe', in *The Twentieth Century in European Memory: Transcultural Mediation and Reception*, ed. by Tea Sindbæk Andersen and Barbara Törnquist-Plewa (Leiden/Boston: Brill, 2017), pp. 27–55.

[19] Stefan Troebst, 'Halecki Revisted: Europe's Conflicting Culture of Remembrance', in *A European Memory? Contested Histories and Politics of Remembrance*, ed. by Małgorzata Pakier and Bo Stråth (New York/Oxford: Berghahn Books, 2010), pp. 56–63.

[20] Aleida Assmann, *Auf dem Weg zu einer europäischen Gedächtniskultur* (Vienna: Picus, 2010), p. 32.

states. In combination with the failure of the Russian Federation to recognize the crimes of Stalinism, the result has been a form of competitive remembering between victims of Nazi and Soviet oppression.[21] Beattie has noted that this division in European memory is mirrored by divisions between West and East in Germany memory. He identifies in both Europe and Germany an 'inaccurate east–west dichotomy [that] legitimises pressure on the eastern side to conform to a seemingly unquestionable but, in fact, contested western norm'.[22] In this chapter, I show how these 'memory regions' construct and are constructed by transnational networking and how these competing discourses of memory are negotiated by an actor who is part of the official structures of a Western European state and yet whose activities focus on the memory of resistance and opposition in the East.

The Method

The first step in the relational approach is to decide which actors and which relationships are to be analysed. For the scholar of transnational memory, this presents both practical and theoretical challenges. Even if time and resources were available to gather data on every single cross-border collaboration by memory activists across the globe (a mammoth undertaking), the researcher would require a large and multilingual team of researchers to read and understand the data. From a theoretical perspective it would be extremely difficult to untangle the different cultures constructing and being constructed by these multiple relationships, especially if we recognize that the national and cultural *does* matter even as we turn to the transnational and transcultural.

Here we can usefully return to our position as students of German Studies: that is, we can conduct transnational German studies without losing sight of the German-language cultures that have formed the focus of our research and training. Thus I take as my starting point a memory-political institution located in Germany and consider the networks created by and through its collaborations with institutions and individuals located in the rest of the world. This limits our data to those relationships created by and through the activities of the selected institution. The method does not capture all of the transnational activity of every actor involved, but it does allow me

---

[21] Assmann, *Auf dem Weg*, p. 41.

[22] Andrew H. Beattie, 'Learning from the Germans? History and Memory in German and European Projects of Integration', *PORTAL Journal of Multidisciplinary International Studies* 4 (2007), pp. 1–22, http://dx.doi.org/10.5130/portal.v4i2.483 [accessed 6 June 2016], p. 17.

to reflect on the ways in which national memory cultures are intertwined and transformed by collaboration across borders and how such collaborative activity shapes and is shaped by transnational remembering.

My focus is on the Federal Office for the Files of the State Security Service of the Former GDR (*Bundesbeauftragter für die Unterlagen des Staatssicherheitsdienstes der ehemaligen DDR*, BStU), across a period of four years, January 2009–December 2012 (divided into two periods, 2009–2010 and 2011–2012). This timeframe has been chosen to allow a comparison over time while limiting data collection to a manageable amount. The year 2009 marked the twentieth anniversary of the fall of the Berlin Wall, the sixtieth anniversary of the founding of the Federal Republic (and the GDR) and the seventieth anniversary of the start of the Second World War. For this reason it was known by some as a 'Supergedenkjahr' [commemoration super year] and we might expect to see a high volume of commemorative activity, especially in terms of European memory. The year 2011 was marked by violent and non-violent protest movements in North Africa and the Middle East, some of which led to the (temporary) end of authoritarian regimes in the region. Collectively, these became known as the 'Arab Spring'. Looking at this period as a whole thus allows us to see if and how German memory culture is intertwined with post-authoritarian reconciliation within and outside of Europe.

The BStU was established in 1991 to manage access to the Stasi files according to the Stasi Records Law passed in December of that year. Alongside its involvement in the vetting of those in positions of authority (known as lustration) and file access, the BStU also has in its remit political education and remembrance. This includes the running of seminars, workshops and other events, as well as the management of regional and national exhibitions relating to the activities of the Stasi. The BStU is also a member or partner of several pan-European networking initiatives: the European Network Remembrance and Solidarity (2005), the European Network of Official Authorities in Charge of the Secret-Police Files (ENOA, 2008) and the Platform of European Memory and Conscience (2011).

Once the approach has been established, the next step is to gather data on the cross-border activities of the institution. This was done through examining activity reports, yearly summaries and press releases. The activity reports and yearly summaries were read in full. Press releases were selected for inclusion where the title indicated cross-border collaboration of some kind. From this data, information on collaborative activities – that is, the institutions or individuals with whom the BStU worked and the connections between them – was extracted and recorded. Given that an institution can be represented by multiple individuals who are nonetheless not acting independently, where the institutional affiliation of an individual was given this was recorded in place of their name. Where the participants were not named, but were simply described as part of a specific group (e.g. Tunisian civil rights activists), this term was used to designate the actor. Both German and non-German participants in the cross-border collaborations were included to capture information on which other German institutions were brought into the transnational networks created by and through the BStU.

The quantitative methods of SNA require the researcher to represent the relationships between actors (or 'nodes') numerically so that they can be explored using mathematical algorithms. The latter can be performed by a range of software, of which one of the most common (and the one used in this chapter) is Ucinet.[23] The data on relationships was recorded in two Excel matrices according to the date of the collaborative activity: 2009–2010 or 2011–2012. The matrices coded numerically the relationships between the BStU and the other actors and between the other actors and one another. The network created by these relationships can therefore be described as an ego-net: that is, the 'network which forms around a particular social actor'. The BStU is the 'ego' in this regard, and the other institutions are 'alters'.[24] One instance of collaboration between the ego and an alter, or between two alters, equalled a single tie. Thus, where there was no evidence of a relationship I entered '0' in the matrix, where there was data showing a single connection I entered '1', '2' for two connections and so on. This allowed the strength of the ties to be taken into consideration in the statistical calculations (where appropriate). All ties were considered to be reciprocal in SNA terms: that is, the relationship between the actors was mutually recognized (though not necessarily in the same way by both partners).

In order to allow statistical analyses relating to geographical location I also created two 'attribute' matrices. Each country represented in the network was ascribed a numeric code. In one column the actors in each network were listed, in a second column the relevant country code. The same process was conducted for region. The regions were defined geographically, but also with a view to different memory-political discourses. The initial list comprised: Western Europe, Central and Eastern Europe/Post-Socialist (CEE), Scandinavia, Southern Europe, Balkans, Post-Soviet, North America, South America, North

[23] Stephen P. Borgatti, Martin G. Everett and Linton C. Freeman, *Ucinet 6 for Windows: Software for Social Network Analysis* (Harvard, MA: Analytic Technologies, 2002).

[24] Nick Crossley, Elisa Bellotti, Gemma Edwards, Martin G. Everett, Johan Koskinen and Mark Tranmer, *Social Network Analysis for Ego-Nets* (Los Angeles: Sage, 2015).

Africa, Middle East, Central and Southern Africa, East Asia, Southeast Asia and multiregional. Given the continued impact of division on contemporary memory politics in Germany, German actors were divided into those that represented former West and/or post-unification Germany (categorized as Western Europe) and those who were socialized in the former East Germany and/or have as their principle focus working through the GDR past (categorized as CEE/Post-Socialist; notably, the BStU falls into this category). The Excel matrices were then converted into datasets using Ucinet, which could be converted into visualizations using the related software Netdraw.[25]

Figs. 8 and 9 show the Netdraw representations of the entire network created by and through the BStU in the respective periods. The different shapes of the individual nodes indicate the regional location of the actor and the size of the nodes indicates their 'degree centrality' in the network (see below). We can already see from these visualizations that the BStU collaborates with actors from a wide variety of geographical locations and that 2009–2010 saw the largest number of relationships built with the largest number of different partners. A basic analysis of 'Ego Composition' – that is, the make-up of the the BStU ego-net in each period – shows this numerically. In 2009–2010 the BStU worked with 148 partners from 40 different countries, creating a total of 729 ties. In 2011–2012 these figures were 90 partners from 33 countries and 440 ties. This confirms the hypothesis that we would see a boom in acts of memory, including cross-border collaborations, in anniversary years, such as the 'Supergedenkjahr' of 2009.

Nonetheless, in order to make these highly complex visualizations more meaningful, we need to extract data on the 'texture' of the networks. SNA provides a number of measures that can be used to reveal different aspects of the network in this regard. I have selected three of these to present here: centrality, components and homophily.

Centrality

Centrality is one of the most basic measurements of SNA and it can take a variety of forms, each of which attempts to capture in some way the importance of an actor in a given network. The simplest of these is 'degree centrality' (DC). DC is a measure of the number of immediate ties a node has. As we have a 'weighted' network (the more frequent the contact between the

---

[25] Stephen P. Borgatti, *Netdraw Network Visualisation* (Cambridge, MA: Analytic Technologies, 2002). An easy-to-follow discussion of creating matrices can be found in Christina Prell, *Social Network Analysis: History, Theory and Methodology* (Los Angeles: Sage, 2012), pp. 13–16.

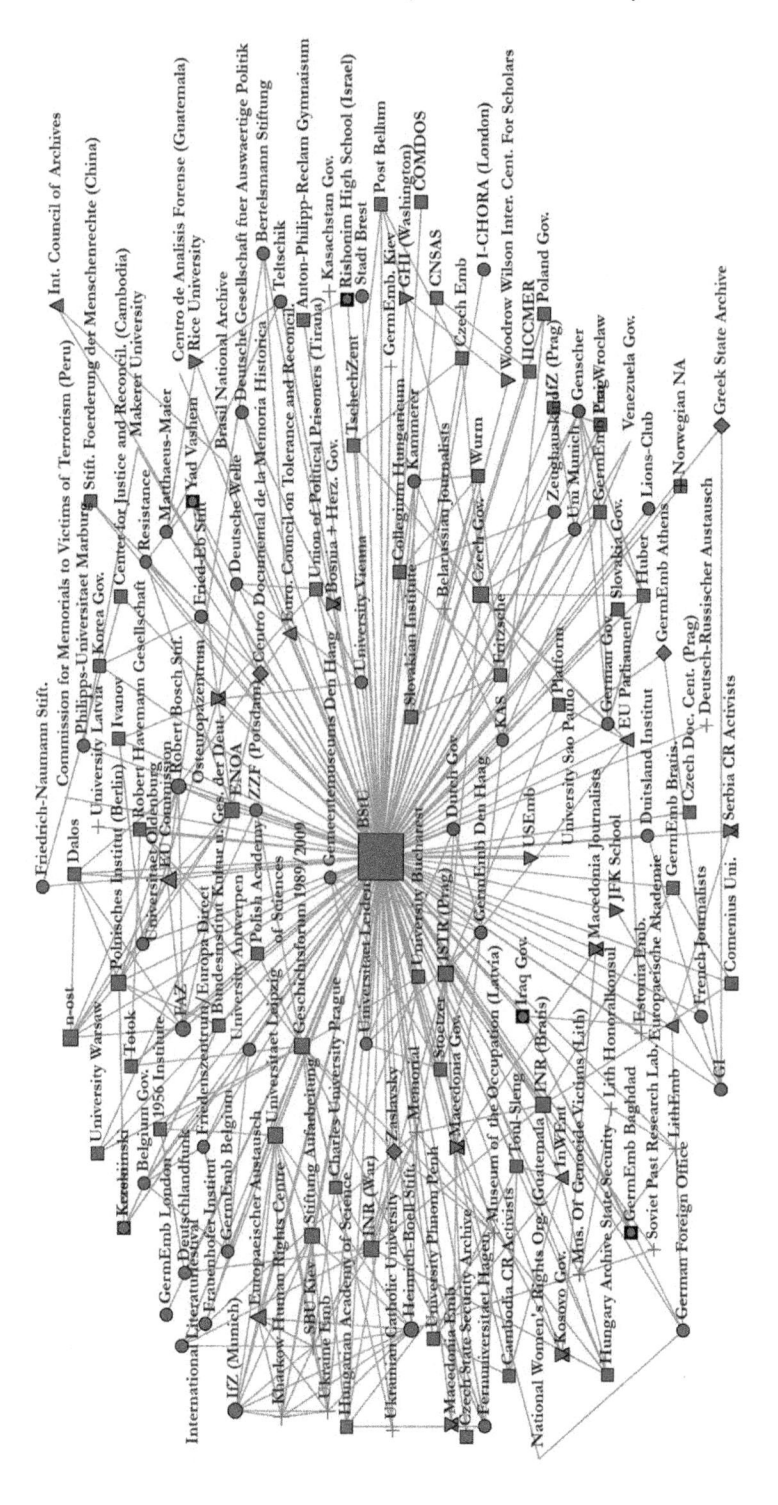

Networks and Relationality in German Memory Cultures 159

Fig. 8. BStU Network 2009–2010.

160 Sara Jones

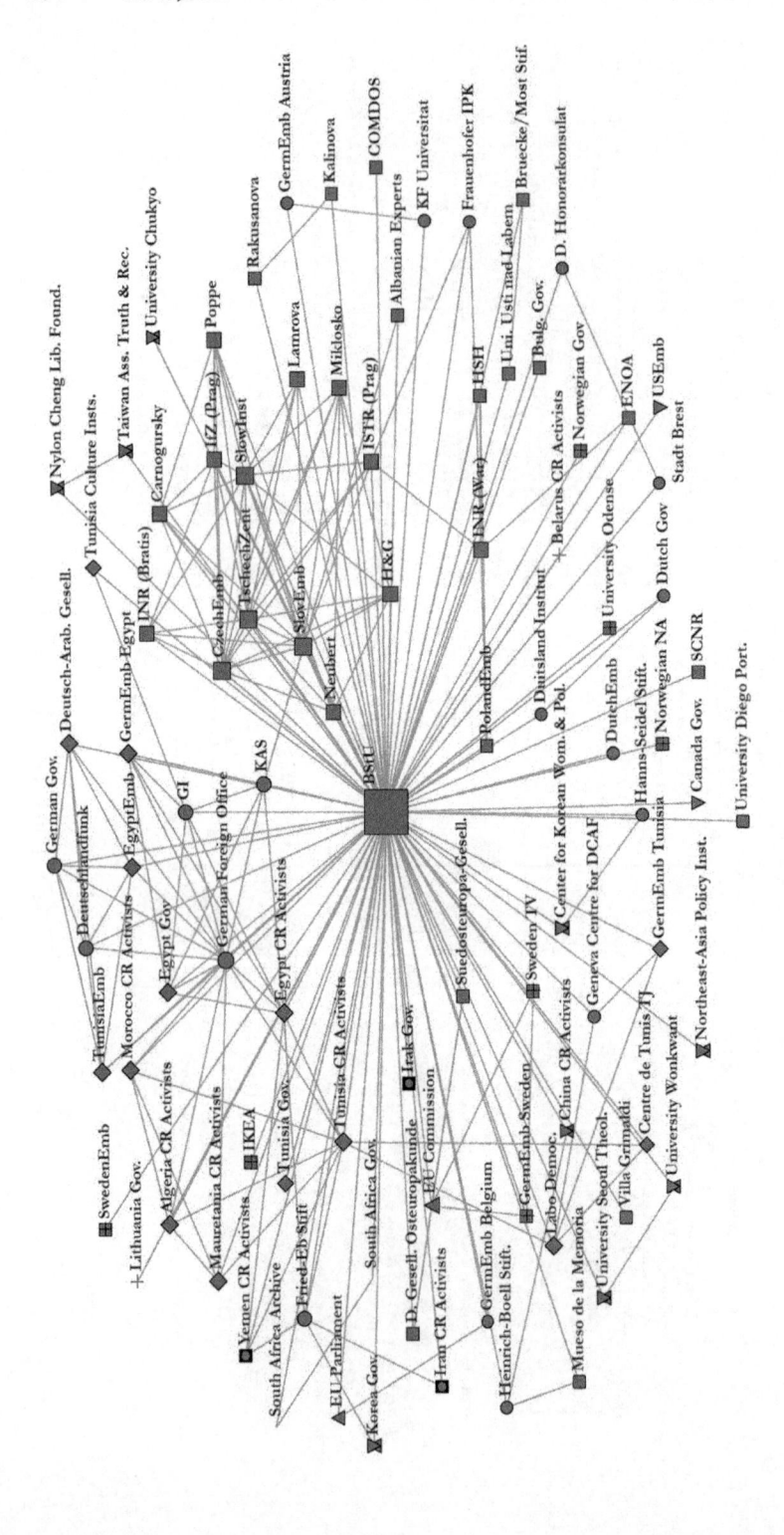

Fig. 9. BStU Network 2011–2012.

nodes the greater the 'weight'), DC is the sum of the value of the ties.[26] In this way, an actor with a high DC is one that is brought into collaboration with the BStU in a large number of events and activities with a range of diverse participants. Identifying the actors with the highest DC in the two networks can thus indicate with whom the BStU collaborated most frequently and/or within the largest and most diverse projects. This can reveal much about the ways in which this transnational network is shaped and function as a starting point for further measurements. Figure 10 shows the top ten most central nodes (excluding the BStU) for the two periods. The figure given in brackets is the DC expressed as a proportion of the maximum possible DC in that network (weighted normalized DC). This allows for an easier comparison of networks with different sizes.

These figures indicate that the network in 2009–2010 was larger in terms of the number of actors but less dense than that in 2011–2012, with even the most central actors having fewer direct ties as a proportion of the total network. This suggests that the larger network was created by a greater number of discrete events or activities, rather than repeated events with the same participants. This contrasts with the network in 2011–2012, in which the top four actors have a DC considerably higher than any others in this network or in that of the previous period. This indicates a sustained and close collaboration between the BStU and these institutions.

It is also striking that the most central actors in the 2009–2010 period are all either German government institutions or political foundations, or represent CEE/Post-Soviet interests. In contrast, the most central actors in the 2011–2012 period are divided between German government institutions and political foundations, representatives of CEE interests and representatives of countries that were part of the 'Arab Spring'. This appears to confirm the hypothesis that political events can shift the focus of transnational collaboration between memory activists. In this case, the shift entails moving from an emphasis on co-operation with other Central and European actors in the context of European memory politics to activities with partners in the countries in North Africa and the Middle East in the process (at this time) of democratic transition. What this data cannot tell us, however, is what shape this takes and how the actors from different regions are connected. For this, we need to look at 'components'.

---

[26] For further discussion of the concept of 'degree centrality' see Prell, *Social Network Analysis*, pp. 96–101; Robert A. Hanneman and Mark Riddle, 'A Brief Introduction to Analyzing Social Network Data', in *The SAGE Handbook of Social Network Analysis*, ed. by Peter J. Carrington and John Scott (Los Angeles: Sage, 2011), pp. 301–69 (pp. 364–65).

2009–2010			2011–2012		
Position	Actor	DC	Position	Actor	DC
=1	ENOA	20 (0.014)	=1	Slovakian Embassy	30 (0.067)
=1	Institute of National Remembrance (INR, Warsaw)	20 (0.014)	=1	Czech Embassy	30 (0.067)
3	Czech Government	16 (0.011)	=1	Slovakian Institute	30 (0.067)
=4	Institute for the Study of Totalitarian Regimes (ISTR, Prague)	15 (0.010)	=1	Czech Centre	30 (0.067)
=4	Geschichtsforum 1989/2009	15 (0.010)	5	German Foreign Office	17 (0.038)
=6	Security Service of Ukraine (SBU)	12 (0.008)	=6	Tunisian Civil Rights Activists	13 (0.029)
=6	Heinrich-Böll-Stiftung	12 (0.008)	=6	Institute for Contemporary History (IfZ, Prague)	13 (0.029)
=8	Polnisches Institut	11 (0.007)	7	Egyptian Civil Rights Activists	11 (0.024)
=8	Memorial	11 (0.007)	8	INR, Warsaw	10 (0.022)
=10	Konrad-Adenauer-Stiftung (KAS)	10 (0.007)	=9	KAS	9 (0.020)
=10	Robert-Bosch-Stiftung	10 (0.007)	=9	ISTR, Prague	9 (0.020)
=10	Institute for National Remembrance (INR, Bratislava)	10 (0.007)	=9	Goethe Institut	9 (0.020)
=10	Goethe Institut	10 (0.007)			

Fig. 10. Degree Centrality in BStU Networks 2009–2012.

Components

A 'component' in SNA terms is a segment of an ego-network in which all actors are linked by a path that does not go through the central node.[27] The components are created by the networking activities of the central node – that is, the BstU – and therefore do not show relationships between the actors beyond those networking activities. What a calculation of components can reveal is which actors the BStU connects with one another and patterns in its approach to collaboration. To calculate the components we need to remove the central node, the BStU, from the Excel matrix and convert the new matrix to a dataset in Ucinet. An analysis for 'components' was run on the matrices for both periods using Netdraw. For 2009–2010 one component was significantly larger than any other (45 nodes, compared with 15 for the next largest). In 2011–2012 there were two larger components with 25 and 18 nodes respectively (followed by five nodes for the next largest). Given the limitations of space, I will focus my analysis on these three, which can be seen in Figs. 11–13. The shape of the nodes indicates the region that they represent and the size is determined by their 'betweenness centrality' (BC) within the component. This measure provides information on the centrality of the node in terms of how often an actor sits between two other actors – that is, the extent to which it functions as a connector.[28]

The fact that in the 2009–2010 matrix the largest component is significantly bigger than any other might be interpreted as evidence of a highly connected network, in which the activities of the BStU create relationships between most of the other actors. However, this is where our analysis of BC can add value. Four actors have a considerably higher (normalized) BC than the remaining nodes in the component: the Institute for the Study of Totalitarian Regimes (ISTR), Prague (nBC = 4.035); the Institute of National Remembrance (INR), Warsaw (nBC = 3.835); the Geschichtsforum 1989/2009, Germany (nBC = 3.646); and the Czech Government (nBC = 3.262). This indicates that it is the BStU's collaborations with these actors on different projects involving different actors that is holding this component together. These institutions are brought into one activity and connect with a particular group of actors, after which they are brought into second and subsequent activities in which they connect with different groups. The first group of

---

[27] For more on 'components' and their significance see Crossley et al., *Social Network Analysis for Ego-Nets*, pp. 12–13; Hanneman and Riddle, 'A Brief Introduction', pp. 352–56; Prell, *Social Network Analysis*, pp. 153–55.

[28] For more on 'betweenness centrality' see Prell, *Social Network Analysis*, pp. 104–07; Hanneman and Riddle, 'A Brief Introduction', pp. 366–67.

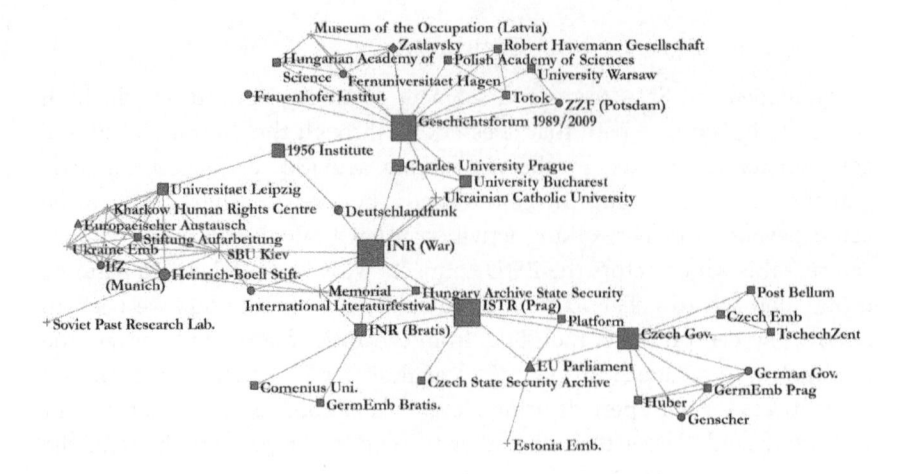

Fig. 11. Component 1, BStU 2009–2010.

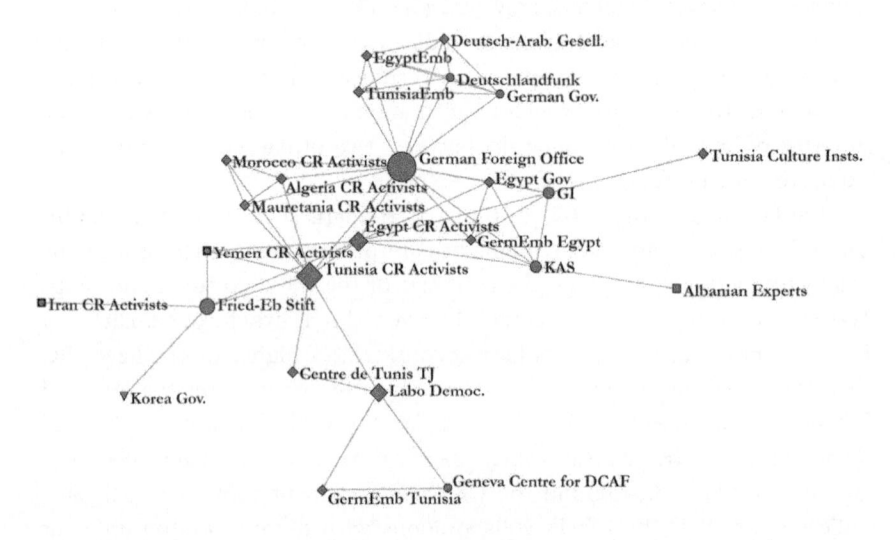

Fig. 12. Component 2, BStU 2011–2012.

actors are not otherwise connected to the second in the network constructed by and through the BStU, thus these institutions lie *between* these different groups of actors – removing them would remove that connection. A high BC is generally considered to indicate that an actor has a high level of control over the flow of information in the network and is influential.[29] In our context, we might interpret this to mean that these actors have the ability to both provide

[29] Prell, *Social Network Analysis*, p. 104.

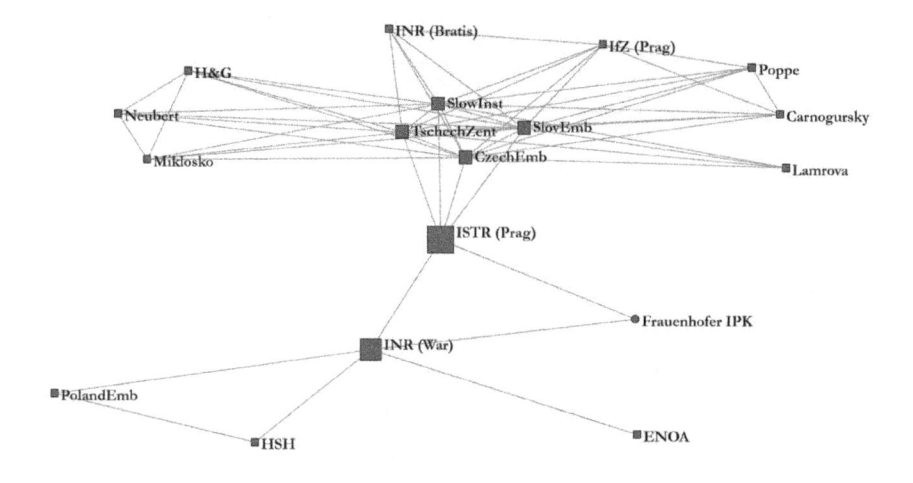

Fig. 13. Component 3, BStU 2011–2012.

and draw resources from the groups they connect. These may be material resources (such as funding), but may also be creative and narrative resources. The connectors can draw on discourses about the past and approaches to memory politics from multiple perspectives and integrate these into their own context. At the same time, they can present their own narratives about the past and the politics of remembering to multiple audiences.

In Components 2 and 3 we can also see that there are actors that appear to play an important connecting function. In Component 2 these are the German Foreign Office (nBC = 3.307); Tunisian Civil Rights Activists (nBC = 2.694) and, to a lesser extent, Egyptian Civil Rights Activists (nBC = 1.302); the Friedrich Ebert Foundation (linked to the Social Democratic Party, nBC = 1.149); and the Tunisian NGO Labo' Démocratique (nBC = 1.124). In Component 3 the connectors are the ISTR, Prague (nBC = 1.532), and the INR, Warsaw (nBC = 1.124). The lower normalized BCs in comparison with Component 1 suggests that these components are smaller, but more cohesive: that is, that actors are connected to one another through multiple pathways, rather than through a single node. This suggests that in 2011–2012 the BStU's collaborative activity took the shape of multiple projects with many of the *same* partners.

Homophily

If we look more closely at the actors in Component 1 we can observe that – although the central actors may indeed have had access to multiple partners – the vast majority are located within CEE memory discourses. This

	2009–2010		
Actor	Country	Region	Region Merged
ENOA	0.125	0.250	0.250
Institute of National Remembrance (INR, Warsaw)	0.000	0.500	0.800
Czech Government	0.400	0.700	0.700
Institute for the Study of Totalitarian Regimes (ISTR, Prague)	0.250	0.750	0.875
Geschichtsforum 1989/2009	0.357	0.643	0.714
Security Service of Ukraine (SBU)	0.200	0.300	0.600
Heinrich-Böll-Stiftung	*0.333*	*0.111*	*0.111*
Polnisches Institut	0.222	0.556	0.556
Memorial	0.000	0.143	0.714
Konrad-Adenauer-Stiftung (KAS)	*0.000*	*0.000*	*0.000*
Robert-Bosch-Stiftung	*0.375*	*0.250*	*0.250*
Institute for National Remembrance (INR, Bratislava)	0.167	0.833	1.000
Goethe Institut	*0.250*	*0.250*	*0.250*
Mean	0.206	0.407	0.525

Fig. 14. Homophily in BStU Networks 2009–2012.
Actors in West Europe region in italics.

includes post-Soviet actors (here, Ukraine and the Russian Federation). As noted above, I had initially coded these actors as located in a separate region; however, the embedding of post-Soviet actors in this component suggests that they are intertwined with the narratives and discourses about the past and the politics of memory that are generated by institutions and individuals based in CEE countries that were not part of the Soviet Union – a hypothesis that I test below. Component 2 is made up almost entirely of North African and Middle Eastern actors in countries that saw popular protests as part of the 'Arab Spring', as well as a number of German government actors and political foundations. Component 3 is made up exclusively of actors from the CEE region, with the exception of the German technology company Frauenhofer IPK.

Networks and Relationality in German Memory Cultures 167

	2011–2012		
Actor	Country	Region	Region Merged
Slovakian Embassy	0.333	0.917	1.000
Czech Embassy	0.333	0.917	1.000
Slovakian Institute	0.333	0.917	1.000
Czech Centre	0.333	0.917	1.000
German Foreign Office	*0.429*	*0.286*	*0.286*
Tunisian Civil Rights Activists	0.222	0.667	0.778
Institute for Contemporary History (IfZ, Prague)	0.286	1.000	1.000
Egyptian Civil Rights Activists	0.125	0.375	0.500
INR, Warsaw	0.200	0.800	0.800
KAS	*0.500*	*0.333*	*0.333*
ISTR, Prague	0.333	0.833	0.833
Goethe Institut	*0.500*	*0.333*	*0.333*
Mean	0.327	0.691	0.739

These groupings can be demonstrated numerically using a measure known as 'homophily'.[30] This provides information on the similarity between an ego and its alters. For our purposes, the original 'ego' (the BStU) is again removed from the network and the relevant Ucinet procedure is run on the other actors in each network. In this way, each actor is treated as an 'ego' and the data reveals the extent to which it shares a specific attribute with those to whom it is connected directly in the context of the network created by the BStU (as noted above, we cannot know about connections beyond this network). I ran homophily measures on the networks using the country and region attribute matrices and subsequently edited the regional attribute matrix to merge the post-Soviet and CEE regions. I then reran the regional homophily measure for each network. The results for the most degree-central actors in each network can be seen in Figure 14: the figure shown is the number of an actor's alters

---

[30] For more on 'homophily' see Crossley et al., *Social Network Analysis for Ego-Nets*, pp. 80–82; Prell, *Social Network Analysis*, pp. 129–31.

that have the same country/regional attribute as that actor, divided by the total number of alters for that actor.

As we can see, there is a significant increase in regional homophily for the post-Soviet actors (the Russian NGO, Memorial, and the Security Service of Ukraine, SBU) in 2009–2010, when the CEE and post-Soviet regions are merged. This indicates that these actors are more often connected to CEE partners than to other post-Soviet ones. It should be noted that this refers to absolute connections. There are more CEE actors in the network than post-Soviet ones, so the probability of connecting with CEE actors is significantly higher in the first place. Nonetheless, we can see, that where post-Soviet actors are included in the network, they are most likely to be included in connection with actors from the CEE region.

A closer look at the homophily table indicates a further pattern. The most degree-central actors from CEE/Post-Soviet contexts and those from the North Africa/Middle East region have a significantly higher (absolute) regional homophily than country homophily. In 2009–2010 the mean country homophily for CEE/Post-Soviet actors is 0.191, versus a (merged) regional homophily of 0.6209. In 2011–2012 the figures for CEE/Post-Soviet are 0.307 and 0.948, and for actors based in North Africa/Middle East 0.174 and 0.639. This indicates that, even where these actors are brought to collaborate with actors outside of their national context, these are more often than not nodes from their regional context (and, in some cases, where the regional homophily is 1, exclusively so). This is not true of the most central West European actors, who – in these networks – are all based in (western) Germany. For these actors, the regional homophily is either equal to the country homophily (at 0 in the case of the Konrad Adenauer Foundation in 2009–2010), or it is a lower figure. The reduction in homophily can be accounted for by the division of German memory actors into two regions – CEE/Post-socialist and Western European. However, the fact that the regional homophily is never higher than the country homophily also suggests that German government and political foundation actors are not typically brought into collaborations with West European partners.

Caught between East and West: Narratives of Memory

What this amounts to is quantitative evidence that, while the BStU acts globally, the network that it constructs through collaboration is essentially regional. The high regional homophily of nodes within the major components indicates that although the BStU may gain access to (and disperse) a variety of material and discursive resources through transnational collaboration, its partners are limited to regional resources in terms of what they can gain through their co-operation with the BStU. In this way, the cross-border collaboration of the BStU may function to reinforce, rather than challenge, regional narratives about the past and the processes of coming to terms with it.

Examining the implications of this finding requires us to turn to qualitative methods, notably the use of hermeneutics, to trace how the relationships constructed in and through the network are given meaning by the BStU. Here I will outline one possible approach to this through a focus on the two distinct regions identified through the SNA of the BStU's collaborative activity in 2011–2012: co-operation with post-'Arab Spring' countries (Component 2) and with countries in Central and Eastern Europe (Component 3). Comparing the ways in which these activities in different regions are given meaning by the BStU can highlight how transnational engagement in different areas of the world is constructed in different ways and for different purposes.

The method I deploy is narrative analysis. This method traces the ways in which actors and events are positioned in a relationship to one another to provide a causal explanation (a 'plot') for the purpose and outcome of the activity. The corpus is the same as for the SNA: that is, activity reports, yearly summaries and press releases. Text relating to transnational collaboration was extracted from this material and gathered in a single document for each region: in this case, material relating to activity with CEE partners in one file and activity with partners in North Africa and the Middle East in another. The files were then uploaded to the content analysis software Nvivo. The narratives were then identified inductively by looking for common patterns in the texts collated in Nvivo. Each activity was coded according to the way in which it is constructed narratively. Narrative analysis does not claim to uncover an extratextual reality – that is, I am not arguing that the BStU's presentation of these actors and events is the 'true' story of that collaboration. However, the ordering of the 'plot' elements (actors, activities, time, place) can demonstrate how this institution chooses to make sense of and present that event and its participants. This in turn can have implications for its institutional identity and consequently its action in the world.[31]

I identified five narratives patterns in the texts in this corpus, which were clearly divided between the two regions. In the texts about collaboration with partners in North Africa and the Middle East, of 21 activities recorded, 13 were coded with a narrative that – borrowing from Andrew Beattie – I will term 'Learning from the Germans'[32] – no other narrative was recorded more than three times. Beattie uses 'Learning from the Germans' to describe the ways in which the construction of a European memory

---

[31] For more on narrative analysis see Barbara Czarniawska, *Narratives in Social Science Research* (London: Sage, 2004).

[32] Beattie, 'Learning from the Germans?'

mirrors that of German national memory culture. In the description of the BStU's collaborative activities in this region, it comes to mean a narrative in which non-European actors seek out German partners in order to learn from their apparently superior methods of working through the past. In this way, collaboration is based not on a model of exchange but on one of the German actor passing (symbolic and material) resources to the non-European partner.

To give just two examples of this way of describing the collaborative activity: regarding the involvement of the BStU in the task force 'Transformationspartnershaft' [Partnership of Transformation] in Egypt in March 2011, organized by the German Foreign Office and including 'Gespräche' [conversations] between German and Egyptian partners, as well as public events in Cairo, we are told:

> The experiences that Germany and this institution [i.e., the BStU] have gathered since 1989 were to be communicated to the Egyptian public and also state organisations. Eventually it was decided that an experienced representative of the BStU should meet multipliers and activists on site [i.e., in Egypt] in order to report on ways of making the archives accessible and on the experiences from the time of the Peaceful Revolution and the upheaval [Umbruch] in Germany.

'Conversations' are not presented as a dialogue between equal partners, but as a method of the German actor instructing the non-German one. Similarly, regarding a visit to the BStU by representatives of the Iraqi parliament, the authors of the activity report state:

> Following a tour through the archives and card indexing rooms, the delegation informed themselves [informiert sich] in a conversation with the Federal Commissioner Roland Jahn and the head of the archive Birgit Salamon about the work of the authority. During the conversation, the different conditions for working through the past in Iraq and Germany became clear. The English translation of the Stasi Records Law was of particular interest to the visitors.

Here we see a conversation that does appear to be more of an exchange about different experiences; and yet, in terms of the distribution of knowledge as a resource, it is only the non-German actors who are 'informed' and gain something materially useful for their own memory-political work (the translation). While actors from this region may be constructed as experts in terms of memory work in their own context, the German partner is not constructed as being changed by the collaboration with them.

In the collaborative activity with CEE partners a quite different mixture of narratives emerges. Of the 28 activities recorded, 13 are coded with the narrative I designate 'common histories': that is, a linking of the actors and events that emphasizes the similarities between the pasts of the countries involved. Twelve activities are coded with the term 'official networks', indicating that the activity is set within the context of the official European networks dedicated to the history and memory of state socialism. In the case of the BStU this is most commonly the ENOA. Two other dominant narratives are 'co-operation' (eight activities) and 'expert exchange' (six activities).[33] Again, I will provide just a couple of examples that highlight how these narratives are interwoven with one another. With reference to a workshop with the Polish INR, the activity report describes the meeting as follows:

> In collaboration with the Polish Institute of National Remembrance (INR) the authority organised a workshop with experts from the sister institutions in the European Network [i.e., the ENOA] on the 27 November 2012, in order to discuss a possible digitalisation and online publication of documents about the multilateral co-operation of the state security services in the former Soviet bloc system.

Here the event is constructed as an opportunity for expert exchange between equal partners ('sisters') based on intertwined common histories. The outcome will be embedded in the activities of both the German and non-German actors and therefore all parties are transformed by the relationship. Similarly, the visit of a delegation from the Lithuanian parliament to the BStU in February 2012 is described as including a conversation at the centre of which 'stood an exchange about the differences and commonalities in the working through of the activities of the secret police in the former Eastern Bloc'. In this case, the different experiences of state socialism in countries across Eastern Europe are acknowledged; however, the idea that these can nonetheless be subsumed within a conversation about 'the former Eastern Bloc' suggests that the partners have a common history. The use of the word 'exchange' (in German, *Austausch*) highlights that the meeting took the form of a dialogue in which symbolic resources (information, ideas and so on) were given and received by both parties.

---

[33] Note that activities could be coded with more than one narrative.

Towards a Collaborative Memory

These observations lead us back to the discussion of divisions in European and German memory outlined above. In its collaborations with partners in North Africa and the Middle East, the BStU identifies itself as part of a 'German' way of coming to terms with the past: that is, as part of what Beattie describes as the 'western norm'.[34] In contrast, in its co-operations with CEE partners, the BStU constructs an eastern region of memory that is based on a sense of shared history that is explored through expertise and co-operation within recognized partnerships. The SNA shows that German or Western European actors are largely excluded from the collaborations with CEE partners captured in Component 3 and to a large extent from the CEE-dominated network in Component 1. This contrasts with the network constructed among the post-Arab Spring countries, represented by Component 2, in which the German Foreign Office, KAS, Friedrich-Ebert Stiftung and Goethe Institut are represented. This indicates that this 'Eastern Bloc' might be set in opposition to 'western norms' of remembrance. This tension can also be seen in the BStU's own assessment of its activities after 20 years of German unity, as laid out in the 2009–2010 activity report. Here the existence of the BStU is described as being one of a set of measures that show Germany 'to have set international standards in the approach to dictatorial pasts' and yet the authors lament that, 'just as the West is still quite some way from seeing the GDR as part of German history, it seems that the history of the countries in Central and Eastern Europe formerly under communist rule are not yet seen as part of European history in Paris, Stockholm and Rome.'

In this way, we can see that the BStU's network of transnational remembering is both constructed by 'culture' – that is, narratives about the past that are defined regionally – and constructs 'culture', through a structure that is likely to reinforce and reshape those narratives, despite a stated wish to overcome the east–west dichotomy in remembrance. In this way, an exploration of relationality and collaboration can demonstrate how transnational memory is constituted not (only) by 'travelling' across borders but through 'transactions' between actors located in different contexts – something I would like to term 'collaborative memory'. Within these transactions, the BStU's presentation of itself and the purpose of its transnational collaboration is transformed, shifting narratively between 'western norms' of working through the past – constructing non-European partners as deficient – and eastern demands for other pasts to be included in European memory cultures,

---

[34] Beattie, 'Learning from the Germans', p. 17.

suggesting that it is European (and German) memory that is lacking. These transformations are fundamentally political, as the narratives define who is qualified to contribute to determining modes of remembrance nationally, regionally and globally. The tracing of collaborative activity through SNA allows us to map and measure the material basis for and outcomes of discursively constructed regions of memory (that is, the actual connections between diverse memory actors). Combining this with qualitative analysis of the texts created by and for collaboration allows us to identify how these actors position themselves within those discourses and how the characteristics of a given collaboration can cause that positioning to shift.

Suggestions for Further Reading

Bond, Lucy and Jessica Rapson (eds.), *The Transcultural Turn: Interrogating Memory Between and beyond Borders* (Berlin: de Gruyter, 2014), 270 pp.

Bond, Lucy, Stef Craps and Pieter Vermeulen (eds.), *Memory Unbound: Tracing the Dynamics of Memory Studies* (New York: Berghahn, 2017), 301 pp.

Carrington, Peter J., and John Scott (eds.), *The Sage Handbook of Social Network Analysis* (Los Angeles: Sage, 2011), 642 pp.

Czarniawska, Barbara, *Narratives in Social Science Research* (London: Sage, 2004), 169 pp.

De Cesari, Chiara, and Ann Rigney (eds.) *Transnational Memory: Circulation, Articulation, Scales* (Berlin: de Gruyter, 2014), 384 pp.

Erll, Astrid, 'Homer: A Relational Mnemohistory', *Memory Studies* 11.3 (2018), pp. 274–86.

Pakier, Małgorzata, and Bo Stråth (eds.), *A European Memory? Contested Histories and Politics of Remembrance* (New York: Berghahn, 2010), 372 pp.

Prell, Christina, *Social Network Analysis: History, Theory and Methodology* (Los Angeles: Sage, 2012), 274 pp.

Sierp, Aline, and Jenny Wüstenberg, 'Linking the Local and the Transnational: Rethinking Memory Politics in Europe', *Journal of Contemporary European Studies* 23.3 (2015), pp. 321–29.

Part 3

Temporality: Experiences of Time

9

It's About Time

The Temporality of Transnational Studies

Anne Fuchs

The Transnational Imaginary: Space without Time

Anyone reading up on the transnational turn in the social sciences and humanities cannot but notice the celebratory tone of a vast body of literature that, as Aleida Assmann puts it, 'seems to encapsulate a vision of a better world'.[1] This vision entails the end of the national and ethnic identifications that have underpinned the nation state ever since its stellar rise in the nineteenth century. To this day, the sovereign nation state relies on notions of boundedness, unity, homogeneity and self-determination that appear to clash with the transnational interconnectedness of our world. Responding to globalization, transnationalism therefore pursues those 'systems of ties, interactions, exchange and mobility' that operate across national borders.[2] The transnational research perspective also entails analysing the 'internal globalisation'[3] of the nation state by way of 'everyday cultural globalisation'.[4] Inspired by diasporic studies and postcolonial theory, transnationalism casts light on processes of creolization, hybridization and cultural translation that, in the era of globalization, have the potential to overcome essentializing notions of identity by way of what is hailed as a new 'transnational imaginary'.[5]

---

[1] Aleida Assmann, 'Transnational Memories', *European Review* 22.4 (2014), pp. 546–56 (p. 546).

[2] Steven Vertovec, *Transnationalism* (London/New York: Routledge, 2009), p. 3.

[3] Ulrich Beck, 'The Cosmopolitan Society and its Enemies', *Theory, Culture, Society* 19 (2002), pp. 17–44 (p. 17).

[4] Regina Römhild, 'Global Heimat Germany. Migration and the Transnationalization of the Nation State', *Transit* 1 (2004), pp. 1–8 (p. 1).

[5] Vertovec, *Transnationalism*, p. 7.

This imaginary transcends the kind of 'methodological nationalism', as German sociologist Ulrich Beck characterized it, that has underpinned much of humanities research, including literary history, which, in the western literary tradition, tended to reify the white and male-dominated national canon at the expense of female writers and minor literary traditions. In German literary history, the rediscovery of female intellectuals and writers (such as Bettina von Arnim, Karoline von Günderrode, Minna Kautsky, Irmgard Keun and Gertrud Kolmar, to name but a few) was instigated by feminist criticism in the 1970s but is still an incomplete project. But transnationalism targets not only the implicit 'cultural racism' of nationalism but also the limited horizon of inter-culturality, which, according to Wolfgang Welsch, merely offers a cosmetic correction of the problematic conception of 'cultures as islands or spheres'.[6] The transnational turn opens up 'a new analytic optic which makes visible the increasing intensity and scope of circular flows of persons, goods, information and symbols triggered by international labour migration'.[7] It thus promises a fresh approach to the construction of placed identity in the twenty-first century by, for example, exploring the morphology, strength, density and durability of the multiple networks people entertain in today's transnationally networked society. Social network analysis deliberately uproots the idea that belonging is always rooted in a durable, bounded and stable culture.

Transnationalism can also be viewed as an offspring of and correction to prevailing theories of globalization, which tend to analyse the geopolitical effects of an interconnected world from a top-down perspective: global capitalism, large-scale migration movements, regionalized wars with global reach, global terrorism, environmental threats, cyber-warfare and real-time information networks are some of the dominant topics of globalization studies. As the flipside of globalization theories, transnationalism foregrounds the messy proximities, dynamic interconnections and multiple entanglements that characterize social reality at a local level. Conceptualizing 'the emerging multipolarity of the twenty-first century [...] and the multidirectionality of cross border flows of people, goods and ideas', transnationalism – in the words of the editors of a recent volume on transnational German Studies – prompts us 'to shift our focus away from the movement of some – migrants, refugees, exiles or trafficked people – across borders towards the implication of all'.[8]

---

[6] Wolfgang Welsch, 'Transculturality: The Puzzling form of Cultures Today', in *Spaces of Culture: City, Nation, World*, ed. by Mike Featherstone and Scott Lash (London: Sage, 1999), pp. 195–213 (p. 196).

[7] A. Caglar cited in Vertovec, *Transnationalism*, pp. 13–14.

[8] Elisabeth Herrmann, Carrie Smith-Prei and Stuart Taberner, 'Introduction:

Reviewing these ambitions of transnationalism, it is striking that the debate is dominated by two interwoven vocabularies: a vocabulary of travel, trajectories, mobility and flows, and a vocabulary of space and place. In the German tradition, the quest for a place in the world was, from the nineteenth century onwards, negotiated through a rich *Heimat* [homeland] discourse that mobilized notions of stable belonging at a time when Germany underwent accelerated modernization, generating widespread anxieties about the direction and pace of change. Linda Shortt suggests that the idea of *Heimat* may be too overburdened with its racist and reactionary baggage to lend itself to the analysis of fluid belonging in our hyper-mobile age.[9] While Shortt focuses on modes of belonging that 'are not conceived as immobile and unchanging attachments', Rosi Braidotti promotes nomadism for its opposition to permanence and stasis.[10] From this perspective, the incessant flow of people, commodities, information and ideas in the global age has created dynamic circuits of exchange, networks of interaction and transnational spaces that constitute a new 'mobility paradigm'.[11]

However, with its sole focus on travel across borders and through space, transnational studies has all but eclipsed time and temporality from its analytic optics. If time features at all in transnational studies, it is conceptualized vaguely, either in terms of non-temporalized flows and dynamics or as 'the real time' of the information age. For example, Steven Vertovec claims that the exchange, mobility and interactions that characterize transnational networks happen in real time and with increasing speed and velocity.[12] But this description is highly misleading because it wrongly suggests that the high speed conventionally associated with the information age is experienced evenly across the globe.

Contemporary German-Language Literature and Transnationalism', in *Transnationalism in Contemporary German-Language Literature*, ed. by E. Herrmann, C. Smith-Prei and S. Taberner (Rochester, NY: Camden House, 2015), pp. 1–15 (p. 4).

[9] Linda Shortt, *German Narratives of Belonging. Writing Generation and Place in the Twenty-First Century* (London: Legenda, 2015), p. 6.

[10] Shortt, *German Narratives*, p. 7. Rosi Braidotti, *Nomadic Subjects: Embodiment and Sexual Difference in Contemporary Theory* (New York: Columbia University Press, 2011).

[11] Thomas Faist, 'Diaspora and transnationalism: What kind of dance partners?' in *Diaspora and Transnationalism: Concepts, Theories and Methods*, ed. by Rainer Bauböck and Thomas Faist (Amsterdam: Amsterdam University Press, 2010), pp. 9–34 (p. 22).

[12] Vertovec, *Transnationalism*, p. 3.

To be sure, digital technologies have revolutionized the relationship between individuals, their worlds and their temporal horizons.[13] Social media platforms have produced new forms of participatory online communication and digital technologies have moved the broadcast age into the post-broadcast era in which production and reception are fundamentally intertwined.[14] And yet, in spite of the radical transformation of the social sphere in networked society, we need to be mindful of the social embeddedness of the experience of time. Our biological body clocks, the natural world with its rhythms of seasons, the passage of day and night, the cycle of birth and death continue to shape our experience of time, even though these spheres have been infiltrated by digital technologies, as Jonathan Crary points out.[15] In social life, notes Barbara Adam, time is clustered around 'timescapes' – that is, context-dependent temporal practices that are tacitly understood. And so it is that in our daily lives we traverse a multitude of places that come with a wide range of temporally inflected behaviours and speeds.[16] If we recognize that the temporality of everyday life involves the conventional clock, biological and psychological needs alongside analogue and digital technologies, then we can ask to what extent and how the 'information ecology' of the digital era has transformed our experience of time and space. Robert Hassan describes the new information ecology as follows:

> Contexts may combine and separate in the space of nanoseconds – or last for hours or days or weeks. Contexts traverse geographic space, dissolving it into the virtuality that is the network society. [...]. Importantly, this digital environment or ecology is as real as the built environment that comprises the cities and towns and as actual as the

---

[13] Tim Berners Lee is credited for the invention of the World Wide Web: in March 1989 he wrote 'Information Management: A Proposal', which formulated his vision of the web. By October 1990 he had written the three cornerstones that remain the foundation of today's web: HTML (Hyper Text Markup Language), URI (Uniform Resource Identifier) and HTTP (Hypertext Transfer Protocol). At the end of 1990 the first web page was launched at CERN and in 1991 the new web community was opened to users outside. See http://webfoundation.org/about/vision/history-of-the-web/ [accessed 27 December 2016].

[14] See Andrew Hoskins, 'Anachronisms of Media, Anachronisms of Memory: from Collective Memory to a New Memory Culture', in *On Media Memory. Collective Memory in a New Media Age*, ed. by Motti Neiger, Oren Meyers and Eyal Zandberg (Basingstoke: Palgrave Macmillan, 2011), pp. 278–88.

[15] Jonathan Crary, *24/7: Late Capitalism and the Ends of Sleep* (London: Verso, 2013).

[16] Barbara Adam, *Time* (Cambridge, MA: Polity, 2004), p. 143.

natural ecology that provides the building blocks (the contexts) for life on earth.[17]

As previously mentioned, the intensification of human–machine interconnectivity is often perceived in terms of the arrival of so-called real time and the cancellation of temporal depth and duration. Originally real time was a technical term designed to capture the speed of computing operating systems. But its transfer to the social sphere is problematic, not least because it promotes a totalizing version of connectivity. Rather than enfolding us in a world of timeless simultaneity, the temporal ecology of the twenty-first century has engendered complex modes of 'connected asynchronicity'. Refugees and migrants experience connected asynchronicity in their daily lives when they communicate by social media with their families and friends, who often inhabit radically different time zones back home. As long as human beings inhabit multi-layered temporal environments that come with different patterns, rhythms and durations, the machine–human interaction will remain inherently asynchronous.

The field of transnational memory studies may give us productive pointers as to how temporal categories can be integrated into the conceptual framework of transnationalism. One of the foremost proponents of the transnational turn in memory studies, Astrid Erll, has rightly argued that the object of memory studies is no longer the container-culture of the nation, as paradigmatically exemplified by Pierre Nora's analysis of a bounded French national memory culture that took no account of the immigrant communities in today's France.[18] Erll proposes to focus instead on the 'production of transcultural mnemospaces' by tracking the routes and journeys of memories through space and time (on this, see too the discussion of mapping memory by Sara Jones in Chapter 8 of this volume). Erll proposed five dimensions of memory – carriers, media, contents, practices and forms – that draw attention to the transnational movement of memory. The most prominent example in this regard is, of course, the memory of the Holocaust, which, as a result of decades of remediation, has emerged as one of the most pervasive global memory icons.[19] Conceived in predominantly spatial terms, Erll's five dimensions of memory are open to a temporal perspective that, for example, focuses

---

[17] Robert Hassan, 'Network Time', in *24/7. Time and Temporality in Network Society*, ed. by Robert Hassan and E. Purser (Stanford, CA: Stanford Business Books, 2007), pp. 37–61 (p. 48).

[18] Astrid Erll, 'Travelling Memory', *Parallax* 17.4 (2011), pp. 4–18 (p. 7).

[19] See Daniel Levy and Natan Sznaider, *Erinnerungen im globalen Zeitalter: Der Holocaust* (Frankfurt a. M.: Suhrkamp, 2001); Aleida Assmann and Sebastain Conrad

on the role of emerging media technologies in the 'remediation' of memories across time.[20] Erll rightly emphasizes that the contents, practices and forms evolve as they travel across space and through time. In this way transnational memory studies aims to foreground temporal trajectories that result in surprising forms of localized, vernacularized and hybridized memories. However, even though the five dimensions discussed by Erll can be temporalized through, for example, the analysis of their historical emergence and transformations, they are in themselves not temporal categories of analysis.

Temporal Categories of Analysis

So how can transnational studies take account of the multiplicity of times in the era of transnational mobility? In the first instance, transnational studies requires temporal categories of analysis that interweave spatial categories of mobility with a temporal perspective. In 1935 the Marxist philosopher Ernst Bloch published *Die Erbschaft dieser Zeit* [*Heritage of our Times*], a work in which he analysed the roots of fascism. Explaining why so many German peasants and the lower middle classes in particular had embraced National Socialism, Bloch came up with the notion of the 'Gleichzeitigkeit des Ungleichzeitigen', the contemporaneity of the non-contemporaneous. At the beginning of his book he writes: 'We do not all inhabit the same present. This is so only on a superficial level because we can all be seen today. But this does not mean that we all live simultaneously.'[21] By this, Bloch referred to the continued sway of archaic beliefs in the modern period. Support of Hitler by the lower German middle classes and peasantry in the 1930s exemplified this

---

(eds.), *Memory in a Global Age: Discourses, Practices and Trajectories* (Houndmills: Palgrave Macmillan 2010).

[20] Erll, 'Travelling Memory', p. 12.

[21] In German: 'Nicht alle sind im selben Jetzt da. Sie sind es nur äußerlich, dadurch daß sie heute zu sehen sind. Damit aber leben sie noch nicht mit den anderen zugleich.' See Ernst Bloch, *Erbschaft dieser Zeit* (Frankfurt a. Main: Suhrkamp, 1962), p. 1. Bloch coined the phrase 'Gleichzeitigkeit des Ungleichzeitigen', but the concept goes back to the late eighteenth century, when European civilization was set as a benchmark for overseas cultures seen as having been left behind. See Reinhart Koselleck, '"Neuzeit": Remarks on the Semantics of Modern Concepts of Movement', in Reinhart Koselleck, *Futures Past. On the Semantics of Historical Time* (New York: Columbia University Press, 2004,) pp. 236–38. See also Hanns-Georg Brose, 'Das Gleichzeitige ist ungleichzeitig. Über den Umgang mit einer Paradoxie und die Transformation der Zeit', in *Unsichere Zeiten. Herausforderungen gesellschaftlicher Transformationen. Verhandlungen des 34. Kongresses der Deutschen Gesellschaft für Soziologie in Jena 2008*, ed. by Hans-Georg Soeffner with Kathy Kursawe, Margrit Elsner and Manja Aldt (Wiesbaden: Springer, 2010), pp. 547–62.

fact. For Bloch their seemingly irrational beliefs were powerful intrusions of unprocessed residual elements from the past in the present. Bloch's notion of the contemporaneity of the non-contemporaneous thus discarded the linear model according to which mankind was uniformly progressing from primitive early stages to modernity. By illuminating the 'multi-temporal and multi-layered contradictions within a single present', he punctured the idea that we all inhabit the same homogeneous time.[22]

Bloch's notion of the 'Gleichzeitigkeit des Ungleichzeitigen' can be usefully connected with the current debate on 'uneven geographical development' that separates the developed world from developing countries, the centre from the periphery, fast-paced urban social life from slower rural existence and the globally mobile elite from local communities. In his seminal book *The Condition of Postmodernity* (1989) the Marxist geographer David Harvey argued that space and time are tied to material practices and processes and hence to social life.[23] Even though space is a seemingly common-sense category in our daily lives and as such part of our tacit knowledge,

> conflicts arise not merely out of admittedly diverse subjective appreciations, but because different objective material qualities of time and space are deemed relevant to social life in different situations. Important battles likewise occur in the realms of scientific, social, and aesthetic theory, as well as in practice. How we represent space and time in theory matters, because it affects how we and others interpret and then act with respect to the world.[24]

Harvey's groundbreaking book analysed the radical readjustment of time and space in the wake of the European crises of 1848 that manifested itself in crop failures, economic depression and revolutionary upheavals which then engulfed 'the whole of what was then the capitalist world'.[25] For Harvey the explosiveness of 1848 called into question the time-as-progress narrative 'as too many people had been caught up in the maelstrom of hopes and fears, not to appreciate the stimulus that comes with participant action in "explosive" time'.[26] These events then also gave rise to the 'insecurities of a

---

[22] Anson Rabinbach, 'Unclaimed Heritage: Ernst Bloch's Heritage of our Times and the Theory of Fascism', *New German Critique* 11 (1977), p. 7.
[23] David Harvey, *The Condition of Postmodernity. An Enquiry into the Origins of Cultural Change* (Cambridge: Blackwell 1989), p. 203.
[24] Harvey, *The Condition of Postmodernity*, p. 205.
[25] Harvey, *The Condition of Postmodernity*, p. 260.
[26] Harvey, *The Condition of Postmodernity*, p. 261.

shifting relative space in which events in one place could have immediate and ramifying effects in several other places'.[27] Even though Germany was a late colonial power, much of nineteenth-century German literature responded to the experience of rapacious capitalist expansion and historical acceleration. The stellar rise of the nineteenth-century *Dorfgeschichte* [the rural story], is a case in point. Berthold Auerbach's popular *Schwarzwälder Dorfgeschichten* [*Black Forest Village Stories*, 1843–1854] seemingly offered idyllic visions of rural life in the Black Forest that were, however, imbued with deep-seated anxiety that this world was in jeopardy or, indeed, already lost. Auerbach's stories could be read as the literary articulation of the contemporaneity of the non-contemporaneous, the unmooring of *Heimat* and of placed identity in a rapidly accelerating world.

In his later work Harvey then asked how globalization affects the contemporary experience of time and space. Rather than declaring the victory of time over space, Harvey argues that, under the conditions of a global market, the uniqueness of local time and local space matters ever more. The dissolution of spatial barriers in the global era results precisely in the emphatic reaffirmation of temporalized local place within the space of the global. Local food production, the revival or invention of local traditions and the focus on local politics are prominent trends that underline 'the search for secure moorings in a shifting world'.[28] Harvey sees such an investment in a place-bound identity that is anchored in tradition as an understandable reaction against globalization. However, these kinds of initiative run the risk of becoming 'a part of the very fragmentation which a mobile capitalism and flexible accumulation can feed upon'.[29] He thus makes the case for a theory of uneven geographical development that is capable of taking account of 'the different ways in which different social groups have materially embedded their modes of sociality into the web of life, understood as an evolving socio-ecological system'.[30] The rich metaphor of the 'web of life' evokes the idea of inhabited places as sites of diverse social, symbolic and temporal practices.

So how do these three interconnected notions of the non-contemporaneity of the contemporaneous, of uneven geographical development and of the connected asynchronicity of network society advance transnational studies? In the first instance, these ideas complicate simplistic notions of real time connectivity and simultaneity that feed into the idea of a uniform global

[27] Harvey, *The Condition of Postmodernity*, p. 261.
[28] Harvey, *The Condition of Postmodernity*, p. 302.
[29] Harvey, *The Condition of Postmodernity*, p. 303.
[30] Harvey, *Spaces of Global Capitalism. Towards a Theory of Uneven Geographical Development* (London/New York: Verso, 2006), p. 77.

time. To be sure, by enabling real time, the digital era has divorced time from space: financial split-second transactions now have an immediate global reach that was unthinkable 30 years ago. Likewise, digital communications technologies have made it possible for many (but not all) people worldwide to communicate with one another at any time they choose and at little cost. And yet these digital transactions and mobile communication networks always engender very varied local effects that are inflected by other social categories such as power, gender, race and class. Or, to put it differently: social reality always folds neutral global time back into local timescapes. In daily social life, global time is experienced as socially inflected and uneven local time.

One of the most prominent concerns in the current debate on time is the idea that the digital technologies of network society have detemporalized historical and social time: according to this view, the information age has destroyed meaningful narration by fostering a surface culture of browsing and net surfing that is without direction and anchorage. A prominent proponent of this argument is the Korean philosopher Byung Chul Han, who believes that the internet has atomized temporality by giving birth to 'point time', the directionless and disconnected experience of isolated moments that are no longer integrated into a coherent story about ourselves.[31] The arbitrary links and countless options of the internet, argues Han, have destroyed the very conditions of temporal duration and narration.[32] Network society has relinquished the possibility of meaningful experience by championing the timeless neutrality of information which savagely annihilates memory.[33] But this type of argumentation is steeped in undialectical technological determinism: it reduces social actors to passive recipients of technological developments without any kind of agency. In the words of Jan van Dijk, it downplays our 'daily struggles over the construction and use of these networks, in the role of managers and employees, producers and consumers or governors and citizens'.[34] The sociologist Judy Wajcman similarly observes that '(t)he relationship between technological change and temporality is dialectical, not teleological'.[35] A proponent of STS (Science, Technology & Society Studies), she rightly emphasizes that the design of technology is not simply the outcome

---

[31] Byung-Chul Han, *Duft der Zeit. Ein philosophischer Essay zur Kunst des Verweilens* (Berlin: transcript, 2009), p. 39.
[32] Byung-Chul Han, *Duft der Zeit*, p. 10.
[33] Byung-Chul Han, *Duft der Zeit*, p. 13.
[34] Jan van Dijk, 'The One-Dimensional Network Society of Manuel Castells', *New Media & Society* 1 (1999), pp. 127–38 (p. 135).
[35] Judy Wajcman, *Pressed for Time. The Acceleration of Life in Digital Capitalism* (Chicago, IL/London: The University of Chicago Press, 2015), p. 9.

of indisputable technical imperatives but rather the product of complex social processes that may reflect gender biases, racial inequality, educational gaps and class differences, as well as the unevenness of geography. Society and technology are, as Wajcman puts it, 'mutually constitutive'.[36] The implication here is that transnational studies too requires frames of analysis that can bring into view the social inflection of digital technologies in everyday life: for example, the analysis of the digital connectivity of migrant, refugees and diasporic communities must go beyond the banal and – as previously argued – misleading observation of real time communication at little or no cost. Such celebratory statements overlook the practical difficulties of communication across different time zones and continents, while also failing to recognize widespread experiences of displacement, alienation and separation.

So when we use concepts such as real time or immediacy we need to bear in mind that they are not neutral technical terms but cultural signifiers that promote a particular vision of connected society. As the British sociologist John Tomlinson argues, this new culture of immediacy nurtures the desire for instant gratification by *ostensibly* closing the gap that separates 'now from later, here from elsewhere, desire from its satisfaction'.[37] In so doing this culture of immediacy displaces the values of patience, experience, duration and reflection as long-term processes over time. Of course, this does not mean that this new cult of immediacy has really overcome temporal delays: broadband congestion, long airport security queues, automated answering loops of service providers and the permanent traffic congestion in and around urban centres continue to bog down everyday life in the twenty-first century. Further to these infrastructural blockages, the reality of millions of displaced populations across the globe is marked by long periods of waiting in detention camps or refugee centres: often barred from employment, these displaced people experience the sheer weight of time as their asylum or immigration applications make their way through over-burdened systems.

A brief glance at Jenny Erpenbeck's semi-documentary and award-winning novel *Gehen Ging Gegangen* [*Go, Went, Gone*, 2015] may illustrate this point. The novel deals with a group of male refugees from African countries who have arrived in Germany and made it to Berlin after highly perilous journeys across the Mediterranean. The title of the narrative – the conjugation of the irregular verb *gehen* [to go] – refers firstly to the language classes that the refugees attend. But it also evokes the refugees' shared experience of displacement: they inhabit an insecure space defined by

---

[36] Wajcman, *Pressed for Time*, pp. 31–32.

[37] John Tomlinson, *The Culture of Speed. The Coming of Immediacy* (London: Sage, 2007), p. 74.

temporary accommodation and enforced mobility, as they cannot settle down or work before their cases have been adjudicated. Here migration designates not Braidotti's liberating nomadism but a disabling experience of stagnation. As they are waiting for their asylum claims to be processed the refugees kill time on social media. On the one hand, social media connect them with a network of friends who are also stranded in different parts of Europe; on the other, this only accentuates significant absences. In Erpenbeck's novel real time connectivity is precarious and often interrupted by blockages.

Another striking symptom of our temporal ecology is the pervasive phrase 24/7 ('twentyfourseven'). Again, the term is anything but neutral: it champions a totalitarian world of uninterrupted connectivity and availability that is totally disconnected from context. As Jonathan Crary argues, 24/7 'announces a time without time, a time extracted from any material or identifiable demarcations, a time without sequence or recurrence'.[38]

> It effaces the relevance or value of any respite or variability. Its heralding of the convenience of perpetual access conceals its cancellation of the periodicity that shaped the life of most cultures for several millennia: the diurnal pulse of waking and sleeping and the long alterations between days of work and a day of worship or rest [...].[39]

However, it is important to note that the ubiquity of the term 24/7 disguises opposing social experiences: for example, in the world of global business, continual connectivity often accentuates the rank, authority and power of an individual within a corporate company. For the globally mobile corporate elite, time scarcity can be a valuable asset that accrues considerable symbolic and social capital. In sharp contrast, the increasingly casualized workforce of the so-called 'gig' economy is likely to perceive the imperative of 24/7 connectivity in terms of relentless economic pressure to hold down insecure and underpaid jobs. Zero-hour and short-term contracts and precarious employment without holiday and pension entitlements or sickness benefits create forms of time scarcity that exacerbate economic inequality.[40] 'To be

---

[38] Crary, *24/7*, p. 29. Crary demonstrates that the time regime of 24/7 even invades our sleep by undermining 'distinctions between day and night, between light and dark, and between action and repose' (p. 17).

[39] Crary, *24/7*, pp. 29–30.

[40] On the exponential rise of global inequality see Thomas Picketty, *Capital in the Twenty-First Century*, trans. Arthur Goldhammer (Cambridge, MA: Harvard University Press, 2014).

precariatised,' comments Guy Standing, 'is to be subject to pressures and experiences that lead to a precariat existence, of living in the present, without a secure identity or sense of development achieved through work and lifestyle.'[41] For those who eke out a precarious living, the future is no longer the object of long-term rational planning: it collapses into the experience of never-ending time pressure. Terézia Mora's novel *Der einzige Mann auf dem Kontinent* [*The Only Man on the Continent*, 2009] thematizes the employment practices in the new gig economy. Set in Berlin at the time of the global financial crisis of 2008, it relates seven days in the life of Darius Kopp, an IT specialist who, by the end of the novel, will have lost his job in a global company.[42] Kopp grew up in the GDR and managed the Wende by quickly embracing capitalism as the only functioning economic system. When, at the beginning of the Noughties, the IT company he has worked for is taken over by the globally operating Fidelis Wireless, most of the employees lose their jobs with the exception of Kopp: he ends up as the only sales rep in Europe on a flexible and highly precarious contract. Kopp turns into a glutton who cannot stop consuming because life in the fast lane is unsatisfactory.[43] The inverse image of his overweight body – he rapaciously consumes consumer goods, food and drink – is his wife Flora's emaciated and tired figure. She needs to complement her underpaid work as a translator by part-time waitressing in a Berlin strand bar. The couple's life in contemporary Berlin exemplifies stagnation at top speed.

This brings me to the final trope of this chapter: the idea that we now inhabit an extended present without the future horizon that defined modernity since its inception around 1800. From the early nineteenth century onward, Western society perceived the present by and large in terms of an ever-accelerating passage en route to a brighter future.[44] The Enlightenment period heralded the advent of modern time as the driver of technological

---

[41] Guy Standing, *The Precariat. The New Dangerous Class* (London: Bloomsbury, 2014), p. 28.

[42] Terézia Mora, *Der einzige Mann auf dem Kontinent. Roman* (Munich: Luchterhand, 2009).

[43] See also Mary Cosgrove, 'The Time of Sloth in Terézia Mora's *Der einzige Mann auf dem Kontinent*', special issue: *The Longing for Time: Ästhetische Eigenzeit in Contemporary Film, Literature and Art*, ed. by Anne Fuchs and Ines Detmers. *Oxford German Studies* 46.4 (2017), pp. 374–87.

[44] On the time in modernity see Anne Fuchs and Jonathan J. Long (eds.), *Time in German Literature and Culture 1900–2015* (Houndmills/Basingstoke: Palgrave Macmillan, 2016); Dirk Göttsche (ed.), *Critical Time in Modern German Literature and Culture* (Oxford/Berne/Frankfurt: Peter Lang, 2016); Anne Fuchs, *Precarious Times: Temporality and History in Modern German Culture* (Ithaca and London: Cornell University Press, 2019).

and economic modernization. By advocating processes of rationalization, the modern time regime pushed the older models of cyclical or liturgical time into the background in favour of a linear conception of past, present and future. Modern time happened in the fast lane of a present that left the past behind to reach into a new and better future.[45] Once the difference between the past, the present and the future was brought into view, the future became the horizon of urgent human planning and action.

However, there is widespread consensus that, by the end of the twentieth century, the future had lost its shiny gloss: environmental degradation – along with the resulting ecological disasters and large-scale displacement of human populations – ongoing warfare in the Middle East and global terrorism are crises that cast doubt on the human ability to realize a better future. No longer the projection screen for opposing teleological narratives, at the beginning of the twenty-first century the future appears as radically menacing and foreshortened. The literary critic Hans-Ulrich Gumbrecht glumly observes that the only horizon of expectation left to humanity is that of the end of all times.[46] For Gumbrecht the lack of an open future turns the present into a past that is made up of the totality of missed final chances.[47] This broad present is not only closed off from the future as an open horizon but it is also flooded by pasts that we can no longer shed in our hyper-mediated world. Gumbrecht's dystopian perspective is echoed up to a point by the French historian François Hartog, who has coined the term 'presentism' for the experience of an omnivorous present that has taken the place of authentic historical time.[48] Like Gumbrecht, Hartog diagnoses a profound crisis of historicity which, in his view, finds expression in the current memory boom. According to Hartog, our memory culture merely reacts to the disappearance of the open future by transmuting memory into a 'theological category'.[49] Our presentism is so deeply pathological because it destroys our historical relatedness to both the past and the future: in Hartog's words, presentism is a 'monstrous time'.[50] Aleida Assmann too foregrounds

---

[45] Reinhart Koselleck, 'Time and History,' in *The Practice of Conceptual History. Timing History, Spacing Concepts*, trans. Todd Samuel Presner, foreword by Hayden White (Stanford: Stanford University Press, 2002), p. 113.

[46] Hans Ulrich Gumbrecht, *Präsenz*, ed. with an afterword by Jürgen Klein (Frankfurt a. Main: Suhrkamp, 2012), p. 42. See also Hans Ulrich Gumbrecht, *Unsere breite Gegenwart* (Frankfurt a. Main: Suhrkamp, 2010).

[47] Gumbrecht, *Präsenz*, p. 17.

[48] François Hartog, *Regimes of Historicity. Presentism and The Experiences of Time*, trans. Saskia Brown (New York: Columbia University Press, 2015), p. xviii.

[49] Hartog, *Regimes of Historicity*, p. 7.

[50] Hartog, *Regimes of Historicity*, p. 203.

a fundamental reconfiguration of our relationship to past, present and future: she argues that the time regime of modernity ended in the 1980s against the backdrop of the extreme violence of twentieth-century history and in the context of emerging ecological threats.[51] But Assmann evaluates the disappearance of modern time in a very different light: even though the future as a horizon of ideological investment has collapsed, the present remains a site where social actors manage to construct and synthesize their experiences of time.[52] Instead of Hartog's and Gumbrecht's alarmist register, she adopts a constructivist perspective that emphasizes human agency in the construction of time. Seen from this perspective, time is always lived, remembered and projected through specific cultural frames that reflect gender, class, age, race and power relations. In sharp contrast, Gumbrecht's and Hartog's respective analyses of the extended present reflect intellectual preoccupations at a remove from the lives of millions of refugees, migrants and precarized workers who experience the lack of a future in very concrete terms. In the last analysis, this discussion shows that the terms of the debate need to be explored, refined and tested with reference to the fractured and entangled timescapes that social actors traverse in their daily lives.

Conclusion

Since the postwar period, the humanities and social sciences have undergone massive epistemological shifts as manifest in the proclamation of countless turns: my own career has spanned the linguistic turn, the cultural turn, the memory turn, the trans/gender turn, the spatial turn, the poststructuralist turn, the postcolonial turn, the temporal turn, the affective turn, the digital turn and – last but not least – the transnational turn, to name but a few. Turns are strategic instruments that trumpet a break with previous methodologies and an epistemological reorientation of an entire field of enquiry. Turns promise to make visible tacit assumptions, correct research biases and uncover neglected areas of research. They often justify new funding calls and initiatives, and produce new generations of specialists who compete over scarce resources and positions. Turns always produce a body of theory legitimizing what we do and how we do it. In so doing they paradoxically produce new orthodoxies and blind spots that require new interventions from outside the field. My chapter has argued that the prescriptive optimism associated with transnational studies as discussed

---

[51] Aleida Assmann, *Ist die Zeit aus den Fugen? Aufstieg und Fall des Zeitregimes der Moderne* (Munich: Hanser 2013), p. 18.

[52] Assmann, *Ist die Zeit aus den Fugen?* p. 273.

in the opening section requires a temporal corrective: by reconnecting the debate on transnational mobility in the twenty-first century with the crises of time as sketched in broad brushstrokes, the field will be able to illuminate and critique the rapid growth of inequality as a major challenge of our transnational era.

Suggestions for Further Reading

Assmann, Aleida, 'Transnational Memories', *European Review* 22.4 (2014), pp. 546–56.

Errl, Astrid, 'Travelling Memory', *Parallax* 17.4 (2011), pp. 4–18.

Feindt, Gregor, Felix Krawatzek, Daniela Mehler, Freidmann Pestel and Rieke Trimçev, 'Entangled Memory: Toward a Third Wave in Memory Studies', *History and Theory* 53.1 (2014), pp. 24–44.

Fuchs, Anne, *Precarious Times: Temporality and History in Modern German Culture* (Ithaca and London: Cornell University Press, 2019), 322 pp.

Hodkinson, James, and Benedict Schofield, *German in the World: The Transnational and Global Contexts of German Studies* (New York: Boydell & Brewer, 2020), 284 pp.

Pettersen, Anders, 'Transcultural Literary History: Beyond Constricting Notions of World Literature', *New Literary History* 39.3 (2008), pp. 463–79.

Rosendahl Thomsen, Mads, *Mapping World Literature: International Canonization and Transnational Literatures* (London: Continuum, 2008), 177 pp.

Vertovec, Steven, *Transnationalism* (London: Routledge, 2009), 216 pp.

10

Transnationalizing Faith

Re-imagining Islam in German Culture

James Hodkinson

Re-imagining East–West Relationships through German Culture

In a quiet corner of the *Beethovenplatz* in Weimar, Germany, stands the 'Hafis-Goethe Denkmal' – the Hafez-Goethe Monument. Unveiled in 2001, it was the work of two sculptors, Ernst Thevis and Fabian Rabsch, and takes the form of two large chairs made out of stone and set to face each other, as if to imply an encounter or meeting of sorts (Fig. 15). Who or what, though, is involved in this meeting? The monument's name implies an imaginary encounter between two figures of world literature – the German poet and intellectual Johann Wolfgang von Goethe (1749–1832) and the fourteenth-century Persian poet Hafez of Shiraz (1325–1390), who lived centuries apart and can never in reality have met. In representing this fictitious encounter, though, the monument does not depict the two poets literally. In a city bristling with statues of important literary figures, especially Goethe, the chairs remain empty. In this way the monument arguably also represents a wider series of encounters: Islam, the Orient, Persia, are shown to meet the occident, Germany and Christianity, across time and space.

What, though, do the chairs have to say in qualitative terms about East–West encounters? The monument might seem to imply that the two cultures are fundamentally separate and different, with each chair representing one of the two. Yet closer attention to the form of the monument and the materials used in its construction imply a less binary reading. Both chairs are situated atop a stone plinth sporting embossed bronze arabesque patterns that connect them physically. And, while the two 'seats', those surfaces of each chair that face the other, are chiselled smooth and show clear lines of definition, the rear surface of each chair has, by contrast, been left rough, almost untreated

Fig. 15. The 'Hafis-Goethe Denkmal' – the Hafez-Goethe Monument, Weimar, Germany. Photo by the author.

in a way that implies some kind of natural state. The chairs' hard edges can be imagined to interlock and thus to re-establish some kind of broken organic whole. In fact, the chairs are identifiably made not only of the same *type* of stone but of the same *piece* of stone.

The plinth also has set into it three plaques, each bearing embossed bronze inscriptions of verses taken from the two poets' works, including two stanzas in German from Goethe and a verse from Hafez in the original Persian script (Figs. 16, 17 and 18). However, the stanzas by Goethe, one of which is taken from his collection of poems that inspired the monument, the *West-östlicher Divan* (1819), flank both ends of the plinth, whilst the *ghazal* by Hafez is set between the chairs: neither culture and neither poet is associated exclusively with one position or one particular chair. Finally, neither of the quotations simply proclaim the merits of their own culture, but each explores images and ideas of openness, connection and interaction with the other.[1] According to

---

[1] The ghazal (Fig. 18), no. 413 from the *Divan* of Hafez, asserts that it was not through force that the ruler's throne was built, though (by implication) through love, and yearns to see what 'magic' experiences will unfold from gazing into the eyes of a friend. The other stanza by Goethe reads: 'Wer sich selbst und andere kennt,/ Wird auch hier erkennen:/ Orient und Okzident/ Sind nicht mehr zu trennen.' It contains categories common to discussion of Orientalism, 'Orient' and 'Occident', 'self' and 'other', yet speaks of connections between these pairings that cannot be severed.

Re-imagining Islam in German Culture 195

WER SICH SELBST UND ANDRE KENNT
WIRD AUCH HIER ERKENNEN
ORIENT UND OKZIDENT
SIND NICHT MEHR ZU TRENNEN

Figs. 16, 17 and 18. Bronze inscription in the plinth of the Hafez-Goethe Monument, Weimar, Germany. Photos by the author.

the monument there is, it appears, as much connecting the chairs, the poets and their cultures as there is dividing them.

At the most basic level the common materials used to build the chairs imply a fundamental unity of the human species: just as both are of one stone, so humanity is united by a shared biological heritage. The chairs can also refer to more specific cultural historical connections, reinforcing the idea that Christianity and Islam are connected in as many ways as they are distinct. For all of their crucial and significant differences, Christianity, Islam and Judaism form the family of Abrahamic faiths and, as such, share many key tenants of belief and moral codes, transmitted through a shared prophetic heritage and embodied in connected scriptural and oral traditions.[2]

Most significant for this chapter, though, is the fact that the monument also represents a particularly nuanced model of how distinct cultures encounter each other. On the one hand, that model preserves the *distinctiveness* of the cultures involved, recognizing their mutual *differences* at the point of encounter while simultaneously preserving, on the other hand, a sense of those characteristics and traditions they have in *common*. This chapter will seek to trace this paradigm, referred to in the following as the *similarity* of cultures, showing how certain German writers of the late eighteenth and early nineteenth centuries began to represent the relationship between the Islamic and non-Islamic worlds in terms of various forms of 'similarity'.[3] Two key literary works from the period will be considered: first, the literary work that gave rise to the monument considered above, Goethe's *West-östlicher Divan* [*West-eastern Divan*, 1819], where the goal is to reinvest insights from the discussion of similarity back into the work itself and use it as a tool for close reading; and, second, G.E Lessing's earlier Enlightenment drama of religious tolerance *Nathan der Weise* [*Nathan the Wise*, 1779], which will be subjected to the same scrutiny. Throughout, similarity is recognized as an emerging paradigm in scholarship and an alternative to more established academic methods that have insistently looked at how Western literature has reduced Islam, Judaism and Oriental cultures generally to its 'other'. The discussion will also explore carefully the limitations of similarity, however, showing how, in the hands of both writers and readers, the concept can become ambivalent and, at times, deeply problematic.

---

[2] Much contemporary interfaith dialogue stresses the commonalities between the faiths, although in theology scepticism about grouping the religions together can be found: Adam Dodds, 'The Abrahamic Faiths? Continuity and Discontinuity in Christian and Islamic Doctrine', *Evangelical Quarterly* 81.3 (2009), pp. 230–53.

[3] Anil Bhatti and Dorothee Kimmich (eds.), *Ähnlichkeit: ein kulturtheoretisches Paradigma* (Konstanz: University of Konstanz Press, 2015).

From Critical Binaries to Ambivalent Similarities

Through the latter half of the twentieth century 'postcolonial' scholarship sought to illuminate the ethical shortcomings, cultural prejudices and imbalanced power relations of European colonialism, documenting histories of the trauma, oppression, misrepresentation and exclusion of colonized peoples. Within this context the figure of Edward Said played a pivotal and specific role, and his first major work, *Orientalism* (1978), is directly germane to this discussion.[4] Said discerned practices of exercising soft cultural power within European literature, art and scholarship, which went in tandem with the politics, militarism and economics of chiefly French and British colonialism in North Africa, the Middle East and Asia. These Orientalist practices amounted to the oft-cited 'othering' of Oriental peoples and cultures, which involved their reductive representation as the binary opposite of European culture and values: where Europe was presented as active, rational, progressive and civilized, the Orient was passive, childishly irrational and in need of civilization or modernization. While, on occasion, the Orient could be positively inflected, according to Said, representing long-lost origins or longed-for exotic locales, it remained outside of and different from European culture, served to undergird Europe's sense of its own cultural supremacy and legitimized its 'civilizing mission' in Africa and Asia.[5]

Said's model has limited application for German culture. Although the only two German writers he examines in any depth, Goethe and the Romantic polymath Friedrich Schlegel (1772–1829), both wrote in the period before German Empire and colonialism, Said does not explore the possibility that their work and German culture generally might reflect different modalities of engagement with the Orient in the period.[6] Alternative approaches have been forthcoming, however.[7] Todd Kontje, for instance, does not lose sight of the fact that German writers produced literary Orients that were effectively 'imaginaries' facilitating reflection on nascent German nationhood,

---

[4] Edward Said, *Orientalism* (London: Penguin, 2003).

[5] See Said, *Orientalism*, pp. 1–28.

[6] See Said's brief treatment of Goethe's *Divan*, *Orientalism*, pp. 167–68.

[7] Responses to Said did not really emerge in German until the mid 1990s, with Nina Berman, *Orientalismus, Kolonialismus und Moderne: Zum Bild des Orients in der deutschsprachigen Kultur um 1900* (Stuttgart: Verlag für Wissenschaft und Forschung, 1996). The early twenty-first century saw a growth in interest, as seen in such works as Debra Prager, *Orienting the Self. The German Literary Encounter with the Eastern Other* (Rochester, NY: Camden House, 2014) and Suzanne Marchand, *German Orientalism in the Age of Empire: Religion, Race and Scholarship* (Cambridge: Cambridge University Press, 2009).

but builds a strong case for reading some German writing as an attempt to resist the 'ideological straightjacketing' of earlier binary models and explores less antagonistic models of German–Oriental encounter.[8] Andrea Polaschegg sought to disentangle what she saw as two separate drives at the heart of the orientalizing process – the drive to 'know' the Orient as an object of hermeneutic endeavour and the drive to co-opt the Oriental to function within processes of European identity formation.[9] These analogous though distinct drives require different conceptual terms, with the former, the drive to know, operating in terms of Oriental culture's relative familiarity ('das Vertraute') and unfamiliarity ('das Fremde') to the European subject, and the latter operating in terms of a sliding scale between 'selfhood' ('das Selbst') and the other ('das Andere') and marked by instances of 'Grenzziehung' – acts of demarcation by which the European writing subject associates and disassociates itself from the Oriental. With this multiaxial framework Polaschegg began to produce multi-layered, less binary and less 'either–or' readings of key German writing on the Orient.[10]

The simple, illuminating, flexible and yet not unproblematic paradigm of cultural *similarity* can be seen as a continuation of this conceptual debate. Similarity has been explored most revealingly by Germanists Anil Bhatti and Dorothea Kimmich. According to Bhatti, similarity should not be misunderstood as the 'harmonisation' or 'levelling out of differences', but as a category that holds onto cultural concepts such as 'identity' and 'difference,' 'proximity' and 'distance', and moves beyond them without breaking with them entirely.[11] It can serve to describe mutually distinct cultural phenomena in terms of how they defy stringently binary categories and rather inhabit the figurative space of the German phrase 'sowohl als auch' [both this and that].[12] Yet similarity remains an ambivalent concept. Kimmich shows how the idea continues to divide scholars owing to its 'fuzzy' qualities – that is, its apparent evasion of philosophically precise language, its radically 'contingent' nature or wholesale dependence upon context for meaning and, thus, its ideologically 'slippery' quality. This latter becomes evident in its apparent applicability to experiences and phenomena such as 'Selbstverlust, Anpassungsdruck und Assimilation', the loss of individual identity and the

---

[8] Todd Kontje, *German Orientalisms* (Ann Arbor: University of Michigan Press, 2004), pp. 1–14 (p. 9).

[9] Andrea Polaschegg, *Der andere Orientalismus. Regeln deutsch-morgenländischer Imagination im 19. Jahrhundert* (Berlin: de Gruyter, 2004).

[10] Polaschegg, *Der andere Orientalismus*, pp. 39–59.

[11] Bhatti and Kimmich, *Ähnlichkeit*, p. 15.

[12] Bhatti and Kimmich, *Ähnlichkeit*, p. 9.

pressure to 'fit in' and to assimilate, rather than integrate, so often viewed as negative in cultural theory.[13]

So, while the term appears an apt concept for discussing our chosen texts, with many of them referring explicitly to the adjective 'ähnlich' or the noun 'Ähnlichkeit' in their representations of German–Oriental encounters, we must proceed with caution. If Lessing and Goethe seek to write themselves free of stark, black-and-white models of Occident and Orient, Christianity, Islam and indeed Judaism, then we must also ask critically how similarity functions in their texts – be it as an explicitly framed concept or as a subtler tendency, and as a progressive notion or a problematic pull towards cultural homogeneity.

Experiments in Similarity in Goethe's *Divan*

Goethe poured much of the knowledge he had amassed on Oriental language and culture into the poems of his *Divan*.[14] The *Divan* is no mere pastiche of Persian verse, however. Rather, Goethe seems to wish to suspend the idea that the collection belongs exclusively to either of the worlds it touches – medieval Persia and nineteenth-century Germany.[15] Many formal aspects of the collection bear testimony to this. The term 'Divan' is a Germanic rendering of the Persian '*divân*', referring traditionally to a collection of a poet's shorter verses. Goethe's *Divan* is such a collection, arranged into 12 books separated by thematic foci and matters of style. The first edition of the collection came with a frontispiece in which the left leaf bore a message in Arabic introducing Goethe and his collection to an Oriental audience, while the second page displays the author's name and publishing details typical of any book in German. The poems are, of course, written in Goethe's native German. They are accompanied, too, by a series of 'Noten und Abhandlungen' ['Notes and Essays', 1819] designed to provide historical facts about and explanations of Persian and Arabic culture and Islam generally to a largely uninformed nineteenth-century German-speaking readership. Despite its obvious status as a great work of German

---

[13] Bhatti and Kimmich, *Ähnlichkeit*, pp. 10–14.

[14] Katharine Mommsen, *Goethe and the Poets of Arabia*, trans. Michael M. Metzger (Rochester, NY: Camden House, 2014).

[15] Goethe describes this as a state of 'hovering between two worlds' ('zwischen zwei Welten schwebend) in a letter to Zelter of May 1820. Cited in Johann Wolfgang Goethe, *West-östlicher Divan. Studienausgabe*, ed. by Michael Knaupp (Stuttgart: Reclam, 1999), p. 622. On this see also Anil Bhatti, '"…zwischen zwei Welten schwebend …". Zu Goethes Fremdheitsexperiment im *West-östlichen Divan*' http://www.goethezeitportal.de/fileadmin/PDF/kk/df/postkoloniale-studien/bhatti_divan.pdf [accessed 17 November 2019].

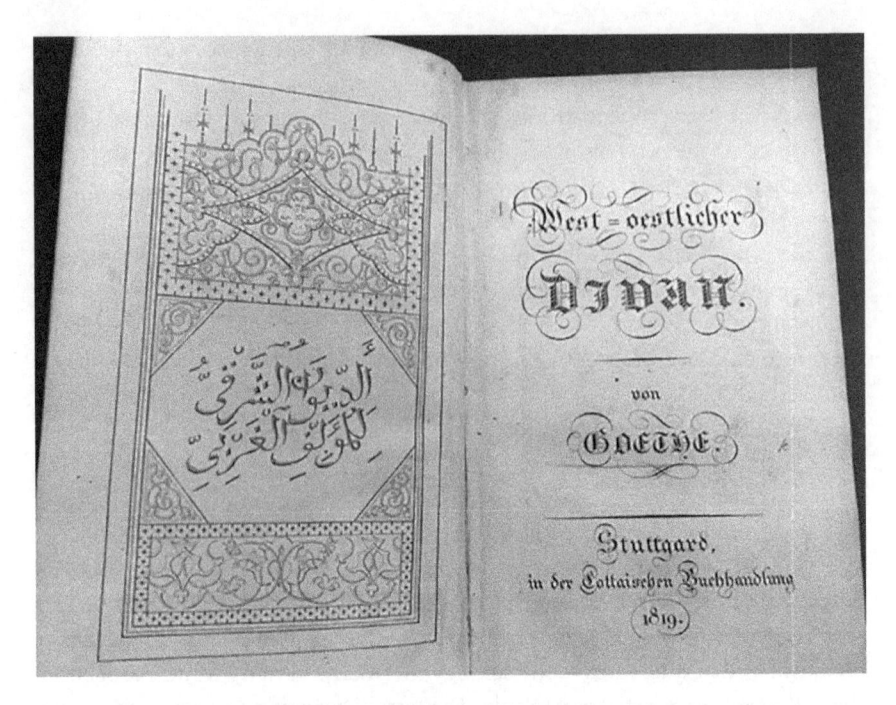

Fig. 19. Frontispiece of first edition of the *Divan* (Stuttgart, 1819).
Photo by the author.

literature, then, as published artefacts the various editions of the *Divan* appeal to a position between two cultures and in some sense reflect elements of both.

For Andrea Polaschegg the collection reflects two different strategic approaches to the Orient on Goethe's part. One the one hand, Goethe addresses and informs his readers so that they might understand his many Oriental allusions. In the 'Notes' Goethe positions himself as a European subject who wishes to mediate the Orient as the object of scholarly knowledge. Secondly, though, the lyrical voice of the poems is seen to undertake a fictional journey directly 'into' the Orient. Here, though, the fictional Orient is no naive fairy-tale alternative to the Occident. This journey is both temporal and spatial, and its destination is a fictional Oriental 'Zeit-Raum', a constructed time-place in which the specifics of cultural and linguistic difference are left behind. The Orient, in this form, can be experienced directly and as a realm of connection and continuity. For Polaschegg, these two strategies coexist and allow Goethe to communicate to his audience aspects of the Orient as known 'other', but also mark his attempt to move beyond the limitations of hermeneutic knowledge. The collection thus treats the Orient in terms of its cultural distinctiveness while simultaneously exploring it from within, through a form of experimental, fictional participation that sidesteps the hermeneutic drive to know and also overcomes difference.[16]

In the collection's opening verse, entitled 'Hegira', for instance, the lyrical voice reflects on its own experiences, exhorting itself to undertake a flight to the East:

> North and South and West
> Thrones are shattered, empires shaking;
> Flee, now, to the purer East
> On patriarchal air to feast:
> Amidst the loving, drinking singing
> Youth from Khiser's well is springing.[17]

Depicted here are not the serene chairs of the monument in Weimar but the shattered thrones and shuddering kingdoms involved in the Napoleonic Wars (1809–1815) that preceded the writing of the collection. Goethe's 'flight' then refers both to his drive to flee the literal destruction, conflict and intellectual poverty of modern Europe and his figurative desire to seek the stability and wisdom he saw as represented by the historical Orient.[18] The lyrical voice longs to breathe the air of the 'purer East' and seeks rejuvenation for itself at the fountain of Al-Khidr's (Khiser) – a figure in the Koran associated with the perennial life of nature. This imagery smacks, one might think, of a fantasy of returning to human origins in the cradle of the Orient and thus of the exoticized form of Orientalism constantly criticized by Edward Said. Things, though, are arguably more complex.

By giving his poem its title, Goethe likens his own flight to the East to that of the Prophet Mohammed, who undertook his hegira to Medina in AD 622. On one level, this naming of the poem begins a pattern within the *Divan* by which Goethe 'participates' in an apparently historical Islamic world. Goethe's poems do not, though, express the simple desire to inhabit the past. The poem alludes both to the Islamic past and to Germany's present: just as the prophetic hegira was both a flight and the beginning of a new historical

---

[16] Polaschegg, *Der andere Orientalismus*, pp. 293–97.

[17] See J. Whaley (trans.), *Goethe's West-Eastern Divan/ West-östlicher Divan, rendered into English by J. Whaley* (London: Oswald Wolff, 1974). Cf. the original: 'Nord und West und Süd zersplittern,/ Throne bersten, Reiche zittern,/ Flüchte du, im reinen Osten/ Patriarchenluft zu kosten,/ Unter Lieben, Trinken, Singen,/ Soll dich Chisers Quell verjüngen' in Johann Wolfgang Goethe, *Sämtliche Werke, Briefe, Tagebücher und Gespräche*, ed. by Hendrik Birus (Frankfurt am Main, 1987 ff), 3.1, p. 12.

[18] Mommsen, *Goethe and the Poets of Arabia*, p. 33.

period for Mohammed and his followers, so the hegira of the *Divan*, too, marks both a flight and a new beginning – one that seeks to renew Germany and Europe through its fictional experience of the Orient. This fictional version of the Orient is thus so overtly trans-historical and multi-temporal – encompassing episodes from the Prophet's life reimagined explicitly as the experiences of a nineteenth-century German, imagined meetings with Koranic figures and glimpses at the fourteenth-century Persia of Hafez – that no stable sense of place or time is established. The product is, rather, a self-reflexive fiction of Orient, one that announces its own fictional status and serves as an experimental literary space for exploring more fluid Occidental–Oriental relationships.[19]

Elsewhere in the *Divan* the lyrical voice exploits the new possibilities offered by this fictional Orient. The lyrical voice's own relationship with the figure of Hafez is cast and recast. In the first poem of 'Hafis Nameh' ['The Book of Hafez'] the lyrical voice, presented as a German poet, engages in a fictional dialogue with Hafez, calling upon him to explain the relevance of the epithet by which he is known (Hafez referring to one who has memorized the Koran). Having configured himself, albeit rhetorically, as a stranger ignorant of the life of Hafez, the 'Dichter' pulls closer to his Persian counterpart, addressing him directly:

> For if we share another's mind
> We shall be the other's equal
> You I'll mirror to perfection
> I who am myself endowed
> With our scared book's reflection
> Like as on that holy shroud
> Our Lord's image was impressed:
> Quickening secret in my breast
> Conquering sceptic, foe, or thief,
> Radiant vision of belief.[20]

---

[19] See also Hamid Tafazoli, '*Heterotopie als Entwurf poetischer Raumgestaltung*', in *External Space – Co-Space – Internal Space. Heterotopia in Culture and Society*, ed. by Hamid Tafazoli and Richard T. Gray (Bielefeld: Aisthesis: 2012), pp. 35–59.

[20] Translation from Whaley, *West-Eastern Divan*, pp. 28–31. Also see the original: 'Denn wenn wir wie andre meinen,/ Werden wir den andern gleichen./ Und so gleich ich dir vollkommen,/ Der ich unsrer heil'gen Bücher/ Herrlich Bild an mich genommen,/ Wie auf jenes Tuch der Tücher/ Sich des Herren Bildnis drückte/ Mich in stiller Brust erquickte,/ Trotz Verneinung, Hindrung, Raubens,/ Mit dem heitern Bild des Glaubens', Goethe, *Sämtliche Werke*, 3.1, p. 28.

Re-imagining Islam in German Culture   203

The poet's desire to resemble Hafez perfectly here does not, though, express a drive to self-negation. The poet persona wishes to become the equivalent of Hafez within his own tradition, carrying with him the spiritual imprint of the Bible in the manner that the Shroud of Turin was said to carry the likeness of Christ's face. In the section entitled 'Unbegrenzt' [Unlimited] within the 'Book of Hafez', the relationship morphs again, and the two poets are no longer mere companions or even kindred spirits. The poet imagines his own fate as so intertwined with that of Hafez that the pair are effectively twins, locked in benign fraternal competition:

> And let the world entirely sink
> Hafez, with you or else with none
> I will compete! Let joy and pain
> Be ours, as twins in common![21]

The fluidity of the fictional relationship between Hafez and the lyrical voice is mirrored in the voice's relationship to Islam generally. In 'Hikmet Nameh' ['The Book of Maxims'], the lyrical voice criticizes those who adhere only to their own beliefs thus:

> Stupid, that each his own special opinion
> Praises as though his case be odd!
> If Islam means submission to God
> We all live and die in Islam's dominion.[22]

The grounds for this criticism is that, according to this stanza, we all live and die within Islam. This deliberately hyperbolic statement plays off the fact that the name 'Islam' is derived from the Arabic verb to submit, where submission refers to the surrender of the self to God's will. Arguably many religions, and certainly the Abrahamic faiths, have this in common, so the poetic voice does not call upon readers literally to become Muslims, but implies that they might think of their own faith in terms of the doctrinal elements it shares

---

[21] Translation from Whaley, *West-Eastern Divan*, pp. 34–35. For the original see 'Und mag die ganze Welt versinken,/ Hafis mit dir, mit dir allein/ Will ich wetteifern! Lust und Pein/ Sei uns, den Zwillingen, gemein!' Goethe, *Sämtliche Werke*, 3.1, p. 32.

[22] Translation from Whaley, *West-Eastern Divan*, pp. 102–03. Cf. the original 'Närrisch, daß jeder in seinem Falle?/ Seine besondere Meinung preist!/ Wenn *Islam* Gott ergeben heißt,/ In Islam leben und sterben wir alle.' Goethe, *Sämtliche Werke*, 3.1, p. 65.

with Islam, drawing itself and an implied readership into an idealistic notion of cross-faith identity.

Elsewhere in the collection the poetic voice speaks as if from a Muslim perspective. In a well-known poem that was never published in the *Divan* but belongs to its paralipomena, 'Süsses Kind, die Perlenreihen' ['Sweetest Child, a pearly row'],[23] the lyrical voice pronounces on the common origins of the Abrahamic faiths, describing how the succession of Abrahamic prophets, including Moses and Jesus, had been united in their experience of one true God.[24] In doing so, however, the poet effectively echoes the Prophet Mohammed's vision of Islam as the restoration of a pure monotheistic faith to supersede Judaism and Christianity. Furthermore, when addressing Suleika, an adored female subject in many *Divan* poems, the poetic voice shows hostility to the 'Zeichen' [sign] of the crucifix she wears, echoing the Islamic dislike of the symbol and the underlying disavowal of Christ as the son of God. However, the voice relents, saying that it will, for the love of Suleika, take on the 'Renegatenbürde', the burdensome role of infidelity to his own faith, by accepting her wearing of the cross.[25] The 'Notes' also contain successive references to and instruction on the Islamic project of restoring 'true' monotheism to the world.[26] On such occasions Goethe-as-commentator writes from a more conventionally German locus to address and inform a German readership about the doctrine of a faith different to their own.

The collection, then, shifts position vis-à-vis Islam. Goethe as author–commentator informs his readership about Islam in his 'Notes', though he also has his lyrical voice speak poetically, through parable and allegory, on Islamic doctrine. That poetic voice also participates in a construction of the Orient that both stands for the historical Orient in itself, though one that also functions as an idealized nexus facilitating cross-cultural, perspectival shifting, and allows the poet to inhabit, at times, an imaginary Muslim persona. From that position the poet explores aspects of belief shared by people of all the Abrahamic faiths, doing so through reference to aspects of specifically Islamic doctrine. At the same time, though, he also moves

---

[23] Mommsen, *Goethe and the Poets of Arabia*, pp. 136–40. Also Goethe, *Sämtliche Werke*, 3.1, pp. 508–10.

[24] Mommsen, Goethe and the *Poets of Arabia*, p. 136. Also Goethe, *Sämtliche Werke*, 3.1, p. 509.

[25] Mommsen, *Poets of Arabia*, p. 138. Also Goethe, *Sämtliche Werke*, 3.1, pp. 509–10. There is also an entire chapter on Goethe's dissent from Islam in Mommsen, *Goethe and the Poets of Arabia*, pp. 174–234.

[26] See Goethe, *Sämtliche Werke*, 3.1, p. 236). See also Mommsen, *Goethe and the Poets of Arabia*, pp. 129–32 (p. 131).

to adopt a position of tolerance towards Christianity and, thus, of religious diversity. It is in this constellation of changing perspectives that Goethe's poems explore forms of cultural similarity, both by communicating the known cultural differences between the Islamic Orient and the West and, simultaneously, by shifting to an imaginary locus from which traditions and doctrines can be re-examined, their mutual differences in turn relativized, dissolved and re-established. The *Divan* has been widely criticized for its exoticism and the fact that Goethe derived much of his information from translations and 'loaded' colonial sources.[27] However loaded those sources may be, the models of cross-cultural encounter in the collection read as many-layered and as attempts to resist starkly polarizing notions of cultural difference.

Faith and Familial Similarity in Lessing's *Nathan the Weise*

G.E. Lessing engaged in religious debates in published essays, private correspondence and literary texts throughout his career, and the comparative theologian Karl-Josef Kuschel has provided a detailed analytical reconstruction.[28] Lessing published on key religious debates within German-speaking Christendom from the 1750s, often striking out against what he saw as the inflexible dogma of orthodox Lutheran theology.[29] He was also well informed on matters of Islam, having cultivated intellectual friendships with leading Orientalists, reading widely in French and English translations of the Koran and writing, again, in defence of the Prophet Mohammed and his followers, countering views of Islam as irrational, praising its 'logical' stance on the topic of miracles, arguing for its compatibility with a model of universal morality and envisioning the possibility of salvation for Muslims in an afterlife.[30] And, of course, he wrote against antisemitism in various forms throughout his life, whether in the early play *Die Juden* [*The Jews*, 1749], which uses the comic tale of a foiled plot and the uncovering of underhand disguises to critique how Christians utilize Jewish stereotypes for their own ends, or in *Nathan*, which had much to do with his interest in the cause of eighteenth-century

---

[27] See Yomb May, 'Goethe, Islam, and the Orient: The Impetus for and Mode of Cultural Encounter in the West-östlicher Divan', in *Encounters with Islam in German Literature and Culture*, ed. by James Hodkinson and Jeffery Morrison (Rochester, NY: Camden House, 2009), pp. 89–107.

[28] Karl-Josef Kuschel, *Vom Streit zum Wettstreit der Religionen. Lessing und die Herausförderung des Islam* (Düsseldorf: Patmos Verlag, 1998).

[29] Kuschel, *Vom Streit zum Wettstreit der Religionen*, pp. 124–56.

[30] Kuschel, *Vom Streit zum Wettstreit der Religionen*, pp. 84–101, 105–24 and 156–65.

Jewish emancipation and his support and admiration for his own friend, the German–Jewish philosopher Moses Mendelssohn (1729–1786), upon whom the figure of Nathan is often thought to be modelled.

Lessing's writing on religion bears the hallmark of the Enlightenment tradition of *tolerance*, and the term, together with its negative inverse, *intolerance*, is strewn throughout his writing[31] (for more on the contemporary significance of Lessing, see Claire Baldwin's discussion in Chapter 15 of this volume). The concept and practice of tolerance is, though, fraught with numerous tensions, including the critical objection that it can be skewed to favour normative values or, more specifically, that members of one community can be seen to tolerate only their own acceptable version of another. Lessing scholars have become critical in their assessment of Lessing's tolerance in this sense. Ritchie Robertson describes what he believes to be a flawed or false idea of tolerance in Lessing's writing, by which members of faiths overcome their mutual prejudices in order to 'tolerate' each other, but do so on the basis of a notion of shared humanity that fails to recognize or respect the importance of religious difference.[32]

The ideal of a universal humanity stretching beyond cultural difference also awakens another tradition with which Lessing's play has been connected – that of *cosmopolitanism*. In its Enlightenment form, cosmopolitanism referred to a core ideal, explored by thinkers and writers in essayistic and literary work in different contexts and disciplines, that tended to conceive of humanity as a substantially unified community, to which ethnic, linguistic and cultural differences were internal.[33] Cosmopolitan thinking and values are seen as an important cornerstone of many eighteenth- and nineteenth-century ethical, philosophical and legal debates. However, many famously cosmopolitan thinkers and writers have been exposed by postcolonial critics as undercutting their own aspirations or simply promulgating racist and hierarchical thinking by presenting European peoples as more capable of reasoned thought than others, and thus as better fulfilling criteria qualifying membership of a nascent world community.[34]

---

[31] See Peter Freimark, Franklin Kopitzsch and Helga Slessnarev (eds.), *Lessing und die Toleranz. Sonderband zum Lessing Yearbook* (Detroit: WSUP; Munich: text + kritik, 1986); also Ritchie Robertson, '"Dies hohe Lied der Duldung"? The Ambiguities of Toleration in Lessing's *Die Juden* and *Nathan der Weise*', *The Modern Language Review* 93.1 (1998), pp. 105–20 (106 and 109); also Adam Sutcliffe, 'Lessing and toleration', in *Lessing and the German Enlightenment*, ed. by Ritchie Robertson (Oxford: Voltaire Foundation, 2013), pp. 205–25.

[32] Robertson, '"Dies hohe Lied der Duldung"', p. 118.

[33] Robert Fine, *Cosmopolitanism* (London/New York: Routledge, 2007), esp. p. x.

[34] For a post-colonial critique of cosmopolitanism see Homi K. Bhabha, 'Unsatisfied:

At the heart of the critical objections to these Enlightenment traditions lies a dissatisfaction with how cultural difference is devalued within ostensibly progressive models of intercultural relationships. If tolerance is to be extended by one culture to another only when the latter culture sufficiently shares the beliefs of the former or, indeed, if one culture insists on defining the standards by which other communities may be included in a model of universal humanity, then cultural differences serve to reinforce hierarchies, or are rejected entirely, and a more problematically normative notion of similarity comes into play. Considering key moments from *Nathan*, then, this chapter will next examine the treatment of religious groupings and the erosion of their mutual prejudices in favour of forms of tolerance, and evaluate critically the apparently cosmopolitan futures on offer, considering in what ways concepts of cultural similarity, however problematic, can be found within the play.

Nathan is set in Jerusalem during the Third Crusade (1189–1192), which saw a failed attempt by European Christian monarchs and their armies to retake the city of Jerusalem following its capture in 1187 by the Muslim forces of Sultan Saladin – known historically as Saladin the Wise (1137–1193). In his play, however, Lessing transfers this epithet to the eponymous central character, a Jewish merchant named Nathan. Nathan's 'wisdom' arguably expresses itself in his ability to recognize and assert the value of tolerance and universal humanity. He schools the incumbent Muslim ruler Saladin in ideals of religious tolerance through his telling of the iconic 'parable of the Ring', and has taken in a Christian orphan girl, Recha, raising her as his own daughter, and maintaining an open and tolerant attitude to the Christian community – especially to one particular Knight Templar, Curd von Stauffen, who had been spared by Saladin following the defeat of the Crusaders and who saves Recha from Nathan's burning house despite his own initially antisemitic views. In a play set in one of the most contested cities on Earth, and at one of the most fraught and violent periods in Christian–Islamic history, Nathan serves as a peacemaker, a mediator and a preacher of human values speaking out against sectarian hatred.

Such hatred, flowing from mutual intolerance and bigotry, abounds in the play. On hearing the 'anonymized' story of a Jew who had adopted a Christian girl and raised her in his own faith, the patriarch, the head of the Christian community in Jerusalem, calls for the Jew to be burned alive in line with papal decrees on apostasy.[35] In speaking, the patriarch is offering

---

Notes on Vernacular Cosmopolitansim', in *Postcolonial Discourses: An Anthology*, ed. by Gregory Castle (Oxford: Blackwell, 2001), pp. 39–52 (esp. p. 41).

[35] All translations are from Stephanie Clennell and Robert Philip (trans.), *Nathan the Wise by Gotthold Emphraim Lessing. Translated from the German Nathan der Weise* (Milton Keynes: Open University Press, 1994), here p. 82. See also the original

advice to the Templar von Stauffen, who is struggling to come to terms with his discovery that Recha is not Nathan's biological daughter but is an adoptee of Christian heritage. Informed of the news by Recha's Christian companion, Daja, his reaction is also negative, referring to her Jewish upbringing as a perversion ('Verlenken') of innately Christian spiritual inclinations that would have otherwise followed 'an altogether different path'.[36] As the action unfolds, though, the Templar appears capable of freeing himself from bigotry and intolerance, confessing to Nathan that he should never have sought advice from the bigoted, villainous patriarch.[37] Indeed, it is only the revelation of Recha as his sister that prevents a full-blown romance from developing between the two, and he ends the play reconciled with Saladin, his uncle, and Nathan.

Although the Muslim ruler Saladdin has spared the Templar's life, he begins the play as an ambivalent figure, having, as Jim Reed reminds us, executed all of von Stauffen's brothers in arms.[38] Yet Saladin's own thinking also evolves beyond binary categories: when Sittah, his sister, condemns Christians for following Christ out of partisan devotion rather than for the ethical content of his teaching, he acknowledges her point, but distinguishes between Christians generally and the militancy of the Knights Templar, with whom he had sought a truce and attempted a treaty.[39] Rather than ask to borrow from Nathan the money that he needs in the third act, he asks for truth about which of the three Abrahamic faiths is the better. Upon being presented with Nathan's parable, he insists that all faiths ought to be distinguishable from each other, citing cultural markers such as diet and clothing: 'I should have thought/ That each of the religions which I named to you/ Were easy to distinguish. Even by/ Their clothing; even down to food and drink', though is forced to follow the conclusion Nathan draws from his own parable, wishing his sister had been privy to this lesson.[40]

---

in Gotthold Ephraim Lessing, *Werke und Briefe. Gesamte Werkausgabe*, 12 vols. in 14, ed. by Wilfried Barner, Klaus Bohnen and others (Frankfurt a.M: Deutscher Klassiker Verlag, 1987 ff), here L, V, p. 578.

[36] Clennell and Philip, *Nathan the Wise*, p. 94. See also Lessing, *Werke und Briefe*, L, IX, p. 571.

[37] Clennell and Philip, *Nathan the Wise*, p. 127. See also Lessing, *Werke und Briefe*, L, IX, p. 610.

[38] T.J. Reed, *Light in Germany. Scenes from an Unknown Enlightenment* (Chicago, IL/London: University of Chicago Press, 2015), pp. 74–76.

[39] Clennell and Philip, *Nathan the Wise*, pp. 47–49. See also Lessing, *Werke und Briefe*, L, IX, pp. 516–18.

[40] See Clennell and Philip, *Nathan the Wise*, p. 82. Cf. the original: 'Ich dächte die Religionen [...] doch wohl zu unterscheiden wären. Bis auf Kleidung, bis auf Speis' und Trank', in Lessing, *Werke und Briefe*, L, IX, p. 557.

Nathan's parable is well known. It tells of a father with three sons, all equally beloved to him. As his life progresses the father struggles to decide which of his sons should inherit his most precious item – a ring that rendered the wearer more beloved of God. His solution is to have two replicas made and to share the three rings out. Over time, the identity of the true ring is lost and, after the father's death, arguments surface as to which ring is the original. Ultimately a judge is called in to arbitrate and suggests that the 'tyranny of the one ring' should be forgotten.[41] Of course, the three rings represent the three Abrahamic faiths, and each son, the judge proposes, should believe in the truth of his own 'ring', effectively entering a form of wager, whereby he prove the truth of his beliefs to the others.[42] The aim of the wager, though, is not for each son to prove the other rings to be fake, but rather to heighten devotion to his own faith, attaining 'deepest of devotion to God'.[43] Devotion to the specifics of one's own faith, teaches the parable, will *also* lead to a *common* experience of unity with and in God and moral improvement for all. In scholarship, the parable has been read in many ways – as the classic Enlightenment proverb calling for tolerance and, more recently, as an allegory of diasporic traditions in which migrant Jewish communities assimilated into local cultures and, at times, necessarily 'hid' their Jewishness.[44] Here, though, it can also be seen as an attempt to place value simultaneously on the specific beliefs and practises of different religions and on the broader ethical goals they appear to share – an approach that frames the three faiths according to our concept of similarity.

Nathan is not the only cultural mediator, however. The figure of Al-Hafi is a Muslim dervish who works as a *de facto* treasurer and intermediary for Saladin. Traditionally played on stage as a comical, bedraggled wanderer, he has come to be seen to as a positive representative of Sufism and the more liberal attitudes towards non-Muslims associated with that form of Islam.[45] In his exchange with Nathan he refers to a community on the river Ganges where he has lived among the 'Ghebern',[46] a community of Zoroastrians, also

---

[41] Clennell and Philip, *Nathan the Wise*, p. 84. See also Lessing, *Werke und Briefe*, L, IX, p. 559.

[42] Clennell and Philip, *Nathan the Wise*, p. 84. See also Lessing, *Werke und Briefe*, L, IX, p. 559.

[43] Clennell and Philip, *Nathan the Wise*, p. 84. See also Lessing, *Werke und Briefe*, L, IX, p. 559.

[44] See Jonathan M. Hess, 'Lessing and German-Jewish culture: a reappraisal', in *Lessing and the German Enlightenment*, ed. by Robertson, pp. 179–204 (p. 187).

[45] See Kuschel, *Vom Streit zum Wetstreit der Religionen*, pp. 231–39.

[46] Clennell and Philip, *Nathan the Wise*, p. 68. See also Lessing, *Werke und Briefe*, L, IX, p. 540.

known as 'Ghebers' or 'Parsees', who fled to India from religious persecution by Muslims.[47] As he leaves the play at the end of the second act, tired of court politics, financial dealings and religious conflict, Al-Hafi invites Nathan to join him on his journey, to live among the Ghebers free of material needs, saying 'On the Ganges, on/ The Ganges only there are human Beings'.[48] Yet is this idyll one that truly tolerates diversity and difference, a cosmopolitan community in which all live as fellow humans without surrendering their heritage? Or does the emphasis placed on humanity imply a community that functions harmoniously only because it overwrites religious and cultural distinctiveness with a generalized vision of collective human identity?

The two moments described here – the parable that seeks to balance precariously a universal ethics against the specifics of faith doctrine, and Al Hafi's cosmopolitan utopia in India in which people are defined more by their humanity than their specific cultural affiliations – both point to a core tension in the text. For all its culturally sensitive ideals, the play seems to veer towards a future peace that flattens out cultural differences and even moves beyond faith *per se*. This tension returns again in the play's famous denouement: the revelation that Recha and Curd are actually twin siblings, offspring of their father Assad, Saladin's (Muslim) brother, and a European Christian mother, though raised separately. Von Stauffen's resemblance to Saladin's brother is mentioned repeatedly throughout, with Daja commenting 'that Saladin has pardoned/ Him because he looks so like one of/ His brothers, one whom he loved dearly'.[49] Explicit references to 'similarity' in the original German text refer here to the literal physical resemblances that often go hand in hand with biological, familial relationships. In seeking to represent a new symbolic human family, Lessing appeals to literal blood ties. Just as the Ganges community downplayed cultural differences, so this new family gestures beyond religious convictions. Notably, though, while Nathan is doubtless involved in the mutual embraces[50] on which the final curtain falls, and which include characters of all faith backgrounds, the newly

---

[47] The threat is perhaps less that Lessing conflates Ghebers and Sufi Muslims, as in Robertson, '"Dies hohe Lied der Duldung"', p. 115, and more that the play appeals to an idealized humanity at the cost of representing faith traditions.

[48] Clennell and Philip, Nathan the Wise, p. 68. See also Lessing, *Werke und Briefe*, L, IX, p. 540.

[49] Clennell and Philip, *Nathan the Wise*, p. 27. See the original German: '[...] dass Saladin den Tempelherrn, Begnadigt, weil er seinem Brüder einem, Den er besonders lieb gehabt, so ähnlich sehe', in Lessing, *Werke und Briefe*, L, IX, p. 493. The sentiment is echoed almost verbatim by Saladin at L, IX, p. 561.

[50] Clennell and Philip, *Nathan the Wise*, p. 142. See also Lessing, *Werke und Briefe*, L, IX, p. 627.

re-established consanguine family, as critics have pointed out, excludes the Jew.

This point in the play can also be seen as the conclusion of a far broader tendency in which none of the major religions are presented, as Robertson and others have noted, in any great detail – certainly in theological terms.[51] In a similar vein, Nicholas Boyle has noted that the characters end up embracing a form of 'agnostic humanism', dedicated to shared ethical values but ambivalent if not indifferent about key tenets of religious belief and observance.[52] The play's main characters, then, become less representative of their respective faiths as they come to resemble each other in their shared humanistic ideals. *Nathan* rightly holds a place as a well-intentioned literary masterpiece of the later Enlightenment, and occupies a place of affection in German cultural history. Yet its idealistic pull towards universal humanity is also a pull away from cultural and religious specificity, and the appeal to genealogical connections arguably threatens the inclusivity and thus the cultural diversity of this model of the wider human family. The drift towards this kind of similarity in the play reminds us that certain groups and traditions can be seen as not similar enough, and thus to belong less.

Conclusion

It was arguably though his work on Goethe's *Divan* that Anil Bhatti's interest in the concept of similarity grew.[53] By constructing shifting relationships between the West and the Islamic Orient, by both communicating with Western readers on Islamic culture and also 'inhabiting' that culture poetically, and by constructing fluid relationships between Islam and other revealed religions and finding commonalities between all while preserving a sense of the distinctiveness of each, Goethe's collection exemplifies a particular model of cross-culturally sensitive similarity. Bhatti's reading of Goethe offers an optimistic vision here – one that might serve to depolarize traditional notions of Occident and Orient, Islam and the West, to illuminate these tendencies in the texts of the past and also provide us with a new critical paradigm as scholars in the present. As we have seen from this chapter, however, different treatments of similarity, be they theoretically pitched or embedded in literary texts, can be more or less sophisticated. They can also contribute to excluding tendencies and end up denying cultural difference and promoting normative

---

[51] Robertson, '"Dies hohe Lied der Duldung"', p. 115.
[52] Nicholas Boyle, *Goethe. The Poet and the Age. Vol 1: The Poetry of Desire* (Oxford: Oxford University Press, 1991), p. 33.
[53] Cf. Bhatti, '... zwischen zwei Welten schwebend ...'.

and hierarchical thinking. This critical insight perhaps informs the final goal of this chapter – namely to remind us as readers of the perhaps obvious, though often forgotten, insight that the conclusions we reach are not simply the results of the conceptual tools we use, but also of how we use them.

Suggestions for Further Reading

Bhatti, Anil, and Dorothee Kimmich (eds.), *Ähnlichkeit: ein kulturtheoretisches Paradigma* (Konstanz: University of Konstanz Press, 2015), 340 pp.

Hodkinson, James, and Jeffrey Morrison (eds.), *Encounters with Islam in German Literature and Culture* (Rochester, NY: Camden House, 2009), 271 pp.

Polaschegg, Andrea, *Der andere Orientalismus. Regeln deutsch-morgenländischer Imagination im 19. Jahrhundert* (Berlin: de Gruyter, 2004), 613 pp.

Robertson, Ritchie, '"Dies hohe Lied der Duldung?" The Ambiguities of Toleration in Lessing's *Die Juden* and *Nathan der Weise*', *The Modern Language Review* 93.1 (1998), pp. 105–20.

Said, Edward, *Orientalism* (London: Penguin, 2003), 396 pp.

11

Transnational Imaginaries

The Place of Palestine in Gershom Scholem, Franz Kafka and Early Cinema

Nicholas Baer

*If I'm never going to leave my bed again,
why shouldn't I travel as far as Palestine?*

– Franz Kafka[1]

The category of the nation is perhaps nowhere more fraught than in the Israeli–Palestinian context, a highly charged force-field of ethno-religious identities, political ideologies and conflicting territorial claims. Overlaid with collective memories and symbolic meanings, the landscape has borne witness to war and imperial conquest, shifting regimes and borders, perpetual occupation and injustice and overlapping yet fundamentally irreconcilable narratives of historical experience.[2] How might one thus envision the relation between the Germanic realm, itself heterogeneous and unstable, and a region as contested and overdetermined as the Middle East? As I will show in the following, cultural formations involving the Holy Land raise enormous conceptual challenges for the study of transnationalism.

A contribution to the growing field of Transnational German Studies, this essay will explore what Edward Said called the 'imaginative geography'[3]

---

[1] Franz Kafka, *Letters to Milena*, ed. by Willi Haas, trans. Tania and James Stern (New York: Schocken, 1953), p. 236.

[2] See Edward W. Said, 'Invention, Memory, and Place', *Critical Inquiry* 26.2 (Winter 2000), pp. 175–92; W.J.T. Mitchell, 'Holy Landscape: Israel, Palestine, and the American Wilderness', *Critical Inquiry* 26.2 (Winter 2000), pp. 193–223; and Judith Butler, *Parting Ways: Jewishness and the Critique of Zionism* (New York: Columbia University Press, 2012), pp. 205–24.

[3] On Said's concept of 'imaginative geography', see his *Orientalism* (New York:

of Palestine among Central European Jews in the early twentieth century. Bringing together multiple prose genres and media, I will consider Gershom Scholem's autobiographical and scholarly writings in tandem with Franz Kafka's parables, letters and diaries, as well as early cinematic productions. My argument is that these works lent expression to the paradoxes of Jewish Messianism, which were tenable so long as the Land of Israel remained a topos, non-localizable space or projected image. The contradictions became unsustainable, however, as Zionism strove to realize the Messianic idea, moving from the 'abstract' to the 'concrete' realm of world history.

The two writers examined in this essay rejected the acculturationist, liberal–bourgeois tendencies of German-speaking Jewry, but also recognized the unavoidable problematics of resettlement in Palestine. A pioneering scholar of Jewish mysticism who made Aliyah in 1923, Scholem quickly became disillusioned with the Zionist movement and theorized the dialectics of Jewish renewal, attributing them to broader tensions between 'restorative' and 'utopian' forces in the Messianic idea. For Scholem, these tensions were given exemplary figuration by Kafka, whose writings postulated the anomalous or even impossible spatiotemporal coordinates of the Messiah's arrival. Unable to visit Palestine before his death in 1924, Kafka nonetheless gained a fleeting vision of the landscape from propaganda films such as Ya'acov Ben-Dov's *Shivat Zion* [*Return to Zion*, 1921], which appealed to incommensurable temporalities in documenting Jewish national revival.

Gershom Scholem and the Dialectics of Jewish Renewal

Galvanizing only a minority of German-speaking Jews, the Zionist movement belonged to a wide array of spiritual renewal efforts in Central Europe following the First World War. Dismissing the tenets of liberal–rationalist Judaism, a younger generation of intellectuals including Gershom Scholem and Franz Rosenzweig advocated the revitalization of a distinct community and cultural sphere, revolting against their fathers' integrationism and embarking on what Stéphane Mosès would deem an 'internal journey of "dissimilation"'.[4] The thinkers assumed disparate conceptions of Jewish solidarity or collective identity, from national revival to diasporic reform,

---

Pantheon, 1978); *Culture and Imperialism* (New York: Alfred A. Knopf, 1993); and 'Invention, Memory, and Place', p. 181.

[4] Stéphane Mosès, 'Scholem and Rosenzweig: The Dialectics of History', trans. Ora Wiskind, *History and Memory* 2.2 (Winter 1990), pp. 100–16 (p. 103). See also Michael Löwy, *Redemption and Utopia: Jewish Libertarian Thought in Central Europe*, trans. Hope Heaney (London/New York: Verso, 2017).

but they shared an investment in reappropriating religious sources and traditions from which acculturated Jews had ostensibly become alienated. And, though avowedly restorative, their endeavours to promote Jewish knowledge were no less innovative, as Michael Brenner has argued.[5] In Brenner's analysis, educational institutions and publications initiated in Weimar Germany – most prominently, Rosenzweig's *Freies Jüdisches Lehrhaus*, Rosenzweig and Martin Buber's translation of the Hebrew Bible, and the multivolume reference works *Jüdisches Lexikon* [*Jewish Lexicon*] and *Encyclopaedia Judaica* [*Jewish Encyclopedia*] – marked a retrieval of Jewish cultural heritage through quintessentially modern modes of expression, transmission and reception.

The dialectics of Jewish renewal were theorized most sustainedly by Scholem, a cultural Zionist who moved to Palestine at the age of 25. In his memoirs of his youth, *Von Berlin nach Jerusalem* [*From Berlin to Jerusalem*, 1977], Scholem addressed the vexed relation between the Zionist idea and the early twentieth-century revival of Judaism:

> If there was any chance of a fundamental renewal whereby the Jews would fully realize their inherent potential, this – so we believed – could happen only over there, where a Jew would encounter himself, his people, and his roots. One's attitude toward religious tradition also played a part here, and had a clear dialectical function. For from the outset the struggle between a striving for continuation and revivification of the traditional form of Judaism and a conscious rebellion against this very tradition, though within the Jewish people and not through alienation from it and abandonment of it, created an ineluctable dialectics that was central to Zionism. Watchwords like 'renewal of Judaism' or 'revivification of the heart' only verbally masked this dialectics. It was bound to break through every attempt to endow it with substance in the concrete process of building a new Jewish community, and in large measure it shaped the inner history of the Zionist movement from my youth to the present.[6]

Scholem thus emphasized the significance of the ancient homeland for spiritual and sociocultural rebirth as well as the inexorable dialectic between Zionism and Jewish religious tradition – a dialectic that remained concealed

---

[5] Michael Brenner, *The Renaissance of Jewish Culture in Weimar Germany* (New Haven, CT/London: Yale University Press, 1996), p. 111.

[6] Gershom Scholem, *From Berlin to Jerusalem: Memories of My Youth*, trans. Harry Zohn (New York: Schocken, 1980), pp. 54–55.

during his youth, when 'a decision in favor of a new beginning [...] appeared clear-cut'.[7] For Scholem, the tensions between continuity and internal revolt, and between religious–mystical regeneration and political self-determination, necessarily materialized as the Zionist movement assumed more concrete historical form over the twentieth century.[8]

Already in 1926 Scholem had expressed his deep uneasiness with the burgeoning yet embattled Zionist movement. In 'Bekenntnis über unsere Sprache' ['On Our Language: A Confession'], written for the occasion of Rosenzweig's fortieth birthday, Scholem acknowledged mounting concern over Arab resistance but focused on an avowedly 'more uncanny' threat: the profanation of the Hebrew language.[9] Scholem's later essays retained this concern over Zionism's inherent problematics, which he related more broadly to the two opposing tendencies crystallized in the Messianic idea. Recalling Sigmund Freud's account of life and death instincts from *Jenseits des Lustprinzips* [*Beyond the Pleasure Principle*, 1920],[10] Scholem characterized the objective of restorative forces as 'the return and recreation of a past condition which comes to be felt as ideal', filtered through collective memory and historical fantasy; utopian forces, by contrast, are 'nourished by a vision of the future', pushing toward conditions that have never yet been achieved.[11] Ever-present and dialectically intertwined, restorative and utopian impulses were able to coexist, Scholem wrote, as long as Messianic hope 'remained abstract, not yet concretized in people's experience or demanding of concrete decisions'.[12] Their latent contradiction nonetheless became palpable during moments of acute 'Messianic activism'[13] across Jewish history – from the Bar Kokhba revolt against the Roman Empire through the seventeenth-century Sabbatian movement to the Zionism of Scholem's own time.

---

[7] Scholem, *From Berlin to Jerusalem*, p. 151.

[8] On this point, see also Gershom Scholem, *Walter Benjamin: The Story of a Friendship*, trans. Harry Zohn (Philadelphia: The Jewish Publication Society of America, 1981), p. 171.

[9] Gershom Scholem, 'On Our Language: A Confession', trans. Ora Wiskind, *History and Memory* 2.2 (Winter 1990), pp. 97–99 (p. 97).

[10] Sigmund Freud, *Beyond the Pleasure Principle*, ed. and trans. James Strachey (New York and London: W.W. Norton & Company, 1961).

[11] Gershom Scholem, 'Toward an Understanding of the Messianic Idea in Judaism', trans. Michael A. Meyer, in Gershom Scholem, *The Messianic Idea in Judaism and Other Essays on Jewish Spirituality* (New York: Schocken, 1995), pp. 1–36 (p. 3).

[12] Gershom Scholem, 'The Crisis of Tradition in Jewish Messianism', in Scholem, *The Messianic Idea*, pp. 49–77 (p. 51).

[13] Scholem, 'Messianic Idea in Judaism', p. 15.

In his studies of Jewish Messianism, Scholem offered what David Biale has called a 'counter-history'[14] to various rationalist tendencies beginning in the Middle Ages that had commonly sought to extract apocalypticism from the realm of rabbinic Judaism. Among these attempts, medieval philosophers and theologians such as Maimonides had foregrounded the restorative aspect of Messianism, whereas later proponents of Enlightenment rationalism instead emphasized the utopian element as they adopted 'the idea of the eternal progress and infinite task of humanity perfecting itself'.[15] For Scholem, nineteenth- and early twentieth-century Jewish scholars – including both historians associated with the *Wissenschaft des Judentums* and later Marburg School philosophers such as Hermann Cohen – had secularized Messianism as a liberal faith in progress in an apologetic effort to present a 'purified and rational Judaism'.[16] In such accounts of Messianism the redemption was no longer conceived of as a miracle, but rather as the inevitable telos of an immanent historical process. Pushing back against this optimistic model of continuous historical development, Scholem recalled the extended tradition of apocalyptic Messianism, which had stressed the catastrophic aspect of redemption and had postulated an unbridgeable chasm between the unredeemed world and 'that which will arise in its ruin'.[17]

At the end of his influential essay 'Zum Verständnis der messianischen Idee im Judentum' ['Toward an Understanding of the Messianic Idea in Judaism', 1959] Scholem addressed the significant cost of the Messianic idea for Jewish historical experience:

> The grandness of the Messianic idea corresponds to the endless powerlessness in Jewish history during all the centuries of exile, when it was unprepared to come forward onto the plane of world history.

---

[14] See David Biale, *Gershom Scholem: Kabbalah and Counter-History* (Cambridge, MA/London: Harvard University Press, 1982). For more recent accounts of Scholem's life and historiographical work see Amir Engel, *Gershom Scholem: An Intellectual Biography* (Chicago, IL: University of Chicago Press, 2017); David Biale, *Gershom Scholem: Master of the Kabbalah* (New Haven, CT/London: Yale University Press, 2018); and Jay Howard Geller, *The Scholems: A Story of the German-Jewish Bourgeoisie from Emancipation to Destruction* (Ithaca, NY/London: Cornell University Press, 2019).

[15] Scholem, 'Messianic Idea in Judaism', p. 26. Scholem argued that this latter view stemmed from the Kabbalah; see Gershom Scholem, 'The Messianic Idea in Kabbalism', trans. Moses Hadas, in Scholem, *The Messianic Idea*, pp. 37–48 (p. 37).

[16] Scholem, 'Messianic Idea in Judaism', p. 9.

[17] Scholem, 'Messianic Idea in Judaism', p. 10. See also Scholem, 'Messianic Idea in Kabbalism', p. 38.

> There's something preliminary, something provisional about Jewish history; hence its inability to give of itself entirely. For the Messianic idea is not only consolation and hope. Every attempt to realize it tears open the abysses which lead each of its manifestations *ad absurdum*. There is something grand about living in hope, but at the same time there is something profoundly unreal about it. It depreciates the singular worth of the individual, and he can never fulfill himself, because the incompleteness of his endeavors depreciates precisely what constitutes their core value. Thus in Judaism the Messianic idea has compelled a *life lived in deferment*, in which nothing can be done definitively, nothing can be irrevocably accomplished. One may say, perhaps, the Messianic idea is the real anti-existentialist idea. Precisely understood, there is nothing concrete which can be accomplished by the unredeemed.[18]

Scholem thus placed a series of terms in contrasting or even paradoxical relation, suggesting that the Messianic idea's 'grandness' correlates to the 'endless powerlessness' of Jewish history; that the condition of hope is both 'grand' and 'profoundly unreal'; and that individual undertakings are 'depreciated' at their very point of 'core value'. Moreover, a moment of realization is either at an indefinite remove in the abstract realm, in the case of 'a *life lived in deferment*', or a figure of absurdity when manifested in world history. Recalling his concern over the 'actualization' of Hebrew in 'On Our Language', Scholem concluded his essay with a conundrum posed by 'the Jew of this age': namely, 'Whether or not Jewish history will be able to endure this entry into the concrete realm without perishing in the crisis of the Messianic claim which has virtually been conjured up'.[19] Following his earlier statement that attempts to realize the Messianic idea inevitably lead '*ad absurdum*', this question suggests a critique of the Zionist movement, which had stirred up irresolvable tensions in initiating a 'utopian return' to the ancient homeland.[20]

---

[18] Scholem, 'Messianic Idea in Judaism', p. 35. Translation modified.
[19] Scholem, 'Messianic Idea in Judaism', p. 36.
[20] Scholem, 'Messianic Idea in Judaism', p. 35. On the essay and its reception history, see also Michael L. Morgan and Steven Weitzman, 'Introduction', in *Rethinking the Messianic Idea in Judaism*, ed. by Michael L. Morgan and Steven Weitzman (Bloomington: Indiana University Press, 2015), pp. 1–20.

Franz Kafka and the Impossible Coordinates of Messianic Arrival

Likewise raised in an acculturated bourgeois family, Franz Kafka shared Scholem's rebellious interest in the Hebrew language and Jewish religious tradition, famously excoriating the 'few flimsy gestures [...] performed in the name of Judaism' in his 'Brief an den Vater' ('Letter to the Father', 1919).[21] In a missive from 1916, Kafka's first fiancée, Felice Bauer, had recounted a fierce dispute at Berlin's *Jüdisches Volksheim* wherein Scholem had encouraged his coreligionists to learn Hebrew and engage directly with historical Jewish sources. (With typical negational irony, Kafka responded, 'theoretically I am always inclined to favor proposals such as those made by Herr Scholem, which demand the utmost, and by so doing achieve nothing'.[22]) Kafka would become a recurring figure in Scholem's own writing in subsequent decades – from his 1934 correspondence with Walter Benjamin through his letter to Salman Schocken, 'Ein offenes Wort über die wahren Absichten meines Kabbalastudiums' ('A Candid Word about the True Motives of My Kabbalistic Studies', 1937) to his 'Zehn unhistorische Sätze über Kabbala' ('Ten Unhistorical Aphorisms on Kabbalah', 1958) and his late autobiographies.[23] Insofar as Kafka's work posited revelation as unrealizable and incomprehensible, it represented what Scholem deemed 'the most perfect and unsurpassed expression of this fine line [between religion and nihilism] [...] a secular statement of the Kabbalistic world-feeling in a modern spirit'.[24]

For Scholem, Kafka's 'heretical Kabbalah' found its most concentrated expression in the author's parables, which – like Jewish mystical tradition itself – postulated the paradoxical or even impossible conditions of Messianic arrival.[25] (For a consideration of the continued contemporary influence of

---

[21] Franz Kafka, *Letter to the Father*, trans. Ernst Kaiser and Eithne Wilkins (New York: Schocken, 2015), p. 77. On this point see also Robert Alter, *Necessary Angels: Tradition and Modernity in Kafka, Benjamin, and Scholem* (Cambridge, MA: Harvard University Press, 1991).

[22] Franz Kafka, *Letters to Felice*, ed. by Erich Heller and Jürgen Born, trans. James Stern and Elisabeth Duckworth (New York: Schocken, 1973), p. 505. See also Scholem, *From Berlin to Jerusalem*, p. 79; and Scholem, *Walter Benjamin*, p. 105.

[23] Walter Benjamin and Gershom Scholem, *The Correspondence of Walter Benjamin and Gershom Scholem, 1932–1940*, ed. by Gershom Scholem, trans. Gary Smith and Andre LeFevere (Cambridge, MA: Harvard University Press, 1992); Biale, *Gershom Scholem*, pp. 31–32; David Biale, 'Gershom Scholem's Ten Unhistorical Aphorisms on Kabbalah: Text and Commentary', *Modern Judaism* 5.1 (February 1985), pp. 67–93; Scholem, *Walter Benjamin*; and Scholem, *From Berlin to Jerusalem*.

[24] Biale, *Gershom Scholem*, p. 31.

[25] Biale, 'Gershom Scholem's Ten Unhistorical Aphorisms', p. 88. See also Scholem,

Kafka's interest in Judaism, see also Claire Baldwin's discussion in Chapter 15 in this volume.) Consider, for example, the first paragraph of Kafka's 'Das Kommen des Messias' ['The Coming of the Messiah', n.d.]:

> The Messiah will come as soon as the most unbridled individualism of faith is possible – when there is no one to destroy this possibility and no one to suffer its destruction; hence the graves will open themselves. This, perhaps, is Christian doctrine too, applying as much to the actual presentation of the example to be emulated, which is an individualistic example, as to the symbolic presentation of the resurrection of the Messiah in the single individual.[26]

Parodying the language of Christology and Hegelian dialectics, this convoluted passage muddles the distinctions between Jewish and Christian doctrine (attributing a passage from the New Testament, Matthew 27:52–53, to the former) and also between particular and universal figures. In the opening sentence the narrative voice places the individual in a series of contradictory relationships: the Messiah's coming is contingent upon both the possibility of an 'unbridled individualism of faith' and the presence of 'no one' who might ruin this very possibility or tolerate its expunction. Furthermore, the 'example' to be followed is characterized as 'individualistic', whereas the mediatory figure of Jesus becomes symbolically manifest in the 'single individual'. On a grammatical level, Kafka also stages the issue of nominalism throughout this passage by alternating between noun, verb and adjective forms of particular cognates (coming/come, destroy/destruction, possible/possibility) as well as by lending reiterated nouns varying modifiers, as in the 'actual' versus 'symbolic presentation'.

In the second and final paragraph of 'The Coming of the Messiah', the narrative voice invokes unmanageable configurations of space and time: 'The Messiah will come only when he will no longer be necessary; he will come only a day after his arrival; he will come, not on the last day, but on the very last.'[27] Impishly suggesting that the Messiah will come only under conditions of needlessness, this statement raises questions about the differences between the Messiah's 'coming' and his 'arrival' and between the 'last' and 'very last' days.

'Messianic Idea in Judaism', p. 34: 'The arrival of the Messiah himself is tied to impossible, or at any rate highly paradoxical, conditions.'

[26] Franz Kafka, 'The Coming of the Messiah', trans. Clement Greenberg, in *Parables and Paradoxes*, ed. by Nahum N. Glatzer (New York: Schocken, 1958), p. 81. Translation modified.

[27] Kafka, 'Coming of the Messiah', p. 81. Translation modified.

Although the spatiotemporal process of 'coming' would seem to culminate in 'arrival', the narrative voice here paradoxically asserts that the latter will be post-dated by the former. Furthermore, by positing the existence of a day following 'the last day', the narrator suggests a time beyond chronology, which assumes a sequence from first to last. Kafka also enacts a temporality of deferral in the parable through verb tense and syntax. Although both paragraphs begin with statements of the conditions of the Messiah's coming, the tense in the subordinate clauses switches from the present ('as soon as [...] is possible') to the future ('when he will no longer be'), and the delayed possibility of the Messiah's coming finds articulation in the increasing length and elaborateness of its conditions: 'will come' (future tense), 'will come only' (future tense with adverb), 'will come only a day after his arrival' (future tense with adverb, indirect object, and prepositional phrase), 'will come, not on the last day, but on the very last' (future tense with correlative conjunction that places two prepositional phrases in parallel form).[28]

Though less explicitly about Messianism, Kafka's parable 'Das Ziel' ['My Destination', n.d.] likewise thematizes the anomalous spatiotemporal coordinates of departure and arrival:

> I gave orders for my horse to be brought round from the stable. The servant did not understand me. I myself went to the stable, saddled my horse and mounted. In the distance I heard a trumpet sounding, I asked him what this meant. He knew nothing and had heard nothing. At the gate he stopped me, asking: 'Where are you riding to, master?' 'I don't know', I said, 'only away from here, away from here. Always away from here, only by doing so can I reach my destination'. 'And so you know your destination?' he asked. 'Yes', I answered, 'didn't I say so? Away-From-Here, that is my destination'. 'You have no provisions with you', he said. 'I need none', I said, 'the journey is so long that I must die of hunger if I don't get anything on the way. No provisions can save me. For it is, fortunately, a truly immense journey.'[29]

In this thwarted exchange – filled with misunderstandings, logical disjunctures and the breakdown of social hierarchy – the eponymous

---

[28] One also notes the switch from a positive-positive ('sowohl [...], als auch') to a negative-positive ('nicht [...], sondern') correlative conjunction between the first and second paragraphs of the parable – an alteration that seems to reduce the potentiality of Messianic arrival and realizability.

[29] Franz Kafka, 'My Destination', trans. Ernst Kaiser and Eithne Wilkins, in *Parables and Paradoxes*, ed. by Glatzer, p. 189. Translation modified.

destination assumes a utopian quality as a site without a pre-established or pre-existing location, even as it is both inconceivable and inarticulable except in terms of what is already known or manifest. The narrator's destination ('Away-From-Here') is impossible as a definite noun, place or telos, and is unable to become a 'here' that is not defined in relation to the point of departure. The parable's alternation between the imperfect and present tenses raises further questions about spatial mobility and temporal progression. Though Kafka evokes infinite movement in the present tense (e.g., 'Always away from here', 'a truly immense [*ungeheuere*] journey'), suggesting an unfathomable future, he stages the entire interaction at an undefined time in the past. Finally, in evoking various biblical topoi, the text both intimates and frustrates a theological reading; the trumpet call is heard only by the narrator, who does not appear to move through the gate into another realm.

Kafka's own mobility became increasingly dubious in the years before his untimely death of tuberculosis in 1924, as Palestine became a perpetually deferred and ultimately impossible destination. In his initial letter to Felice Bauer from 1912, Kafka recalled her 'promise to accompany him next year to Palestine', and he insisted on discussing and planning their upcoming trip.[30] By the following decade Palestine had lost its status as a promised, imminent or even potential destination, appearing fugitive and unreachable. Kafka dismissed travel plans to Palestine in 1921 as 'dreams'[31] and, after moving to Berlin in 1923, he wrote in the past subjunctive: 'In any case Palestine would have been beyond me; in view of the possibilities in Berlin it would not even be urgent.'[32] During Kafka's final year he referred to his planned trip to Palestine as an unrealistic and unrealizable idea that provided him with a vague, sustaining hope: 'I saw that if I somehow wanted to go on living, I would have to do something fully radical, and I wanted to go to Palestine. I surely would not have been capable of it and am also pretty unprepared in Hebrew and in other respects, but I needed to hold out some kind of hope.'[33] In one of his final letters to Milena Jesenská, Kafka fatalistically wrote of his plans to visit her in Palestine as 'a phantasy, the kind of phantasy someone has who is convinced he will never again leave his bed'.[34] Over the course of

---

[30] Kafka, *Letters to Felice*, p. 5.

[31] Franz Kafka, *Briefe an Ottla und die Familie*, ed. by Hartmut Binder and Klaus Wagenbach (Frankfurt am Main: S. Fischer, 1974), p. 111.

[32] Franz Kafka, *Letters to Friends, Family, and Editors*, trans. Richard and Clara Winston (New York: Schocken, 1977), p. 380.

[33] Kafka, *Briefe an Ottla und die Familie*, pp. 145–46.

[34] Kafka, *Letters to Milena*, p. 236.

these letters, Kafka's vision of Palestine thus sheds its potential for actualization and becomes increasingly intangible, phantasmagorical, fleeting and always-already. For Kafka, in other words, the space of Palestine adopts the qualities of a film.[35]

Incommensurable Temporalities in Early Cinema

In a laconic diary entry from 23 October 1921 Kafka wrote, 'Afternoon: Palestine film'.[36] Through scrupulous archival research, Hanns Zischler has ascertained that Kafka attended a private screening of Ya'acov Ben-Dov's *Shivat Zion* [*Return to Zion*, 1921] that day at Prague's Lido-Bio, presented by the Zionist organization and journal *Selbstwehr*. For Zischler, the film allowed Kafka to retain a cinematic vision of the place he would never visit before his death: 'Palestine remains for Kafka an unreachable terrain, a ground he is unable to tread, near enough to touch and far away – an imaginary space, a film.'[37] While Zischler's thesis has been faulted for overdetermining visual media, overlooking Kafka's manifold encounters with Palestine through written and oral accounts,[38] contemporary articles on the screening nonetheless indicate that cinema was distinguished through the vividness of its representations: 'The event demonstrated how important showings of this kind would be for our cause, how through scenes like these we come much closer to the reality of Palestine than through all the reports.'[39]

Emerging contemporaneously with the Zionist movement at the *fin de siècle*, cinema was likewise characterized by a fundamental opposition between irrevocable change and cyclical return to an originary state. In

---

[35] On the relationship between Kafka and the moving image, see also Peter-André Alt, *Kafka und der Film: Über kinematographisches Erzählen* (Munich: C.H. Beck, 2009); Shai Biderman and Ido Lewit (eds.), *Mediamorphosis: Kafka and the Moving Image* (London/New York: Wallflower, 2016); Brook Henkel, 'Kafka's Animations: Trick Films, Narrative, Reification', *New German Critique* 45.2 (Autumn 2018), pp. 67–97; and Kata Gellen, *Kafka and Noise: The Discovery of Cinematic Sound in Literary Modernism* (Evanston, IL: Northwestern University Press, 2019).

[36] Franz Kafka, *The Diaries of Franz Kafka, 1914–1923*, ed. by Max Brod, trans. Martin Greenberg (New York: Schocken, 1949), p. 197. Translation modified.

[37] Hanns Zischler, *Kafka Goes to the Movies*, trans. Susan H. Gillespie (Chicago, IL: University of Chicago Press, 2003), p. 115.

[38] Judith Butler, 'Who Owns Kafka?', *London Review of Books* 33.5 (3 March 2011), pp. 3–8.

[39] *Selbstwehr* (28 October 1921); quoted in Zischler, *Kafka Goes to the Movies*, p. 111.

its traditional form, film emerges from the photochemical registration of reflected light and the technological reproduction of strips of still frames that produce the illusion of continuous movement when projected in rapid succession. The medium's paradoxical basis in movement and stasis was doubled in early representations of the train, which similarly deploys both linear and rotating mechanical parts to effect the experience of 'simultaneous motion and stillness'.[40] As the 'cinema of attractions' gave way to one of 'narrative integration',[41] trains and other vehicles featured prominently in filmic narratives, which – like railway journeys and filmic form itself – are structured around forward progression and ultimate return to stasis. Drawing on Freud's theory of life and death instincts, Laura Mulvey has argued that cinematic narrative is dually propelled by 'stimulation to movement' and the 'aim to return, to rediscover the stillness from which it originally departed'.[42] For Mulvey, the basic antinomies of both narrative and cinema are often figured through tropes of movement and stasis, desire and marriage, animacy and death.

The ontological duality of cinema found visual expression in the earliest moving images of Palestine. In one of cameraman Alexandre Promio's travelling actualities for the Lumière Brothers, *Départ de Jérusalem en chemin de fer* [*Leaving Jerusalem by Railway*, 1896], the camera is mounted to the end of the train, as is typical of early cinematic 'phantom rides', such that the movement of the train is synonymous with that of the camera. The illusion of movement produced by the filmic medium is duplicated not only through the camera's backward tracking movement but also through the forward motion of individuals within the frame, many of whom direct their gaze at the camera and raise their hats to the departing passengers. Capturing men, women and children of varying ethno-religious backgrounds, who wear a mix of modern dress and traditional religious garb, the film depicts a veritable *Altneuland*, with old ruins alongside the Montefiore Windmill and the Jerusalem Railway Station. On a formal level, the backwards movement of the camera and the retrospective gesture of the farewell are juxtaposed with the ceaseless forward motion of the train – and, with it, of cinematic

---

[40] Lynne Kirby, *Parallel Tracks: The Railroad and Silent Cinema* (Durham, NC: Duke University Press, 1997), p. 2. See also Dimitris Eleftheriotis, *Cinematic Journeys: Film and Movement* (Edinburgh: Edinburgh University Press, 2010).

[41] Tom Gunning, *D. W. Griffith and the Origins of American Narrative Film* (Urbana, IL/Chicago, IL: University of Illinois Press, 1991), p. 43; see also Tom Gunning, 'The Cinema of Attraction: Early Cinema, Its Spectator and the Avant-Garde', *Wide Angle* 8.3–4 (Fall 1986), pp. 63–70.

[42] Laura Mulvey, *Death 24x a Second: Stillness and the Moving Image* (London: Reaktion, 2006), p. 71.

time – creating a Janus-faced duality of temporal orientation. As a passenger-cum-spectator, the filmic viewer is both looking back and moving forward, recalling Walter Benjamin's Messianically tinged figure of the angel of history, 'turned toward the past' and yet propelled 'into the future to which his back is turned'.[43]

A dual temporal perspective also characterizes the aforementioned *Return to Zion*, a propaganda film that was presented at the Twelfth Zionist Congress in Carlsbad in September 1921, one month before the Prague screening that Kafka attended.[44] The third work by Zionist film pioneer Ya'acov Ben-Dov, *Return to Zion* documents aspects of Jewish national revival in Palestine, including various kibbutzim (e.g., Degania Alef, Hulda, Kiryat Anavim, Kvutzat Kinneret), schools (Alliance Israélite Universelle, Bezalel Academy of Arts and Design, Herzliya Hebrew Gymnasium), organizations (Assefath Hanivcharim, Jewish Legion) and dignitaries (Winston Churchill, Ze'ev Jabotinsky, Alfred Mond, Herbert Samuel, Nahum Sokolow, Chaim Weizmann), as well as the work of *chalutzim* in regions such as Galilee and Jezreel Valley. In an extended sequence, the film also features the historic 1921 excavation of the Hamat Tiberias Synagogue (deemed the 'first Hebrew excavation'), led by archaeologist Nahum Slouschz and sponsored by the Jewish Palestine Exploration Society. Following a series of shots detailing a menorah, a mosaic floor and marble panels and columns, Ben-Dov presents the uncovering of a Roman-era sarcophagus containing a skeleton and glass cup (described as 'masonry from the time of Hebrew rule').[45] Defying the halachic prohibition against excavating graves, the opening of the

---

[43] Walter Benjamin, 'On the Concept of History', trans. Harry Zohn, in *Selected Writings: Volume 4, 1938–1940*, ed. by Howard Eiland and Michael W. Jennings (Cambridge, MA: Harvard University Press, 2003) pp. 389–400 (p. 392). On the work of Alexandre Promio see also Michael Allan, 'Deserted Histories: The Lumière Brothers, the Pyramids and Early Film Form', *Early Popular Visual Culture* 6.2 (2008), pp. 159–70.

[44] Multiple versions of the film circulated in the 1920s. I am using the print contained on the DVD that accompanies Hanns Zischler, *Kafka geht ins Kino* (Berlin: Galiani, 2017). A title card reading 'Pesach 5680 to Hanukkah 5681' suggests that this print is a later version than the one Kafka viewed. On the film's history, see Hillel Tryster, *Israel Before Israel: Silent Cinema in the Holy Land* (Jerusalem: Steven Spielberg Jewish Film Archive, 1995). On the history of German–Israeli film relations, see Tobias Ebbrecht-Hartmann, *Übergänge: Passagen durch eine deutsch-israelische Filmgeschichte* (Berlin: Neofelis, 2014).

[45] On this excavation, see Steven Fine, *Art and Judaism in the Greco-Roman World: Toward a New Jewish Archaeology* (Cambridge: Cambridge University Press, 2005), pp. 22–27.

Fig. 20. Cinema as 'a torn-open grave'. Still from Ya'acov Ben-Dov's *Shivat Zion* [*Return to Zion*, 1921].

sarcophagus indicates the iconoclasm of Zionist engagement with Jewish tradition and presages the common trope of cinema as an uncanny form of preservation and reanimation – or what Joseph Roth would call 'a torn-open grave' (Fig. 20).[46]

Insofar as Ben-Dov's film maintains a twofold focus on an ancient past and modern revival, on Hebrew ancestors and Zionist settlers, it exemplifies the ideological patterns of the Zionist movement as well as the dialectic that Scholem later identified between 'restorative' and 'utopian' tendencies. Yet *Return to Zion* appeals to a further array of often-incommensurable temporalities, rooted in cycles of nature and human life, individual and collective milestones, decisional politics and religious rituals, and secular and messianic time. Divided into three parts ('Moments', 'The High Commissioner in the Land of Israel', 'The Chalutzim') and structured around Herbert Samuel's

[46] Joseph Roth, 'The Uncovered Grave', trans. Nicholas Baer, in *The Promise of Cinema: German Film Theory, 1907–1933*, ed. by Anton Kaes, Nicholas Baer and Michael Cowan (Oakland: University of California Press, 2016), pp. 98–99 (p. 99). Fig. 20 is from the print contained on the DVD that accompanies Hanns Zischler, *Kafka geht ins Kino* (Berlin: Galiani, 2017).

first year as inaugural High Commissioner of Palestine, the film depicts a wine harvest, marriages, religious holidays and celebrations (Pesach, Tu BiShvat, Shabbat Nachamu, Hanukkah) and noteworthy developments in the British Mandate and Zionist movement. Such heterogeneity is duplicated on a formal level, as the film alternates between prosaic, descriptive intertitles and ones that quote from biblical verses and Jewish blessings (Psalm 13:1, Isaiah 40:1 and 43:6, Jeremiah 31:17, the Kiddush). Finally, though retaining many elements of the 'cinema of attractions' (e.g., non-narrative variety format, frontal mode of exhibition, direct address to the camera), Ben-Dov also explores cinema's potential in tracking broader historical developments, culminating in Colonial Secretary Winston Churchill's 1921 reaffirmation of the Balfour Declaration – the statement from 1917 that, in Edward Said's words, 'has long formed the juridical basis of Zionist claims to Palestine'.[47]

Conclusion

As I have argued, works by Scholem, Kafka and early filmmakers betray the paradoxes of Jewish Messianism – whether formulated in terms of the ineluctable dialectics of Jewish national revival, the impossible conditions of arrival or the disparate and even incommensurable temporalities of the Zionist movement. The works complicate established understandings of transnational studies, encouraging scholars to move beyond a focus on 'trans-societal and trans-organizational realities'[48] to consider abstract places, linguistic topoi and imagistic phantasmagoria that are tenable as long as they remain unrealized. What happens, however, when a population seeks to complete an unfathomable journey to a non-localizable place, or to actualize an unmanageable configuration of space and time? As the past century has indicated, the paradoxes of the Messianic idea are borne out with grave consequentiality, entailing a devastating geopolitical conflict well beyond the pale of redemption.[49]

---

[47] Edward W. Said, 'Zionism from the Standpoint of Its Victims', *Social Text* 1 (Winter 1979), pp. 7–58 (p. 9).

[48] Peggy Levitt and Sanjeev Khagram, 'Constructing Transnational Studies', in *The Transnational Studies Reader: Intersections and Innovations*, ed. by Sanjeev Khagram and Peggy Levitt (New York and London: Routledge, 2008), pp. 1–18 (p. 10).

[49] I would like to thank Judith Butler for her invaluable comments on an earlier version of this essay. Doron Galili also served as a generous interlocutor.

Suggestions for Further Reading

Allan, Michael, 'Deserted Histories: The Lumière Brothers, the Pyramids and Early Film Form', *Early Popular Visual Culture* 6.2 (2008), pp. 159–70.

Biale, David, *Gershom Scholem: Master of the Kabbalah* (New Haven, CT/London: Yale University Press, 2018), 251 pp.

Butler, Judith, 'Who Owns Kafka?' *London Review of Books* 33.5 (2011), pp. 3–8.

Ebbrecht-Hartmann, Tobias, *Übergänge: Passagen durch eine deutsch-israelische Filmgeschichte* (Berlin: Neofelis, 2014), 300 pp.

Engel, Amir, *Gershom Scholem: An Intellectual Biography* (Chicago, IL: University of Chicago Press, 2017), 241 pp.

Kafka, Franz, *Parables and Paradoxes* (New York: Schocken, 1958), 190 pp.

Said, Edward W., 'Invention, Memory, and Place', *Critical Inquiry* 26.2 (2000), pp. 175–92.

Scholem, Gershom, *From Berlin to Jerusalem: Memories of My Youth* (New York: Schocken, 1980), 178 pp.

Scholem, Gershom, *The Messianic Idea in Judaism and Other Essays on Jewish Spirituality* (New York: Schocken, 1995), 400 pp.

Zischler, Hanns, *Kafka Goes to the Movies* (Chicago, IL: University of Chicago Press, 2003), 172 pp.

12

Securing the Archive

On the Transience of (Latin) American German Identities

Paulo Soethe
Translated by Sarah Pybus

Introduction

Who would have thought that Brazil, a country typically associated with tropical lifestyles, Carnival and samba, would have a heritage strongly influenced by German immigration? Between 1824 and 1952 around 350,000 people immigrated to Brazil from the German-speaking region, giving Brazil the world's second-largest population of German immigrants after the USA.

In Rio Grande do Sul, Brazil's most southerly state, people of German origin now make up 12 per cent of the total population (around 9.5 million inhabitants). In 1930, Joinville – now the third-largest city in southern Brazil, with almost 600,000 inhabitants – had 35,000 German-speaking residents (of a total population of 54,000). Of the 931,000 people living in the state of Santa Catarina, 160,000 spoke German in their everyday lives. Curitiba, the capital of the state of Paraná, is now home to 1.9 million people, making it the largest city in southern Brazil and the eighth-largest in the country as a whole; in 1919, Curitiba had a population of 85,000 people, 13,000 of whom spoke German.

The development of medium-sized cities in southern Brazilian settlement zones (such as Joinville) and internal migration by Germans or people of German origin to existing large cities (such as Porto Alegre (the capital of Rio Grande do Sul), Curitiba, São Paulo and Rio de Janeiro) made the German language a key component of urban cultural life, particularly from the end of the nineteenth century. Brazilian institutions integrated the language and culture of the *alemães* up to 1937, laying the foundations for a well-developed school system (around 1,000 schools), social and cultural music, gymnastics and theatre groups and a German-language press. German-language literature was also written and distributed in Brazil, and German-speaking academics played a notable role in organizing institutions within Brazil's emerging scholarly world. German language and culture was held in high esteem, and its presence shaped everyday city life and the consolidation of institutions.

Even in this instance of transnational experience – lesser-known worldwide and even in Germany – examining the history of the melting pot that is Brazil immediately raises interesting questions about the epistemological implications of often conflict-ridden processes of movement and the collective imaginations circulating in this context. The questions raised by the colonization that took place from the sixteenth century and the mass forced immigration of Africans from the seventeenth century were compounded during the accelerated globalization of the nineteenth century by huge migration flows from Europe, including its German-speaking regions. This migration took place against the backdrop of socio-historic events on both sides of the Atlantic: restoration policies on the 'old continent' and the state-building process in Brazil. Unlike South America's Hispanic American countries, Brazil did not become a republic until 1889 and not as a result of revolutionary grassroots movements, but through military action.

From 1852 to 1940 Brazil's coordinated immigration programmes encouraged a major German presence in the country, leading to culturally intensive German-speaking life. As was usual at the time, an equally extensive German-language press was established relatively quickly, with more than 600 different media.

The voices in the newspapers and political magazines varied greatly. Together with debates in other languages – above all, Portuguese, but also Italian, Polish, French, Spanish and Arabic, among others[1] – they formed

---

[1] See Martin N. Dreher, Arthur Blásio Rambo and Marcos Justo Tramontini (eds.), *Imigração e Imprensa* (Porto Alegre: EST; São Leopoldo: Instituto Histórico de São Leopoldo, 2004). Tania Regina de Luca and Margarete Alves Antunes, *A presença de jornais em língua estrangeira em algumas bibliotecas paulistas e na Biblioteca Nacional do Rio de Janeiro, Escritos. Revista da Fundação Casa de Rui Barbosa (Dossier Transfopress: A imprensa de língua estrangeira publicada no Brasil)*, vol. 9, no. 9 (2015), pp. 223–87. Tania Regina de Luca and Valéria Guimarães (eds.), *Imprensa estrangeira publicada no Brasil – primeiras incursões* (São Paulo: Rafael Copetti, 2017). Further information can be found on the website of the 'Transfopress Brasil' research project: http://transfopressbrasil.franca.unesp.br [accessed 4 May 2018]. The work of Hans Gehse on the German-language press in Brazil remains essential: Hans Gehse, *Die deutsche Presse in Brasilien von 1852 bis zur Gegenwart. Ein Beitrag zur Geschichte und zum Aufgabenkreis auslanddeutschen Zeitungswesens* (Münster i. W.: Aschendorffsche Buchdruckerei, 1931). See also Karl Arndt and May Olson, *Die deutschsprachige Presse der Amerikas 1732–1968. Geschichte und Bibliographie. 3 Bde* (Munich: Dokumentation, 1973–1985).

a continuum that is sadly no longer known or recognized: at the end of the 1930s these documents were eradicated from Brazilian historiography by a right-wing, populist, dictatorial policy of nationalization. Almost 50 years after being declared a republic, Brazil was plagued by a nationalistic dictatorship under Getúlio Vargas from 1937 to 1945 that forbade all foreign languages, even in such a multicultural country.[2]

Nevertheless, many Brazilian families, communities and institutions maintained a link to the German language that is again generating great interest as a new sense of identity develops. These German roots continue to influence modern Brazilian society and its relationships with Europe and several American countries.

Now, the discovery of documents and cultural contexts allows these submerged German-language layers within Brazilian culture, society and history to be made visible once again and re-evaluated. Print texts produced in Brazil in various languages acted as a cultural meeting point, as the polydiscursive medium for complex knowledge of developments within processes of migration, integration and even isolation. With their variety of forms, languages and themes, publications in different languages form an archive of knowledge that does not just depict individual migration experiences but opens up far more complex opportunities to reflect on cultural experiences of movement. At that time, the press was the only public medium preserved in detail to this day to reflect political, cultural and everyday life. This is the only medium to have preserved specific discourses that can now be reconstructed to the great benefit of scholarship and society.

Collections inaccessible for decades – be it owing to language barriers, their rarity, containment in relatively small, non-university archives or lack of visibility in academia – are now beginning to be presented in digital format both for the country's general population and for international researchers. Documents are to be recorded, digitized and catalogued using the latest technology and based on the latest academic findings according to the form in which they were stored, created and regulated. Materials are to be made available in digital format and, in networked institutions, to form the basis for research projects conceived and realized across various disciplines (see also the discussion of digital networks by Sara Jones in Chapter 8 of this volume).

Over the last 15 years integrating large sections of the Brazilian population into organized society by overcoming social inequalities has played an important role in the continuously growing interest in German language and literature. People seeking social advancement look for new educational

---

[2] See Cynthia Machado Campos, *A política da língua na era Vargas: proibição do falar alemão e resistências no Sul do Brasil* (Campinas: Unicamp, 2006).

opportunities; however, they often also seek ways to establish their own identity and to find meaning in a new social context. The country's history – right down to the level of family histories – is becoming increasingly important in this context.

Historical aspects that – given the growing interest in German – highlight the role the language has played in the development of Brazilian society are being brought to light by German Studies research projects and made available to scholars around the world.

Internationalization and Democratization through Digitization: New Research Landscapes for Transnational German Studies

The interdisciplinary revival of academic and social appreciation for Brazilian German-language texts creates a new space for Brazil to confront its own history, and a new research landscape for German Studies worldwide. As Gerhard Lauer prominently claimed in 2013, digitization reinforces and expands the philological ethos of serving the text. To encourage the appreciation of long-forgotten materials, German philologists begin by gathering the texts, cataloguing and labelling, comparing and interrelating.[3]

In researching the work of German-language newspapers in Brazil (and the Americas), scholars must negotiate uncommon quantities of data and master new methods to achieve important new findings in the fields of history, literature and cultural studies. Mediating and determining the languages of these documents creates another area of field work for foreign-language philology and forms the starting point for a new self-perception: that which was *foreign*-language philology must be viewed as a discipline with its own *multi*lingual communications network. More than ever, the archives of institutions and private individuals are an invaluable source in gaining a more comprehensive picture of the social and intellectual discourses taking effect within these processes of exchange and cultural contact. A great deal of material has sadly been lost over the past decades, but there is still time to collate, tap into and research the existing documents – and to make them accessible. The few, largely fragmentary collections of newspapers in existence must be brought together and completed in digital format in Brazil and overseas.[4]

---

[3] See Gerhard Lauer, 'Die Vermessung der Kultur. Geisteswissenschaften als Digital Humanities', in *Big Data. Das neue Versprechen der Allwissenheit*, ed. by Heinrich Geiselberger and Tobias Moorstedt (Berlin: Suhrkamp, 2013), pp. 99–116.

[4] In Germany, for example, the Stuttgart Institute for International Relationships (*Stuttgarter Institut für Auslandsbeziehungen*, IfA) has a large collection of German-language Brazilian newspapers on microfiche that can be further enhanced using

By presenting the public with digitized newspaper and magazine collections, scholars forge closer contacts and enter into greater dialogue with society. The expectations of the general public play a role in the topics and questions prioritized and the documents chosen for digital access. In any case, digitizing documents leads to the greater democratization of the humanities,[5] demanding new practices, questions and approaches depending on the context. Within the interdisciplinary and international field of German studies in the Americas, digitizing and researching the German-language press in various countries opens up perspectives that describe more fully, understand more deeply and, in the best case, more greatly appreciate Germans' local presence and its social significance.

To ensure this work is successful, standardized guidelines are crucial for the digital presentation of German-language historical texts. The *Deutsches Textarchiv* [German Text Archive] project, or DTA, of the Berlin-Brandenburg Academy of Sciences and Humanities has taken a great step in this direction, producing a standardized base format for presenting reference corpora in the Modern High German language. The DTA base format (DTA-Bf)[6] is the perfect foundation for gradually integrating German-language digital collections and researching these collections through international teams who can work together from different locations and time zones using digital tools.[7]

DTA-Bf allows all documents to be presented as images and as XML text, metadata to be created for a particular document, and the coding of text content and metadata in accordance with the guidelines of the international Text Encoding Initiative (TEI). The standardized, digital and user-friendly

the collections in Brazil. Few Brazilian institutions – such as the Martius-Staden Institute in São Paulo, the Joinville City Archive in Santa Catarina and the Delfos Archive of the Pontifical Catholic University of Rio Grande do Sul in Porto Alegre – preserve newspaper collections in German. However, these still need to be scanned and systematic work is required by researchers skilled in German (or supported by German-language professionals) equipped with the latest tools. The constant rise in isolated initiatives shows that there is a public interest in this material being gradually released and made accessible to the academic community. The State University of São Paulo (UNESP), for example, digitized a small number of titles from the collection of the Martius-Staden Institute. The National Library Foundation in Rio de Janeiro has also begun to systematize and display its German-language newspaper collection.

[5] See Lauer, 'Die Vermessung der Kultur'.

[6] http://www.deutschestextarchiv.de/doku/basisformat/introduction_en.html [accessed 4 May 2018].

[7] The European DARIAH initiative is one example of how digital infrastructure is organized for research purposes: https://www.dariah.eu/tools-services/tools-and-services [accessed 4 May 2018].

environment also allows each document (or parts thereof) to be presented in other languages if a translation is available or being prepared, enabling the international team to annotate documents in optimal fashion: authorized scholars log into the repository containing the digital copies to enter notes and comments about the documents. Their annotations are saved and become part of the collection. As they work, scholars can also search for and mark sections of text specific to their interests, generating new, more specific documents for the relevant database. For example, this allows the researchers to gradually tackle graphically complex printed newspapers, which present particular technical and methodological challenges. This interdisciplinary work between philologists, historians, computer scientists and librarians is as necessary as it is exciting and fruitful.[8]

Dimensions of German Presence in Brazil

Until 1940 the German-language press comprised 121 newspapers, around 415 magazines, newsletters and periodical reports (religious, educational, humorous and political) and 65 almanacs.[9] While many of these publications were sporadic and short-lived, a quarter endured and for decades were a part of life in communities that have now become the country's key centres. For example, Joinville's *Kolonie-Zeitung* [*Colony Newspaper*] was published continuously from 1862 to 1940.

One of the few works to focus specifically on the German-language press in Brazil, Hans Gehse's 1931 thesis, includes a graphic showing the concentration of newspapers published in the region (Fig. 21). An 'x' indicates the number of titles published before Gehse's doctoral thesis was published, while a '+' shows the number of titles still in circulation at the time. The other major cultural centre of the German language, around 800 kilometres to the south, is the aforementioned state of Rio Grande do Sul. The major cities of Rio de Janeiro (with Petrópolis) and São Paulo were further hubs in the network of German-language print media at that time.

There was an astonishing degree of networking between newspapers in the various regions. References to publications in other, distant regions of

---

[8] A September 2016 workshop entitled 'Working with Digital Collections of Newspapers', part of the CLARIN-PLUS project, aimed 'to examine ways in which online language technology services can help to search, connect, analyse and visualize the language data in newspaper collections'. https://www.clarin.eu/event/2016/clarin-plus-workshop-working-digital-collections-newspapers [accessed 4 May 2018].

[9] This detailed list is all thanks to the meticulous work of Dr Thomas Gernot Keil, who has been researching in this field for many years.

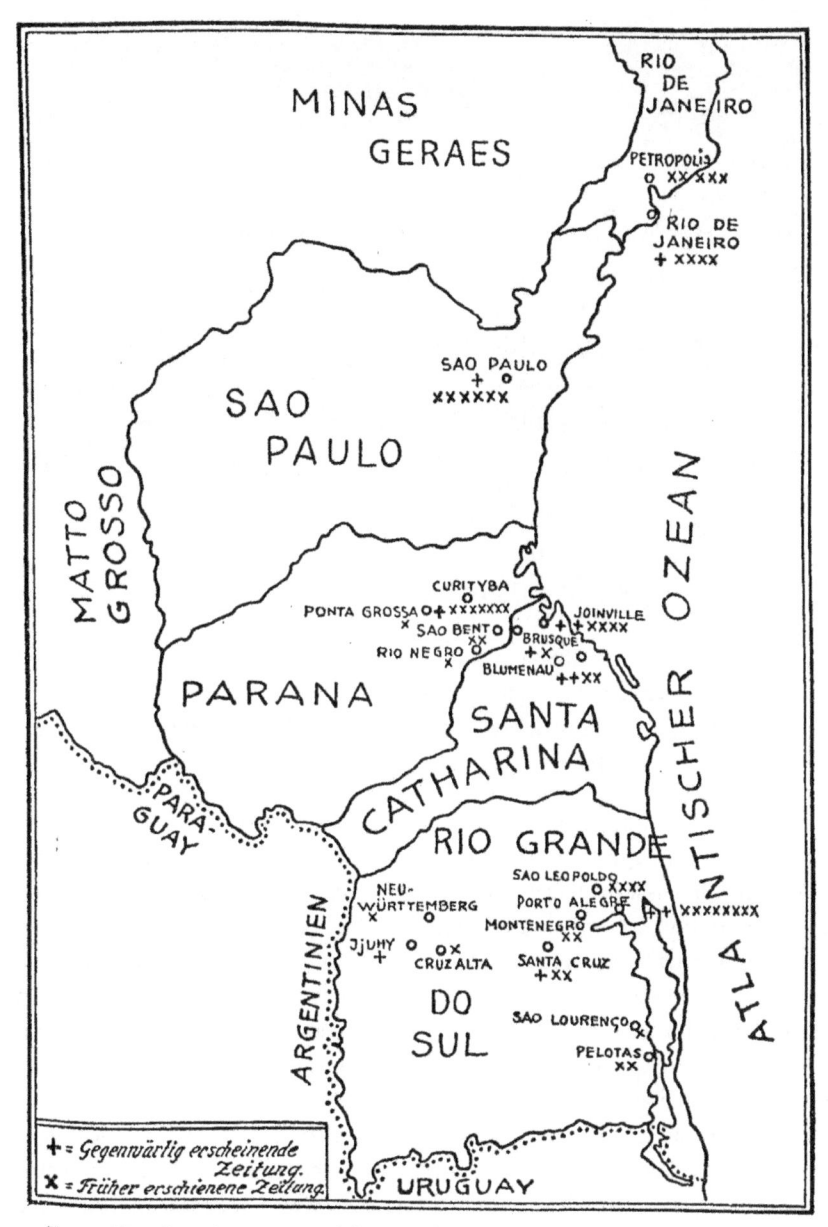

Fig. 21. The concentration of German-language newspapers in Brazil, in Hans Gehse, *Die deutsche Presse in Brasilien von 1852 bis zur Gegenwart. Ein Beitrag zur Geschichte und zum Aufgabenkreis auslanddeutschen Zeitungswesens* (Münster i. W.: Aschendorffsche Buchdruckerei, 1931), p. 177.

Fig. 22. 17 March 1888 issue of *Der Pionier*. Image taken from the freely available public domain digitization of *Der Pionier* from the Brazilian Digital Press Library: http://bndigital.bn.br/acervo-digital/der-pionier/814873 [accessed 4 May 2018].

Brazil and far beyond its borders – for example, in Argentina and the USA – illustrate the integrated discourse that was taking place. For example, the 17 March 1888 issue of *Der Pionier* [*The Pioneer*, see Fig. 22] announced the reproduction of an article published by its 'partner newspaper', the *Deutsche Zeitung* [*German Newspaper*], based in Porto Alegre, about imports permitted by Brazil's imperial government that were harming artisans in southern Brazil's German colonies and would damage the local economy.[10]

Such cross-references between documents are an inexhaustible source of information about the discursive processes of the time and about the development, circulation and transformation of content, ideas and forms of social, cultural and political interaction. The hope is that, in the foreseeable future, the document collections will be completely digitized and analysed using the methods and tools of the digital humanities. This will enable the precise diachronic examination – with no geographical boundaries – of all this material, which was far more important for Brazil than one might realize:

[10] For this specific issue in full, see: http://memoria.bn.br/pdf/814873/per814873_1888_00011.pdf [accessed 4 May 2018].

according to Rudolph Peschke's report in volume XI of *Der Auslandsdeutsche* [*The German Abroad*] from 1928, 'the number of people influenced by German newspapers, with an estimated total circulation of 50,000 – 55,000' was 'around 800,000 or more, a significant proportion of the cultivated section of the overall population, calculated at around 36–37 million'.[11] Copies were passed from home to home and from hand to hand, being highly valued sources of information and mediators (much more than mere intermediate links[12]) for communal, interpersonal 'associations'.

In 1900, 65 per cent of the 9.7 million people over the age of 15 living in Brazil were illiterate. In 1940, 56.1 per cent of the 23.6 million citizens in this age group were still unable to read.[13] Compulsory education had been introduced in Europe's German-speaking regions at an early stage via the establishment of educational institutions (for example, through Frederick the Great's General Rural School Regulation), meaning that 'officially [...] illiteracy has been eradicated in Germany since 1912 at the latest. The last census was conducted in this year, recording an illiteracy rate of 0.01% to 0.02%.'[14] The illiteracy rate among the German–Brazilian population was, therefore, presumably much lower than in the rest of Brazil.

Digitizing the newspapers and processing them using digital humanities methods and tools is an opportunity to gain insights into the role of German-speaking citizens in the development of Brazilian society.

The following examples, which demonstrate the academic importance of the German-speaking press in Brazil, include the multidisciplinary topic of reciprocal depictions in Brazilian/North American relationships.[15]

---

[11] Arndt and Olson, *Die deutschsprachige Presse der Amerkias*, p. 100.

[12] This distinction refers to Bruno Latour's Actor-Network-Theory (ANT), which is ideally suited to researching the importance and social achievements of the press in their societal context. See Bruno Latour, *Re-Assembling the Social: An Introduction to Actor-Network-Theory* (Oxford: Oxford University Press, 2005).

[13] See Ministério da Educação/Instituto Nacional de Estudos e Pesquisas Educacionais Anísio Teixeira (INEP), *Mapa do Analfabetismo no Brasil* (2003), 6 (http://portal.inep.gov.br> [accessed 4 May 2018]).

[14] See Peter Eisenberg, 'Arbeiterbildung und Alphabetisierung im 19. Jahrhundert', in *Analphabetismus in der Bundesrepublik*, ed. by H.W. Giese, vol. 1, pp. 13–32 (*Osnabrücker Beiträge zur Sprachtheorie* 23/1983).

[15] Further examples in the narrower field of German studies would include German-language (layman) theatre in Brazil, languages in contact, changes to German in the lusophone environment, German as a medium for debating the history of ideas, and the circulation of literary texts in German in the Brazilian press. A specific example of the latter: in 1883 the journal *The Pioneer* published a German translation of Samuel Adams Drake's work *Yankee Jim* as a serialized novel-story. Other, similar texts were also published in the press, including foreign works and Brazilian novels translated

Networked Thinking: The German-language Press in North and South America

Examining the history of immigration in the Americas immediately raises questions about complex and conflict-ridden processes such as injustices in the world of work. Brazil and the USA have both been shaped by the mass forced immigration of people from Africa. The situation did not change until globalization accelerated at the end of the nineteenth century, not least owing to mass migration from Europe. The material, social and cultural traits these societies now possess were borne from the coming together of millions of migrants of extremely varied provenance and from negotiations – between these people and the existing power structures in the countries, between the different groups and, above all, among themselves. From the mid-nineteenth century, German immigrants and their descendants gradually became more involved in processes of change and in the relevant German-language (and therefore multilingual) public debates. This field has yet to be researched in detail.

From a political perspective, the immigration of German-speaking Europeans – particularly in the context of the failed bourgeois revolution of 1848 – was in many cases a gust of wind that set the pages of a liberally minded, German-speaking press all a-flutter. Debates about the liberal development of economy and society and the abolitionist stance of many journalists of German provenance are connected to their engagement with German-speaking regions overseas; many people who left Europe in the mid-nineteenth century did so because of its political situation. In the USA, Carl Schurz was the most prominent representative of this political tradition.[16] Fleeing Restoration Europe, these 'Forty-Eighters' found new spaces in both North and South America to spread their ideas and for their own social, political and often economic activities.

One example for Brazil would be Ottokar Dörffel, who founded the *Colony Newspaper* in Joinville; this was one of Brazil's most important and longest-lasting German-language papers.[17] Liberally minded but not at all revolutionary,

into German, novels written in Germany and local works produced by recently arrived German immigrants or German–Brazilians. This vast collection of novels has not yet been identified.

[16] See Carl Wittke, *Refugees of Revolution. The German Forty-Eighters in America* (Westport, CT: Greenwood, 1970) and Frank Baron, 'Abraham Lincoln and the German Immigrants: Turners and Forty-Eighters', in *Yearbook of German-American Studies. Supplemental Issue*, vol. 4 (Lawrence: University of Kansas, 2012).

[17] https://dokumente.ufpr.br/en/dbpdigital.html [accessed 17 November 2019]. The *Kolonie Zeitung* is currently being digitized within the 'dbp Digital' project, a collaboration between the Federal University of Paraná (UFPR) and the historical archive of

the newspaper – like many of Brazil's other German-language publications – criticized slavery from the viewpoint of Brazil's disorganized and ineffective economic order. For example, issue 35, published on 2 September 1865 after the end of the American Civil War, contains the news from North America – most worrying for the publisher – that the stronger freed slaves were 'refusing to work' and abandoning the 'largely deserted' plantations 'in droves'. The 'planters' freed themselves of the 'old, infirm' ones left behind, 'leaving them with no means of living, so that the cities swarm with Negros in need of support'.[18] Without wishing to ignore the now extremely problematic wording, opinions and statements in the reports of the time, we should also recognize that, in describing the unplanned abolition of slavery, as the article goes on to do on its second page, it seems to deliberately contrast with a report on the *following* page of the same edition. This report publicizes a pamphlet from the *Revista Commercial* [*Commercial Magazine*] of the coastal city of Santos entitled *Gedanken und Fingerzeige, um die Sklaverei in Brasilien aufzuheben, das Eigenthum zu retten und die Freigelassenen zu nützlichen Bürgern zu erziehen* [*Thoughts and pointers to abolish slavery in Brazil, save property and teach the freedmen to become useful citizens*].[19]

The Santos pamphlet proposes the foundation of an '"Evangelical, patriotic, national brotherhood" in all areas of the country that shall gradually buy the slaves' freedom from their masters through joint contributions'.[20] After a transition period of 'about six years' in which the 'free-bought slaves' would 'remain the property of the brotherhood', the budding citizens would work to repay the brotherhood, amass their own fortune, receive their 'letter of manumission' and finally gain their 'freedom'.[21] From a modern perspective, it is extremely difficult to see the quest for justice in such reasoning; however, given the prevalent conditions and brutal 'logic' of the time, a small step forward was taken when Ottokar Dörffel, who had immigrated from Germany almost ten years before, began a dialogue with the Santos initiative and clearly declared that 'slavery must end'. The German-language publications are fearful of the 'chaos of misfortune for both the masters and the

---

the city of Joinville. The archive in Joinville has an almost complete physical collection of the newspaper. Several copies are already available in the 'Digital Newspaper Collection' of the 'dbp Digital' project. The project was supported by the Fritz Thyssen Foundation from June 2016 to December 2018; I would like to take this opportunity to thank the foundation.

[18] *Kolonie Zeitung*, 35 (2 September 1865), p. 138.
[19] *Kolonie Zeitung*, 35 (2 September 1865), p. 139.
[20] *Kolonie Zeitung*, 35 (2 September 1865), p. 139.
[21] *Kolonie Zeitung*, 35 (2 September 1865), p. 139.

slaves';[22] more detailed research is required into the concern that all people may be integrated into formal society and become citizens in a dignified manner, something the country has thus far failed to achieve.

When considering how important research into the German-language press from the perspective of Transnational German Studies could be for the development of German Studies in the Americas, we must mention the impressive number of publications in German in the United States. In their book *German? American? Literature? New Directions in German-American Studies* (2002), Fluck and Sollors wrote:

> New electronic bibliographic research has shown that in the Harvard University library system there are more than 25,000 German-language titles published in the United States, making German by far the largest single non-English language group among American imprints. How many more might the Library of Congress, The New York Public Library, and the University of Chicago Archives hold? In addition, more than 5,000 German newspapers and periodicals have been identified.[23]

Indeed, a remarkable amount of specific research has been carried out in the United States, such as the research registered in the *Yearbook for German-American Studies* since 1969 or Karl Arndt und May Olson's seminal work *Die deutschsprachige Presse der Amerikas* [*The German Language Press of the Americas*, 1973]. Given the volume of work yet to be explored, ample scope remains for further investigation, particularly with new approaches that could aim to link research into the sources with the use of digital resources.

The role of the German-language press in links between Brazil and the United States should not be disregarded. Comparing sample issues of the aforementioned *The Pioneer* with a periodical available at the University of Chicago,[24] interestingly titled *Der deutsche Pionier* [*The German Pioneer*], we can see many correlations that provide a deeper insight into similarities between Brazil and the United States.

---

[22] *Kolonie Zeitung*, 35 (2 September 1865), p. 139.

[23] Winfied Fluck and Werner Sollors, *German? American? Literature? New Directions in German-American Studies* (New York: Peter Lang, 2002), pp. 3–4.

[24] I would like to thank David Wellbery and Brodwyn Fischer, who in June 2017 invited me to visit the University of Chicago and to present on this topic as part of the CLAS Tinker Field Research Grant programme. I would also like to thank Hans Joas for first encouraging me to take part. The visit prompted me to write the first version of this text for a presentation at the Center for Latin American Studies, University of Chicago.

However, rather than simply comparing the conditions in both countries or the two countries' relationships with German-speaking Europe, a *histoire croisée* approach must be taken to these publications, as first proposed in 2002 by Michael Werner and Bénédicte Zimmermann, along with other reviving trends within historiography.[25] According to these authors, '[histoire croisée] invites us to reconsider the interactions between different societies or cultures, erudite disciplines or traditions (more generally, between social and cultural productions). [It] focuses on empirical intercrossings consubstantial with the object of study, as well as on the operations by which researchers themselves cross scales, categories, and viewpoints.'[26] German-language newspapers in the Americas are highly involved in networks of international discourse that cannot be described as merely 'national'; it is therefore obvious, even unavoidable, that publications of varying provenance from such transnational perspectives should be considered to set these texts in motion and to prompt new perspectives on them.

For example, the first page of *The Pioneer* from 24 July 1886 (published in Curitiba) presents a lengthy review of Andrew Carnegie's *Triumphant Democracy; or, Fifty Years' March of the Republic*, which highlights the economic grandeur of the United States (modern readers will correctly associate the author's name with that of Carnegie Hall, the result of one of the American industrialist's many philanthropic donations). The newspaper's review contains a list of data regarding North America's economic productivity and wealth of natural resources. This text, entitled 'An example for Brazil', was clearly designed to provoke the government authorities and social elite in Brazil, by then in the midst of a profound financial crisis triggered in particular by the lack of productive and labour activities and by the collapse of the slave-production model, which was almost exclusively agricultural.

Indirectly, the German-speaking communities of Brazil – just like its other advanced, Portuguese-speaking powers – demanded a boost from the promotion of economic activities based on free work and the guarantees granted to the relevant small and medium-sized businesses. Without drawing detailed comparisons, the review attempts to suggest that Brazil's natural resources, if correctly managed, could facilitate a whole new form of wealth production, as well as new perspectives on work relations and

---

[25] See also Gunilla Budde, Sebastian Conrad and Oliver Janz (eds.), *Transnationale Geschichte. Themen, Tendenzen und Theorien* (Göttingen: Vandenhoeck & Ruprecht, 2006).

[26] Michael Werner and Bénédicte Zimmermann, 'Beyond Comparison: Histoire Croisée and the Challenge of Reflexivity', *History and Theory* 45.1 (2006), pp. 30–50 (p. 30).

individual property. This shows how the Brazilian German-language liberal press viewed the United States as a space of projection and as a valid point of comparison for the internal problems being discussed within Brazilian society.

On the other hand, the monthly periodical *The German Pioneer* – published in Cincinnati, Ohio, from 1869 to 1887 – published two articles about Brazil as a destination for German immigrants in its February 1886 issue (Issue 2, Volume 17) and its April 1886 issue (Issue 4, Volume 17). These two articles reveal that Brazil's German-speaking communities were interested in attracting new German immigrants. The travel and migratory agencies of the period fought hard to secure investments from German citizens who decided to leave their home country in search of a fruitful beginning on the new continent.

The first of these articles focuses on the many recent initiatives and measures that have favoured immigrants in Brazil. It also states that, with German immigrants choosing Brazil over North America, this must be considered of 'national interest to the German people'.[27] The article also praises Brazil's economic prospects and opportunities thanks to 'its mild and healthy climate, fertile soil, existing and easily expandable railways, navigable rivers and the proximity of the coast', all of which will allow it to link up with global transportation networks. Finally, the article highlights the fact that a commission from the *Deutscher Kolonialverein* [German Association of Immigration] had been sent to the states of Santa Catarina and Paraná (at that time known as 'provinces').

This eulogistic review was followed two months later by an article entitled 'Der Deutsche in Brasilien' ['The German in Brazil'], in *The German Pioneer*, No. 4, April 1886. Clearly contradictory in tone, this article vehemently criticized those who depicted Brazil in favourable terms, ultimately blaming Prussia and its embassies for promoting immigration. The author then begins to describe Brazil, stating that in no other country was 'public security ... threatened to such a great extent'.[28] Not only were a great majority of its citizens apparently keen on 'stealing, assaulting, burning and murdering',[29] but the policemen of the time were well known for their threats and extortion. The author works on the assumption that praise for Brazil as a destination for German immigrants ultimately proves to be false and is due solely to the individual interests of profit-focused initiatives. He therefore recommends that readers in the United States choose independent periodicals published

---

[27] *Der deutsche Pioneer* 2.17 (February 1886), p. 103.
[28] *Der deutsche Pioneer* 4 (April 1886), p. 303.
[29] *Der deutsche Pioneer* 4 (April 1886), p. 303.

in the German language in Brazil that offer more neutral reports and present a more appropriate picture of the difficulties experienced by immigrants. Giving a (vague) example of a reliable source of information, he mentions an article published in Porto Alegre that encourages readers to beware of the police and to create 'a civil guard body for the defence of the citizens against the authorities of state security'.[30] The author goes on to describe in detail the precarious legal system and its incredible 'lack of rights', above all as a corpus of corruption and violent repression against immigrant workers who tried to fight for their rights. In the same vein, the author dedicates a whole paragraph to the inequality seen in private property and production conditions.

Finally, the article condemns the attachment to Brazil widely felt by German–Brazilians. In words of Mr Spielberg (the German deputy), originally taken from the *Colony Newspaper*, from 1885 (No. 15), these immigrants or descendants of immigrants (the German–Brazilians) reject their German nationality. Mr Spielberg, who advocated immigration to Brazil from his position in Germany, states that: 'In Brazil, farmers who are not even naturalized can be heard to say: We come from Germany, we speak German, but we are not Germans!'[31] The North American journalist argues that it would be naive to expect Germans who have immigrated to Brazil and their descendants to have a sense of national identity that would maintain their connection to the German Empire in the long term. In attempting to fight German immigration to Brazil, he himself indirectly advocates immigration to North America and gets to the heart of the argument that, ultimately, cultural identity and assimilation processes are related to material and economic conditions. Nevertheless, a hybrid cultural form develops throughout the article as the deputy continues to voice the words of the German–Brazilian immigrants: 'We speak German, but we are not Germans.' In a time of emerging colonialism, this was a highly charged issue that drew the attention of significant literary figures and intellectuals in other contexts too, as in Heinrich Mann's Brazilian novel *Zwischen den Rassen* [*Between Races*, 1907].[32]

---

[30] *Der deutsche Pioneer* 4 (April 1886), p. 303.

[31] *Kolonie Zeitung* 15 (1885), p. 304.

[32] See Heinrich Mann, *Zwischen den Rassen* (Frankfurt am Main: Fischer, 1987). Gabriele Dürbeck, 'Rassismus und Kosmopolitismus in Heinrich Manns "Zwischen den Rassen" (1907)', in *Heinrich Mann-Jahrbuch*, ed. by Ariane Martin and Hans Wisskirchen, vol. 25 (Lübeck: Schmidt-Römhild, 2007), pp. 9–30. Karl-Josef Kuschel, Frido Mann, Paulo Soethe, *Mutterland. Die Familie Mann und Brasilien* (Düsseldorf: Artemis & Winkler, 2009).

The issues of identity and assimilation are themselves of vital interest; the cultural process is quite fascinating and leaves considerable scope for further investigation in comparative studies between Brazil and the United States, which may still be conducted solely on the basis of documents in the German language and in dialogue with the discourses of the time within German-speaking Europe. Indeed, willing researchers could study how the circulation of opinions and news influenced the formation of stereotypes or the diffusion of objective knowledge about the foreign country in question, each in its respective public sphere, and how the circulation of these texts in German-speaking Europe influenced its perception of Brazil and the USA.

From this intercultural perspective and from the perspective of the aforementioned debates about work relations and the development of the economy and legal system, German-language journals published in Brazil, the USA and other American countries are a promising source of new academic discoveries.

Summary and Outlook

The now historic German-language newspapers remain a vivid and colourful reflection of social and cultural life at the time of their creation. These publications frequently offer unexpected and progressive statements as well as information on topics and perspectives of political and social transformation within their particular context. For example, they helped to alter the stereotypical image of Germans in South America, an image that became more complex and long-lasting and was represented in a wide range of historical and cultural formats.

Germanist approaches, a closer linguistic examination of the documents and digital processing can help to overcome the methodological, epistemological and quantitative limitations of previous research into the history of immigration, which was required to focus more on the depiction of individual migration experiences and has not yet been able to consider in detail how this material is embedded in complex discursive contexts or to view it as part of a multilingual continuum in the society of the time. Modern interdisciplinary and digital research processes bring together editing, digital text preparation and the development of subprojects with different, mutually enriching focal areas.

The digitization of and research into old copies of German-language newspapers in the Americas have little to do with a 'virtual' reality: in fact, this process lends a more specific, tangible form to social and cultural processes that can be traced far back into the past and reconstructed in discursive form. The past is becoming the subject of innovative research approaches. With the transnational approach of a philological, digital German Studies founded on cultural studies, materials from Brazil, North America and other American countries can be used to gain and disseminate insights into an early, highly complex phase in the development of our modern global society.

Suggestions for Further Reading

Arndt, Karl, and May Olson, *Die deutschsprachige Presse der Amerikas 1732–1968. Geschichte und Bibliographie* (Munich: Dokumentation, 1973–1985), 845 pp.

Fluck, Winfied, and Werner Sollors, *German? American? Literature? New Directions in German-American Studies* (New York: Peter Lang, 2002), 419 pp.

Gehse, Hans, *Die deutsche Presse in Brasilien von 1852 bis zur Gegenwart. Ein Beitrag zur Geschichte und zum Aufgabenkreis auslanddeutschen Zeitungswesens* (Münster i. W.: Aschendorffsche Buchdruckerei, 1931), 174 pp.

Lauer, Gerhard, 'Die Vermessung der Kultur. Geisteswissenschaften als Digital Humanities', in *Big Data. Das neue Versprechen der Allwissenheit*, ed. by Heinrich Geiselberger and Tobias Moorstedt (Berlin: Suhrkamp, 2013), pp. 99–116.

Le Blanc, Clara Isabell, 'Authentisch-historisches Material als Basis zur Entwicklung eines diskursiven DAF-Unterrichts an Hochschulen im brasilianischen Kontext: zur Arbeit mit Zeitungsartikeln der deutschsprachigen brasilianischen Presse über die Abolitionsfrage um 1888'. Magisterarbeit - Universidade Federal do Paraná, Curitiba (2019) https://acervodigital.ufpr.br/handle/1884/65795 [accessed April 4 2020].

Wittke, Carl, *Refugees of Revolution. The German Forty-Eighters in America* (Philadelphia, PA: University of Pennsylvania Press, 1952), 384 pp.

Part 4

Subjectivity: Ideology and the Individual

Part I

13

Radical Germans and Their Anglophone Interpreters

Exploring and Translating 'The Unconscious' and Psychoanalysis

Angus Nicholls

Introduction: 'German' Solutions to a 'French' Problem

Despite being predominantly associated with the intellectual history of German-speaking Europe, the cardinal and defining concept of psychoanalysis – 'the unconscious', *das Unbewusste* – had distinctively transnational origins, and has enjoyed a most virulent transnational reception. In fact, this reception has been so florid that many people in the Western world may still feel that they possess, in some manifestation or other, an 'unconscious', normally understood to be a dynamic component of the individual's mental life of which that individual is not directly aware, but which may nevertheless influence their behaviour. The unconscious is the central 'object' of a purported 'science' of which Sigmund Freud (1856–1939) declared himself the inventor. Yet to describe the unconscious as an 'object', 'container' or 'place' – as Freud initially attempted to do when founding his new 'science' – is problematic, as the development and reception of psychoanalysis have shown, and as we shall see below.

Traditionally, sciences form themselves around observations of empirical objects or experimentally verified phenomena, describing these through the invention of technical concepts that have a systematic relation to one another. The unconscious emerged as a term in German thought around the middle of the eighteenth century, partly in response to the ideas of the French philosopher René Descartes (1596–1650), a figure widely viewed as the founder of modern European thinking about the human 'subject' or self. Descartes's most famous philosophical dictum – *cogito ergo sum*, 'I think therefore I am' – was introduced to overcome his radical scepticism concerning the external world. Even if the external world is a dream, or an illusion created by an evil genius to trick us, we can at least be sure, argues Descartes, that there is a thinking substance that doubts and that may be being deceived. Seen in this way, our thinking subjectivity is the only foundation that enables us to arrive at an argument that may, in the end, ascertain the reliability of our best controlled cognitions. With the *cogito* as his starting point, Descartes establishes an argument that can then claim that 'clarity' and 'distinctness' are epistemic qualities that guarantee the reliability of our cognitions.[1]

While this argument formed one of the dominant epistemological frameworks for continental philosophy, at least until its critique by empiricists such as the Scottish philosopher David Hume (1711–1776), it also failed to answer some important questions: What goes on in the human mind when it is not consciously thinking – for example, during sleep? And what role is played by those human perceptions that fall below Descartes's truth threshold of clarity and distinctness? As Matthew Bell and Günter Gödde have shown in important studies on the history of German psychology, it was the German tradition of psychology that, especially during the eighteenth and nineteenth centuries, attempted to provide answers to these questions, inaugurating what Gödde has called 'tradition-lines' of German-language thought on the unconscious that would go on to influence Freud.[2] The main purpose of these tradition-lines was to show that the human mind or soul (in German the equivalent terms normally used are *Geist* or *Seele*) is more than just the conscious mind, and that mental activity is constantly going on beneath the threshold of our conscious awareness. While these German thinkers were 'radical' insofar as they forced European thought to examine the darker and less-than-rational regions of the self, their radicalism was tempered by the fact that they undertook these explorations largely from within the Enlightenment framework of the Western subject delineated by Descartes. Being a 'radical German' thus meant contributing to what Max Horkheimer and Theodor W. Adorno – clearly writing under the influence of Freud – have described as the 'dark' Enlightenment: the attempt to radicalize the Enlightenment by

---

[1] René Descartes, *Meditations on First Philosophy: With Selections from the Objections and Replies*, ed. by and trans. John Cottingham (Cambridge: Cambridge University Press, 1996), pp. 16–23 (Mediation II).

[2] Matthew Bell, *The German Tradition of Psychology in Literature and Thought, 1700–1840* (Cambridge: Cambridge University Press, 2005); Günter Gödde, *Traditionslinien des 'Unbewussten': Schopenhauer, Nietzsche, Freud* (Tübingen: edition diskord, 1999). See also Angus Nicholls and Martin Liebscher (eds.), *Thinking the Unconscious: Nineteenth-Century German Thought* (Cambridge: Cambridge University Press, 2010).

exposing its 'dark side', which lies in 'the fate of the human instincts and passions repressed and distorted by civilization'.³

The inaugurator of what Gödde describes as the *cognitive* tradition-line of theories about the unconscious was Gottfried Wilhelm Leibniz (1646–1716), a German philosopher who wrote predominantly in French, and who argued that some impressions on the human mind are insufficiently intense to become *apperceptions* – objects of conscious awareness – rather than just *perceptions*.⁴ 'The Cartesians', Leibniz writes in his *La Monadologie* [*Monadalogy*, 1714], 'have fallen far short, as they have given no thought to perceptions which are not apperceived' (§14).⁵ Leibniz elaborates upon this idea in the *Nouveaux essais sur l'entendement humain* [*New Essays on Human Understanding*, completed in 1705 but not published until 1765], where he observes that 'there is in us an infinity of perceptions [...] of which we are unaware because these impressions are either too minute and too numerous, or else too unvarying, so that they are not sufficiently distinctive on their own'. Referring to these perceptions as 'small' or weak perceptions [*petites perceptions*], Leibniz notes that, although they do not fulfil the Cartesian criteria of clarity and distinctness, they are still to be regarded as perceptions.⁶

Thus, when the term 'unconsciousness' [*Unbewußtseyn*] first enters German philosophy in 1776, it does so within the context of this cognitive Cartesian-cum-Leibnizian framework. The philosopher who first deployed this term was Ernst Platner (1714–1818), in his *Philosophische Aphorismen* [*Philosophical Aphorisms*, 1776–1782]. In a similar way to Leibniz, Platner characterizes those ideas within consciousness as apperceptions and those beneath consciousness as 'dark' or 'obscure' representations [*dunkle Vorstellungen*].⁷ Similarly, Immanuel Kant (1724–1804), in part three of his *Versuch, den Begriff der negativen Größen in die Weltweisheit einzuführen* [*Attempt to Introduce the Concept of Negative Magnitudes into Philosophy*, 1763], argues that when we focus on something within our consciousness then

---

³ Max Horkheimer and Theodor W. Adorno, *Dialectic of Enlightenment: Philosophical Fragments*, ed. by Gundelin Schmid Noerr, trans. Edmund Jephcott (1947; Stanford, CA: Stanford University Press, 2002), p. 192.

⁴ Gödde, *Traditionslinien des 'Unbewussten'*, pp. 29–34.

⁵ Gottfried Wilhelm Leibniz, *Leibniz's Monadology: A New Translation and Guide*, ed. by and trans. Lloyd Strickland (Edinburgh: Edinburgh University Press, 2014), p. 16.

⁶ Leibniz, *New Essays on Human Understanding*, ed. by and trans. Peter Remnant and Jonathan Bennett (Cambridge: Cambridge University Press, 1996), pp. 54–55.

⁷ Ernst Platner, *Philosophische Aphorismen nebst einigen Anleitungen zur philosophischen Geschichte* (Leipzig: Schwickertscher Verlag, 1776), pp. 7–9.

the other things surrounding it may accordingly be obscured or 'darkened' [*verdunkelt*].[8] In a famous passage that presages the way in which the use of metaphor and simile would go on to determine German-language discourses on the unconscious, Kant then goes on to propose that only 'infinitely few points' [*unendlich wenige Punkte*] 'on the great map of our mind' [*auf der großen Karte unseres Gemüts*] are illuminated, with most representations falling below the threshold of clarity and distinctness.[9] This cartographic metaphor was not lost on the romantic author Jean Paul (Johann Paul Friedrich Richter, 1763–1825), who, influenced by the European colonial explorations of his era, refers in his novel *Selina* (1827) to 'the enormous kingdom of the unconscious' [*das ungeheure Reich des Unbewussten*] as 'this true inner Africa' [*dieses wahre innere Afrika*].[10]

Exploring these darker regions of the self also involved understanding how human subjectivity relates to 'nature', and this question formed a separate, though related, tradition-line of thinking about the unconscious that tended to focus on the irrational 'drives' [*Triebe*] or 'inclinations' [*Neigungen*] within the human subject.[11] Here Kant proposes that our natural or physiological inclinations, such as sexual desires, are often 'obscure' [*dunkel*] to us.[12] Similarly, Arthur Schopenhauer (1788–1860) argues – in *Die Welt als Wille und Vorstellung* [*The World as Will and Representation*, vol. 1, 1819; vol. 2, 1844] – that all of nature, including human beings, is determined by the will [*der Wille*], a blind, irrational and unconscious drive for reproduction present in all nature, ranging from plants to human beings.[13] Humans experience this will most directly through the sex-drive [*Geschlechtstrieb*], which is 'the most complete manifestation of the will-to-live',[14] no matter how disturbing or unpalatable it may be to the conscious mind.

---

[8] Immanuel Kant, *Theoretical Philosophy, 1755–1770*, trans. David Walford and Ralf Meerbore, *The Cambridge Edition of the Works of Immanuel Kant* (Cambridge: Cambridge University Press, 1992), p. 234.

[9] Immanuel Kant, *Anthropology from a Pragmatic Point of View*, trans. Robert B. Louden (Cambridge: Cambridge University Press, 2006), pp. 23–25.

[10] Jean Paul, *Selina oder über die Unsterblichkeit der Seele* (1827), quoted in *'Dieses wahre innere Afrika': Texte zur Entdeckung des Unbewussten vor Freud*, ed. by Ludger Lütkehaus (Gießen: Psychosozial Verlag, 2005), p. 77.

[11] Gödde, *Traditionslinien des 'Unbewussten'*, pp. 57–80.

[12] Kant, *Anthropology*, p. 25.

[13] See Christopher Janaway, 'The Real Essence of Human Beings: Schopenhauer and the Unconscious Will', in *Thinking the Unconscious*, ed. by Nicholls and Liebscher, pp. 140–55.

[14] Arthur Schopenhauer, *The World as Will and Representation*, trans. E.F.J. Payne, 2 vols. (New York: Dover, 1969), vol. 2, p. 514.

But during the second half of the nineteenth century, metaphysical ideas such as Schopenhauer's 'will' came to be seen as unacceptably vague and speculative, and German philosophy accordingly attempted to orientate itself towards the empirically verifiable methods of the natural sciences.[15] The emergence of the psychoanalytic idea of the unconscious can be properly understood only in light of this attempted reorientation, since, as we shall shortly see, Freud originally saw psychoanalysis as outlining a 'scientific psychology' – by which he meant a *natural-scientific* psychology.

In this respect, a significant forerunner to Freud was the German psychologist Gustav Theodor Fechner (1801–1887), the founder of 'psychophysics'.[16] The research programme of psychophysics – outlined in Fechner's *Elemente der Psycho-Physik* [*Elements of Psychophysics*, 2 vols., 1860] – posited what came to be known as 'psycho-physical parallelism' – the idea that all mental phenomena have an underlying physiological correlate.[17] This notion became a general postulate of natural-scientific psychology of the late nineteenth century, having key adherents in figures such as Wilhelm Wundt (1832–1920) in Germany and William James (1842–1910) in the United States.[18] Fechner continued the threshold model of consciousness inaugurated by Leibniz and later developed within an explicitly psychological framework by Johann Friedrich Herbart (1776–1841) in his *Lehrbuch zur Psychologie* [*Textbook on Psychology*, 1816].[19] Following the lead of Herbart, while also criticizing his metaphysical tendencies, Fechner sought to underpin the threshold model with a modern experimental method focused on the measurement of sensations.[20] Applying his so-called 'formula of measurement' [*Maßformel*], Fechner showed that physiological stimuli must reach a certain level of intensity to cross the threshold of consciousness.

---

[15] See Herbert Schnädelbach, *Philosophy in Germany, 1831–1933*, trans. Eric Matthews (Cambridge: Cambridge University Press, 1984), especially chapter 3, pp. 66–108.

[16] For context, see Michael Heidelberger, *Nature from Within: Gustav Theodor Fechner and his Psychophysical Worldview*, trans. Cynthia Klohr (Pittsburgh, PA: University of Pittsburgh Press, 2004).

[17] Gustav Theodor Fechner, *Elemente der Psychophysik*, 2 vols. (Leipzig: Breitkopf und Härtel, 1860), vol. 1, p. 8, quote trans. Simon Thomas; quoted from Michael Heidelberger, 'Gustav Theodor Fechner and the Unconscious', trans. Simon Thomas, in *Thinking the Unconscious*, ed. by Nicholls and Liebscher, pp. 200–40 (p. 211).

[18] Heidelberger, 'Gustav Theodor Fechner and the Unconscious', pp. 212–13.

[19] Johann Friedrich Herbart, *Lehrbuch zur Psychologie* (Königsberg: Unzer, 1816), p. 105.

[20] Heidelberger, 'Gustav Theodor Fechner and the Unconscious', pp. 207–10, 223–25.

Crucially, Fechner also – albeit only inferentially, as his many critics pointed out[21] – demonstrated the existence of stimuli that do not cross this threshold and which are accordingly to be regarded as unconscious. While the idea that unconscious representations could sink below the threshold of consciousness must in no way be conflated with Freud's idea of psychological 'repression' [*Verdrängung*], Fechner's attempted natural-scientific charting of the unconscious would serve as one of the models for Freud's new 'science' of psychoanalysis.

The problem raised by these tradition-lines – and a problem that became acute when Freud attempted to characterize psychoanalysis as a natural science – lay in the fact that 'the unconscious' is neither an empirical object nor a phenomenon that is susceptible to positive observation by way of scientific experiment. The unconscious or 'unconscious' effects – and, as we shall see, a strong distinction is necessary between the substantive form of *the* unconscious and adjectival uses of the term 'unconscious' – is much more an *inference* concerning something that cannot be directly observed. But inferences – even if they cannot be verified experimentally – can be powerful things, providing human beings with orientation and perhaps even with a narrative about their lives in times of difficulty. And, precisely because of their orientation-giving power, they also move readily across cultural and linguistic boundaries. The purpose of this chapter will therefore be to show how the modern inference of the unconscious began to be theorized in scientific psychology, how it entered psychoanalysis and how the psychoanalytic discourses on the unconscious travelled beyond German-speaking Europe, in this case through the highly successful – but also highly contested – translation of Freud's works into the English *Standard Edition of the Complete Psychological Works of Sigmund Freud*. Here some preliminary drawing of boundaries is necessary: the focus here is primarily on German-language *thought* (meaning philosophy and psychological theory), rather than on other equally important traditions to do with the unconscious, such as literature, hypnotism, somnambulism and occult practices.[22] And, for

---

[21] See the discussion in Heidelberger, 'Gustav Theodor Fechner and the Unconscious', pp. 221–26.

[22] For a discussion of hypnotism, the occult and religious practices of psychological healing related to the unconscious, see Henri F. Ellenberger, *The Discovery of the Unconscious: The History and Evolution of Dynamic Psychiatry* (New York: Basic Books, 1970), chapters 1–4 (pp. 3–253). Some analysis of the unconscious as a theme in German literature before Freud is offered by Rüdiger Görner in 'The Hidden Agent of the Self: Towards an Aesthetic Theory of the Non-Conscious in German Romanticism', in *Thinking the Unconscious*, ed. by Nicholls and Liebscher, pp. 121–39.

reasons of space, the psychoanalytic tradition will be examined only through its founder, Freud, and not his colleagues and successors, such as Carl Gustav Jung and Jacques Lacan, to mention just two prominent names.

Freud's Conceptions of the Unconscious

Freud's conceptions of the unconscious were influenced by a range of sources: by his general absorption of the romantic and German idealist notion – found, for example, in Schopenhauer – that the unconscious emerges from aspects of 'nature' within the subject; and by the cognitive tradition-line of the unconscious that begins with Leibniz and receives its modern scientific formulation in the works of Fechner.[23] But, because of his wish to establish psychoanalysis as a modern science modelled along natural-scientific lines, Freud was less inclined to acknowledge figures such as Schopenhauer,[24] while at the same time ostentatiously displaying his proximity to the scientific tradition of Fechner, whose ideas he claims to have followed closely.[25] Here our purpose is not to offer an exhaustive account of Freud's ideas about the unconscious; rather, we will focus on a particular tension within them that would have a profound effect on their transnational reception: namely, the tension between Freud's 'will to science', on the one hand, and his inevitable recourse to metaphorical modes of expression to communicate his ideas about the unconscious, on the other. It was arguably the attempt to resolve this tension that shaped some of the choices made by Freud's Anglophone translators – choices that would play a determining role in the global reception of psychoanalysis.

Freud's 'will to science' can be found in the ambitious early manifesto for psychoanalysis that in English has come to be known as the 'Project for a Scientific Psychology' but which in German simply bears the title of 'Entwurf einer Psychologie' (draft or sketch of a psychology). Composed in 1895, the

---

[23] Günter Gödde, 'Freud and Nineteenth-Century Philosophical Sources on the Unconscious', in *Thinking the Unconscious*, ed. by Nicholls and Liebscher, pp. 261–86.

[24] As Günter Gödde shows, Freud's self-relation to Schopenhauer is characterized by a complex mixture of acknowledgement and attempts at differentiation: see Gödde, 'Freud and Nineteenth-Century Philosophical Sources on the Unconscious', pp. 281–84.

[25] Freud writes: 'I was always open to the ideas of G.T. Fechner and have followed that thinker on many important points.' Sigmund Freud, 'An Autobiographical Study', in *The Standard Edition of the Complete Psychological Works of Sigmund Freud*, ed. by and trans. James Strachey and Anna Freud et al., 24 vols. (London: The Hogarth Press, 1953–1974), vol. 20, pp. 7–74 (p. 59); the *Standard Edition* is hereafter cited as SE followed by volume and page numbers.

'Project' bears the influence of Fechner and of Freud's early mentor in physiology, Ernst Brücke (1819–1892), when it outlines a plan for a psychology that would 'represent psychical processes as quantitatively determined states of specifiable material particles'.[26] Based on this model, it appears that Freud may have initially believed that psychoanalysis could map the movement of physical energies within the actual anatomy of the human brain.[27] But Freud was at the same time developing, in collaboration with Josef Breuer, the psychoanalytic idea of unconscious 'repression', which arose from Freud's and Breuer's analysis of Bertha Pappenheim (otherwise known as 'Anna O.') between 1880 and 1882.[28] As a result of this highly controversial 'breakthrough' analysis of 'Anna O.'[29] – just one of many important female patients and theorists in the history of psychoanalysis[30] – Freud then began to use decidedly non-positivist and highly metaphorical modes of expression to outline an openly abstract and speculative model of human mental functioning.

Thus, when Freud attempts to introduce his idea of the unconscious to a lay audience in *Vorlesungen zur Einführung in die Psychoanalyse* [*Introductory Lectures on Psychoanalysis*, 1916–1917], he uses architectural metaphors to make his ideas accessible:

> Let us [...] compare the system of the unconscious to a large entrance hall, in which the mental impulses jostle one another like separate individuals. Adjoining this entrance hall there is a second, narrower, room – a kind of drawing-room – in which consciousness, too, resides. But on the threshold between these two rooms a watchman performs his function: he examines the different mental impulses, acts as a censor, and will not admit them into the drawing-room if they displease him.[31]

In this extended metaphor, while the entrance hall [*Vorraum*] represents the unconscious [*das Unbewußte*], the idea of the preconscious [*das Vorbewußte*] is also introduced via the concept of the threshold [*Schwelle*] inherited

---

[26] Freud, 'Project for a Scientific Psychology', in SE, vol. 1, pp. 295–410 (p. 295).

[27] See Richard Wollheim, *Freud*, 2nd edn (London: Fontana, 1992), p. 44.

[28] See vol. 2 of the SE, *Studies in Hysteria*.

[29] For an (at times) polemical critique of this analysis see Mikkel Borch-Jakobsen, *Remembering Anna O.: A Century of Psychoanalytic Mystification*, trans. Kirby Olsen and Xavier Callahan (New York: Routledge, 1996).

[30] For an overview see Nancy Chodorow, 'Freud on Women', in *The Cambridge Companion to Freud*, ed. by Jerome Neu (Cambridge: Cambridge University Press, 1991), pp. 224–48.

[31] Freud, 'Resistance and Repression', in SE, vol. 16, pp. 286–302 (p. 295).

from Fechner. Here Freud's crucial innovation lies in the idea that active censorship of unacceptable mental contents takes place upon this threshold, which is an intermediate point between the unconscious and the civilized 'drawing room' [*Salon*] of the conscious mind or consciousness [*das Bewußte, Bewußtsein*]. Whereas Fechner's threshold model relates only to the intensity of the stimuli and whether this is sufficient for them to cross over the threshold, Freud introduces emotional and cultural criteria according to which mental representations may or may not gain entry into the *Salon* of consciousness.

The model unconscious–preconscious–conscious is known as Freud's first topographic model of the human mental apparatus. Its general basis was to be found in Freud's sexual theory and in the initially androcentric idea of the Oedipus complex, according to which the young male – usually at around the age of between three and five years, during the so-called *phallic* stage of psychosexual development – wishes to expel the father from the family situation so that he can enjoy the full sexual affections of the mother. These ideas give rise to guilt and psychological repression, which involves unacceptable mental representations being pushed below the threshold of consciousness.[32] But, following the horrors of the Great War, Freud introduced a second topographic model [*zweite Topik*], which Gödde sees as having been heavily influenced by Schopenhauer's ideas about the unconscious will,[33] and which emphasized both the erotic and the aggressive drives in human beings.

In this second model, the unconscious is far more pervasive and far less localized to a certain area of the mental apparatus. In other words, Freud starts to refer more to 'unconscious' elements in the psyche and concomitantly less frequently to *the* unconscious as an actual place or container with definitive boundaries. The origin of unconscious 'drives' [*Triebe*] is now described by Freud as the *Es* (translated into English as the *id*), which exists in dynamic tension with the conscious mind or *Ich* (English: ego) and with that aspect of the personality that represents the dictates of civilized morality and societal norms: the *Über-Ich* (English: superego). Whereas *the* unconscious was previously associated predominantly with the repression of unacceptable sexual wishes related to the Oedipus complex, in this new model the *Es* or id is the source of two dynamic and conflicting drives: *Eros*, or the sex-drive [*Geschlechtstrieb*], and *Thanatos*, or the death drive [*Todestrieb*], the latter being an addition that reflected Freud's new theorization of aggression and

---

[32] See Freud, 'A Special Type of Choice of Object Made by Men', in SE, vol. 11, pp. 163–75.

[33] Gödde, 'Freud and Nineteenth-Century Philosophical Sources', pp. 281–82.

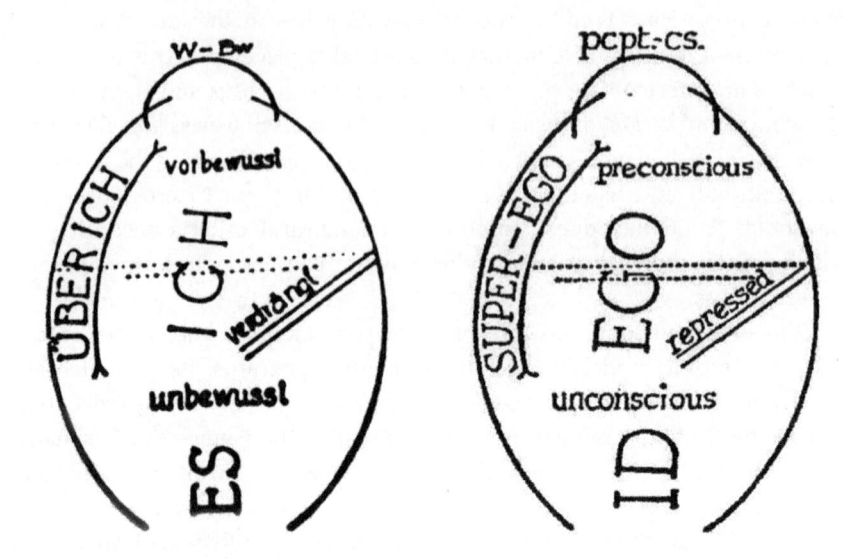

Figs. 23 and 24. Freud's diagrams for the second topographic model [zweite Topik] of the human psyche in its German and English versions. Taken from: Freud, *Neue Folge der Vorlesungen zur Einführung in die Psychoanalyse* (Vienna: Internationaler Psychoanalytischer Verlag, 1933), p. 110; Freud, *New Introductory Lectures on Psychoanalysis*, SE, vol. 22, p. 78.

war.[34] And, in this new model, unconscious elements can potentially pervade all areas of the mental apparatus, as Freud now speculates that aspects of both the ego [*Ich*] and the superego [*Über-Ich*] may be unconscious, as can be seen in Freud's sketch of the second topographic model (Figs. 23 and 24).

In the later stages of his career, Freud retreated from the ambitious natural-scientific aims found in the 'Project for a Scientific Psychology', emphasizing the abstract and heuristic character of his topographic models. Here, again, metaphor and analogy play a role in describing how the different aspects of the second topographic model relate to one another. 'In thinking of this division of the personality into an ego, a super-ego and an id,' Freud advises his readers in the *Neue Folge der Vorlesungen zur Einführung in die Psychoanalyse* [*New Introductory Lectures on Psychoanalysis*, 1933],

---

[34] This second topography is chiefly developed in 'Das Ich und das Es' ['The Ego and the Id', 1923], in SE, vol. 19, pp. 3–66; whereas the distinction between *Eros* and *Thanatos* was outlined slightly earlier in *Jenseits des Lustprinzips* [*Beyond the Pleasure Principle*, 1920], in SE, vol. 18, pp. 3–64.

you will not, of course, have pictured sharp frontiers like the artificial ones drawn in political geography. We cannot do justice to the characteristics of the mind by linear outlines like those in a drawing or in primitive painting, but rather by areas of colour melting into one another as they are presented by modern artists.[35]

Thus, a project that had begun in 1895 with the aim of representing 'psychical processes as quantitatively determined states of specifiable material particles' was now, nearly 40 years later, invoking analogies from modern art to describe an openly speculative mental topography designed to be used only as a heuristic basis for treatment in the clinical setting. And Freud was now also prepared to admit, again in the *New Introductory Lectures*, that the idea of unconscious drives [*Triebe*] – translated in the *Standard Edition* as 'instincts' for reasons that will be explored below – have only an inferential or hypothetical status, in that they can be viewed only indirectly, by way of their putative effects. 'The theory of instincts [*Triebe*]', he writes, 'is so to say our mythology. Instincts are mythical entities, magnificent in their indefiniteness. In our work we cannot for a moment disregard them, yet we are never sure that we are seeing them clearly.'[36]

Freud's oscillation between two basic models of psychoanalysis – the first being the natural-scientific or biological model of the 'Project', the second the philosophical, speculative, mythological or what Freud would call 'metapsychological' model of the later works – presented the Anglophone translators of Freud with two choices about how to render his writings. Was Freud a natural scientist of the mind, a speculative conquistador of the human soul, or both?[37] And is it even *possible* to be both, or does the second model fundamentally contradict the first one? In their desire to establish psychoanalysis as a serious medical profession in early twentieth-century Britain, Freud's English translators understandably sought to avoid this ambivalence, and chose to interpret Freud in line with the first model. But in doing so they created a different, now global, Freud: a Freud that is very much a case of translation as *interpretation*.

---

[35] Freud, 'The Dissection of the Personality', in *New Introduction Lectures on Psychoanalysis*, SE, vol. 22, pp. 57–80 (here: p. 79).
[36] Freud, 'Anxiety and Instinctual Life', in SE, vol. 22, pp. 81–111 (here: p. 95).
[37] For the former view see Frank J. Sulloway, *Freud: Biologist of the Mind* (New York: Basic Books, 1979); for the latter view see Bruno Bettelheim, *Freud and Man's Soul* (London: Penguin, 1982), discussed below.

'A Darwin of the Mind': Translating Freud for the *Standard Edition*

In his classic study concerning cultural transfers, the French Germanist Michel Espagne identifies the *transferrant* or *Vermittler* (mediator) as a key figure in processes of intercultural exchange (for more on the role of the translator as *Vermittler*, see the discussion by Charlotte Ryland in Chapter 4 of this volume). Focusing on such mediators allows one to see not only in what contexts specific cultural forms are taken up but also how these cultural forms are activated in and transformed by the home society of the mediator. The question here is not simply one of linear and unidirectional influence, according to which foreign cultural forms have an impact upon the host society; rather, the focus is also upon how the 'imported' form is itself transformed by the process of importation. Such transformations may affect the status of cultural forms in the new host society but also may in turn change their status within the society from which they originally emerged, or indeed their status on a global level.[38] This 'feedback loop' situation arguably characterizes the Anglophone reception of Freud's ideas about the unconscious, since their translation into English fundamentally changed their status not only in the Anglophone world but arguably also in German-speaking Europe, not to mention globally.

When it comes to Anglophone mediators of Freud's work, two figures played a key role in the translation of psychoanalysis into English: Ernest Jones (1879–1958) and James Strachey (1887–1967). Although the translation of Freud into English involved multiple actors in both the United States and Britain, not to mention Freud himself and his daughter Anna (1895–1982), Jones and Strachey were nonetheless the leading figures behind the *Standard Edition of the Complete Psychological Works of Sigmund Freud*, a 24-volume edition that appeared between 1956 and 1974 under the general editorship of Strachey. Following Freud's death in 1939, Jones – who at that time was the leading figure in psychoanalysis in Britain, having founded the London Psychoanalytical Society in 1913 – saw the importance of producing an edition of Freud in English, which he hoped would be the definitive edition in any language. In a letter written in January 1940 to interested parties in the United States, who Jones hoped would fund his proposed translation project,

---

[38] See Michel Espagne and Michael Werner, 'Deutsch-Französischer Kulturtransfer im 18. und 19. Jahrhundert. Zu einem neuen interdisziplinären Forschungsprogramm des C.N.R.S', *Francia. Forschungen zur westeuropäischen Geschichte* 13 (1985), pp. 502–10; Michel Espagne, *Les transferts culturels franco-allemands* (Paris: Presses universitaire de France, 1999).

one of Jones's American supporters underlined the urgent wartime context of this undertaking. Owing to Freud's recent death, as well as to the 'definite loss of Central Europe to further contributions to the development of psychoanalytic science', this author opined that the 'English speaking countries in the future [...] will have to carry the full burden of responsibility for the fate of this science'.[39] While this letter no doubt overstates the case in order to raise funds for Jones's project, it also underlines the new importance of the English-speaking world for the future of psychoanalysis, since Freud himself was forced to emigrate to Britain in 1938 following the German annexation of his native Austria in that year. Thus, for Freud, according to his recent biographer Élisabeth Roudinesco, Jones was 'historically, politically, and geographically the man of the future of psychoanalysis'.[40]

The biography of Jones provides important contextual information for the manner in which Freud is translated in the *Standard Edition*. Trained as a medical doctor within the scientific tradition of Darwinism and materialist positivism, Jones saw Freud as a 'Darwin of the mind' who had replaced the metaphysical speculations of German philosophy with a 'biological theory of mental evolution'.[41] This may partially explain why the 'Project for a Scientific Psychology' – quickly abandoned by Freud and thrown into question by the later development of psychoanalysis, while also being relegated to the final supplementary volume [*Nachtragsband*] of the German edition of Freud's works – is prominently placed in volume one of the *Standard Edition*.

The case of Freud's other important Anglophone mediator – James Strachey – is, however, rather more complex. As a member of the Bloomsbury group, Strachey would have discussed Freud and his works in conversations with Virginia and Leonard Woolf, among others, whose Hogarth Press published the *Standard Edition*. But Strachey – a graduate of Cambridge and a contemporary there of Leonard Woolf and John Maynard Keynes – had already encountered the ideas of Freud when, in his capacity as assistant editor of *The Spectator*, he read the work of Frederic William Henry Myers (1843–1901), who invoked Freud in the context of his theories concerning the 'subliminal self', and who was founder of the Society for Psychical Research in

---

[39] Letter to Jones dated 28 January 1940 by an unnamed author, *Archives of the British Psycho-Analytical Society*, quoted in Riccardo Steiner, 'A World Wide International Trade Mark of Genuineness? Some Observations on the History of the English Translation of the Work of Sigmund Freud, Focusing Mainly on His Technical Terms', *International Review of Psycho-Analysis* 14 (1987), pp. 33–102 (p. 46).

[40] Élisabeth Roudinesco, *Freud in His Time and Ours*, trans. Catherine Porter (2014; Cambridge, MA: Harvard University Press, 2016), p. 139.

[41] Ernest Jones, *Papers on Psycho-Analysis* (London: Baillière, Tindall and Cox, 1913), p. xii.

Cambridge.[42] This in turn led Strachey to Freud's couch in Vienna, where he was sent in 1920 on the recommendation of Jones, and where he would soon begin trial translations of Freud's works in collaboration with his wife, Alix Strachey (1892–1973, née Sargent-Florence), a graduate in modern languages from Newnham College, Cambridge, who also underwent analysis with Freud in Vienna and later with his disciple Karl Abraham in Berlin.[43]

Although, therefore, the Stracheys came from rather more literary backgrounds than did Jones, their reception of Freud was nevertheless filtered through the decidedly natural-scientific focus of Cambridge University. Between 1920 and 1922 no fewer than four Cambridge graduates were in analysis with Freud, making up 40 per cent of Freud's caseload, according to the estimate of John Forrester. In addition to the Stracheys and Joan Riviere (1883–1962, another early translator of Freud), the psychiatrist John Rickman (1891–1951) and the botanist and later acclaimed ecologist Arthur Tansley (1871–1955) were among Freud's patients. Upon returning to Britain, the Stracheys, Rickman and Tansley formed part of a group that met regularly to discuss Freud's ideas from 1925 onwards – a group which Forrester describes as largely 'natural scientific' in orientation.[44]

Although that natural-scientific orientation certainly played a role in determining the translation choices made within the *Standard Edition*, it should be noted that Strachey already had precedents to rely on, in particular Freud's 'Five Lectures on Psychoanalysis', which had been translated, in collaboration with Freud himself, by Henry W. Chase – a Fellow in Psychology at Clark University – for a lecture tour of the USA that Freud undertook in 1909.[45] Further to this, Jones's own *Papers on Psycho-Analysis* (1913) had already rendered many of Freud's key terms into English. In this way, cardinal terms such as 'preconscious' [*vorbewusst*], 'repression' [*Verdrängung*], 'resistance' [*Widerstand*] and 'transference' [*Übertragung*] were already established in English prior to the Great War, with Jones later claiming that 'repression' was in fact Freud's own suggestion.[46] Freud's solution of 'repression' for *Verdrängung* set the tone for later translations, which tended to favour Latinate endings: 'interpretation' for *Deutung*, 'sublimation' for *Sublimierung*, 'condensation' for *Verdichtung*, to

---

[42] See Frederic William Henry Myers, *Human Personality and Its Survival of Bodily Death*, 2 vols. (London: Longmans, Green and Co., 1903).

[43] Roudinesco, *Freud in His Time and Ours*, pp. 275–80.

[44] John Forrester, 'Freud in Cambridge', *Critical Quarterly* 46.2 (2004), pp. 1–26 (pp. 2–4).

[45] See Sigmund Freud, 'The Origin and Development of Psychoanalysis', trans. H.W. Chase, *The American Journal of Psychology* 21.2 (1910), pp. 181–218.

[46] Ernest Jones, *Free Associations: Memories of a Psychoanalyst* (1959; New Brunswick, NJ: Transaction, 1990), p. 169.

mention just three of many examples. Since Greek and Latin served as models for natural-scientific terminology in English, this translation strategy served to reinforce the natural-scientific and medical image of Freud that Jones, and following him the Stracheys, wished to reinforce. This was an especially important component of Jones's 'cultural policy' for the promotion of Freud's ideas in the comparatively more prudish Anglophone world, since the medicalizing of Freud's language would serve to present Freud's controversial sexual theories in a reassuringly abstract and scientific light.[47] To this end, a 'Glossary Committee' for the translation of Freud was established, comprised of the Stracheys, Jones, Rickman and Riviere. According to James Strachey's retrospective account in his obituary for Riviere, this 'quite irresponsible body', in which 'Greek terminology was all the rage', was tasked with deciding 'for all time how the technical terms of psychoanalysis were to be translated'.[48]

Many of those decisions shocked the German-speaking emigrants who came to form part of the psychoanalytic establishment in the United States following the Second World War, most notably the Austrian-born professor of psychology at the University of Chicago, Bruno Bettelheim (1903–1990). In Bettelheim's view, 'the English renditions of Freud's writings distort much of the essential humanism that permeates the originals', transforming Freud's ideas into 'abstract, depersonalized, highly theoretical, erudite and mechanized – in short "scientific" – statements'.[49] For Bettelheim, the most egregious of the numerous errors that he attributes to Freud's English translators is their rendering of the German *Seele* not as 'soul', but as 'mind', with the adjective *seelisch* also becoming 'mental' in the *Standard Edition*. The root-word for psychoanalysis is the Greek ψυχή (*psyche*), which can mean spirit, breath, ghost, soul, self. Freud, notes Bettelheim, chose to translate this term into German as *Seele* (soul), describing psychoanalysis as both 'treatment of the soul' [*Seelenbehandlung*] and 'knowledge of the soul' [*Seelenkunde*]. In the *Standard Edition*, much to Bettelheim's understandable horror, these instances are coldly translated as 'mental treatment' and 'mental science' respectively.[50]

---

[47] For detailed context see Steiner, 'A World Wide International Trade Mark of Genuineness?' pp. 54–58, 63–65.

[48] James Strachey, 'Obituary: Joan Riviere (1883–1962)', *International Journal of Psychoanalysis* 44 (1963), pp. 228–30 (p. 229). For context on the 'Glossary Committee' see Darius Ornston, 'The Invention of "Cathexis" and Strachey's Strategy', *International Review of Psychoanalysis* 12 (1985), pp. 391–99 (pp. 391–92).

[49] Bettelheim, *Freud and Man's Soul*, pp. 4–5.

[50] Bettelheim, *Freud and Man's Soul*, pp. 70–75; see also Freud, 'Psychical (or Mental) Treatment', in SE, vol. 7, pp. 283–302 (p. 283); Freud, 'Some Elementary Lessons in Psychoanalysis', in SE, vol. 23, pp. 281–86 (p. 282).

This was clearly a decision in favour of a medicalized Freud that at the same time played down the humanist, poetic and philosophical elements of his thought, and was very far from being an isolated case. A similar example can be found in the *Standard Edition*'s rendering of *Trieb* – the term that Freud used to describe the motivating energies or 'drives' of the psyche – as 'instinct': a word associated first and foremost with biology and with the writings of Darwin.[51] Another is the rendering of *Verdichtung* – the expression that Freud uses to describe the way in which one dream symbol can bring together and express multiple emotions or affects – as 'condensation': a term suggestive of chemical solutions in a laboratory, which also fails to communicate the sense of *Dichtung* (poetic composition) in Freud's German original.[52] Finally, evidence of Strachey's mania for abstract-sounding ancient Greek formulations can be found in his bizarre rendering of Freud's *Besetzung* – the sense in which an object can become charged, invested or occupied [*besetzt*] by the subject's libido or mental energy[53] – into the word 'cathexis', which Strachey invented from the ancient Greek word for 'occupation'.[54] In this case, a perfectly everyday German word is replaced with an abstract neologism endowed with an aura of technical authority. Much like the *Standard Edition* in general, the scientific aura of 'cathexis' seems – despite its distortion of Freud's idea of *Besetzung* – to have been part of its wild success: today a search for 'cathexis' in Google Scholar generates over 29,000 results.

Although it is beyond the scope of this chapter exhaustively to determine the global impact of the *Standard Edition*, a quick perusal of Freud in just two other languages yields telling results. When it comes to the *Standard Edition*'s significant impact on psychoanalysis in German-speaking Europe, one need only note the influence exerted by Strachey and the *Standard Edition* on the 11-volume German *Studienausgabe* of Freud's works, the closest thing to a commented critical edition of Freud's works in German, which appeared between 1969 and 1975. Strachey himself was the senior editor of this project up until his death in 1967, and its first volume opens with a sketch of Freud's life and works originally written by Strachey for the *Pelican Freud Library*.[55]

---

[51] See, for example, the SE's rendering of Freud's essay 'Triebe und Triebschicksale' as 'Instincts and Their Vicissitudes', in SE, vol. 14, pp. 109–40.

[52] See especially pp. 279–304 of *The Interpretation of Dreams* (SE, vol. 4).

[53] See, for example, Freud's usage in 'Group Psychology and the Analysis of the Ego', in SE, 18, pp. 69–143 (p. 111).

[54] See Ornston, 'The Invention of "Cathexis"', pp. 392–94; see also Jean Laplanche and Jean-Bertrand Pontalis, *The Language of Psychoanalysis*, introd. by Daniel Lagache, trans. Donald Nicholson-Smith (1967; London: Karnac, 1988), pp. 62–65.

[55] James Strachey, 'Sigmund Freud. Eine Skizze seines Lebens und Denkens', trans. Käte Hügel, in Sigmund Freud, *Vorlesungen zur Einführung in die Psychoanalyse*

Furthermore, this edition's critical apparatus (introductory commentaries on texts, editorial notes, bibliography and index) is based upon that found in the *Standard Edition*, as noted by Angela Richards, the editor of the *Pelican Freud Library*, in her opening editorial remarks in volume one of the *Studienausgabe*.[56]

Turning to French psychoanalysis, it is noteworthy that the former scientific director of the French edition of Freud's *Oeuvres Complètes*, Jean Laplanche (1924–2012), refers to the *Standard Edition* as the 'psychoanalytic vulgate', regarding it as an indispensable resource that is a 'model of unity of style and terminology', even if it sometimes 'flattens the meaning'.[57] In their highly influential *Vocabulaire de la Psychoanalyse* [*Language of Psychoanalysis*, 1967], which formed the linguistic basis for the preparation of the French complete edition (still an ongoing project), Laplanche and his colleague Jean-Bertrand Pontalis hail the *Standard Edition* as the unsurpassed critical edition of Freud's works in any language, stating that its 'translations, editorial commentary, critical apparatus and indexes make this great enterprise an unrivalled source of references for the scholar'.[58] Thus, in terms of global impact – and for better or worse in light of the distortions mentioned above – a case can be made that Freud in English came to eclipse Freud in German: today a Google Scholar search for 'unconscious Freud' yields over 376,000 results, whereas 'unbewusst Freud' produces around 32,000. In this way, the translation of Freud into English launched the global career of the unconscious.

Conclusion: On the Orientating Power of Metaphors

Taking the long view of German discourses on the unconscious allows one to observe certain recurring phenomena. One of these – which stretches from the psycho-physical unconscious of Fechner, via Freud's 'Project for a Scientific Psychology', to Jones's image of Freud as a 'Darwin of the mind' – is the attempt to characterize the unconscious as a natural-scientific 'object'

---

und neue Folge, Studienausgabe, vol. 1, ed. by Alexander Mitscherlich, Angela Richards and James Strachey, 11th edn (1969; Frankfurt am Main: S. Fischer, 1989), pp. 7–18.

[56] Angela Richards, 'Erläuterungen zur Edition', trans. Käte Hügel, in Freud, *Vorlesungen zur Einführung in die Psychoanalyse und neue Folge, Studienausgabe*, vol. 1, pp. 26–31.

[57] Jean Laplanche, Pierre Cotet and Andre Bourguignon, 'Translating Freud', in *Translating Freud*, ed. by Darius Ornston (New Haven, CT: Yale University Press, 1992), pp. 63–74 (p. 136).

[58] Laplanche and Pontalis, *The Language of Psychoanalysis*, p. xv.

susceptible to observation under experimental conditions, or, failing that, at least to technical adumbration through the scientific vocabulary of psychoanalysis. That Freud himself eventually conceded the merely heuristic and tentative character of many of his ideas concerning the unconscious demonstrates the pathos of his 'will to science' – something that found belated expression in the Graeco-Latin vocabulary of the *Standard Edition*.

Another long-term and rather obvious phenomenon lies in the bare persistence of the idea of the unconscious despite the failure of psychoanalysis to establish itself in natural-scientific terms. The philosopher of science Karl Popper (1902–1994) – someone who knew Freud's Vienna and the culture of psychoanalysis very well – famously concluded in his *Conjectures and Refutations* (1963) that psychoanalysis cannot be regarded as a science because it does not generate falsifiable hypotheses. Even if the patient refuses to accept the interpretations of their analyst, such refusals can, in psychoanalytic terms, always be put down to their unconscious 'resistance' [*Widerstand*] towards the purported truth of the analyst's statements.[59] In this way, psychoanalysis would always be able to explain away results or phenomena that do not coincide with its theories, precisely because its central 'object' – the unconscious – can only be inferred by way of its surface effects. Or – to put this in the language of Descartes's epistemology – no 'clear' and 'distinct' observations of the unconscious are possible.

But the fact that the unconscious cannot be directly observed, and that hypotheses about it cannot be falsified, does not prevent it from having explanatory and orientating power. Part of this power can be found in its metaphors – a recurring one being the 'dark' or 'unilluminated' map of the mind, which we find in Kant, in Jean Paul, and again in Freud's topographic models. Seen in this way, the unconscious is less susceptible to being fixed by conceptual history, and perhaps more amenable to what the German philosopher Hans Blumenberg (1920–1996) termed 'metaphorology' – the task of tracking those persistent metaphors in Western thought that do the pre-conceptual and orientating work that cannot be carried out by 'clear' and 'distinct' concepts.[60] In naming the unconscious, or in attributing certain events or phenomena to its purported underlying existence, a certain kind of narrative is created that may be of therapeutic value. In Blumenberg's words, elaborated in his posthumously published *Theorie der Unbegrifflichkeit* [*Theory of Non-Conceptuality*, 2007]:

---

[59] Karl Popper, *Conjectures and Refutations: The Growth of Scientific Knowledge* (London: Routledge and Kegan Paul, 1963), pp. 34–37.

[60] See Hans Blumenberg, *Paradigms for a Metaphorology*, trans. Robert Savage (Ithaca, NY: Cornell University Press, 2010).

Concepts do not only refer to objects, rather they also constitute objects [...] So it is with the *concept of the unconscious* [...] Strictly speaking, the concept of the unconscious is a procedural rule which specifies how one should react when confronted by a particular form of consciousness. [...] The unconscious is an auxiliary concept [*Hilfsbegriff*] used for specific technical operations [...] it indicates a totality of consciousness which no memory or expectation, and no form of self-consciousness, can verify.[61]

If, therefore, the unconscious is not a concept that refers to definitive things in the world but, rather, an auxiliary construct that might helpfully inform reactions to particular kinds of consciousness, then perhaps the guiding question of psychoanalysis should not be *ontological*, but rather *functional*; not 'Does the unconscious exist?' but rather: 'Is it helpful for me to infer that I have an unconscious?' The historian of psychoanalysis Sonu Shamdasani recently observed, in this vein, that the unconscious has in this way become an 'optional' ontology, which many people, especially those in the metropolitan West, continue to find useful.[62] But this is surely not the fate that Freud, or for that matter the translators of the *Standard Edition*, wished for their 'science' of psychoanalysis.

Suggestions for Further Reading

Bell, Matthew, *The German Tradition of Psychology in Literature and Thought, 1700–1840* (Cambridge: Cambridge University Press, 2005), 316 pp.

Bettelheim, Bruno, *Freud and Man's Soul* (London: Penguin, 1982), 128 pp.

Ellenberger, Henri F. *The Discovery of the Unconscious: The History and Evolution of Dynamic Psychiatry* (New York: Basic Books, 1970), 932 pp.

Espagne, Michel, *Les transferts culturels franco-allemands* (Paris: Presses universitaire de France, 1999), 296 pp.

Forrester, John, 'Freud in Cambridge', *Critical Quarterly* 46.2 (2004), pp. 1–26.

Gödde, Günter, *Traditionslinien des 'Unbewussten': Schopenhauer, Nietzsche, Freud* (Tübingen: edition diskord, 1999), 688 pp.

Laplanche, Jean, and Jean-Bertrand Pontalis, *The Language of Psychoanalysis* (1967; London: Karnac, 1988), 691 pp.

Neu, Jerome (ed.), *The Cambridge Companion to Freud* (Cambridge: Cambridge University Press, 1991), 372 pp.

---

[61] Hans Blumenberg, *Theorie der Unbegrifflichkeit* (Frankfurt am Main: Suhrkamp, 2007), pp. 40–42, my trans.

[62] Sonu Shamdasani, 'Epilogue: The "Optional" Unconscious', in *Thinking the Unconscious*, ed. by Nicholls and Liebscher, pp. 287–96 (pp. 293–96).

Nicholls, Angus, and Martin Liebscher (eds.), *Thinking the Unconscious: Nineteenth-Century German Thought* (Cambridge: Cambridge University Press, 2010), 341 pp.

Ornston, Darius (ed.), *Translating Freud* (New Haven, CT: Yale University Press, 1992), 272 pp.

14

Patterns of Global Exile

Exploring Identity through Art

Birgit Lang

Migration and exile form essential elements of the German-speaking experience from the Middle Ages until today. While migrants move for a range of reasons, including for relationships, in an attempt to better their economic situation or to gain valuable life experience abroad, exiles are expelled by political means by the very society they were part of. In the history of the German-speaking world the largest forced migration concerns the expulsion of half a million citizens who were deemed 'un-German' under National Socialism: they included German and Austrian Jews, political activists and religious minorities. The most prominent representatives of this group were members of the German and Austrian intellectual elite, such as Thomas Mann (1875–1955), Bertolt Brecht (1898–1956) and Stefan Zweig (1881–1942), all of whom were avid critics of the National Socialist regime.

Exile is a traumatic experience. It commonly leaves its subjects with a sense of disempowerment and alienation, though to varying degrees. Stefan Zweig, for example, committed suicide in 1942 with his second wife Lotte, even though he found a safe haven in his country of refuge, Brazil, while the émigré painter and artist Louis Kahan (1905–2002), the subject at the heart of this chapter, showed remarkable resilience in the light of adversity. The exile experience also often engenders a sense of distrust and a conflicted relationship between exiles and their former home country, even once exile has 'ended'. Following the war, Thomas Mann, for example, never returned to Germany to live, but took residence in Switzerland, while Bertolt Brecht became a GDR citizen, albeit with a foot in the door to his former homeland thanks to his Austrian, i.e. Western passport. Kahan survived the war in Paris and Algeria, and later reunited with his family in Australia, where he eventually settled.

Mann's and Brecht's return to the German-speaking world was motivated in part by their reliance on the German language as their means of creative expression and German-speakers as their readers. As a visual artist Kahan was more easily able to transcend national and linguistic boundaries than writers and thespians and to take his art places (on this, see too Elizabeth Anderson's discussion of how the visual can transcend boundaries in Chapter 1 of this volume). In line with recent research on global migration, this chapter examines the motivations behind Kahan's global artistic self-positioning as a cosmopolitan in the aftermath of exile: among them, his professional identity, his family life and his lifelong love of a third culture – that of France. In a second step this chapter explores how Kahan's artistic practice as a portraitist became 'a passport' or 'a currency' that opened doors to art, society and the new world around him, as his daughter, Melbourne artist Dena Kahan, poignantly put it.[1] Analysis of selected artworks reveals how Kahan's unique artistic perception shaped the life of Allied soldiers in Algeria as well as the Australian art world; and how this in turn fashioned the Australian view of Kahan as a Viennese émigré. Finally, this chapter generates reflections on the role Austrian origins play in Kahan's cosmopolitan life and transnational artwork.

To answer these large identity questions this biography-led research is based on a wide source base and employs a range of methods, including historical contextualization of Kahan's life and oeuvre and interviews with his widow Lily and his daughter Dena Kahan, along with analysis of a previous interview with the painter, select artworks and newspaper reviews from the period in question.

Louis Kahan: Biography

In order to explore wider issues around biography and portraiture from a transnational perspective, it is necessary to identify and investigate how Kahan's life experience shaped his sense of identity at a range of crucial points: his birth in the Habsburg Empire and subsequent childhood as a 'third culture kid'; his choice of 'cultural affinity' rather than national or ethnic cultural belonging; the ideal of cosmopolitanism in Paris; his exilic existence; and his life in Australia.

---

[1] Lily and Dena Kahan interviewed by Birgit Lang: personal interview, Melbourne, 31 October 2016. The author would like to warmly thank the Kahan family for their willingness to be interviewed, for providing access to Louis Kahan's Private Collection of newspaper clippings and for granting permission to publish Fig. 26. Portrait of a young man as part of this publication.

The first child of Wolf and Dinah Kahan, Louis Kahan was born in Vienna in 1905. His parents had moved to Vienna from Russia just months before his birth. Their journey was part of a larger movement of Jews who migrated to Vienna around the turn of the century. Most of these migrants came from Habsburg Galicia, an area of Central–Eastern Europe (today's Ukraine). Galicia was a multicultural landscape in the north of the Habsburg Empire, most vividly portrayed in literature by Leopold von Sacher-Masoch (1836–1895). Under Habsburg rule, the number of Galicia's Jews grew sixfold to about 872,000 in 1910. This was due to high birth rates, as well as the steady influx of refugees from nearby Russia fleeing a series of anti-Jewish pogroms, first in 1881–1884 and again in 1903–1906.[2] Kahan's parents also left their native Russia after witnessing such a pogrom, deciding to start their family in the safer environment of the capital of the Habsburg Empire.[3]

The Kahans were a successful migrant family and eventually established themselves as master tailors for the Viennese middle and upper classes. At the fashionable address of Neuer Markt 14, their tailoring business was located close to its clientele – the Burgtheater, or Imperial Court Theatre, and the government ministries in the centre of Vienna were all nearby. Louis Kahan and his sister Valerie grew up in an acculturated Jewish household. They were second-generation Jewish immigrants who lived in a city that was shaped by a multicultural reality – as was to be expected in the capital of a multiethnic empire. They grew up as part of a society that in 1867 had granted Jews the unrestricted right to reside and practise their religion, a society that saw Jews become leading figures in the arts, law and medicine. At the same time, Austrian society discriminated against Jews, as observed by writers such as Arthur Schnitzler (1862–1931), and the Kahan children belonged to a generation that witnessed the rise of political anti-Semitism in Vienna.[4]

Amid these contradictions Louis Kahan's passions evolved, and these can be interpreted as attempts to negotiate his own sense of belonging in a

[2] Paul Robert Magocsi, 'Galicia: A European Land', in *Galicia: A Multicultured Land*, ed. by Christopher Hann and Paul Robert Magocsi (Toronto: University of Toronto Press, 2005), pp. 3–21 (p. 11).

[3] Lily and Dena Kahan interviewed by Birgit Lang: personal interview, Melbourne, 31 October 2016.

[4] Oxford émigré historian Peter G.J. Pulzer was the first to discuss this in his seminal work *The Rise of Political anti-Semitism in Germany and Austria* (1964). Discussions of political anti-Semitism in Vienna often focus on the city's influential mayor Dr Karl Lueger, who was in office between 1897 and 1910. Compare Richard S. Geehr, *Karl Lueger: Mayor of Fin de Siècle Vienna* (Detroit, MI: Wayne State University Press, 1990), pp. 171–207.

complex world. As Jews living outside their biblical homeland, the Kahans were part of the Jewish diaspora. As the child of immigrants, Kahan shared only part of the cultural background of his Russian-born parents. This implied a set of characteristics that are typical for 'third culture kids': an expanded worldview contrasted by potentially confused loyalties; a three-dimensional view of the world and an at times painful view of reality; and cross-cultural enrichment contrasting with ignorance of the home culture.[5]

In terms of cultural affinity Kahan was drawn not to his native Austria, to Russia or to Palestine, but to France. On account of his Francophilia his family called him 'Louis', the French version of his birthname Ludwig.[6] In 1925, as a young man, Kahan followed his calling and left Vienna for Paris, after having learned the family trade rather than studying art, as his father had insisted (possibly a consequence of the latter's own experience of anti-Semitism and migration).[7] Paris had been a magnet for foreign artists and writers since the turn of the century. Americans, Italians, Poles, Hungarians, Russians, Japanese and Jews of different nationalities flocked to the city, where the bohemian and artistic lifestyle in the Montparnasse district allowed foreign artists to form a cosmopolitan identity and to escape expectations of assimilation otherwise imposed on migrants.[8] Kahan's migration to Paris coincided with this heyday of Jewish artistic life. He began taking life drawing classes at the Académie de la Grande Chaumière in Montparnasse, which attracted a range of French and many international artists. As would become a pattern during his life in times of need, Kahan supported himself by working as a tailor and then as a designer for the leading French fashion designer and couturier Paul Poiret (1879–1944). He designed costumes for the famous expressionist dancer Josephine Baker (1906–1975) and for the French writer Colette (1873–1954) in the stage adaptation of Colette's novel *La Vagabonde*, as well as for the iconic Follies Bergères cabaret music hall. In addition, he contributed freelance illustrations to newspapers and magazines.[9]

---

[5] David C. Pollock and Ruth E. Van Reken, *Third Culture Kids. Growing Up Among Worlds* (Boston, MA/London: Nicholas Brealey Publishing, rev. edn 2009), p. 95.

[6] Lily and Dena Kahan interviewed by Birgit Lang: personal interview, Melbourne, 31 October 2016.

[7] Louis Kahan interviewed by Hazel de Berg, 9 December 1965: audio interview (sound recording) in the Hazel de Berg collection, National Library of Australia http://trove.nla.gov.au/work/18511887 [accessed 10 October 2017].

[8] Richard D. Sonn, 'Jewish Modernism: Immigrant Artists of Montparnasse 1905–1914', in *Foreign Artists and Communities in Modern Paris, 1870–1914*, ed. by Karen L. Carter and Susan Waller (Burlington: Ashgate, 2015), pp. 125–40 (p. 126).

[9] Lou Klepac, *Louis Kahan* (Sydney: The Beagle Press, 1990), pp. 8–9.

When Hitler came to power in Germany in 1933, 20,000 German refugees poured into France, many of whom took refuge in Paris. France had been a haven of safety for German artists and intellectuals throughout the nineteenth century, and in 1933 liberal immigration politics promised similar concessions. Next to Prague, Paris became the centre for émigré political activity. Political parties oppressed in National Socialist Germany established their headquarters in Paris and cultural organizations founded by German refugees included publishing houses, newspapers, journals and bookshops.[10] The nature of Kahan's relationship with the German refugee community in Paris is unknown. He was, however, keenly aware of the fate of Austrian Jews after the annexation of Austria into Germany in March 1938. As a consequence of the Anschluss, Kahan's sister Valerie and her husband left Vienna and Austria. They arrived in Fremantle, Australia, on 20 September 1938, followed seven months later by the Kahan parents, as can be seen in the ship arrival lists from that time.[11]

In the meantime, Kahan's beloved France changed from a country of asylum to one of internment: in 1938 the French parliament passed legislation that enabled the internment and deportation of refugees.[12] After the outbreak of the Second World War on 1 September 1939, émigrés were classified as enemy aliens owing to their German citizenship, and they were interned in a range of camps across the country. Kahan was interned for a short time and volunteered for the French army.[13] Like other foreign Jews he was not permitted to join the regular French army, but only the French Foreign Legion, a unique French military branch created in 1831 and based in North Africa.[14] Kahan left for Oran, Algeria, where he served with about 3,500 other German and Austrian refugees who enlisted for the duration of the war.[15] Kahan's deployment ended with the invasion of French North Africa by English and American troops on 8 November 1942 ('Operation Torch'). He then found himself stranded in Oran, with Vienna and Paris, the European

[10] Barbara Vormeier, 'Frankreich', in *Handbuch der deutschsprachigen Emigration 1933–1945*, ed. by Claus-Dieter Krohn, Patrik von zur Mühlen, Gerhard Paul and Lutz Winkler (Darmstadt: Primus, 1988), pp. 213–50 (pp. 226–28). Paris also became the home of the Czechoslovak, Polish and Spanish Republican governments in exile.
[11] National Archives Australia, Canberra: A12508, 21/2172.
[12] Vormeier, 'Frankreich', p. 233.
[13] Klepac, *Louis Kahan*, p. 9.
[14] Zosa Szajkowski, *Jews and the French Foreign Legion* (New York: Ktav, 1975), p. 60.
[15] Szajkowski mentions that the Jewish community of Algeria prepared Passover for 1,500 Jewish legionnaires. Szajkowski, *Jews and the French Foreign Legion*, p. 83. Vormeier, 'Frankreich', p. 234 states that the majority of the 3,000 émigré members of the French Foreign Legion were transferred to North Africa in 1939–1940.

cities he could call home, under National Socialist rule, and unable to join his family in Perth, Australia, because of immigration restrictions that followed the outbreak of the war.

Kahan's Portraits

Kahan started to paint in exile. He began to exhibit in group shows in Algiers and in Casablanca, depicting the landscapes and people of North Africa. His largest North African art project concerned portraiture. But why did he again take up art, and specifically portraiture, then? The art of portraiture is defined by an intimate exchange between artist and sitter (whether over a short or long period), and by the artist's interpretation of his object. While the relationship between artist and sitter can vary greatly – from family member to stranger, from private person to public figure – the representational intent of this genre is commemorative. Art historians regularly identify the key artistic tension at the heart of portraiture as the contradiction between a need for the image to resemble the sitter (likeness) and the 'normative function of a representation to produce something clearly distinct and distant from the person represented'.[16]

For Kahan this commemorative function was not at odds with the artist's freedom of aesthetic choice and vision. Rather, as a transnational artist, the paradigm of likeness provided him with an opportunity to connect to, blend in with and understand the new worlds he encountered during the course of his migrations. Likeness was of utmost importance to him because in this transient context it presumably provided him with a sense of authenticity. Yet, this never stopped him depicting the portraits of his subjects in different styles, appropriate to their persona and the situation in which the portrait was taken, as this chapter shows.

The first example of Kahan's adaptation of portraits to suit his need as a transnational artist is actually a category of works: portraits of wounded Allied soldiers in Algeria made during 1943–1945 that witness the trauma of the war. Over the period 1942–1945 Kahan drew some thousand portraits of wounded American and British soldiers. For his portraits of soldiers Kahan worked with pencil, and quickly. The portraits that he made in Algeria were not intended for the general public. Because sending photographs was prohibited during the war, carbon copies of Kahan's portraits that were mailed to the soldiers' families were the only 'snapshots' available to soldiers and families alike.[17] These images must have been comforting to see: comforting for the soldiers, to whom they represented both a reassurance of individual existence,

---

[16] Richard Brilliant, *Portraiture* (London: Reaktion Books, 2013), p. 23.
[17] Klepac, *Louis Kahan*, p. 10.

and a record of their physical injuries; comforting for the soldiers' families for the same reasons, albeit in a different way.

Kahan considered this artistic practice a contribution to the war effort. These portraits were an intimate undertaking, an attempt to witness the hardship experienced by the Allied soldiers. His refusal of remuneration represented a gesture of his gratitude to the Allied forces for rescuing him and so many others.[18] Much has been written about the role and importance of the witness in the context of the Holocaust,[19] yet accounts of bearing witness to the suffering of Allied soldiers have been sparse. Such accounts have tended to focus on the experiences of soldiers who survived prisoner-of-war camps, or those who freed Holocaust survivors at the end of the war, and only occasionally have soldiers' experiences of being wounded been discussed.[20] Kahan's portraits of soldiers can be seen as an act of witnessing the effects of the soldiers' experience of combat, including the bodily harm and near-death experiences they suffered. He did so through visiting them in hospital and, importantly, at the same time by paying tribute to their individuality through his portraits. As such these portraits had life-affirming potential, in that they provided soldiers with an opportunity to acknowledge their experience and to transform unformulated traumatic experiences into formulated psychic material, thus relieving the effects of trauma.[21] Most of these portraits Kahan did not sign by name, but with the signature 'by a guy from Paris'. This indicates the documentary character of his tremendous project: such a signature all but erases the role of the artist in an attempt to highlight the drawing as an act of service to the welfare of fellow soldiers. The signature also proposes that, in geopolitical terms, Kahan still viewed himself as a Parisian, yet it gives away little about his inner motivations.

Kahan's family attests that he described his time in North Africa as driven by a sense of adventure.[22] This was a very different experience from many of his fellow émigrés in the same situation, who found exile deeply troubling, such as Stefan Zweig. The literature on adult 'third culture kids' underlines how the chronic loss of relationships as well as the related anger

---

[18] Klepac, *Louis Kahan*, p. 10.

[19] For a historical contextualization see Arlene Stein, *Reluctant Witnesses: Survivors, Their Children, and the Rise of Holocaust Consciousness* (New York: Oxford University Press, 2014).

[20] Compare Peter Leese and Jason Crouthamel (eds.), *Traumatic Memories of the Second World War and After* (Cham: Palgrave Macmillan, 2016).

[21] Donnel B. Stern, 'Partners in thought: a clinical process theory of language', *The Psychoanalytic Quarterly* 78.3 (2009), pp. 701–31 (p. 715).

[22] Email by Dena Kahan to author 25 November 2017.

and sadness can result in an individual's withdrawal from his or her parental culture, and from surroundings more broadly. Studies about the mental health of refugees underline the higher rates of psychopathology (including depression, dissociation, anxiety or post-traumatic stress disorder) found in this cohort.[23] Additionally, refugees often experience difficulties securing employment because of their visa status and the non-transferability of their educational and professional qualifications. Generally speaking, 'many experience underemployment and downward vocational and socioeconomic mobility'.[24]

In other words, the accumulated loss that Kahan experienced during the war could have been deeply challenging, emotionally as well as in relation to his employment. Arguably, drawing allowed him to deal with the ill-effects of adverse change in a range of ways: first and foremost, he was able to work and exhibited in shows, and, with the drawing of portraits, he gained important artistic experience. Secondly, being a witness to the suffering of soldiers provided Kahan with a sense of purpose, artistically as well as emotionally. He experienced creative mastery and expanded his drawing skills, and simultaneously his art made it possible to reach out to individual soldiers, creating a human connection. His witnessing constituted an act of empathy and, although the encounters with soldiers were undoubtedly intense, psychologically Kahan was more or less in control of the situation. In turn this would have provided him with a salutary sense of control in a world where he, like other refugees, was manifestly vulnerable.

Australian Portraits

Portraits remained crucial to Kahan's artistic practice long after the war. Kahan joined his family in Perth in 1947, from where he moved to Melbourne in the late 1950s.[25] He quickly established himself there as an artist, painting in a range of genres, and was able to build on his previous expertise gained in Algeria. Portraits for Melbourne's middle and upper classes provided him with a steady income, and soon he also became the portraitist of choice for members of Australia's creative and intellectual circles.[26] His own background,

---

[23] Pollock and Van Reken, *Third Culture Kids*, p. 162; Fred Bemak and Rita Chi-Ying Chung, 'Refugee Trauma: Culturally Responsive Counseling Interventions, *Journal of Counseling & Development* 95.3 (2017), pp. 299–308 (p. 300).

[24] Bemak and Chi-Ying Chung, 'Refugee Trauma', p. 301.

[25] Klepac, *Louis Kahan*, pp. 15–16.

[26] Louis Kahan, *Great Music Makers* (Melbourne: Macmillan Publishers Australia, 2005); Louis Kahan, *The Face of Literature* (Melbourne: Melbourne University Press, 1981).

Fig. 25. Louis Kahan, Portrait of Australian writer Patrick White, reproduced by kind permission of the Art Gallery of New South Wales.

his European identity and his love for French culture – a love shared with the old Australian elites who were the descendants of mainly British migrants themselves – meant that Kahan was able to embrace and shape the rich intellectual tapestry that defined the postwar era 'Down Under'. To speak with Pierre Bourdieu, his cosmopolitan identity raised his 'symbolic capital': that is, he held more leverage in the social arena based on his prior experience.[27]

Kahan's impulse to chronicle and shape Australian intellectual life can perhaps best be seen through his 1962 portrait of Australian writer Patrick White (1912–1990) (Fig. 25; here reproduced in black and white). At the time

[27] Pierre Bourdieu, *Distinction. A Social Critique of the Judgement of Taste* (Cambridge, MA: Harvard University Press, 1984), p. 168.

of the portrait in the early 1960s, Patrick White was famous in particular for his novel *Voss*, which was based on the life of the nineteenth-century Prussian explorer and naturalist Ludwig Leichhardt, who disappeared while on an expedition into the Australian outback. Kahan shared with White a cosmopolitan experience of related geographical worlds: White had served in North Africa and the Middle East during the war; he had lived in London and New York for many years, and returned to Australia in the postwar period. The omnipresence of the exile/immigrant experience and its cosmopolitan and deeply transnational nature also became a motivating factor in Kahan's choice of White for his subject for the Archibald Prize. White's interest in painters in general and in Australia's immigrant history, and his intense and at times ambivalent friendships with a range of Jewish émigrés and Holocaust survivors, might, in return, have aroused further curiosity about Kahan as a fellow cosmopolitan creative mind.[28]

The purpose of the Archibald prize is to foster portrayals of Australians distinguished in art, letters, science or politics. Winning the Archibald Prize solidified Kahan's reputation as an Australian artist. Thus Arnold Shore, art critic for the Melbourne daily *The Age*, stated that 'intensity of effect, plus likeness, thoroughly earned Louis Kahan his first Archibald prize'.[29] Yet the portrait of White also elicited responses from a range of artist–critics, some of them previous winners of the Archibald Prize who enjoyed high public regard, and who commented with acrid defensiveness, questioning the status of Kahan's work as a portrait. Three topics dominate their critique: theatricality, artistic technique and superficiality. Prominent art critic James Gleeson (1915–2008), a foremost Australian surrealist painter and poet, attacked Kahan's painting as 'certainly not a true portrait', rather 'grossly theatrical – a stage prop meant to be read across footlights, a declamatory, unsubtle over-stated poster-portrait'. He opined that the image may have borne 'a considerable but superficial likeness but its attempts to go beyond the skin [are] a resounding failure'.[30]

Another provocative voice was that of the young Robert Hughes (1938–2012), who would become one of the most well-known art critics of his generation. When he wrote about Kahan, Hughes was about to leave Australia for London and New York and become the art critic for *Time* magazine.

---

[28] David Marr, *Patrick White. A Life* (Sydney/Melbourne/London/Auckland: Random House, 1991), p. 296; p. 384.

[29] Arnold Shore, untitled, newspaper clipping, undated, Archibald Folder, Private Collection of Louis Kahan.

[30] James Gleeson, 'Decay of the portraits', *Sun-Herald*, 20 January 1963, Archibald Folder, Private Collection of Louis Kahan.

Throughout his career Hughes considered modernism an affront to the curative and cathartic powers of art, and resented its underlying emotional darkness – a view he already expressed with reference to Kahan's portrait. In Hughes' description it was 'a tribute of bombast to the grey eminence of Australian writing', and superficial in the tension between the realist drawing and 'the congested textures that decorate it'.[31] Former Archibald Prize winner William Pigeon (1909–1981) characterized Kahan's painting as 'more of a coloured drawing', denying it its status as a portrait.[32]

Historian of the Archibald Prize Peter Ross has summarized the debate in terms of the shift 'from the early preponderance of formal, academic portraits' to 'modernist, even abstract, attempts [...] made to meet the expectations of a more critically aware public and an arts community determined to keep up with contemporary art expression'.[33] Indeed, the Archibald Prize has always triggered 'debates about biographical representation in Australia'.[34] In the early 1960s the controversy focused on the question of whether a portrait in a modernist style could serve as the likeness needed for the image 'to be called a portrait at all'. Some critics at the time understood that artists such as Kahan were 'grappling with the problem of integrating portraiture with the modern movement'.[35] That White himself was a modernist writer and that Kahan's choice of portrait style was defined by his subject went unnoticed. White himself expressed satisfaction with the portrait and stated that 'I think Mr Kahan has succeeded in expressing the feeling of my books'. When asked about the description of the portrait as 'over-theatrical' the accomplished playwright replied, 'Well, I think perhaps I am a bit theatrical!'[36] It is insightful to speculate on the sources for White's ironic defence of his portrait, presumably directed at the above-mentioned James Gleeson. More specifically, White knew from personal experience what it meant to be critiqued for the fictional portrayal of Australian characters and Australian society – as such, he might well have recognized Kahan as a fellow portraitist.

[31] Robert Hughes, 'This banal collection is the Archibald', *Sunday Mirror*, undated [1963], Archibald Folder, Private Collection of Louis Kahan.

[32] 'Dargie's kick misses the mark', newspaper clipping, undated, Archibald Folder, Private Collection of Louis Kahan.

[33] Peter Ross, *Let's Face It. The History of the Archibald Prize* (Sydney: Arts Gallery of NSW, rev. edn 2013), pp. 55–56.

[34] Gillian Whitlock, 'Pictures at an Exhibition. The Year in Australia', *Biography* 39.4 (2016), pp. 565–72 (p. 565).

[35] James Olefson, 'Portrait painters' new aim', *Sun-Herald*, 19 January 1964, Archibald Folder, Private Collection of Louis Kahan.

[36] 'Prized portrait "good likeness"': newspaper clipping, undated, Archibald Folder, Private Collection of Louis Kahan.

Winning the Archibald Prize established Kahan as a successful Australian artist, while paradoxically also making him more Viennese. The public disputation about the White portrait contributed to the hype that drew in crowds of 6,000 visitors to the Art Gallery of New South Wales in a single day. Gallery visitors joined the critics in expressing a diversity of opinions – 'from "world-ranking masterpiece" to "humbug"'.[37] The ambivalence towards the White portrait was strangely reflected in the ambivalence towards Kahan's status as an Australian. It was not unusual for the media to draw on the Archibald Prize-winner's life story, especially when the prize was given to a particular artist for the first time. In Kahan's case, reports varied from a simple 'Viennese-born'[38] to more detailed statements, such as 'born in Vienna and spent much of his early life in France'; the latter often included mention of Kahan's wartime period in Algeria.[39] Overall, these accounts demonstrate a distinct tendency to subsume his biography into a focus on his Viennese émigré experience – this was true for media outlets as different as *The Sun* (the highest-circulating daily in Australia) and the *Sydney Jewish News*. In *The Sun* Kahan was presented as follows: '[t]he artist whose name now goes down in our art history is in Australia today only because his family fled here from Nazi-oppressed Austria just before the war.'[40] The *Sydney Jewish News* likewise foregrounded Kahan's connection with Vienna in an article titled 'Australian Prize Far Cry from Vienna Fashions' – an allusion to the Kahan family business as master tailors.[41]

This foregrounding of Kahan as a Viennese émigré artist can be explained by a need in Australian society to make sense of the life story of their now accoladed fellow citizen. In his ground-breaking study *Imagined Communities*, Benedict Anderson has argued that nations conceive themselves 'as a deep, horizontal comradeship' that exists regardless 'of the actual inequality and exploitation that may prevail in each'.[42] Migrants and refugees often serve to mark the boundaries of imagined communities, and it seems that one consequence of Kahan's symbolic acceptance into the Australian community was a concurrent oversimplification of his biography as well as an insistence on

---

[37] '6,000 visit Art Gallery', newspaper clipping, undated, Archibald Folder, Private Collection of Louis Kahan.

[38] Arnold Shore, untitled, newspaper clipping, undated, Archibald Folder, Private Collection of Louis Kahan.

[39] 'Louis Kahan wins Archibald Prize', newspaper clipping, undated, Archibald Folder, Private Collection of Louis Kahan.

[40] Patrick Tennison, 'Brush with fate', *The Sun*, 19 January 1963.

[41] Greer Fay Cashman, 'Australian prize far cry from Vienna fashions', *The Sydney Jewish News*, 25 January 1963.

[42] Benedict R. Anderson, *Imagined Communities. Reflections on the Origin and the Spread of Nationalism* (revised and extended edition, London: Verso, 2010), pp. 6–7.

remembering his origins. The former was partly a consequence of the fact that, in post-war Australia, Vienna became synonymous with the Central European Jewish heritage of an increasingly influential group of refugees, even if their life stories prove more complex than accounted for in the Vienna–Australia dyad. The latter is an expression of the tension in the Australian mind as to whether an outsider such as Kahan could portray an Australian subject authentically. While such contentions were not raised publically in the context of the Archibald Prize, Kahan's 1963 exhibition *Waltzing Matilda*, named after Australia's best-loved bush ballad, was not received well on such an account. As Shmuel Gorr, the Director of the Jewish Art Museum Melbourne, commented, 'It didn't work. The Melbourne non-Jewish critics wouldn't accept this presumption [of embracing an Australian theme] for [sic] a non-Australian.'[43] This case study of Kahan reveals, therefore, how exile identities can be hybrid and hyphenated, but also (still) reside in the eye of the beholder.

Kahan as a Transnational Artist

Transnational artists retain more than one sense of home, yet, as argued by Anne Ring Peterson, 'the multiple cultural references in their works also raise the difficult question of the provenance of their art'.[44] For the present discussion, the 'difficult question' becomes: what is gained and what is lost by considering Kahan's Austrian origins when studying his life and oeuvre? Kahan was Viennese, but already in the first decades of his life he imagined himself as a Parisian. Towards the end of his life he saw himself as Australian. Nonetheless, Australian society – or at least Australian society as reflected in the local media – perceived him as a hyphenated Australian, a Viennese émigré, thus underlining his migrant and refugee status.

Kahan's life story evinces many similarities with those of other Austrian and German émigrés, yet, among German-speaking émigrés in Australia of the 1930s, the majority came on a direct route from Europe. By comparison, Kahan's identity was more cosmopolitan, owing to his experiences in France and Algeria; it was also a more clearly defined diasporic Jewish identity. Kahan's wife Lily, whose family is of Iraqi Jewish origin, had grown up in Indonesia and Malaysia and come to Australia as a consequence of the Second World War. Kahan was well connected to the Viennese émigré community

---

[43] Shmuel Gorr, 'Letter to the editor. Art group needs no justification', *Canberra Times*, 6 October 1964.

[44] Anne Ring Peterson, 'The Locations of Memory: Migration and Transnational Cultural Memory as Challenges for Art History', *Crossings: Journal of Migration & Culture* 4.2 (2013), pp. 121–37 (pp. 121, 123).

and was friends with Alfred Baring (d. 1982) and Else Baring (1908–1999), as well as Karl Bittman (1911–1996), the founders of the émigré Viennese Theatre (*Kleines Wiener Theater*) in Sydney.[45] Yet, rather than émigrés, his closest group of friends in Australia included Lillian Wightman (1903–1992), Melbourne fashion designer and owner of the iconic Le Louvre boutique, a 'mecca of Parisian fashion'.[46]

Kahan identified his love for music as his 'most Viennese' trait, which raises the question of other early artistic influences, including, perhaps most poignantly, the new modern Viennese portraiture. Regarding the 'New Viennese' – the fin-de-siècle generation of Viennese painters – art historian Gemma Blackshaw has argued that their portraits 'reveal the modern body that lay behind [the screen of historicism and inherited culture] in all its shocking physicality'.[47] This cannot be said of Kahan's early portrait of a young man made in 1928, which shows a dapper figure dressed in 1920s fashion and stylized more along the lines of New Objectivity, with his smooth haircut and fashionable clothes (Fig. 26). More than four decades later Kahan's portrait of White tells a different story, however, with the writer's large hands, rugged from farm labour, representing both White's connection to the country and the writer's artisanal craft, and his clothes carrying a quality of disintegration and decay about them.

These exaggerated features were registered by Australian viewers of the portrait in 1962, and not always in a positive manner. A short newspaper article recorded snippets of audience feedback, such as: 'The eyes look like golf balls'; 'There seems to be a lot of the illustrator visible, particularly in the pullover'; 'Did he get the pullover at the South pole'.[48] The powerful modernist style that Kahan employed (soft in comparison to Pablo Picasso's abstract portraits) honours the literary modernism of White and concurrently references the school of new modern Viennese portraiture – notably portraits by Oskar Kokoschka created around and after 1910, such as those of William Wauer (1910) and Baron Viktor von Dirsztay (1911), or Kokoschka's 1917 self-portrait. This observation neither makes Kahan's portrait of White an *Austrian* portrait nor Kahan an *Austrian* artist. Indeed, to classify Kahan as Austrian could be perceived as problematic in light of the expulsion of his family and

---

[45] Birgit Lang, *Eine Fahrt ins Blaue. Deutschsprachiges Theater und Kabarett im australischen Exil und Nach-Exil (1933–1988)* (Berlin: Weidler, 2006), pp. 62–69.

[46] Susannah Walker, 'A nice little frock shop', *The Age*, 26 February 2010.

[47] Gemma Blackshaw, 'On stage: The New Viennese', in *Facing the Modern. The Portrait in Vienna*, ed. by Gemma Blackshaw (London: National Gallery Company, 2014), pp. 13–34 (p. 30).

[48] 'Views on art!', newspaper clipping, undated, Archibald Folder, Private Collection of Louis Kahan.

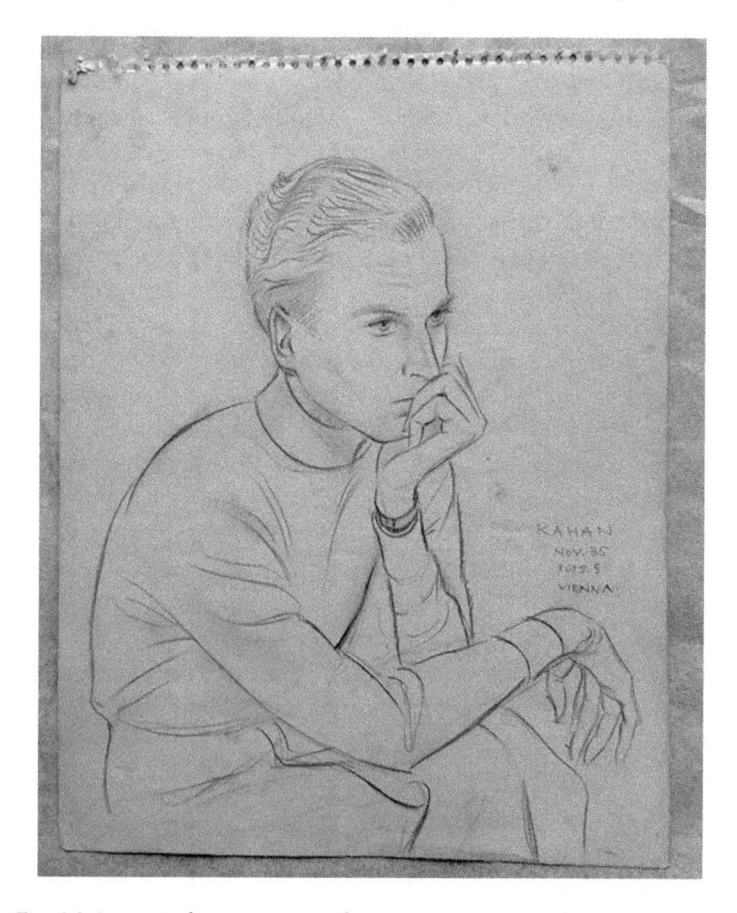

Fig. 26. Louis Kahan, Portrait of a young man, reproduced by kind permission of the Kahan family.

the fact that the Austrian state took many decades to come to terms with its past. Rather, it recollects that transnational artists tend to possess a greater capacity for referencing a particular style or form of expression that is part of their wider cultural repertoire. While Kahan's borrowings or echoes are authentic, simultaneously their meaning becomes reinterpreted in the artist's specific, local context, which is itself subject to change over time.

As we have seen through the case study of Kahan, the parallel investigation of biography and artistic genre can help to reveal the intricate ways of the creation and reception of transcultural art. The portraits that Kahan made in Algeria resulted from an exchange with each sitter and its intimate audience was – via reproduction and postal service – the sitter's family. This exchange created new, intricate and intimate layers of meaning for the drawings. Kahan's decision to submit his portrait of White to the Archibald Prize meant that the negotiation between artist and viewers became more pronounced and public; as did the exchange with his viewers. Again, the portrait as a genre granted him a significant opportunity to connect to and shape the world around him. Kahan's wide painterly register meant that he confidently chose the style for his portrait, depicting the modernist writer by modernist means.

Kahan's example is significant because his biography helps us to see the way in which his life and work is both unique but also part of a larger émigré experience. The challenge of this approach is to carefully form an understanding of the complex intersections between exile experience, the changing ways in which transnational artists position themselves and how they are perceived by their audiences. In hindsight it might seem ironic that the Australian audience perceived Kahan as a Viennese émigré, although his life story was more complex than that of other émigrés and although they had only limited knowledge of the specific Viennese modernist artistic traditions Kahan was able to draw upon. Yet such simplified readings, which are based on a mixture of a lack of knowledge and biographical overgeneralizations, can occur relatively easily, not only in the public eye but also in academic research. At the same time, biography-led research contributes to a multi-faceted understanding of the transnational realm and sheds a new light on the global exile experience.

Suggestions for Further Reading

Blackshaw, Gemma (ed.), *Facing the Modern. The Portrait in Vienna* (London: National Gallery Company, 2014), 192 pp.

Brilliant, Richard, *Portraiture* (London: Reaktion Books, 2013), 194 pp.

Carter, Karen L., and Susan Waller (ed.), *Foreign Artists and Communities in Modern Paris, 1870–1914* (Burlington: Ashgate, 2015), 280 pp.

Klepac, Lou, *Louis Kahan* (Sydney: The Beagle Press, 1990), 128 pp.

Lang, Birgit, *Eine Fahrt ins Blaue. Deutschsprachiges Theater und Kabarett im australischen Exil und Nach-Exil (1933–1988)* (Berlin: Weidler, 2006), 346 pp.

Leese, Peter, and Jason Crouthamel (eds.), *Traumatic Memories of the Second World War and After* (Cham: Palgrave Macmillan, 2016), 313 pp.

Marr, David, *Patrick White. A Life* (Sydney: Random House, 1991), 720 pp.

Peterson, Anne Ring, 'The Locations of Memory: Migration and Transnational Cultural Memory as Challenges for Art History', *Crossings: Journal of Migration & Culture* 4.2 (2013), pp. 121–37.

Pollock, David C., and Ruth E. Van Reken, *Third Culture Kids. Growing Up Among Worlds* (Boston, MA: Nicholas Brealey Publishing, 2009), 480 pp.

Soussloff, Catherine M., *The Subject in Art. The Birth of the Modern* (Durham, NC: Duke University Press, 2006), 192 pp.

15

Representative Germans

Navid Kermani and the German Literary Tradition of Critical Cosmopolitanism

Claire Baldwin

In 2016 German politicians and the public debated who would be appointed the next president of the Federal Republic of Germany. The candidacy of prominent author Navid Kermani generated particular excitement and concern, captured in an opinion piece by Paul Ingendaay:

> Admittedly, an outsider and a man from the outside. [...] Many might take offense that Kermani is Muslim. But he does not have to serve as poster boy for a dreamy multi-cultural Germany, a cliché-ridden idea he himself criticizes; to the contrary, he would instead stand for the best German tradition of social engagement – not despite, but rather precisely because he combines political and religious thought as does no one else. [...] it would be a different model, a reliable mirror of the new German reality.[1]

The opposing perspectives on Kermani's suitability for the highest diplomatic office of the country reflect fundamental debates over the understanding of contemporary Germany, the symbolic representation of the state and the identity of the nation. These issues provoke deep uncertainties in a society that is, as Stuart Taberner argues, still coming to recognize its transnational

---

[1] Paul Ingendaay, 'Muslim und moderner Patriot', *Frankfurter Allgemeine Zeitung*, 30 September 2016 www.faz.net/aktuell/feuilleton/debatten/kermani-als-bundespraesident-ein-muslim-und-patriot-14459501.html [accessed 2 November 2017]. The reader comments to the article further capture these debates, as does the Facebook page *Navid Kermani als Bundespräsident* www.facebook.com/kermanipraesident [accessed 1 March 2018].

and multi-religious character as one of its constituent features affecting all its inhabitants.[2]

Although he did not become president, Navid Kermani is indeed an eloquent representative and influential interpreter of Germany as an 'exemplary transnational space' in which the manifestations of globalization in everyday life permeate society and culture.[3] A renowned scholar of Islamic Studies, prolific journalist and author of narrative fiction and wide-ranging essays, Kermani is much in demand as a public voice on the current conditions faced by refugees, on Islam in Europe and as a defender of the European Project.[4] He illuminates diversity within religious traditions and intersections between them and combats polarizing discourse on religious and ethnic differences to explore the question posed succinctly in his book title *Wer ist Wir? Deutschland und seine Muslime* [*Who is We? Germany and its Muslims*, 2009].[5] Multi-perspectivism and the dialogic exploration of the self and social contexts characterize his novels. In speeches such as '*Über die Grenzen – Jacques Mourad und die Liebe in Syrien*' ['Beyond the Borders: Jacques Mourad and Love in Syria', 2015],[6] Kermani emphasizes the world's transnational interconnectedness and the moral and political failure of a narrow construal of self-interest, calling on political actors to address terrorism and the ravages of war. His journalism – for example, on refugee routes from Izmir to Germany in *Einbruch der Wirklichkeit* [*Upheaval: The Refugee Trek through Europe*, 2016][7] – prompts soul-searching about Europe's political responsibilities towards individuals fleeing violence, persecution and economic misery, as he reminds readers that the ideals of transnational human rights are fundamental to the European project. In *Entlang den Gräben* [*Along the Trenches*, 2018][8] he charts traces of

---

[2] Stuart Taberner, *Transnationalism and German-Language Literature in the Twenty-First Century* (London: Palgrave Macmillan, 2017), pp. 51–55.

[3] Taberner, *Transnationalism*, p. 19.

[4] For an overview of Kermani's work see the bibliography compiled by Torsten Hoffmann, 'Navid Kermani – Auswahlbibliografie', in *Text und Kritik* Heft 217 (2018), ed. by Torsten Hoffmann, pp. 87–92.

[5] Navid Kermani, *Wer ist Wir? Deutschland und seine Muslime* (Munich: Beck, 2009).

[6] Navid Kermani, 'Über die Grenzen – Jacques Mourad und die Liebe in Syrien', in *Navid Kermani: Friedenspreis des deutschen Buchhandels 2015. Ansprachen aus Anlass der Verleihung* (Frankfurt: Börsenverein des Deutschen Buchhandels, 2015), pp. 49–71.

[7] Navid Kermani, *Einbruch der Wirklichkeit. Auf dem Flüchtlingstreck durch Europa*. Mit dem Magnum Photographen Moises Saman (Munich: Beck, 2016).

[8] Navid Kermani, *Entlang den Gräben. Eine Reise durch das östliche Europa bis nach Isfahan* (Munich: Beck, 2018).

war and political and cultural rifts along national, subnational and transnational fault-lines from Germany across Eastern Europe to Iran. His dialogue with many individuals informs these investigations into varieties of cultural memory, new manifestations of nationalism and challenges to supporting a harmonious diversity of cultures, languages and religions.

Kermani's prominence as a public intellectual is reflected in his membership of literary, scholarly and civic institutions. Numerous honours recognize his academic and literary achievements and political and social engagement.[9] He speaks in many venues and writes frequently for newspapers. His work is circulated widely in translation; for example, 'Beyond the Borders', his acceptance speech of the Peace Prize of the German Book Trade, appears on its homepage in German, Arabic, French and English with links to translations into seven further languages.[10] He is, to speak with Rebecca Braun, embedded in networks and processes of world authorship that extend his audience globally.[11] These augment his role as a cultural mediator and moral arbiter, while furthering the critical public discourse on politics, literature and society he promotes in Germany and beyond. Through his extensive authorship, rich expertise and lived experience as a child of immigrants and a dual German and Iranian citizen, Kermani thus effectively represents transnational Germany in the public eye and engages expansively with what Elisabeth Herrmann calls the contemporary transnational shared horizon of experience.[12]

Yet Kermani is still frequently perceived, as in the article above, as 'an outsider and a man from outside'. The adjective 'transnational' itself sometimes reinscribes the ethnic or minority status of authors and their

---

[9] These recognitions reflect the breadth of his literary, journalistic and political resonance, as even a selective list documents: the European Prize of the Heinz Schwarzkopf Foundation for Scientific and Journalistic Work (2004); Hannah Arendt Prize for Political Thought (2011); Heinrich von Kleist Prize (2012); Cicero Speaker's Prize (2012); Gerty Spies Literature Prize (2014); The Peace Prize of the German Book Trade (2015); Marion Dönhoff Prize for International Understanding and Reconciliation (2016); ECF Princess Margriet Award for Culture (2017). For a fuller listing of Kermani's awards see his website: www.navidkermani.de.

[10] *Friedenspreis des deutschen Buchhandels* www.friedenspreis-des-deutschen-buchhandels.de/445722/?aid=970665 [accessed 1 March 2018].

[11] Rebecca Braun, 'Introduction: The Rise of the World Author from the Death of World Literature', *Seminar* 51.2 (2015), pp. 81–99 (p. 98).

[12] Elisabeth Herrmann, 'How does Transnationalism Redefine Contemporary Literature?' in *Transnationalism in Contemporary German-Language Literature*, ed. by Elisabeth Herrmann, Carrie Smith Prei and Stuart Taberner (Rochester, NY: Camden House, 2015), pp. 19–42 (pp. 24–25).

literatures.[13] Kermani affirms his multiple cultural and linguistic affiliations as a German-born son of Iranian immigrants, while rejecting any essentialist label that might 'co-opt' his identity to insist on full recognition as part of the German literary tradition.[14] Kermani's own reflections on his position as a German author, the focus of my further analysis here, belie his declarations of disinterest in questions of national belonging, as he explores what it means for him to be a representative author with cosmopolitan commitments in the Germanophone literary tradition and the transnational public sphere. Indeed, his persistent critique of the category of 'nation' places him squarely within these debates that are so characteristic of German intellectual and cultural life. He emphasizes that any individual or cultural identity always exceeds the categories used to describe it and rejects national clichés and nationalist sentiments, not least in his literary work to deconstruct them. He contrasts such ideas of identity with an inclusive cultural and civic sense of belonging, one embedded in transnational contexts and defined as cosmopolitan, yet nonetheless also marked by Kermani as specifically German.[15]

Citing iconic German literary figures in his statements of professional affiliation, Kermani advances a claim to the heritage of critical cosmopolitan thought in German culture. He is not alone in constructing an illustrious literary genealogy to define himself as a German author, but is notable for his analytic attention to what such affiliation means and how it shapes his contemporary authorial practice and sense of succession within the tradition he constructs. Moreover, he links his embrace of this tradition to a further dimension of German cultural belonging, namely the recognition and condemnation of National Socialist crimes as an obligation for all Germans. Underscoring the personal and cultural losses inflicted through Nazi violence and ideology, he connects his cosmopolitan ethos explicitly to the topics of mourning and remembrance that characterize so many of his works.[16] By

[13] Yogita Goyal, 'Introduction: The Transnational Turn', in *The Cambridge Companion to Transnational American Literature*, ed. by Yogita Goyal (Cambridge: Cambridge University Press, 2017), pp. 1–15 (p. 1).

[14] 'Navid Kermani', in Helga Druxes and Karolin Machtans, 'Interview with Navid Kermani', in *Navid Kermani*, ed. by Helga Druxes, Karolin Machtans and Alexandar Mihailovic (Bern: Peter Lang, 2016), pp. 35–48 (pp. 36–37).

[15] David Coury underscores the European vision of this cosmopolitanism in David N. Coury, 'Kafka and the Quran: Patriotism, Culture, and Post-National Identity', in *Navid Kermani*, ed. by Helga Druxes, Karolin Machtans and Alexandar Mihailovic (Bern: Peter Lang, 2016), pp. 49–68.

[16] Thomas Anz, 'Kunst der Emotionalisierung. Navid Kermanis Poetik des Todes', *Text und Kritik* Heft 217 (2018), ed. by Torsten Hoffmann, pp. 6–13 (p. 6).

locating himself in a German tradition of cosmopolitan literary engagement and transnational critique, Kermani thus not only asserts his own belonging as a German author but simultaneously promotes a conception of German culture that recognizes the cosmopolitan contestation of nationalist ideologies as a central feature of its canonical history. Instead of emphasizing his marginality to German culture by identifying with such opposition, Kermani ensconces himself firmly within its traditions and advocates for the significance of literary work in probing the multivalent meanings of German culture and of national and transnational identities.

The German Cosmopolitan Cultural Tradition

Kermani's speech of 23 May 2014, presented to the German parliament on the 65th anniversary of the Basic Law, exemplifies his invocation of German cosmopolitan thought to define his authorial position on the political stage. In a speech focused on the status of migrants in Germany, Kermani lauds the constitutional ideals and accomplishments of the Federal Republic that protect them and condemns the violence perpetrated against perceived foreigners in Germany and restrictions of their constitutional rights. He explains both his praise and his censure of Germany as the cultural work of critique, anchored in a German tradition of self-critical appraisal directed particularly to operative ideas of nationhood: 'Since the late 18th century, at the latest since Lessing, who disdained patriotism and who was the first German to use the word "cosmopolitan", German culture has often stood in an antipodal relation to the nation.'[17]

Here, as elsewhere, Kermani defines 'this cosmopolitan line of German thought'[18] and what David Coury aptly calls Kermani's 'cultural patriotism'[19] by naming authors he counts as his literary forefathers (and it is a decidedly patriarchal lineage) and by analysing their common ethos. Stefan Zweig, Walter Benjamin, Franz Kafka and Heinrich Heine are among them, yet also Jean Paul and Thomas Mann, to list but several. The German tradition he constructs prominently includes, but is not exclusive to, Jewish authors of the nineteenth and twentieth centuries: 'I am concerned here not with a specifically Jewish impetus in German literature but with a cosmopolitanism that the Jewish authors merely emphasized more often than other

---

[17] Navid Kermani, 'Zum 65. Jahrestag der Verkündung des Grundgesetzes. Rede vor dem Deutschen Bundestag am 23. Mai 2014', in *Zwischen Koran und Kafka. West-östliche Erkundungen*, Navid Kermani (Munich: Beck, 2014), pp. 341–49 (p. 346).

[18] Kermani, 'Grundgesetzes', p. 346.

[19] Coury, 'Kafka and the Quran', p. 51.

Germans.'[20] Kermani neither ignores circumstances that temper authors' relationships to dominant German culture nor countenances a reductive biographical interpretation of authors and their literature based on religion, citizenship, ethnicity or ancestry. What signals belonging to this distinct German cosmopolitan heritage is, for Kermani, an author's professional and personal choice to produce literature in German that takes up its specific 'legacy, with the authority and responsibility that arise from it'.[21]

Kermani's understanding of this German cultural tradition has been read through the concept of the *Kulturnation* [cultural nation], an idea of German cultural commonality transcending the instability and political divisions of German states.[22] The opposition between *Kulturnation* and *Staatsnation* [political nation] codified by Friedrich Meinecke in 1908 remains an influential and controversial conceptual framework for questions of German identity. It generated renewed interest in response to the complications of German division and unification in the 1980s and 1990s, as Stephen Brockmann analyses,[23] represented perhaps most prominently by Günter Grass. In Cold War political writings, Grass employs the term *Kulturnation*, in opposition to a political nation-state, to mark a superior form of national identity 'free of typical claims to power'; he claims its authors are 'cosmopolitans' and 'the better patriots' and calls on many of the same literary predecessors as does Kermani to authorize and elucidate his practice of anti-nationalist political and moral engagement in the public sphere.[24] And in his vociferous opposition to German reunification, Grass advocates for a political confederation of German states linked by cultural commonalities,

---

[20] Navid Kermani, 'In eigener Sache', in *Zwischen Koran und Kafka. West-östliche Erkundungen*, Navid Kermani (München: Beck, 2014), pp. 7–18 (p. 9). English translation: Navid Kermani, 'Preface. A Personal Note', in *Between Quran and Kafka. West-Eastern Affinities*, trans. Tony Crawford (Malden, MA: Polity Press, 2016), pp. viii–xv (p. ix).

[21] Kermani, 'A Personal Note', p. viii.

[22] Helga Druxes and Karolin Machtans, 'Introduction: The Intercultural Project of Navid Kermani', in *Navid Kermani*, ed. by Helga Druxes, Karolin Machtans and Alexandar Mihailovic (Bern: Peter Lang, 2016), pp. 1–14 (p. 1).

[23] Stephen Brockmann, *Literature and German Reunification* (Cambridge: Cambridge University Press, 1999).

[24] Günter Grass, 'Die deutschen Literaturen' (1979), in Günter Grass, *Essays und Reden II: 1970–1979*, ed. Daniela Hermes (Göttingen: Steidl, 1993), pp. 518–27 (p. 520). Rebecca Braun illuminates the shifting forms of Grass's political self-staging over the course of his career in Rebecca Braun, *Constructing Authorship in the Work of Günter Grass* (Oxford: Oxford University Press, 2008), especially chapter 2 (pp. 38–64).

a 'Kulturnation in confederative multiplicity'.[25] More recent debates over the idea and capaciousness of the German *Kulturnation* have arisen in the context of the increased immigration to Germany that challenges and transforms its self-understandings.[26] Indeed, many facets of the discourse on the *Kulturnation* do resonate in Kermani's writing: these include the centrality of the German language in the definition of the cultural tradition; the relationship of opposition between *Geist* [spirit; intellect] and *Macht* [political power]; the idea of the cultural work of social and political critique as a meaningful form of patriotism; and the assertion of cosmopolitan interests and perspectives, long a feature of German cultural self-perception. Kermani himself, however, explicitly disavows the term *Kulturnation* as a useful concept. This rejection illuminates his distinctive effort to dissociate the discussion of German cultural identity emphatically from any framework of nation by identifying the cultural commonality he embraces as the German cosmopolitan tradition.

The incongruity of 'culture' and 'nation' in the German-speaking world prohibits recourse to the idea of a *Kulturnation*, Kermani asserts.[27] Moreover, the modern construct of nationhood itself obscures and represses the layered experiences of individual and communal identity, proving it an inadequate concept through which to interpret belonging:

> I question the contemporary concept of nation [...] as a point of reference for identity [das Eigene]. Historically, the nation almost always led to a leveling of established or newly emergent cultural, linguistic, ethnic or religious differences and contains an enormous potential for violence, as shown throughout the entire 20th century.[28]

German culture is especially well poised to recognize these limitations, given the non-identity of political and cultural alignments in German-speaking lands, as well as the experienced history of German nationalist ideologies as instruments of violence and political repression directed both across and within political borders.

---

[25] Günter Grass, 'Kurze Rede eines vaterlandslosen Gesellen' (1990), in Günter Grass, *Essays und Reden III: 1980–97* (Göttingen: Steidl, 1997), pp. 230–34 (p. 234). See also Grass, 'Lastenausgleich' (1989), in *Essays und Reden III*, pp. 225–29.

[26] Arndt Kremer, 'Transitions of a Myth? The Idea of a Language-Defined Kulturnation in Germany', *New German Review* 27 (2016), pp. 53–75.

[27] Klaus Nüchtern, 'Über den Zufall', *Falter* 44/2012, www.falter.at/falter/rezensionen/buch/454/9783446239937/ueber-den-zufall [accessed 23 May 2018].

[28] Nüchtern, 'Über den Zufall'.

Kermani opposes *Kulturnation* with his conception of a shared German-language culture that neither projects nor compensates for the idea of nation, but is instead independent of it. This alternative view of commonality is grounded in the cosmopolitan values and practices of the form of authorship Kermani specifies and promotes through his analyses of his literary predecessors. Not only is its cosmopolitanism expressed through its respect for foreign cultures, but it significantly highlights the vitality of the internal diversity within German-language culture that the ideological and political force of the idea of nation suppresses, and it explores such a multiplicity of perspectives as a salient strength of the cultural tradition. Kermani also contests the capacity of the term *Kulturnation* to indicate the relationship of culture to politics. Instead of framing the work of social and political critique as a competing form of nationhood, he defines it as a constituent feature of the cosmopolitan ethos expressed in the German cultural tradition; he thereby draws on a European understanding of cosmopolitanism that has long evoked the commitments to speak truth to power and to skewer social complacency as attributes of the cosmopolitan intellectual. The critique of one's own society and politics from the standpoint of a German cultural tradition defined not by nation but by its cosmopolitan spirit is for Kermani a form of local civic engagement – or, to speak with Coury, a form of cultural patriotism commensurate with the constitutional patriotism and hopes for a post-national Europe theorized by Jürgen Habermas.[29]

Kermani's conception of the legacy of the German cosmopolitan tradition and of its concrete meaning for his authorial practice becomes especially clear through his discussions of Kafka, Lessing and Heine. Kafka offers a model of demonstrative choice of authorial affiliation with German literature from a position of multiple cultural attachments. Kermani champions Lessing's intellectual integrity as a cosmopolitan critic. In Heine, Kermani finds a paragon of solidarity with those who experience suffering and injustice, as he contemplates the role of author as *Stellvertreter* or representative within the cosmopolitan literary tradition. His analysis throughout engages with questions of language, identity and representation, and with the literary critique of nationalist ideologies and their repressive force. The values and cultural work of the German cosmopolitan tradition Kermani lauds include

---

[29] Jürgen Habermas, "Geschichtsbewußtsein und posttraditionale Identität. Die Westorientierung der Bundesrepublik", in *Eine Art Schadensabwicklung. Kleine politische Schriften VI* (Suhrkamp: Frankfurt am Main, 1987), pp. 159–79 (especially pp. 168–69 and 173–74). See also his later essays, such as those in Jürgen Habermas, *Die postnationale Konstellation. Politische Essays* (Suhrkamp: Frankfurt am Main, 1998).

national self-critique, openness to cultural plurality and diversity, and a vision of transnational relationships and obligations that support universal human rights.

Kafka: The Exemplary German Author

Kermani's essay collection *Zwischen Koran und Kafka: West-östliche Erkundungen* [*Between Quran and Kafka: West-Eastern Affinities*, 2014][30] features Kafka as one figure of orientation for Kermani's own authorship. Kafka stands for German literary cosmopolitanism as an individual not defined by German national belonging and a writer who exemplifies a demonstrative choice of literary affiliation: 'Kafka can also mean a way of participating in German literature, upholding it all the more resolutely for being ever uncertain of one's social and political affiliation.'[31] Kermani finds in Kafka a model for his own identity as a German author writing from a position of biographical otherness. 'Not unlike Kafka [...] I partook of German literature as my own and was an especially motivated student of it, perhaps not in spite but because of my origins.'[32] If the distance from an ethnic and Christian German identity prove an incentive to delve more deeply into German literature, the study that ensues in turn motivates Kermani to engage more fully with the religious and cultural traditions of his heritage, a development he parallels to Kafka's interest in Judaism (for more on this theme in Kafka, see Nicholas Baer's discussion in Chapter 11 of this volume). Kermani's reading of Kafka leads from aesthetic and philosophical investments to an engagement with the Quran 'and the religion and culture of Islam along with it'. Both Kafka and the Quran ground his 'insistence, religious or not, on the continuing relevance of metaphysical questions in a radically secularized environment'.[33] In commentary on Kafka, Kermani speaks of an archive that nurtures the cosmopolitan dimensions of German literature: 'Jewish authors in particular bestowed on German literature a cultural, religious and biographical archive that has been a vital contribution to its worldwide importance.'[34] Kermani's

---

[30] Navid Kermani, *Zwischen Koran und Kafka. West-östliche Erkundungen* (Munich: Beck, 2014).
[31] Kermani, 'A Personal Note', p. xiii.
[32] Kermani, 'A Personal Note', p. xiv.
[33] Kermani, 'A Personal Note', p. xiv.
[34] Navid Kermani, 'Nachmittag Schwimschule. Kafka und Deutschland', in *Zwischen Koran und Kafka*, pp. 211–28. English: 'Swimming in the Afternoon: Kafka and Germany', in *Between Quran and Kafka*, pp. 141–54 (p. 152). This is a revised version of 'Was ist deutsch an der deutschen Literatur?' *Wespennest* (2007), pp. 22–28.

discussion of his intellectual development as an author and a scholar of Islam in relation to his analysis of Kafka as a literary forefather resonates with this idea of an archive of diverse expression, a foundation of the cosmopolitan German literature that Kermani perpetuates and claims as his authorial inheritance.

Kafka's engagement with this archive in his literary explorations of alienation together with his plural identity markers define his prominence in the cosmopolitan tradition and belie an equivalence of German-language authors with the German nation. Instead, his status as 'not only German' (a phrase Kermani frequently employs) makes him the 'exemplary German writer',[35] an apt representative of that German literature characterized precisely by its self-aware distance from an untroubled sense of national identity. Referencing Thomas Mann, Kermani writes: 'the distinguishing feature of Germany's poets remains their strained relationship with Germany.'[36] In framing the relationship between the German nation and the German culture he admires as oppositional and marking this antagonism as a constituent aspect of the tradition he calls upon (as he similarly does in his speech to the German parliament), Kermani is careful not to exculpate all forms of German culture from a suspect political nationalism. He instead emphasizes that an author's intellectual and ethical choice to engage critically through literature with reductive ideas of nationhood can be a form of conscious cosmopolitan practice. Literature's capacity to probe political and cultural discourses through concrete stories that influence readers' horizons of empathy, imagination and reflection entails great authorial responsibility, in Kermani's view. He champions writing that contests a nationalist appropriation and asserts a moral cosmopolitanism: 'the Nazis' monopolization of German literature ran up against its limits wherever the motifs of self-criticism, openness to the world, European unity and humanism began.'[37] This is the ethos defining the German literary genealogy Kermani evokes when he avows: 'there is no greater obligation for me than to belong to the same literature as the Jew Franz Kafka of Prague. His Germany is also my homeland.'[38]

Kermani's consciousness of professional commitments and his notable authorial pathos is itself, he reflects, an aspect of his German literary and intellectual inheritance. The tendency towards metaphysical seriousness, he attests, is a characteristic of his writing that is 'certainly of German

---

[35] Kermani, 'Swimming in the Afternoon', pp. 141–42.
[36] Kermani, 'Swimming in the Afternoon', p. 147.
[37] Kermani, 'Swimming in the Afternoon', p. 150 (translation amended).
[38] Kermani, 'Swimming in the Afternoon', p. 154.

origin' – as is the self-ironic skewering of that trait.[39] The moral gravity attending this literary legacy is underscored by the way Kermani positions himself historically in relation to it, emphasizing its losses: 'The lineage I followed ends with the Second World War.'[40] The caesura results from violent cultural suppression, the Holocaust perpetrated in Germany's name and the 'totalitarian ideology of Nazism [that] seemed to have discredited all overarching projects and all concepts of the collective'.[41] The weight of the National Socialist past and a vigilant consciousness of its political and moral failures and cultural losses are thus central to the legacy of the cosmopolitan cultural lineage in the present. The obligation of belonging to the same literature as Kafka entails the imperative to resist ethnic nationalism and help develop shared understandings through cosmopolitan literary practice. While Kafka and the compatriots of 'his Germany' represent a literary genealogy that is indeed, as Yasemin Yildiz notes, oppositional, if only in part minoritarian, Kermani evokes it not to position himself as marginal to German culture or free from German historical guilt:[42] rather, he asserts a place of belonging squarely within a German cultural tradition defined through its probing self-critique and its examination of German national identity in dialogue with the wider world. Kermani's demonstrative choice to inherit this German cultural past and take on its obligations is not a means of avoiding the burden and significance of the Holocaust for the present, but instead a perspective through which to engage it.

In 2005, in discussion with 'four not quite German authors', the interviewer from the magazine *Literaturen* [*Literatures*] insisted to his interlocutors, including Kermani, 'that you simply are not German authors like Goethe and Thomas Mann'. Kermani retorted, 'But perhaps German rather in the sense of Kafka'. In Kermani's shorthand, as elaborated here, Kafka stands for a full belonging to German literature as a professional and personal choice, and for a commitment to use the heightened linguistic and cultural perspectives of being 'authors who do not have a purely German biography' to further what Kermani identifies as German literature's best traditions.[43] The distinctive

---

[39] Kermani, 'In eigener Sache', p. 9 ('A Personal Note', p. viii, translation amended).
[40] Kermani, 'A Personal Note', p. viii.
[41] Kermani, 'A Personal Note', p. x.
[42] Yasemin Yildiz, *Beyond the Mother Tongue: The Postmonolingual Condition* (New York: Fordham University Press, 2012), pp. 167–68.
[43] 'Fremde Leben in anderen Welten – "Ich bin ein Teil der deutschen Literatur, so deutsch wie Kafka"; Vier nicht ganz deutsche Autoren: Terézia Mora, Imran Ayata, Wladimir Kaminer und Navid Kermani im Literaturen-Gespräch', *Literaturen: die Zeitschrift für Leser*, 4 (2005), pp. 26–31. www.cicero.de/ich-bin-ein-teil-der-deutschen-literatur-so-deutsch-wie-kafka/45292 [accessed 1 March 2018].

linguistic precision from a position of 'foreignness' that is exemplified by Kafka's literature is, Kermani muses, a quality contemporary authors from immigrant backgrounds may likewise develop, while reclaiming 'something of the worldliness, the outward awareness or the metaphysical foundations' of the German cosmopolitan tradition: 'We will see, not today, not tomorrow, but in twenty or fifty years, how the foreignness that has now entered German literature once again as a result of immigration influences its orientation and its qualities.'[44] When Kermani points to Kafka as his literary compatriot to illustrate the folly of a merely ethnic or national idea of German identity and authorship and to push back against categorization as a minority author, he also means to evoke the complex ethos and practice of the cosmopolitan German literary tradition as he defines it in his essays and seeks to carry it forward in his own literary work.

Lessing: The Cosmopolitan Critic

Kermani also claims Lessing, a canonical founder of modern German literature, as an intellectual model and literary ancestor, while emphasizing two of his qualities: his cosmopolitanism and his power as a critic (for more on Lessing and Islam, see the discussion by James Hodkinson in Chapter 10 of this volume). Lessing's incisive polemics have always been a cornerstone of his reputation, and Lessing is frequently considered an exemplary cosmopolitan author, as well as a quintessentially German one; his work pillories bigotry and dogmatism, and especially *Nathan der Weise* [*Nathan the Wise*, 1778] is still performed as a dramatization of reciprocal respect and recognition of human commonality across diverse cultures and religions. In Kermani's analysis, Lessing's practices as a critic and a cosmopolitan define his authorship and his relationship to his society and culture, as well as his contemporary relevance. Moreover, Kermani's reception of Lessing is novel in drawing an explicit and trenchant connection between these two roles and thus between the commitments that cosmopolitan and critical practices exemplify.

Kermani posits the necessary conjunction of two characteristics of Lessing's writing – a rigorous critique of his own cultural context and a generous interest in what is foreign – as a crucial foundation of the cosmopolitan literature he promotes:

> Lessing is correctly praised for his knowledge of foreign cultures and his advocacy of tolerance. He was one of the first German authors to

[44] Kermani, 'Swimming in the Afternoon', pp. 152–53.

employ the expression 'cosmopolitan' and its German counterpart 'Weltbürger' [world citizen]. More seldom seen is that this openness to the world goes together with a consistently critical relationship to his own society.[45]

Kermani reveres Lessing's twinned practices of self-critique and knowledgeable openness towards other cultures (notably including Islamic cultures) as reliable measures of intellectual integrity, both of which reflect forms of love as an engaged commitment for the common good.[46] These affective and analytic dimensions together reflect Lessing's Enlightenment values that Kermani aims to rehabilitate.[47] They are the requisite grounding for authorship that furthers an intellectual tradition Lessing helped inaugurate, a German cosmopolitan literature as an expression of engaged world citizenship:

> To learn from Lessing therefore means not only to elevate self-criticism to a principle, to contradict the status quo. It equally means to value the foreign, to support the weak. That is, I believe, a fundamental requirement of every intellectualism and literature still today: respect for the Other and rigor against oneself; the defense of the marginalized and the contestation of dominance.[48]

In upholding Lessing as a paragon of this engaged intellectual ethos, Kermani emphasizes Lessing's resistance to dichotomies between the self and the other: 'We – for Lessing that means each person'.[49] Lessing's recognition of each individual's belonging to the collective 'we' is far from the idea of tolerance that has become, Kermani writes, a ubiquitous and complacent societal 'corporate identity'.[50] To stay true to Lessing's ethos one must reclaim the critical introspection of his radical social analysis, as found in *Nathan the Wise*, but

---

[45] Navid Kermani, *Vergesst Deutschland! Eine patriotische Rede* (Berlin: Ullstein Verlag, 2012), p. 24. This text also appears in revised form in Kermani, *Zwischen Koran und Kafka*, as 'Die heroische Schwäche. Lessing und Terror', pp. 90–120.

[46] Nora Bossong, 'Die Grenzen des Himmels. Navid Kermani als Mittler zwischen Politik und Poetik', in *Text und Kritik* Heft 217 (2018), ed. by Torsten Hoffmann, pp. 52–56, pushes back against Kermani to insist that sometimes critique of what is foreign is imperative.

[47] Coury, 'Kafka and the Quran', pp. 54–58.

[48] Kermani, *Vergesst Deutschland*, p. 27.

[49] Kermani, *Vergesst Deutschland*, p. 28.

[50] Angelika Overath, Navid Kermani and Robert Schindel, *Toleranz. Drei Lesarten zu Lessings Märchen vom Ring im Jahre 2003* (Göttingen: Wallstein, 2003); Kermani's untitled contribution encompasses pp. 33–45 (p. 33).

often smoothed over in its contemporary reception. Kermani upbraids Claus Peymann's twenty-first-century staging of this drama (in the *Berliner Ensemble* repertoire since the 2001 attacks on the World Trade Center) to expose an interpretation of tolerance that reverses Lessing's message: 'Where Lessing wrote against the intolerance of the West, tolerance becomes westernized in today's theater. Its representative is not *one of them* as in Lessing, but rather *one of us*: Nathan the White.'[51] Kermani scorns the theatrical commercialization of tolerance as a bath in collective self-affirmation, and urges his readers instead to embrace Lessing's 'provocative humanism' and his critical focus on the western European treatment of Islam.[52]

Kermani elaborates on the contemporary relevance of Lessing's criticism of his own culture in *Vergesst Deutschland! Eine patriotische Rede* [*Forget Germany! A Patriotic Speech*, 2012]. In discussion of the contemporary xenophobic violence of the National Socialist Underground, Kermani turns to Lessing's drama *Philotas* (1759) as a reflection on proto-nationalist sentiment in German lands. Lessing portrays the misguided self-sacrifice of the captured prince Philotas in the name of his kingdom, Kermani explains, as a tragic cost of the powerful ideology of country loyalty. Lessing rejects such patriotic heroism and, by emphasizing the prince's choice not to question his father's wisdom or his country's legitimation in war, Lessing warns against what Kermani calls the 'ideologizing of the sense of commonality' – 'the immunity of collective truth against individual experience and insight'[53] – as a root cause of many social and political ills. Kermani directs attention to the value he, with Lessing, ascribes to individual observation and insight as the engines of cultural self-critique and betterment, a core Enlightenment position. His interpretation of *Philotas* underscores how the pressures of ideological conformity, especially in the name of aggressive patriotism, distort or repress forms of knowledge founded on personal experience, critical appraisal and independent judgement. Lessing's rejection of a static truth in favour of the dynamic pursuit of truth as an ongoing development of human potential is well known, and is articulated most succinctly in *Duplik* [*A Rejoinder*, 1778]. Lessing's dialogical and antithetical critical method reflects

---

[51] Kermani, 'Die heroische Schwäche', p. 111. In the 2016/17 season, Peymanns's production of *Nathan the Wise*, billed by him as a 'crusade for tolerance', was still in repertoire, and on tour to acclaim. Carsten Heil, 'Claus Peymann im Gespräch', *Neue Westfälische Zeitung*, 22 November 2016 www.nw.de/kultur_und_freizeit/theater_und_kunst/20987055_Claus-Peymann-im-Gespraech-ueber-Nathan-Politik-und-Provinz.html [accessed 1 March 2018].

[52] Overath et al., *Toleranz*, p. 34.

[53] Kermani, *Vergesst Deutschland*, p. 19.

this epistemological conviction and infuses his literary and essayistic practice that is emulated by Kermani.

Kermani's reception of Lessing thus calls attention to the interconnected roles of critic and cosmopolitan and defines his own authorial profile as an ethical and professional choice of affiliation with a tradition of literary cosmopolitan practice that Lessing significantly shaped. Lessing's contemporary relevance lies in how he models and links an incisive critique of his own cultural ills and a generous interest in other cultures and their denizens as a path to substantive literary and cultural engagement with issues from dogmatism, prejudice and zealous patriotism to religious diversity and human rights. Like Lessing, Kermani cultivates a critical public persona that is open to the world and self-critically engaged with it, and demands a similar stance of his audience. He champions such literary practice as an ongoing project born of the Enlightenment, and contests the distorted vision of the Enlightenment sometimes invoked today to reinforce a rejection of Islam in Germany, as scholars have detailed.[54] Rather, he projects the vision of an encompassing cosmopolitan Enlightenment that finds expression in Christian, Jewish and Islamic traditions alike, and, with recourse to Lessing, he aspires to reclaim and revitalize its project in contemporary German letters.

Heine: The Writer as a Representative

Kermani turns to 'the Jewish cosmopolitan Heine'[55] to illustrate the idea of representation or *Stellvertreterschaft*, a term he explores to crystallize his own relationship to the literary tradition he posits. When a friend suggests that Kermani is, by virtue of his authorial pathos and humanitarian commitment, a representative of the Jewish German cosmopolitan literary tradition, he tentatively accepts this assessment in a limited way: 'Not in the sense of an identification, familial relation, or even equal status, but in the sense of a succession and the authority and responsibility that derive from it'.[56] Kermani aligns the role of representative with his consistent emphasis on a vocational affiliation and professional responsibility. He refuses to arrogate

---

[54] David N. Coury, 'Enlightenment Fundamentalism: Zafer Şenocak, Navid Kermani, and Multiculturalism in Germany Today', in *Ethical Approaches in Contemporary German-Language Literature and Culture*, ed. by Emily Jeremiah and Frauke Matthes (Rochester, NY: Camden House, 2013), pp. 139–57; Karolin Machtans, 'Navid Kermani: Advocate for an Antipatriotic Patriotism and a Multireligious, Multicultural Europe', in *Envisioning Social Justice in Contemporary German Culture*, ed. by Jill E. Twark and Axel Hildebrandt (Rochester, NY: Camden House, 2015), pp. 290–311.

[55] Kermani, 'A Personal Note', p. x.

[56] Kermani, 'In eigener Sache', p. 8 (my translation).

to himself a facile identification and is aware of the pitfalls of appropriating another's voice. Kermani's use of the word *Stellvertreter* rather than *Vertreter* seems to underscore this cautious remove and the nonequivalence it entails. A *Stellvertreter* is perhaps but a proxy, responsible to and standing in for another, yet recognized as different from an immediate group member.[57] By accepting the attenuated designation and positioning himself in the legacy of these authors, Kermani aims not to supplant their voices but to add his own as a respectful successor. This role bestows honour and authority as a spokesperson for this tradition, but also entails the responsibility to uphold its characteristic literary practices. His authorial alignment with German cosmopolitanism, the very possibility of his *Stellvertreterschaft*, in turn reflects its transnational purview as well as its capacity for creative renewal and its continued relevance for contemporary literature.

Kermani develops the concept of representation as itself a distinctive element of cosmopolitan literary practice. Heine's writing exemplifies the literary expression of solidarity with others in need and a call for justice on behalf of those beyond one's own narrowly defined tribe. 'None other than Heine introduced the perspective of the oppressed, the conquered, into German literature. However, he precisely does not become the voice of his own people, but instead Heine bore witness to the catastrophes of other, foreign peoples.'[58] For Kermani, Heine's literary practice represents, as a kind of non-identical modern proxy, past Jewish traditions and their religious pathos that resonate in modern cosmopolitan literature through protest against 'the suffering, the pain, the disease of all creatures', a protest of pathos 'in the literal sense of the word'. But, in addition, by giving voice to the suffering of other peoples Heine carries forth the secularized pathos of the Enlightenment, in defence of its vision of equality and 'against the narrow Protestant version of it, against the practice of ascribing character to nations and against hypertrophic rationalism'.[59] Heine testifies against the enslavement of Africans or the decimation of Mexican Indians in the Spanish conquest by employing capacities of literature to guide the imagination beyond the self and to foster recognition of our common humanity, as a function not of identity but of solidarity as a potent literary and political tool (for more on this theme in Heine, see the discussion by Benedict Schofield in Chapter 6 of this volume). Bearing such literary witness is inherent in the cosmopolitan literary tradition Kermani champions, always accompanied

---

[57] Translator Tony Crawford translates 'Stellvertreter' as 'representation of advocacy' in 'A Personal Note', p. viii.

[58] Kermani, 'In eigener Sache', p. 15 (my translation).

[59] Kermani, 'A Personal Note', p. xiii.

by authorial awareness of the non-identity that representation entails. Such solidarity can be endangered by the circumscriptions of identity politics, whether from a refusal to seek mutuality with others or a fear of appearing to speak for them. Heine's lesson for those who would perpetuate this tradition is that 'we do not have to have experienced comparable need, discrimination or oppression to become pathetic in the literal sense of the word',[60] but can and should attend to the suffering of others and extend the scope of our imagination and engagement to the world beyond what is most familiar.

The concept of *Stellvertreterschaft* of the cosmopolitan German literary tradition and as a literary practice within it unites authorial commitments in the present with a multivalent relationship to the German past. The centrality of the idea of pathos, the focus on suffering, in discussion of representing others reflects the belief in fundamental human commonality and the advocacy for transnational human rights that underpin Kermani's writing. The focus on the Jewish heritage within the cosmopolitan tradition connects the legacy of a proud German cultural history with the obligation to remember Germany's national crimes of the ideology and violence of Nazism. Kermani casts his relationship to the literary genealogy he constructs as one of authorial responsibility, with consciousness and knowledge of the Holocaust and its losses, to take up literary practices that contest ethnic nationalism and promote transnational democratic pluralism within and beyond German borders. Such work is simultaneously a form of literary memorialization and contemporary social and political engagement: 'what needs to be done in Germany is to fill, to the extent possible, with our limited means, experience and words, the space that became so vacant in the twentieth century.'[61] Both the aspect of cultural memory and that of present advocacy for human rights are presented as duties that pertain to the role of author as *Stellvertreter* and help define a contemporary transnational literary practice inspired by the cosmopolitan German authors of the past. Kermani ends these reflections with emphasis on both the honour and the task this vision of 'the writer as representative' entails, to again acknowledge as cultural loss: 'that role in Germany is appallingly vacant.'[62]

Kermani's readings of Kafka, Lessing and Heine illuminate his commitments to mark and help fill that empty place of the cosmopolitan writer. The professional ethos Kermani cultivates as a form of participation in this tradition of German culture so significantly shaped by Jewish authors forges a profound connection with and inheritance from the German past, something

---

[60] Kermani, 'A Personal Note', p. xiii (translation amended).
[61] Kermani, 'A Personal Note', p. viii.
[62] Kermani, 'A Personal Note', p. xv.

often considered a conundrum for authors without a long family history in Germany. His belonging within this tradition attests to the inclusive power of this shared German cultural tradition and to its internal diversity. His authorial work helps interpret and invigorate its cosmopolitan vision through his multifaceted perspectives as German and more than German and his contributions to its pluralistic archive. Kermani also feels a particular responsibility to engage this tradition and particularly its Jewish dimension anew in order to honour the Jewish European heritage as a contemporary Muslim German author:

> Along with the Judaeo-Arabic heritage of the Enlightenment, Heine and scholars of Judaism after him felt a responsibility to uncover its Islamic heritage as well. And it would be a good thing if Muslim authors today, whether religious or not, would reciprocate by standing up for [*mitvertreten*] Europe's Jewish heritage.[63]

Auschwitz and German Belonging

Kermani expressly stands up for and 'co-represents' the European Jewish heritage as a German Muslim and develops his conception of non-identical solidarity and commemoration in a speech celebrating the twentieth anniversary of the Munich University Chair of Jewish History and Culture, 'Auschwitz morgen: Die Zukunft der Erinnerung' ['Auschwitz tomorrow: The Future of Memory', 2017].[64] Kermani believes that a shared cultural and political memory of the Holocaust remains foundational for contemporary Germany (see also the discussion of this theme by Stuart Taberner in Chapter 16 of this volume). He emphasizes literature's capacities to cultivate that memory and addresses issues of identity and representation, responsibility and belonging, loss and commemoration that resonate with his study of Kafka, Lessing and Heine.

Kermani insists that Germans with immigrant backgrounds must recognize their stake in German responsibility for past national crimes and he identifies challenges of such 'migration to the past'.[65] As Germany's

---

[63] Kermani, 'A Personal Note', p. xiii (translation amended).

[64] Navid Kermani, 'Auschwitz morgen: Die Zukunft der Erinnerung', *Frankfurter Allgemeine Zeitung*, 7 July 2017 www.faz.net/aktuell/feuilleton/debatten/auschwitz-morgen-navid-kermani-ueber-die-zukunft-der-erinnerung-15094667.html?printPagedArticle=tr%E2%80%A6 [accessed 11 July 2017].

[65] Andreas Huyssen, 'Diaspora and Nation: Migration into Other Pasts', *New German Critique* 88 (2003), pp. 147–64.

population gains in diversity of ethnic, religious and national backgrounds, it becomes difficult for many people to perceive the Nazi past as relevant to their lives. Yet Kermani rejects the conclusion that this diverse society introduces a qualitatively new aspect into debates on the collective memory of Auschwitz: 'One need not treat immigrants or their children and children's children as a disruption in the politics of memory. The question of how a past remains present when biographical references are lacking presents itself the same way whether these references slowly disintegrate or were never there.'[66] Far from an anomaly, the distance of immigrants to the German past instead resembles that of younger ethnic Germans with loosening familial bonds to history. The analysis of each group's relationships to German history and each other itself highlights the moral and political question 'Who is we?' as it relates to historical guilt and responsibility, directing a critical transnational consciousness to ideological constructs of nationhood then and now. Through this lens, Kermani insists that the responsibility to acknowledge the Nazi past as a national history with personal significance is indeed incumbent on all Germans today regardless of background. This follows logically from the rejection of ethnicity as the basis for contemporary German belonging: 'Whoever contests an ethnic understanding of nation cannot narrow the historical responsibility ethnically. Whoever chooses to attain German citizenship will also have to carry the burden of being German. In Auschwitz at the latest he will feel it.'[67]

The future of the memory of Auschwitz in its relevance for the present depends on forging personal connections to this German history. Kermani relates his own visit to Auschwitz as a moment of forceful understanding that his German belonging also makes this shameful history his own, despite his non-German heritage and more viscerally than his German citizenship:

> Yes, I belonged with them, not through heritage, through blond hair, Aryan blood or such crap, but simply through the language, and thereby through culture. If there is a single moment in which I became German [...] it was last summer when I affixed the sticker to my chest, before me the barracks, behind me the visitor's centre: German.[68]

Visiting sites of National Socialist violence is one way to seek an experiential sense of the scope and lasting significance of these crimes. Insight into 'the blackness into which people are thrown by ideologies' can also be gleaned

---

[66] Kermani, 'Auschwitz morgen'.
[67] Kermani, 'Auschwitz morgen'.
[68] Kermani, 'Auschwitz morgen'.

through literature and art that represent the circumstances of individuals' lives concretely. Aesthetic works have a crucial role to play in the 'dialectics of the culture and critique of remembrance'[69] through their power, indeed, for Kermani, their task to help their audience imagine and attempt to understand others' experiences; even this effort's inherent limitations can alter the audience's critical and emotional awareness. Aesthetic forms of mediating individual stories thus bring contour and urgency to the political responsibility of accepting past German guilt and defending contemporary human rights and an inclusive democracy in Germany and beyond.[70]

Literary engagement with the Holocaust not only makes German shame and collective responsibility palpable for individual understanding but also conveys a sharply felt sense of loss 'for us who are German today' – loss of individual lives, of a rich German Jewish culture and of a potent cultural conception of Germany that exceeds national categories, namely 'the Germany of Goethe and Heine, this intellectual world in which concepts like world literature, Enlightenment, Europe and cosmopolitan were more common than patriotism, fatherland or pride [...] Therefore, the Holocaust is not only a history of guilt for Germany. It is also a history of loss.'[71] As seen, Kermani defines his ethos of critical cosmopolitanism as one built on his consciousness of this history of loss, the 'abrasion marks' left by Jews within German history and culture, in Leslie Morris and Jay Howard Geller's terms.[72] This is one dimension of the prominence of 'commemorative texts' throughout Kermani's oeuvre that chart personal and communal relationships of remembrance.[73] Marking the space of absence is a ritual way to

---

[69] Kermani, 'Auschwitz morgen'.

[70] This position speaks to the need to interweave the abstraction of human rights discourses with the concretization of memory presented by Andreas Huyssen, 'International Human Rights and the Politics of Memory: Limits and Challenges', *Criticism* 53.4 (2011), pp. 607–24.

[71] Kermani, 'Auschwitz morgen'. This focus on the dimension of loss distinguishes Kermani's view of German identity and authorship after Auschwitz. Günter Grass, for example, also asserts that the shame of the Holocaust underlies the German author's literary production and moral task to 'reflect on Germany'. Yet, whereas Grass argues darkly that to learn from Auschwitz is to 'finally know ourselves', warning his readers to fear a unified Germany, Kermani emphasizes that the German moral responsibility for the Holocaust, and the awareness of its losses, should drive the work of embracing an inclusive German cultural identity for the future. See Günter Grass, 'Schreiben nach Auschwitz' (1990), in Grass, *Essays und Reden III*, pp. 235–56 (pp. 255–56).

[72] Jay Howard Geller and Leslie Morris, 'Introduction', in *Three-Way Street. Jews, Germans, and the Transnational*, ed. by Jay Howard Geller and Leslie Morris (Ann Arbor: University of Michigan Press, 2016), pp. 1–23 (p. 8).

[73] Thomas Anz, 'Kunst der Emotionalisierung'.

hold space for memory and share grief, acknowledging their influence on the bereft community. A fresh cultural consciousness of the losses of the Holocaust reverberating in the present, mediated by newer, non-ethnic Germans as a dimension of their civic participation,[74] benefits the collective German memory and its responsiveness to contemporary transnational challenges:

> Therein lies, perhaps, a chance for Germany not only to recognize the guilt in the extermination of the Jews, but simultaneously to feel the loss. Dschâ-ye schân châlist, one says in Persian, when someone is missed, when he is absent at a party, at a funeral or simply in one's own everyday life. That means, translated literally, 'their place is empty' or also 'their place is free', in the sense of being held open. Dschâ-ye schân châlist, may this speech of a German about Auschwitz be concluded in Persian.[75]

Kermani contributes to such representation of loss with a view to a humane transnational future. Through his work as a cosmopolitan German author he honours the Jewish victims of National Socialism and the values of cultural plurality and human rights and mourns and resists their violent political repression.

In his avowals of professional affiliation, Kermani elaborates on two interconnected factors shaping his belonging to German culture and his role as one of its representatives. His commitments to identify with the German responsibility for the crimes of the Holocaust and to remember its victims, as well as his intellectual work examining constructs of Germanness through a critical transnational lens, serve the recognition 'that precisely in the fractures [*Gebrochenheit*] of Germany lies the identity and, yes, strength and vitality of the Federal Republic'.[76] Through his professional ethos and the authorial profile he presents on the public stage Kermani advocates for a contemporary conception of an inclusive German culture adequate to its fractures and heterogeneity, responsive and responsible to its past. He reminds his audiences that modern German culture has never been isomorphic with a single German nation-state or ethnicity; he exposes the flawed premises of cultural and national uniformity to emphasize forms of transcultural mobility, interactions and influences within and across political borders. Such analysis

---

[74] Michael Rothberg and Yasemin Yildiz, 'Memory Citizenship. Migrant Archives of Holocaust Remembrance in Contemporary Germany', *Parallax* 17.4 (2011), pp. 32–48.
[75] Kermani, 'Auschwitz morgen'.
[76] Kermani, 'Auschwitz morgen'.

underpins transnational methodology as, in Claudia Breger's definition, a 'perspective that foregrounds a critique of nationalist mythologies' and 'the legacy of essentialist, racialized concepts of national belonging'.[77] Kermani regards this kind of ideological critique as a defining feature of his own authorship, influenced by a long history of German cosmopolitan intellectual culture that inspires him to write in its succession.

Suggestions for Further Reading

Adelson, Leslie A., *The Turkish Turn in Contemporary German Literature: Toward a New Critical Grammar of Migration* (New York: Palgrave Macmillan, 2005), 273 pp.

Biendarra, Anke, *Germans Going Global. Contemporary Literature and Cultural Globalization* (Berlin: De Gruyter, 2012), 256 pp.

Druxes, Helga, Karolin Machtans and Alexandar Mihailovic (eds.), *Navid Kermani* (Bern: Peter Lang, 2016), 221 pp.

'Forum: Migration Studies', *The German Quarterly* 90.2 (2017) (with contributions by Gizem Arslan, Brooke Kreitinger, Deniz Göktürk, David Gramling, B. Venkat Mani, Olivia Landry, Barbara Mennel, Scott Denham, Robin Ellis, Roman Utkin), pp. 212–34.

Herrmann, Elisabeth, Carrie Smith Prei and Stuart Taberner, *Transnationalism in Contemporary German-Language Literature* (Rochester, NY: Camden House, 2015), 293 pp.

Hoffmann, Torsten (ed.), *Navid Kermani, Text und Kritik*, Heft 217 (2018), 95 pp.

Rothberg, Michael, and Yasemin Yildiz, 'Memory Citizenship. Migrant Archives of Holocaust Remembrance in Contemporary Germany', *Parallax* 17.4 (2011), pp. 32–48.

Taberner, Stuart, *Transnationalism and German-Language Literature in the Twenty-First Century* (London: Palgrave Macmillan, 2017), 365 pp.

Yildiz, Yasemin, *Beyond the Mother Tongue: The Postmonolingual Condition* (New York: Fordham University Press, 2012), 375 pp.

---

[77] Claudia Breger, 'Transnationalism, Colonial Loops, and the Vicissitudes of Cosmopolitan Affect: Christian Kracht's Imperium and Teju Cole's Open City', in *Transnationalism in Contemporary German-Language Literature*, ed. by Elisabeth Herrmann, Carrie Smith Prei and Stuart Taberner (Rochester, NY: Camden House, 2015), pp. 106–24 (pp. 106, 115).

16

Contrite Germans?

The Transnationalization of Germany's Memory Culture

Stuart Taberner

The election of Donald Trump as president of the United States in late 2016 confirmed a tectonic shift in global affairs that had been underway since at least the Al Qaeda attacks on the Twin Towers in New York on 9/11 and the ensuing 'war on terror', and which was accelerated by the global financial crisis of 2008 and its chaotic aftermath. It seems that the postwar era is now definitively over and that we are entering a new epoch in which it is no longer axiomatic that purportedly western values of liberal democracy, tolerance of diversity and free trade will in the end surely triumph. Of course, the teleological assumption of the universal benefits of the West's domination of the postwar world order in any event often scarcely disguised western nations' pursuit of their own interests. But the current revolt against globalization – including Britain's vote to quit the European Union, growing hostility across the continent to the EU's inept handling of the Eurozone crisis and 2015 refugee crisis, and President Trump's 'America First' rhetoric – have caused many people to fear that the world is about to return to something much worse. This would be a jolt back to the 1930s, with its combustive mix of ethno-nationalism, trade protectionism and geopolitical rivalry.

To people over 40 with a scholarly interest in Germany it probably felt strange when, in the wake of Donald Trump's surprise victory, the Federal Republic was invoked as the last bastion of the western liberal order in newspaper editorials around the world, and even in *Foreign Affairs*, that most august American periodical on international relations.[1] For British, American

---

[1] Thorsten Benner, 'Germany Can Protect the Liberal Order', *Foreign Affairs*, 16 November 2016 https://www.foreignaffairs.com/articles/germany/2016-11-16/germany-can-protect-liberal-order [accessed 21 November 2016].

and indeed German academic specialists who came of age during the postwar division of Germany following its genocidal nationalism between 1933 and 1945, this recent lionization stands in stark contrast to their received understanding of the country as a nation of penitents, dutifully apologizing for their forebears' crimes, especially the Holocaust. Yet the enlightened globalism that Germany is now widely considered to embody has long been a feature of postwar and especially post-unification German politics, culture and society. It is both a corollary and expression of what Karl Wilds has aptly called Germany's 'culture of contrition'.[2] The preamble to the country's 1949 basic law (*Grundgesetz*, or constitution) stipulates that Germany's role is to promote world peace as an equal partner in a united Europe, and still today the country's external relations are driven by a moral imperative to atone for Nazi crimes by pursuing a 'policy for peace', including human rights and humanitarian assistance for conflict resolution and civil-society projects. As Hungarian author Péter Esterházy once put it, Germany is the 'Weltmeister der Vergangenheitsbewältigung' [world champion in coming-to-terms with the past].

Following Trump's election, former foreign minister Joschka Fischer suggested that Germans' internalization of the lessons of the Nazi past meant that there could be no slogan 'Make Germany Great Again!' to match 'Make America Great Again!' This is almost certainly (still) true, but it does not mean that Germany is immune to the global pressures described in the opening paragraph of this chapter. The mass organization PEGIDA (Patriotic Europeans Against the Islamization of the West) was bolstered by popular resentment of Chancellor Merkel's decision to allow more than one million refugees to enter the country in the summer of 2015, and by September 2016 the upstart anti-Euro party *Alternativ für Deutschland* [Alternative for Germany] had morphed into an anti-immigration party and entered 10 out of 16 German state parliaments. After 9/11, a long postwar history of discrimination against Turks had become transformed into a more overt Islamophobia, and hostility toward Muslims was further inflamed by a series of terrorist attacks inspired by the Islamic State, including in Berlin in December 2016, when 12 people were killed by a Tunisian failed asylum seeker driving a truck into the crowd at a Christmas market. More generally, German nationalism seems to be on the rise, whether as anti-foreigner rhetoric or euroscepticism, popular pride in the national football team (Merkel is a big fan) or a new willingness to fly the German flag after decades when it was thought unseemly to do so (elements of the left still object).

---

[2] Karl Wilds, 'Identity Creation and the Culture of Contrition: Recasting "Normality" in the Berlin Republic', *German Politics* 9.1 (2000), pp. 83–102.

In September 2017 Germany suddenly appeared even more 'normal' – if 'normal' means that its political discourse now appeared just as febrile, unpredictable and susceptible to being captured by popularists as that of Britain, the United States and other western countries in the era of Brexit and Trump. In the 2017 Federal elections support for far-right party *Alternativ für Deutschland* – which inveighs against burkhas, minarets and the call to prayer – more than doubled to 12.6 per cent of votes cast, even as several of its most prominent figures decried the 'besmirching' of German soldiers who fought for Hitler and today's ongoing 'obsession' with German guilt. Months later, as this chapter was being finalized in December 2017, a new government had still not been formed, as coalition talks between the much weakened centrist parties broke down. In Germany, as in other countries, the past continues to be contested, and a worldly orientation for the nation – simply put, the embrace of diversity and universal human rights – remains a fragile achievement.

This chapter takes seriously the premise of the book in which it appears. Germany – and all other nations today – can only be properly understood transnationally. The Federal Republic is unavoidably defined by the opportunities that cross-border flows of people, products and ideas give rise to, but also by threats such as climate change, disease and terrorism that do not respect national jurisdictions. In this chapter, it is argued more particularly that the specific form of contemporary Germany's self-understanding as a nation and as an advocate for human rights and multilateral engagement in world affairs emerges out of the interaction of an established domestic discourse of *Vergangenheitsbewältigung* [coming-to-terms with the past] and the Federal Republic's transnational imbrication in the world at large, including its growing global presence and its ongoing dramatic demographic transformation. Germany's 'culture of contrition' is changing rapidly as it takes on a more explicit leadership role in Europe and as successive waves of migrants infuse German memory culture with their own memories of conflict and trauma from elsewhere.

Germany in Europe and the World

The foreign policy of the Federal Republic – particularly since unification – has been powerfully informed by the country's embrace of human rights, the peaceful resolution of conflict, multilateralism and 'commitment to Europe', specifically the European Union. As noted above, these principles express Germany's internalization of its historical responsibility for the crimes of National Socialism. But they also signal the Federal Republic's desire to reassure its neighbours – as it re-emerged after 1990 as a potentially hegemonic power in Europe – that the newly enlarged economic powerhouse at the heart of the continent need not be feared. Foreign policy experts have referred to unified Germany's 'culture of restraint',[3] reflexive anti-militarism,[4] and status as a 'civilian power'[5] or 'semi-sovereign state'.[6] Even as the deployment of German troops in support of UN mandates or NATO actions (notably to remove Serbian forces from Kosovo in 1999 and later in Afghanistan) has to some degree 'normalized' the use of force,[7] as Beate Neuss notes, Germany is always far more cautious than its allies, and it prefers diplomatic to military solutions. In 2003 Germany did not take part in the invasion of Iraq, disappointing the United States. Popular opinion was strongly against intervention, and Chancellor Gerhard Schröder turned this to his advantage during the 2002 elections by pledging that a re-elected SPD government would not participate. Some commentators also perceived anti-Americanism, or at least a desire for Germany to free itself from its postwar dependency upon the United States. In 2011 Germany also declined to join its American and European allies in toppling Libya's Colonel Gaddafi.

Even after the Eurozone crisis – following the global financial crisis of 2008 – confirmed Germany's undisputed standing as 'first among equals' in the EU, the Federal Republic remains, as William Paterson puts it, a 'reluctant hegemon'.[8] Certainly, leadership has been thrust upon Germany rather than enthusiastically seized. Contrition has been internalized to such a degree that it now manifests as a reflexive modesty, even diffidence. Some of Germany's allies – European partners as well the United States – have even complained in recent years about its timidity, especially its reluctance to intervene more decisively in regional and global crisis such as Russia's

[3] Rainer Baumann and Gunther Hellmann, 'Germany and The Use of Military Force: "Total War", The "Culture of Restraint" and The Quest for Normality', in *New Europe, New Germany, Old Foreign Policy? German Foreign Policy since Unification*, ed. by Douglas Webber (London: Frank Cass, 2001), pp. 61–82.

[4] Thomas Berger, *Cultures of Anti-Militarism. National Security in Germany and Japan* (Baltimore, MD: Johns Hopkins University Press, 1998).

[5] See Kerry Longhurst, *Germany and the Use of Force* (Manchester: Manchester University Press, 2004). See also Hanns W. Maull, 'Germany and the Use of Force: Still a "Civilian Power"?' *Survival* 42.2 (2000), pp. 56–80.

[6] Peter J. Katzenstein, *Policy and Politics in West Germany: The Growth of a Semisovereign State* (Philadelphia, PA: Temple University Press, 1987).

[7] Beate Neuss, 'The Normalization of Humanitarian and Military Missions Abroad', in *United Germany: Debating Processes and Prospects*, ed. by Konrad H. Jarausch (New York/Oxford: Berghahn, 2015), pp. 231–51.

[8] William Paterson, 'The Reluctant Hegemon? Germany Moves Centre Stage in the European Union', *JCMSL: Journal of Common Market Studies* 49.1 (2011), pp. 57–75.

annexation of Crimea in 2014. However, the internalization of contrition – its elevation to a guiding principle of foreign policy – does not necessarily preclude the pursuit of national interest. Indeed, it might be argued that repentance defines the *manner* of the Federal Republic's efforts to advance its global agenda, even as this agenda appears ever more normal – that is, more or less similar to the aims of its peers. Contrition is a habitus – that is, an instinctive behaviour, a way of 'being in the world' – rather than a specific kind of content.

Today, this habitus of contrition makes Germany more comfortable in enforcing its values on its partners, and even legitimizes this imposition. During the Eurozone crisis, allusions to the catastrophic consequences of spiralling inflation in the early Weimar Republic and the economic dislocations of the late 1920s – presaging Hitler's rise, it was suggested – justified the German government's insistence on the need for other countries to stick to budget deficit rules, even if this meant painful austerity and high unemployment in Greece, Spain and Portugal. Germany's ostentatious references to lessons learnt from its genocidal past reiterated its postwar commitment – born of contrition – to the 'idea of Europe' *and* validated its imposition of German ordo-liberalism (that is, robust financial discipline and a strong bias against inflationary policies) on the Eurozone. Further afield, the Federal Republic's exercise of 'soft power' – overseas aid, the growing involvement of the Goethe Institute and the German Academic Exchange Service in post-conflict regions and/or fragile states, and work with civil society organizations in developing countries on promoting human rights – expresses contrition but clearly also more generally burnishes the country's global reputation. And German firms' (for the most part) strikingly self-critical appraisals of their historical implication in National Socialism, including the exploitation of slave labour or of Jewish concentration camps inmates, confirm their reputation as global leaders in 'corporate social responsibility' and may even bestow a competitive advantage.

The fact that the Federal Republic may deploy contrition to its own advantage does not mean that the habitus is wholly cynical, however, any more than Chancellor Merkel's reluctance to raise human rights abuses during her visits to China – an increasingly important trading partner – entirely discredits her defence of liberal values. It simply means that contrition sometimes expresses German interests, but at other times it exists in tension with them. This is true of all countries that aspire to conduct 'value-led' foreign policy. In the case of Germany, however, it might be argued that contrition has at least remained a constant of how the country engages with the world, even as its peers have waxed and waned far more dramatically in their commitment to international cooperation and partnership.

From 'National Memory' to 'Cosmopolitan Memory'

The habitus of contrition is not simply a matter of Germany's external relations, of course. It is also expressed within and around the country itself – in the thousands of memorials to the murdered mandated by the state or constructed by private citizens, in public discussion and the media, and in literature, film and theatre. This intense engagement with the Nazi past, and especially with German guilt for the Holocaust, has been extensively examined by scholars at least since the late 1960s, when the discourse of *Vergangenheitsbewältigung* began to shape or even define the public culture of the Federal Republic. For some observers, today's Germany might even be a model for other nations confronting dark episodes in their recent pasts. Postwar Japan and post-apartheid South Africa are often mentioned, but other countries – and atrocities – as diverse as Cambodia, Bosnia and Nicaragua are also cited.

The habitus of contrition is not fixed, of course. In the mid-1980s much was made of the biblical resonances of the 40 years that had passed since the end of the war. In his 1985 address to commemorate the German surrender, President Richard von Weizsäcker noted the 40-year exile of the Israelites and how this span of time entails both a generational change and a reassessment of memory. More recently, Jan Assmann has written of the progression from 'communicative memory' to 'cultural memory', as younger Germans, without direct knowledge of the events, take on the task of memorializing Nazi crimes and the victims.[9] Assmann, and memory-studies scholars following in his footsteps, have generally focused on successive generations' gradual institutionalization of contrition, but it is important to emphasize that this institutionalization has also entailed dynamic change and some dramatic shifts in emphasis. For example, even in the late 1980s few observers would have predicted that a rather rigid – even 'politically correct' – insistence on responsibility for the Holocaust would, in the course of just a few years after unification in 1990, give way to a more inclusive focus on German perpetration *and* German suffering, including the devastation of German cities by Allied aerial bombing from 1942, the mass rapes of German women as the Red Army advanced on Berlin, and the expulsion of ethnic Germans from across eastern Europe from late 1944. To the extent that unification appeared to 'resolve' what author Martin Walser had once called the 'Strafprodukt Teilung' – German division as a 'punishment' for German crimes – the

---

[9] Jan Assmann, 'Communicative and Cultural Memory', in *Cultural Memory Studies. An International and Interdisciplinary Handbook*, ed. by Astrid Erll and Ansgar Nünning (Berlin: New York, 2008), pp. 109–18.

1990s would inaugurate an 'ongoing process of broadening understanding', as Bill Niven puts it.[10] Writers and intellectuals of Walser's generation – for whom the degree of implication or innocence in Hitler's regime depended on whether one was born in 1927, 1928, 1929 or afterwards – began to ask for greater indulgence of their adolescent enthusiasm for Nazism, often with a view to their imminent passing and post-mortem reputation. Nobel-Prize-winning author Günter Grass, for instance, confessed in 2006 that he had been a member of the elite Waffen SS, an episode that he also thematized in his autobiographical novel *Beim Häuten der Zwiebel* [*Peeling the Onion*, 2006] in the same year. Even more striking, prominent representatives of the generation of '68 – the onetime student radicals who in the late 1960s had forced West Germany to confront its ugly past – were now exploring the complicity of older brothers and mothers and fathers in a far more nuanced fashion. Uwe Timm's autobiographically inspired *Am Beispiel meines Bruders* [*In My Brother's Shadow*, 2003], for example, included extracts from letters that his older brother had sent home from the eastern front in the months before he was killed in action and invited unexpected empathy for the diehard SS corporal, who had been pressured to join up by a domineering father and seduced by Nazi ideology.

Literature and film, in fact – embodying more dynamic responses to changing sensibilities than memorials, museums and other institutions – provide the best evidence of recent modifications in the habitus of German contrition. A wave of texts and films from the mid-1990s attempts to balance Germans' internalized sense of responsibility for Nazi crimes with a new emphasis on the *human* dimension of the country's horrific past – ordinary Germans' complicity in terrible crimes, but also their weakness, fear, suffering and occasional kindness. Nico Hofmann's TV series *Unsere Mütter, unsere Väter* [*Generation War*, 2013], for example, relates the wartime experiences of five young friends, including the Jewish Viktor Goldstein, and suggests that each suffered in one way or another. The 'immersive historicism' that Helmut Schmitz identifies is characteristic of a trend to universalize – and perhaps even sentimentalize – the suffering of *all* as they endure circumstances that no single individual could be expected to withstand, much less change. More generally, immersive historicism suggests the '*literarisation* of historiography', to borrow Ulrich Schmid's term for the mixing of techniques and genres that characterizes recent representations of the Nazi past.[11] In some cases, 20 or more years after unification and 70 or so years after the end of the war,

---

[10] Bill Niven, *Facing the Nazi Past* (London: Routledge, 2002), p. 5.
[11] Ulrich Schmid, 'Literarisierung der Geschichtswissenschaft *Moskau 1937*: Karl Schögels Meistererzählung', *Osteuropa* 59.1 (2009), pp. 61–67.

literarization turns to comedy, or even farce. The fact that Timur Vermes' novel *Er ist wieder da* [*Look Who's Back*, 2012], which appeared as a film in 2015, caused little controversy suggests just how confident Germans now feel about the stability of German democracy and their internalization of contrition. Vermes' book imagines that Hitler has come back to life in contemporary Berlin, but today the *Führer* just seems ridiculous. At the same time, of course, the novel also warns its readers against becoming complacent about the threat posed to the Federal Republic's liberal constitutional order by neo-Nazis.

Recent German-language literary texts and films also align with transnational trends and developments. Central to the worldwide success of Bernhard Schlink's novel *Der Vorleser* [*The Reader*, 1995] was that it both replicated a dominant international – or Anglo-American – literary style that emphasized plot and 'readability' *and* embodied an 'ongoing process of broadening understanding' that was not only a German but also a global phenomenon. Schlink's focus on the all too human weakness of the onetime concentration camp guard Hanna was not uncontroversial – critics argued that to accept that her complicity was a consequence of her illiteracy was to relativize her cruelty – but *The Reader* clearly catered to its international readership's interest in how ordinary people could turn on their neighbours and become killers. The global context for the novel's reception was the explosion in ethnic hatred after the end of the Cold War, including genocide in Srebrenica and Rwanda. More generally, *The Reader* might be seen as an early example of a wave of texts and films that respond to an emerging global sensitivity to *all* episodes of atrocity as an affront to universal human rights. After the end of the Cold War, sociologists Daniel Levy and Natan Sznaider argue, the globalization of Holocaust memory has contributed to the development of a 'cosmopolitan memory' that transcends national borders and emphasizes the essential indivisibility of human suffering.[12] Certainly, Schlink's *The Reader*, Timm's *In My Brother's Shadow*, Hofmann's *Generation War* and other recent books and films align the German habitus of contrition (now emphasizing German perpetration *and* German suffering) with a global discourse that frames the deliberate traumatization of 'others' as challenges to our common humanity.

Cosmopolitan memory emerges from the complex interplay of a large variety of factors, including new digital technologies and what Ulrich Beck calls the new 'world risk society'[13] – threats such as climate change and

---

[12] Daniel Levy and Natan Sznaider, *Erinnerung im globalen Zeitalter: der Holocaust* (Frankfurt am Main: Suhrkamp, 2001). In English: *Memory and the Holocaust in a Global Age* (Philadelphia, PA: Temple University Press, 2006).

[13] Ulrich Beck, *World Risk Society* (Cambridge: Polity Press, 1999).

terrorism that do not respect national borders – that compels us to be aware of the interconnectedness of the world we inhabit even if popularist nationalism is on the march once more. More than this, however, cosmopolitan memory is a statement of *values* – a commitment to acting as a global citizen and an embrace of 'worldly' virtues such as tolerance, openness and critical self-reflection.

Demographic Transformation and the Changing Habitus of German Contrition

At the same time, another key feature of globalization has been just as important in transforming Germany's habitus of contrition. In the first half of the 1990s, following the end of the Cold War, mass immigration resulted in a net influx of around two and a half million people, including ethnic Germans and others from central and eastern Europe, people with a Jewish background from the former Soviet Union and some 350,000 refugees fleeing the wars in the former Yugoslavia. In an influential essay of 2003, literary scholar Andreas Huyssen – paraphrasing the question posed by Turkish–German writer Zafer Senoçak shortly after unification in 1990 – asked whether it is 'possible or even desirable for a diasporic community to migrate into the history of the host nation'.[14] Huyssen's focus, which reflected growing academic interest at the time in so-called minority writers' relationship to 'the nation', was on Germany's settled communities, especially second- and third-generation Turkish–Germans. Today, we might pose the question somewhat differently. As Germany becomes ever more diverse – in 2016, every third German under 15 had a migration background, against the backdrop of an aging 'native German' population – it is surely more likely that migrants are reshaping German memory culture than simply integrating into it (see too the discussion by Claire Baldwin in Chapter 15 of this volume). How are the most recent new arrivals transforming Germany's habitus of contrition?

The most obvious manifestation of the impact of demographic diversity on German memory culture has been a significant expansion of its purview beyond its conventional postwar focus on German perpetration (the Holocaust) and German suffering (the bombing of German cities, the rape of German women and the expulsion of Germans from across central and eastern Europe). This enlargement of German memory culture had in fact already been underway since the late 1980s, but it accelerated in the first decade after unification in 1990.

---

[14] Andreas Huyssen, 'Diaspora and Nation: Migration into Other Pasts', *New German Critique* 88 (2003), pp. 147–64; here p. 154.

Once again, literature offers a way of exploring a broader transformation of social and cultural practice. Libuše Moníková's *Verklärte Nacht* [*Transfigured Night*, 1992], for example, has its Czech protagonist return from the Federal Republic to Prague in 1992, where she sees how Russian troops have departed, witnesses the anger directed against collaborators with the communist regime and bemoans the city's transformation into a tourist destination for pleasure-seeking westerners. Šasa Stanišic's *Wie der Soldat das Grammofon repariert* [*How the Soldier Repairs the Gramophone*, 2006], which tells of how Aleksandar Krsmanovic fled to Germany from the fighting in the Balkans, informs about the conflict that prompted the largest arrival of refugees in Germany since the Second World War – until the summer of 2015, of course, when more than one million arrived in the space of a few months from Syria and other conflict zones across North Africa, the Middle East and as far away as Afghanistan. Likewise, in *Titos Brille* [*Tito's Glasses*, 2011], the Croatian–Jewish writer Adriana Altaras provides a potted history of the former Yugoslavia and its disintegration, just as Catalin Dorian Florescu depicts Ceaușescu's Romania and immigration to Germany in *Wunderzeit* [*Time of Miracles*, 2001]) *Der kurze Weg nach Hause* [*The Short Way Home*, 2002] and *Der blinde Masseur* [*The Blind Masseur*, 2006]. Herta Müller depicts the brutality of the Romanian security services more graphically in a series of novels published from the 1990s, including *Der Fuchs war damals schon der Jäger* [*The Fox Was Ever the Hunter*, 1992]. Müller's *Reisende auf einem Bein* [*Traveling On One Leg*, 1989] had already described arriving in the Federal Republic, while also insinuating parallels between National Socialism and the communist persecution she had just fled. Müller's ex-husband Richard Wagner has also depicted life in the Banat (the German-speaking region of Romania).

In *Habseligkeiten* [*Belongings*, 2004], Wagner covers two centuries of German Romanian history, including emigration to America, return to the Banat, postwar confinement in Soviet gulags and immigration to Germany after 1990. Dana Grigorcea's *Das primäre Gefühl der Schuldlosigkeit* [*The Primary Feeling of Innocence*, 2015] also casts back to Romania before the violent overthrow of the Ceaușescu regime in 1989. In *Das achte Leben* [*The Eighth Life*, 2018], Nino Haratischwili presents five generations of Georgians from 1900 into the twenty-first century, and in *In guten Händen, in einem schönen Land* [*In Good Hands, In a Beautiful Land*, 2013] Eleonora Hummel – who is descended from ethnic Germans in Russia deported by Stalin to Kazakhstan – tells of gulags and persecution by the Soviet authorities. In *Sophia oder der Anfang aller Geschichten* [*Sophia, or The Beginning of all Stories*, 2015], in contrast, the Syrian–German writer Rafik Schami responds to a perceived urgent need to 'know' the refugees arriving in Germany in the summer of 2015. Schami depicts the brutality of the Syrian regime from the postwar period to the Arab spring of 2010–2011. Also published in 2015 was Ilija Trojanow's *Macht und Widerstand* [*Power and Resistance*], a novel based on the author's conversations with victims of the Bulgarian secret police during the Communist period. The title most immediately suggests the Nazi period, and it may be that Trojanow's novel – along with many of those mentioned above – responds to German readers' interest in *other* dictatorships and even a desire to contextualize Germany's Nazi past within the broader sweep of Europe's disastrous early twentieth-century history. Certainly, *Power and Resistance* is part of an emerging trend to focus less on the *uniqueness* of the Nazi dictatorship and to emphasize instead the wider transnational phenonomen of extreme nationalism and violence in Europe a century ago – a harbinger, perhaps, of what many believe is taking place today too.

These and other similar novels contribute to what I have described elsewhere as contemporary German-language fiction's 'literary archive of transnational trauma'.[15] Within this archive, a conventional postwar focus on the Holocaust is expanded to include histories of suffering from across Europe and the world. Russian immigrant Katja Petrowskaja's *Vielleicht Esther* [*Perhaps Esther*, 2014] sends its protagonist to Kiev, Berlin, Warsaw and Moscow in search of evidence of the murder of her great-grandmother at Babyn Jar on 29–30 September 1941, when 30,000 Jews were killed, but the novel's implied ethical injunction that human rights abuses *everywhere* must be confronted resonates throughout its chapters. Ukrainian Marjana Gaponenko's 2012 novel *Wer ist Martha?* [*Who is Martha?*, 2014] also relates central and eastern European history, as the elderly Ukrainian Jew Lewadski casts back in his Vienna hotel over a century of expulsions. In an example of what Michael Rothberg terms 'multidirectional memory',[16] the protagonist relates his story of displacement and dispossession to a Palestinian waiter, Habib, who also lives in exile from his homeland – the juxtaposition of moral outrage with moral outrage amplifies the resonance of both.

It can be argued that their internalization of the lessons of the Nazi past predisposes Germans to be responsive to the stories of oppression, persecution and conflict that migrants bring with them. This would be an optimistic – but not entirely unrealistic – prognosis for Germany's ability to allow its habitus of contrition to be reshaped by demographic diversity. The

---

[15] See chapter 2 ('Transnationalism in Contemporary German-language Novels') of my *Transnationalism and German-Language Literature in the Twenty-First Century* (Basingstoke: Palgrave Macmillan, 2017).

[16] Michael Rothberg, *Multidirectional Memory: Remembering the Holocaust in the Age of Decolonization* (Stanford, CA: Stanford University Press, 2009).

transnationalization of German memory culture, we might have cause to hope, seems likely to reaffirm its essentially liberal quality and emphasis on universal human rights.

The Future of Contrition?

Many would challenge this characterization of the evolution of German memory culture, of course. Certainly, it has been suggested that after 9/11 western countries' aggressive assertion of liberal values, whether a particular *Erinnerungskultur* [culture of remembrance], women's rights or gay marriage, is as much about the exclusion of 'others' – i.e. Muslims who are just 'too backward' to be successfully integrated – as it is about social solidarity. In essence, we may be seeing the emergence of a potent 'liberal nationalism' that, paradoxically, trumpets its embrace of universal human rights to reinforce its global dominance. (This might still be preferable to more primordial nationalist discourse that eschews liberal values and human rights altogether and instead simply indulges the fantasy of ethnic or racial supremacy).

In Russian–Jewish writer Vladimir Vertlib's *Am Morgen des zwölften Tages* [*On the Morning of the Twelfth Day*, 2009], the novel's emancipated female protagonist Astrid accuses her Muslim lover Adel of planning a terrorist attack and further hints that he might even be anti-Semitic. Astrid's ostentatious display of western values scarcely disguises and may even legitimize the scapegoating of Muslims – moreover, it is not entirely clear whether the novel endorses or critiques this scapegoating, insofar as the narrative closes with a bout of sensationalizing speculation about Adel's possible implication in bomb-making activities. In this regard, other recent novels are less ambivalent. Olga Grjasnowa's 2014 *Die juristische Unschärfe einer Ehe* [*The Judicial Uncertainty of a Marriage*], for example, suggests that the spectacularly rapid new acceptance of homosexuality and even gay marriage in Germany and other western countries in recent years embodies a strident liberal nationalism that purposely and purposively excludes Muslims. Similarly, in Austrian writer Marlene Streeruwitz's *Entfernung* [*Distance*, 2006], Selma initially reacts negatively to the 'ethnic others' that she encounters on her journey to London on what turns out to be the day of the 7/7 terrorist attacks, and especially the Muslim women in headscarves, whom she perceives as an affront to her sense of what it means to be Austrian, including liberal values and feminism. Indeed, she even sees them as an imminent threat: 'Selma thought, it could happen any moment. One action. A reaction. Any moment something could happen.'[17] In time, however, Selma comes to realize – and

---

[17] Marlene Streeruwitz, *Entfernung* (Frankfurt am Main: S. Fischer, 2006), p. 50.

here *Distance* is part of a sizeable corpus of post-9/11 novels that suggest something similar – that the real threat to her physical and psychological well-being is the neo-liberal orthodoxy of the 1990s and early 2000s up to the global financial crisis of 2008, that, operating across borders without regard for democratic accountability, forces nations into a competitive downward spiral of ever worse conditions of employment, welfare and consumer protections. (Navid Kermani's 2007 *Kurzmitteilung/The Memo*, for example, hints that Islamophobia distracts from the reality that globalization, in its neo-liberal variant, is eroding *all* social bonds and authentic interaction.) At the same time, Selma's transnational resistance to neo-liberalism – symbolized at the end of *Distance* by her joining hands with a black man, a white woman and an Asian Briton – also reinstates the nation. In the novel's closing pages she feels a renewed attachment to her Austrian 'home' and it is implied that the *nation* offers the only possibility of refuge in what the conservative writer Botho Strauß once called the 'floods of globality',[18] even if there is also some comfort in gestures of cosmopolitan solidarity across borders.

The culture of contrition, in short, may now underpin an unexpected nationalism, notwithstanding its reflexive gesturing towards cosmopolitan ideals. In one version of this potentially self-congratulatory affirmation of contrition as a form of *national* identity, a strident assertion of liberal values may conceal the exclusion of Muslims and other 'others'. Indeed, it may be the case that Germans' successful internalization of the 'lessons of the Holocaust' has become the basis for renewed national pride – German–Jewish writer Maxim Biller has spoken of the 'Holocaust trauma as the mother of a long-sought-after German national consciousness'[19] – and it is often noted that the very 'Germanness' of the culture of contrition may insinuate that so-called *Mitbürger* [fellow citizens] of non-German extraction can never fully participate in its rituals or truly 'belong'.[20] More generally, contrition – along with, say, the 'German economic model' – defines what is quintessentially 'German' against the perceived threat of globalization or neo-liberalism.

In any event, it would be a mistake to believe that the transnationalization and cosmopolitanization of German (or Austrian) memory culture is inevitable or, for that matter, irreversible in the uncertain future described in the opening paragraphs of this chapter. Even demographic diversity is

---

[18] Botho Strauß, 'Zeit ohne Vorboten', in *Der Aufstand gegen die sekundäre Welt*, Botho Strauß (Munich: Hanser, 1999), pp. 93–105, p. 96.

[19] Maxim Biller, 'Heiliger Holocaust', in *Deutschbuch* (Munich: Deutscher Taschenbuch Verlag, 2001), pp. 27–29 (p. 28).

[20] Michael Rothberg and Yildiz Yasemin, 'Memory Citizenship: Migrant Archives of Holocaust Remembrance in Contemporary Germany', *Parallax* 17.4 (2011), pp. 32–48.

no guarantee of a 'world-oriented' memory culture, or more broadly of what Saskia Sassen calls a 'postnational and denationalized citizenship'.[21] In the Federal Republic, as elsewhere in the contemporary world, isolationism, nationalism and the renewed upsurge of xenophobia may encourage the re-emergence of national memory cultures that emphasize rivalry over solidarity – that is, the proposition that one nation's history can be validated only when another's is denied or denigrated. This is one possible future for German memory culture suggested by Russian writer Nellja Veremej's 2013 German-language novel *Berlin liegt im Osten* [*Berlin Lies in the East*]. In this book, a Russian care assistant in Berlin finds common cause with her elderly German charge when they narrate their individual stories of national humiliation – the disintegration of the Soviet Union and Russia's descent into chaos, and German wartime suffering – and set *these* memories against what they see as the post-Cold War hegemony of the United States. For the Russian migrant Lena, Germans have repented enough. Quite unexpectedly, Veremej's novel may even suggest that it will fall to recent arrivals such as Lena to become the custodians of national memory culture and to assert a more potently *German* perspective on the past – even if this means a shift from a culture of contrition towards a culture of combativeness.

At the same time, *Berlin Lies in the East* also hints at an altogether larger timescale, namely what David Christian calls the 'big history' of our species' decisive impact on the natural environment.[22] The novel's increasingly insistent allusions to rising sea levels, vanishing rainforests and poisoned skies probably suggest that its characters' myopic focus on the nation is woefully inadequate to the planetary scale of the hazards that we – global humanity – confront. Specifically, Veremej's novel cites W.G Sebald, the German author (deceased 2001) whose books situate the industrialized killing of the Holocaust within the larger and longer history of western modernity, especially the plundering of the natural environment to turbo-charge first imperialism and then the global triumph of capitalism. Indeed, Sebald – along with his imitators in a variety of languages – has come to embody a *global* sense of melancholic regret for the damage we have inflicted on ourselves and our planet through our reckless exploitation of the earth's resources. In common with other recent texts in German and other languages thematizing humankind's impact on the earth's geology and

---

[21] Saskia Sassen, 'Towards Post-National and Denationalized Citizenship', in *Handbook of Citizenship Studies*, ed. by Engin F. Isin and Bryan Turner (London: Sage, 2003), pp. 277–91.

[22] See David Christian, *Maps of Time: An Introduction to Big History* (Berkeley: University of California Press, 2004).

ecosystems (the so-called Anthropocene), Veremej perhaps suggests that a habitus of contrition may today be necessary for humankind as a whole, and not just for Germans.

Suggestions for Further Reading

Adelson, Leslie, *The Turkish Turn in Contemporary German Literature: Toward a New Critical Grammar of Migration* (Houndsmills: Palgrave Macmillan: 2005), 273 pp.

Boos, Sonja, *Speaking the Unspeakable in Postwar Germany: Toward a Public Discourse on the Holocaust* (Ithaca, NY: Cornell University Press, 2014), 244 pp.

Denham, Scott, and Mark McCulloh (eds.), *W. G. Sebald. History – Memory – Trauma* (Berlin: de Gruyter, 2006), 393 pp.

Fachinger, Petra, *Rewriting Germany from the Margins: Other German Literature of the 1980s and 1990s* (Montreal: McGill-Queens University Press, 2001), 176 pp.

Müller, Jan-Werner, *Another Country: German. Intellectuals, Unification and National Identity* (London: Yale University Press, 2000), 332 pp.

Nicosia, Francis R., and Jonathan Huebner (eds.), *Business and Industry in Nazi Germany* (New York/Oxford: Berghahn Books, 2004), 234 pp.

Niven, Bill (ed.), *Germans as Victims* (London: Palgrave, 2006), 304 pp.

Seyhan, Azade, *Writing Outside the Nation* (Princeton: Princeton University Press, 2001), 201 pp.

Rothberg, Michael, and Yasemin Yildiz, 'Memory Citizenship: Migrant Archives of Holocaust Remembrance in Contemporary Germany', *Parallax* 17.4 (2011), pp. 32–48.

Webber, Douglas (ed.), *New Europe, New Germany, Old Foreign Policy: German Foreign Policy since Unification* (London: F. Cass, 2001), 240 pp.

Index

Abonji, Melinda Nadj 66
Abrahamic faiths 196, 203, 204
Actor-Network-Theory (ANT) 106, 107, 237n12
agents 82
Algeria 269–70, 273, 274, 276, 280, 281, 283
Alsace, writers 64, 65
Altaras, Adriana 316
alterity 12
Alternative für Deutschland [Alternative for Germany] 308, 309
And Other Stories (AOS) 85
anglicisms 67
anti-militarism 310
anti-Semitism 120, 125, 205, 271
Arab Spring (2011) 156, 161, 166
Archibald Prize 278, 279
archives 8, 12, 46, 170, 231, 232, 240, 306, 321
artificial language 71
artists 112, 259, 272–73, 279, 281, 283–84
assimilation 66, 198, 243–44, 272
Assmann, Aleida 189, 190
Auerbach, Berthold 184
Auschwitz 302–05

Australia 1, 269–70, 272–74, 276–82, 284
Austria 1, 4, 5, 13, 25, 26, 64, 78, 81, 82, 115, 122, 130, 261, 272, 273, 280
Austro-Hungarian Dual Monarchy 5, 64
authorship 9, 101, 103, 112, 292, 296
  see also world authorship
Azerbaijan 92

Balkans 122, 157, 316
Basel 21, 36–37, 39
Bavaria 51
Bavaria Film 147
Bavarian dialect 46, 48
Bell, Anthea 87, 88
Ben-Dov, Ya'acov 223, 225, 226, 227
Berlin 45, 53, 71, 89, 136, 141–42, 145, 147, 156, 186, 188, 219, 222, 308, 312, 314, 317, 320
Berlin Academy 100
Berners Lee, Tim 180n
Bernofsky, Susan 86, 87
bestsellers 37, 62, 86, 118, 127
Bettelheim, Bruno 263
Bhatti, Anil 198, 211

323

biography 47, 54, 66, 102, 103, 106, 107, 109, 261, 270, 280, 283–84, 295
Birgittine Order 31, 35
Bloch, Ernst 182, 183
Blumenberg, Hans 266
book trade 21, 62, 85, 117
booksellers 82
Bosnia 62, 92, 312
Brant, Sebastian 36, 37, 39
Brazil 128, 229, 230, 231, 232, 234, 236, 241, 244, 245, 269
    German immigration to 242
    German-language press 230, 232, 233, 234, 235, 237, 239, 240, 242, 244
    German-speaking communities 237, 241
Brecht, Bertolt 269, 270
Breuer, Josef 256
Brice, Pierre 144, 145
Brockhaus (printing house) 104
BStU *see* Federal Office for the Files of the State Security Service (BStU)
Bulgaria 62, 63, 66, 143, 317
burgomaster 26, 27, 28, 30

Cambridge University 262
Canetti, Elias 63, 66
canon 5–7, 73, 98, 108, 110, 117–19, 178
Carlyle, Thomas 99, 100, 107–08
Celan, Paul 63
Cemetery of the Holy Innocents, Paris 25
Central and Eastern Europe (CEE) region 166, 167, 168, 169, 171, 172
CGE (French consortium) 145
Chamisso, Adelbert von 65
Chamisso Prize 65, 66
Chase, Henry 262
Christianity 193, 196, 199, 204–05
Church of St Mary, Lubeck 26–27

Church of St Nicholas, Reval 26–27
cinema 8–9, 11–12, 133, 142, 146, 148–49, 223–24, 313
    East German 141–44
    silent 133
    West German 141–44
Cold War 142
Collins, Charlotte 89–90
colonialism 128–29, 184, 197, 243, 252
colonization 230
commemoration 154, 156, 302
communication 51–52, 75, 186
consciousness 110, 116, 251–57, 267, 294, 295, 301, 303, 304, 305, 319
contrition 308–09, 311–15, 317–19, 321
Cooper, James Fenimore 128–29, 131
cosmopolitanism 206, 270, 288–97, 299–302, 304, 306, 314–15
creolization 70
cultural belonging 270, 288
cultural exchange 31, 101, 260
cultural memory 116, 284, 287, 301, 302, 312
Curitiba, Brazil 229, 241

Dance of Death (concept) 25
    see also danse macabre
danse macabre 25, 27, 30
Death, as figure 27, 29, 30
DEFA (studio) 142, 143, 144, 145, 146
Derbyshire, Katy 79, 89, 90
Descartes, Réné 249, 250
Deutsches Textarchiv [German Text Archive] project (DTA) 233
Devotio moderna (religious reform movement) 24, 25
dialects 5, 7, 8, 18, 20, 21, 43, 45, 67
    see also High German, Low German
Dickens, Charles 125, 126, 127, 129, 131
Diet of Cologne (1512) 17

digital technologies 180, 185, 186, 314
digitization 232, 233, 237, 244
displacement 186, 189, 317
Dörffel, Ottokar 238, 239
Dorfgeschichte [rural story] 184

East Germanic languages 20
East Germany 134, 158
    see also cinema, German Democratic Republic (GDR)
East-West encounters 193
Eckermann, Johann Peter 98, 100, 101, 102, 103, 104, 105, 106, 107, 108, 109, 111, 112
ego 157, 158, 163, 167, 257, 258
émigrés 273, 275, 280, 281, 284
employment 186, 187, 188, 276, 319
England 25, 44–45, 55, 85, 117, 126, 130
English (language) 43, 44, 46, 53, 93
Enlightenment 188, 196, 206, 207, 209, 211, 217, 250, 297, 298, 299, 300, 302, 304
environment 57, 58, 146, 180, 234, 237n15, 271, 293, 320
epigenetics 52
Epler, Barbara 86
Erpenbeck, Jenny 86, 87, 186, 187
ethnicity 6, 58, 60, 64, 73, 144, 145, 177, 206, 270, 286, 287, 290, 291, 293, 295, 296, 301, 303, 305, 312, 314, 315, 316, 318
European memory 152, 155, 156, 161, 172
European Project 286
Eurozone crisis 310, 311
exile 43, 63, 64, 67, 123, 124, 217, 269–84, 312, 317
experimental writing 7, 69, 73–74, 201, 202

Fanck, Arnold 134, 138, 139, 140, 141

Fechner, Gustav Theodor 253, 254, 255, 256, 257
Federal Office for the Files of the State Security Service (BStU) 156, 158, 159, 160, 161, 163–72
film *see* cinema
First Sound Shift 20
Fisser, Christoph 146
Florescu, Catalin Dorian 316
forced migration 238, 269
foreign policy 309, 310, 311
France 5, 25–26, 45, 65, 91, 115–16, 120–23, 125, 129–30, 142, 181, 270, 272, 273, 280, 281
    1789 revolution 121, 122
    1848 revolution 123
France-Germany communication 120
Frankfurt Book Fair 78, 82, 83
Franzen, Jonathan 108, 109, 110, 111, 112
Free and Imperial cities 26
freedom 121–23, 131, 239, 274
French (language) 64, 121, 123
French Foreign Legion 273
Freud, Sigmund 9, 249, 250, 253, 254, 255, 256, 257, 258, 259, 261, 263, 266
    English translations of works 255, 259, 260, 261, 262, 263, 264, 265, 267
    French translations of works 265
Freytag, Gustav 7, 118, 124, 125, 126, 127, 128, 129, 130, 131
future 119, 120, 121, 122, 123, 182n21, 188, 189, 190, 207, 210, 216, 221, 222, 225, 261, 302, 303, 305, 318, 319, 320

Galicia (Eastern Europe) 63, 271
Gaponenko, Marjana 317
Gardi, Tomer 7, 70, 71, 72, 74
gay marriage 318
Geist [spirit] 291
Georg Büchner Prize 63, 64

George, Stefan 67
Georgia 92, 316
German (language) 3, 44, 46, 229, 230, 231, 232, 270, 291
  as bridge language 92, 93
  as lingua franca 61, 72, 75
  as national language 58, 59, 60, 61
  study of 1, 2
  see also German studies
German Democratic Republic (GDR) 9, 45, 49, 134, 144, 156, 158, 172, 188, 269
German House, New York University 109, 110
German studies 1, 2, 3, 5, 6, 7, 11, 13, 57, 60, 149, 151, 155, 213, 232, 233, 237n, 240, 245
Germanistik see German studies
German-Japanese co-production 134, 138, 139
Germanness 4, 13, 60, 73, 305, 319
German-Oriental encounters 198, 199
gig economy 187, 188
Gleeson, James 278, 279
globalization 5, 59, 61, 67, 94, 113, 177, 178, 184, 230, 238, 286, 306, 307, 314, 315, 319
Goebbels, Joseph 141
Goethe, Johann Wolfgang von 7, 97, 98, 99, 100, 101, 102, 103, 104, 105, 106, 107, 109, 110, 111, 112, 120, 125, 128, 193, 194, 196, 197, 199, 200, 201, 202, 203, 204, 205, 211
Goethe Institute 111
Grass, Günter 290, 313
Great Britain *see* United Kingdom
Greece 115, 311
Greek 263, 264, 266
Grigorcea, Dana 316
Grjasnowa, Olga 92, 318

guest workers 62, 72
guilt 52, 257, 295, 303, 304, 305, 309, 312
Gumbrecht, Hans-Ulrich 189, 190

Habsburg Empire 64, 270, 271
Hafez of Shiraz 193, 194, 202, 203
Hafez-Goethe Monument 7, 193, 194, 195
Hamat Tiberias Synagogue 225
Han, Byung Chul 185
Hanse see Hanseatic League
Hanseatic League 8, 21, 22, 23, 40
Hanser Verlag (publisher) 77, 89
Haratischwili, Nino 92, 316
Hartog, François 189, 190
Harvey, David 183, 184
Harvey, Kate 89, 90
Hebrew 219
hegira 201
Heimat [homeland] 47, 48, 50n4, 51, 126, 179, 184
Heine, Heinrich 7, 64, 118, 119, 120, 121, 122, 123, 124, 125, 131, 292, 299, 300, 301
Herbart, Johann Friedrich 253
High German 18, 19, 20, 21, 36, 46
Hollywood 134, 135, 136, 137, 146, 147, 149
Holocaust 52, 55, 66, 154, 181, 275, 278, 295, 301, 302, 304, 305, 306, 308, 312, 314, 315, 317, 319, 320, 321
Holy Roman Empire 5, 17, 21, 36, 39, 64, 115
home 45, 47–51, 62, 84, 100, 116, 119, 126, 181, 237, 242, 260, 269, 272, 274, 281, 313, 316, 319
homeland *see Heimat*
homosexuality 318
Hoppe, Felicitas 9, 110, 111, 112, 113
Hughes, Robert 278, 279
Hugo, Victor 125

human rights 286, 293, 299, 301, 304, 305, 308, 309, 311, 314, 317, 318
Humanism 36, 37, 39, 211, 263, 294, 298
Hummel, Eleonora 316
Huyssen, Andreas 315
hypnotism 254n22

id 257, 258
identity 45, 53, 54, 58, 59, 60, 73, 74, 178, 244, 288, 289, 290, 291, 293, 295, 296, 302
idiolects 70
idioms 44, 59, 61, 67–72, 74
  see also dialects
Ilf, Ilja 111
immigration 63, 186, 229, 230, 238, 242, 243, 244, 273, 274, 291, 296, 308, 315, 316
  to Brazil 242, 243
  to North America 243
incunables 24
Ingeborg Bachmann Prize 62, 68
internet 185
Islam 193–212, 286, 293, 294, 296, 298, 299
Islamophobia 308, 319
Israel 213

Japan 138–41, 312
Japanese 61–62, 86
Jews 72, 122, 154, 205, 214, 215, 269, 271–73, 304, 305, 317
  diaspora 271, 281
  writers 289, 293, 301
Joinville, Brazil 229, 234, 238
Jones, Ernst 260, 261, 263
Joyce, James 53
Judaism 196, 199, 204, 215, 217, 218, 219
Junges Deutschland [Young Germany] 121

Kafka, Franz 8, 64, 214, 219, 220, 221, 222, 223, 225, 227, 292, 293, 294, 295, 296
Kahan, Louis 7, 269, 270, 276, 277, 282, 283
  art 274, 275, 276, 278, 279, 280, 281
  biography 270, 271, 272, 273, 280, 281, 284
Kaminer, Wladimir 62, 66
Kant, Immanuel 251, 252
Kawakita, Nagasama 139
Kehlmann, Daniel 9, 108, 109, 110, 112
Kermani, Navid 7, 285, 286, 287, 288, 289, 290, 291, 292, 293, 294, 295, 296, 297, 298, 299, 300, 301, 302, 303, 304, 305, 306
Kimmich, Dorothea 198
Kleist Prize 61
Koran 205, 293
Kraus, Karl 108, 109, 110
Kulturnation [cultural nation] 290, 291, 292

Lang, Fritz 135
languages 46
  assimilation 66
  choice 58
  and identity 58, 59, 73, 74
  see also individual languages by name, e.g. German
Laplanche, Jean 265
Latin 21, 24, 31, 40, 75, 263, 266
Latour, Bruno 80, 106, 107, 108, 237n12
Leibniz, Gottfried Wilhelm 251
Lessing, Gotthold Ephraim 7, 196, 199, 205, 206, 208, 209, 210, 211, 292, 296, 297, 298, 299
literary prizes 57, 61–65, 108
Locher, Jakob 37
Low German 18, 19, 20, 21, 24, 26, 31, 32, 36, 40

Lübeck 8, 21, 24, 25, 26, 30, 31, 37, 39, 40
Ludwig I of Bavaria 115
Lumière Brothers 224

Macht [political power] 291
Mann, Klaus 64
Mann, Thomas 269, 270
Mansaku, Itami 138, 140, 141
May, Karl 142, 143, 144, 145
media 8, 9, 62, 84, 101, 108–12, 134, 145, 181, 182, 214, 223, 230, 234, 280, 281, 312
  see also social media
mediators 107, 109, 112, 260
memorials 312
memory 54, 153, 155, 171, 172, 181, 303, 305, 315
memory culture 156, 170, 181, 189, 318, 319, 320
memory politics 158, 166
memory regions 154, 155, 172, 173
memory studies 151, 152, 153, 154, 170, 181
Merkel, Angela 308, 311
Messianism 214, 216, 217, 219, 220, 221, 227
Metro-Goldwyn 134, 135, 136
Middle East 63, 64, 156, 158, 161, 166, 168, 169, 172, 189, 197, 213, 278, 316
migrants and migration 67, 121, 130, 187, 230, 238, 269, 272, 274, 280
  status in Germany 289
  writers 58, 72, 75
Mitić, Gojko 134, 142, 143, 144, 145
mobile communications 185
modernism 279, 282
Mohammed (prophet) 201, 202
Mohnkopf Press 24, 30, 31, 32, 39, 40
Moníková, Libuše 316
monuments 12, 193, 196
Mora, Terézia 188

Müller, Herta 63, 316
multilingualism 43, 44, 45, 51, 53, 57, 58, 59, 63, 64, 66, 67, 68, 69, 70
Muslims 7, 204, 207–10, 285, 302, 318
Myers, Frederic William Henry 261

Nabokov, Vladimir 53
national poets 118, 121
National Socialism 138, 182, 288, 295, 301, 303, 305, 311, 312, 313, 317
National Socialist Underground 298
nationalism 5, 11, 32, 118, 119, 123, 129, 131, 151, 178, 287, 294, 295, 301, 307, 308, 315, 317, 318, 319, 320
nationhood 116, 118, 130, 152, 177, 181, 213, 288, 291, 292, 294
Native American culture 143–45
Nazism *see* National Socialism
Netdraw (software) 158, 163
networks 8, 9, 20, 78, 79, 80, 81, 85, 87, 88, 90, 91, 92, 93, 100, 102, 106, 107, 108, 111, 130, 154, 155, 157, 158, 161, 163, 164, 167, 169, 171, 178, 179, 180, 185, 234
New Books in German (NBG) 77, 78, 79, 81, 82, 83, 84, 85, 86, 88, 89, 91, 93
New Spanish Books 83n
newspapers *see* press
nodes 157, 158, 161, 163, 165, 168
nomadism 179
North Africa 156, 161, 166, 168, 169, 172, 197, 273–75, 278, 316
North America 8, 245
North Germanic languages 20
Notke, Bernt 25, 26, 27
Nvivo (software) 169

occult 254n
Oedipus complex 257
oppression 122, 128, 131, 155, 197, 301, 317

Orient 193, 197, 198, 199, 200, 202, 204, 211
Orientalism 197, 205
othering 196, 197, 198
Otoo, Sharon Dodua 62
Özdamar, Emine Sevgi 62, 68, 69

Palestine 213, 214, 222, 223, 224, 225, 227
Panthéon, Paris 116
Parafumet (distribution company) 134, 136, 137, 146
Paramount 134, 135, 136
Paris 64, 116, 120–21, 147, 172, 269–70, 272–73, 275
pathos 300, 301
patriotism 289, 291, 292, 298, 299, 304
Paul, Jean 252
PEGIDA [Patriotic Europeans Against the Islamization of the West] 308
Peirene Press 84, 85
Persia 193, 199, 202
Petrow, Jewgeni 111
Petrowskaja, Katja 317
philosophy 2, 36, 120, 250, 251, 253, 254, 261
Pigeon, William 279
Platner, Ernst 251
Poet's Corner, Westminster Abbey 116, 126
Poland 43, 46–47, 129, 131
Polish 46, 54, 67, 230
Pollock, Channing 137
Pontalis, Jean-Bertrand 265
Popper, Karl 266
post-Soviet region 157, 161, 166, 167–68, 171
Prague 64, 162, 163, 165, 166, 167, 223, 225, 273, 294, 316
presidency (Germany) 285
press 8, 85, 86, 87, 117, 231
printers and printing 21, 24, 25, 31, 32, 39, 40
    see also individual printers by name
psyche 263, 264
psychoanalysis 249, 253, 254, 255, 256, 259, 260, 261, 263, 264, 265, 266, 267
psychology 250, 253, 254, 256, 258, 263
psychophysics 253
publishers 82, 84, 85, 93
    see also individual publishers by name

redemption 217
refugees 48, 178, 181, 186, 187, 190, 245, 271, 273, 276, 280, 281, 286, 308, 315, 316
Reitter, Paul 108, 109, 110
remembrance 154, 156, 172, 173, 304
representation 299, 300, 301, 302
repression 120, 243, 254, 256, 257, 262, 291, 305
Rickman, John 262, 263
Rilke, Rainer Maria 7, 64
Rio de Janeiro, Brazil 234
Rio Grande do Sul, Brazil 229, 234
Riviere, Joan 262, 263
Rock, Zé Do 7, 70, 73
Romania 63, 316
Russia 122, 271, 272, 316, 320
    see also post-Soviet region, Soviet Union
Russian Federation 155, 166

Said, Edward 197, 213
St Birgitta of Sweden (1303–1373) 30, 31, 32, 35, 36
St Katherina of Sweden (1332–1381) 31, 32, 35
Santa Catarina, Brazil 229, 242
Santos pamphlet 239
São Paulo, Brazil 234

Schami, Rafik 316, 317
Schiller, Friedrich 99
Schlegel, Friedrich 197
Schlink, Bernhard 314
Schlöndorff, Volker 146
Schmidt, Julian 125
Scholem, Gershom 8, 214, 215, 216, 217, 218, 219, 227
Schopenhauer, Arthur 252, 255
science 2, 8, 9, 60, 101, 107, 151, 185, 249, 253, 254, 255, 261, 263, 266, 267, 278
Scotland 99, 100
Sebald, W.G. 320
Second Sound Shift 20
Second World War 154, 273, 274, 275
Seethaler, Robert 89, 90
Sellar, Niall 89
Şenocak, Zafer 73
Shurz, Carl 238
Silesia 48, 49, 51, 64
    dialect 6–7, 43, 46
similarity 196, 198, 199, 205, 211
slavery 239, 240
SNA *see* Social Network Analysis
social media 79, 180, 181, 187
Social Network Analysis (SNA) 153, 154, 157, 158, 163, 169, 172, 173, 178
    actors 157, 158, 161, 163–71, 173
soldiers, portraits of 274, 275, 276
solidarity 123, 142n32, 156, 214, 292, 300, 301, 302, 318, 319, 320
soul 52, 120, 250, 259, 263, 267
South America 8, 157, 230, 238, 244
Soviet Union 50, 315, 316, 320
Stanišić, Saša 92, 316
Stasi 156
Stein, Kurt M. 69
Strachey, Alix 262, 263
Strachey, James 260, 261, 262, 263
Streeruwitz, Marlene 318, 319

Studio Babelsberg 134, 146, 147, 148
Stuttgart Institute for International Relationships 232n
suffering 275, 276, 292, 300, 301, 312–17, 320
superego 257, 258
Switzerland 1, 5, 13, 25, 64, 78, 81, 82, 269
Syria 316, 317

Tabori, George 64
Tansley, Arthur 262
Tawada, Yoko 61, 68, 86, 87
temporality 3, 10, 11, 12, 25, 179, 180, 185, 191, 221
Timm, Uwe 313
Tobler, Stefan 84, 85
Tokyo 63, 140–41
tolerance 140, 196, 205–09, 296–98, 307, 315
trade 1, 21, 78, 98, 99, 127–30, 139, 272, 287, 298, 307
translation 9, 78, 79, 80, 81, 82, 83, 84, 85, 86, 87, 88, 89, 90, 91, 92, 93, 98, 99, 118, 134
translators 82, 86, 87, 88, 89, 91, 92, 93, 99
translingualism 58, 59, 63, 67, 68, 72, 74, 75, 118, 120, 123, 130
transnationalism 78, 81, 93, 98, 101, 108, 118, 120, 121, 122, 123, 131, 133, 134, 138, 139, 141, 142, 144, 145, 147, 148, 149, 152, 169, 177, 178, 179, 181, 183, 241, 286, 287, 288, 309
    artists 281, 283, 284
    exchange 126, 127, 129, 131
    memory 153, 155, 172, 181, 182
    networks 99, 155, 161
    studies 179, 184, 186, 190, 191, 213
trauma 49, 52, 54, 197, 274, 275, 309, 317, 319, 321

travel blogs 111
Treuhand 145
Trojanow, Ilja 317
Trump, Donald 307
Turkey 62, 69, 122
Turkish 62, 69, 70, 148n
Turkish-Germans 62, 315

Ucinet (software) 157, 158, 163, 167
Ukraine 162, 166, 168, 271, 317
unconscious 249, 251, 252, 253, 254, 255, 256, 257, 259, 265, 266, 267
Unification (1871) 116, 130, 131, 290
Unification (1990) 145, 146, 148n52, 290, 309, 312, 313, 315, 321
United Kingdom 1–2, 64, 77–88, 90–93, 100, 142
United States of America (USA) 45, 64, 77–86, 91, 108, 128, 131, 134, 136–38, 142, 144, 229, 236, 238, 240, 241, 244, 262, 307
Universum-Film (UFA) 134, 135, 136, 142

Veremej, Nellja 320, 321
Vermes, Timur 314
Vertlib, Vladimir 318
Vienna 108, 262, 266, 271–73, 280–81, 317
von Wolkenstein, Oscar 63

Wager, Richard 316

Walhalla monument 7, 115–21, 124, 130
Walser, Martin 312, 313
Weiss, Peter 64
Welskopf-Heinrich, Liselotte 144
West 199, 200, 205, 211
West Germanic languages 20
West Germany 43, 134, 143, 158, 309, 310, 311, 313
   cinema 141, 142, 143, 144
westerns 142, 143, 144, 145
Westminster Abbey 116, 126
White, Patrick 277, 278, 279, 280, 282, 284
Whiteside, Shaun 89
Woebcken, Carl 146
Woolf, Virginia 53, 54
world authorship 80, 101, 103, 104, 107, 109, 110, 112, 113, 287
world literature 9, 13, 59, 61, 74, 97–113, 124, 128, 129, 131, 191, 193, 304
World Wide Web 180n

xenophobia 320

Yugoslavia 143, 144, 315, 316

Zaimoğlu, Feridun 7, 69, 70
Ziervogel, Meike 84
Zionism 214, 215, 216, 218, 226, 227
Zweig, Stefan 269, 275